Edwards

Britain and the
Weimar Republic

F.L. CARSTEN

Britain and the Weimar Republic

the British documents

Schocken Books · New York

First American edition published by Schocken Books 1984
10 9 8 7 6 5 4 3 2 1   84 85 86 87
Copyright © F. L. Carsten 1984
Published by agreement with B T Batsford Ltd, London

Library of Congress Cataloging in Publication Data

Carsten, F. L. (Francis Ludwig)
  Britain and the Weimar Republic.

  Bibliography p.
  Includes index.
  1. Germany—History—1918–1933—Sources.
I. Title.
DD234.C37   1984   943.085   84-5613

Designed by Ken Williamson
Manufactured in Great Britain
ISBN 0–8052–3840–5

CONTENTS

PREFACE

Over many years the Weimar Republic has attracted the interest
of historians and other writers and the volume of literature on its
history is ever growing. Yet the voluminous British records on
Germany for the years 1918 to 1933 have not been investigated
in detail. It is true that many documents from them have been
published in the series of *Documents on British Foreign Policy
1919–1939* (quoted as DBFP), but their accent naturally is on
issues of foreign policy; and all the documents are unfortunately
printed without the minutes which the permanent officials of
the Foreign Office made on the incoming reports, and which
often illuminate the shaping and conduct of foreign policy.
Quite apart from that, the British records also contain innumerable documents on internal German affairs, factual reports by
the numerous British officers and officials serving in Germany,
as well as their comments and criticisms. Owing to the occupation of the Rhineland and the several Allied Commissions
working in Germany – partly military, partly supervising the
various plebiscites – British officers and officials were in an
almost unique position to observe the German scene. Many of
their reports make fascinating reading and shed new light on
Weimar Germany. In addition, some German ministers, above all
Stresemann, were in the habit of talking confidentially to British
diplomats in Germany, of unburdening their hearts and expressing their secret worries to them. The bulk of the information in
the following chapters thus comes from the vast files of the
Foreign Office, but the files of the War Office too contain much
new and interesting information, from the days of the Inter-
Allied Armistice Commission to the years of clandestine

German rearmament in the later years of the Weimar Republic. The stress in the following chapters is more on internal developments in Germany than on foreign affairs, but it was of course impossible to separate the one from the other. Only the very technical problem of German reparations has not been covered in any detail.

My thanks are due to the staff of the Public Record Office who without complaint produced more than 1300 files for me and succeeded in recovering most of those files which were lent to various government departments, and equally to my wife who read the entire draft manuscript and commented on many points of detail.

F.L.C.
London, May 1983

I

DEFEAT AND REVOLUTION IN GERMANY

Before November 1918 the British authorities had hardly any indications that the German collapse was near, that a revolution was imminent and would engulf the whole of Germany. In late October revolutionary movements had broken out in the capitals of the Habsburg Monarchy; in Prague, Budapest and Vienna, National Councils were founded by the different nationalities of the 'multi-national Empire', and its disintegration and that of the Austrian army were proceeding apace.[1] But as yet there was no indication that Germany too would be affected by a similar movement, that the slow fighting retreat of the German army in France and Belgium would lead to a quick Allied victory at the western front, that the German request for an armistice meant the end of the war. Apparently it was assumed on the Allied side that the morale of the German army was still unimpaired, that resistance would continue into the winter of 1918, and little importance was attached to the mutiny of the German sailors which prevented the High Seas fleet from launching a last desperate attack on the British navy. It was noted, however, that disillusionment and anti-monarchical feelings were spreading in Germany on account of the military situation and the request for an armistice. On 1 November the Political Intelligence Department of the Foreign Office considered the 'Internal Conditions of Germany' and stated that it seemed doubtful whether the constitutional changes enacted by the German parliament which limited the 'arbitrary power' of the Emperor William II would 'suffice to save his crown and his dynasty'. German newspapers, such as the *Frankfurter Zeitung* and the social-democratic *Vorwärts*, were suggesting that he should 'draw the

1

necessary consequences' from the momentous changes in the political and military situation; speakers of the Independent Social Democrats (the USPD, which had broken away from the SPD on the issue of the war) were violently denouncing the Emperor; 'workmen are execrating him in the streets and, in one place, his statue has been attired with grotesque habiliments by way of insult and of invitation to take his departure.' Yet the assessment of the Political Intelligence Department was still extremely cautious: 'It remains to be seen whether the old Prussian loyalty, which till recently extended far into the middle and working classes, will survive the strain . . . and whether there exists a corps of officers who can interpose as a bodyguard of the Army between William II and his disillusioned people.' In that case, civil war might break out, and 'the momentous events in Austria' were likely to intensify the political crisis in Germany.[2]

Only a few days later the German revolution started, workers' and soldiers' councils sprang up all over the country and took over political power on the local level, and in Berlin a revolutionary government was formed by the two social-democratic parties and confirmed in office by a plenary meeting of the workers' and soldiers' deputies. The Emperor fled to Holland and there was no loyal corps of officers eager to defend his throne. A British officer who visited Berlin soon after was able to report that 'things are outwardly more or less normal. The ordinary bureaucratic machine is working, most of the Ministers remain at the head of their respective departments, each under the supervision of two socialists, one from each party, appointed by the Cabinet of six People's Commissaries.'[3] It was indeed the continuity of the Prussian bureaucracy which proved the decisive element in the volatile conditions which existed in Berlin and throughout the country; the control of the bureaucracy by the workers' and soldiers' councils did not seriously interfere with the working of the well-established machine but in practice upheld its authority. Law and order did not break down and discipline was maintained to a surprising extent. In December a senior British officer who had been a prisoner of war in Germany added: 'During our stay in Germany we saw no signs whatever of rioting. Guards under the orders of the Workmen's and Soldiers' Council lounged up and down the streets [of Berlin] with rifles over their arms. They were well turned out in new uniforms and wore a red brassard.'[4] This officer was able to observe the return of the front line troops to Berlin, a division of the Prussian Guards. Their reception was 'not such as would be given to a victorious army. There was no cheering, there was only a certain amount of hat and handkerchief waving... I estimated the companies at from 90 to 100 strong, chiefly consisting of very young soldiers. The machine guns limbering behind the companies were drawn by the most disreputable horses I have ever seen.... The troops, horses, guns, etc., were garlanded with flowers and leaves, but the general impression left on one's mind was that of a very pitiful display.'[4] If the High Command of the army had intended to use these troops against the workers' and soldiers' councils and to carry out a purge in Berlin,[5] they were clearly quite unsuitable for the purpose.

The British officers in the west and those reporting from inside Germany were naturally concerned about the condition of the German army (until 1920 there were no diplomatic reports from Germany). An armistice was signed on 11 November – two days after the outbreak of the revolution in Berlin – but a renewal of hostilities seemed possible then and in 1919, before the signature of the Treaty of Versailles. One officer who had an excellent opportunity to watch the retreating German units to the west of the Rhine was Lieutenant-General R. Haking, the British representative on the International Armistice Commission which met at Spa in Belgium, where the German High Command had worked during the war. From his reports to the War Office it emerged clearly that discipline had not broken down (as it had done in the Austrian army), that the units marched back into Germany in comparatively good order and under the command of their officers. 'So far as I have seen', Haking wrote on 16 November, 'the German men look sullen, but they are undoubtedly behaving in an orderly manner. The officers have no real control over them, but the men appear to recognize that somebody must give orders in order to get them back to their own country, which appears to be their main idea at the moment. . . . A great many soldiers and a great many vehicles carry red badges or a red revolutionary flag, and it appears that most of the officers or men have removed their decorations which do not appear to be popular. As regards the troops on the road, march discipline was fairly well maintained, and the men were moving in proper formation.' He added that the Germans had no petrol at all and were forced to leave their lorries wherever they ran out of petrol.[6] Four days later, on 20 November, Haking reported that German infantry, cavalry and artillery had been passing through

3

Spa since the early hours of the morning and were still marching through 'in excellent order, the infantry are singing and in a few cases bands have been playing. . . . The German Town Major, whom I happened to meet during the day, told me they were some of the best troops they had. Some of the officers saluted as we walked past, and the men obeyed orders very well when they were ordered to fall in and march off after a short halt.' Haking also mentioned that the infantry were not from Prussia but from Württemberg, and comparatively few in number.[7]

It is interesting that a German staff officer provided a some-what different picture. He described the arrival at Spa 'of a magnificent, highly disciplined storm battalion' in a state of high morale and efficiency, and how it 'immediately collapsed and lost all discipline and control' under the influence of 'another battalion infected with indiscipline and political chaos' (sic). The German officer also told General Haking that the units in the interior of Germany consisted almost exclusively of either very young or old men 'and their discipline has almost disappeared'. There the soldiers' councils had great power, 'in some cases having complete control of military matters and of Government'; but in the front line units discipline was on the whole still good, for there the authorities limited the soldiers' councils to 'advisory powers only'. The officer admitted that Germany had collapsed completely, but he and his like 'hoped to save their country and Europe from irretrievable disaster, if it were still possible'.[8] That the soldiers' councils in the west had only very limited powers was confirmed to Haking by two members of such a council attached to the German High Command who called on him to inform him of their views. The High Command, they told him, retained all executive powers and they themselves only acted as advisors; they knew 'that the only salvation for the army and the nation is that discipline and order are maintained and that Bolshevism must be kept down.' As to the mood among the troops, the two emissaries declared that the terms of the armistice were so severe that it was impossible to comply with them, 'that the Entente wished to crush the whole German nation, both militarily and economic-ally by letting loose the worst Bolshevik elements and thus increasing the disorder in Germany which would then be quite uncontrollable. These disorders would then certainly spread to other countries and the blame would be on the Allies.' The Allied governments, they added, 'had always said that they were

4

prepared to deal fairly with the German nation if they threw over the military regime but that now . . . there was no moderation in the terms imposed upon Germany; this would rankle for ever in the minds of the German nation.'[9] The two delegates had clearly been well primed by their superiors of the High Command. As early as mid-November the principal lines of German military propaganda with regard to the peace terms and the danger of Bolshevism were conveyed to Britain, not by members of the Prussian officer corps, but by delegates of a soldiers' council. There was no comment from the British side.

Nor was there when a German naval officer volunteered the information that 'the whole machinery still works, the administrative business still goes on for the time being, but there is no head, no energy and the whole nation is "pumped out" and sucked dry.' According to this officer, the German government had no real power and the permanent officials were like 'rabbits fascinated by a snake' poised to devour them, namely Bolshevism; in Berlin a movement was afoot to transfer supreme control to a soldiers' and workers' council; if these councils took over the future was hopeless because they did not represent the nation; the situation was so critical that even Hindenburg, a 'demi-god still in the eyes of half the country', was forced to have his papers stamped by a soldiers' council; the front-line officers, on the other hand, were convinced that they had not been defeated but were 'let down by the revolutionaries at home'; they were full of resentment against the munition workers and the troops at home 'who have lived in ease while they fought'; they wanted 'to take charge and to get a representative government on which they were represented.'[10] Towards the end of November General Haking again noted that very good order was maintained among the troops passing through Spa, that their march discipline seemed to improve, which confirmed his earlier opinion 'that the troops in the front line are less affected by the revolution than those behind'.[11]

Similarly a British officer who had observed the political scene in Berlin wrote: 'The troops, particularly the troops back from the front, are, I think, an element making for safety and order. Their general attitude is that they have been fighting for over four and a half years in the field and do not want to have fighting at home. Their demand is for peace, quiet and order.' In general, they loyally supported the new government and were strongly opposed to the extreme Left, the Spartacists (the followers of Karl Liebknecht and Rosa Luxemburg). Even the German troops on the Eastern Front, 'so far from having been corrupted by the proximity of Bolshevism, are among its most determined opponents' and had recently refused to allow some Bolshevik delegates to pass through their lines to go to Berlin. He added that, so far as he knew, in the garrison towns the soldiers' councils were 'on the whole working smoothly and contributing to the maintenance of order and discipline.'[12] This picture is confirmed by numerous accounts from the German side. In general, the soldiers' councils often consisted of professional NCOs and were an element of order in an often disorderly atmosphere.[13]

A Canadian engineer, who during the war had been interned near Berlin, was able to attend two meetings of the Berlin soldiers' council and emphasized 'the thoroughness of the support of the *moderate* tendency within the Revolution'; a proposal to form a 'Red Guard' to defend the revolution, which was supported by some members of the Executive Council of the Berlin workers' and soldiers' councils, 'was turned down by a very large majority, and nearly all the speakers were vigorous in their denunciation of Liebknecht and his group.' According to this report, Liebknecht lost the sympathy of the soldiers when his followers stormed the military magazines on 9 November and distributed the rifles indiscriminately, thus causing much shooting during the first days of the revolution; the soldiers 'resented Liebknecht's attempt to utilise the opportunity to make himself supreme'. With regard to 'the existing Soviets' (the workers' and soldiers' councils), the engineer stated that they varied greatly 'as regards the relative strength of the radicals and the moderate elements within them' and that in November the Leipzig council was by far the most radical (it was dominated by the Independent Social Democrats, but in reality some others were much further to the Left). The general situation, he thought, could be saved if the provisional government managed to bring enough provisions into Berlin and other towns; so far it had 'received the most effective support from the soldiers in Berlin, and from the fact that almost without exception the entire machinery of the old officialdom remained intact. . . . These officials, who might have been expected from their traditions to have offered the most determined resistance to the Revolution, have apparently been overwhelmed by the suddenness and the strength of the revolutionary movement.'[14] It was a realistic assessment, considerably more so than that provided by the German representative on the Armistice Commission, Edgar von Haniel, who claimed that 'there is no properly constituted Government in Germany', that 'the extreme socialists' were in power, that there were 'no reliable troops in Germany, except a few who are only reliable to a limited extent', that it was necessary 'to get back into Germany the front line troops . . . to safeguard the populace against anarchy'.[15] All this was propaganda, meant for Allied ears.

Towards the end of November one of Germany's most important industrialists, Hugo Stinnes, added his voice to that of the other Germans. According to him, at least 85 per cent of the population wanted peace and quiet, but they were terrorized by the remaining 15 per cent, 'and as these were armed and the rest were not, they did exactly as they liked.' When General Haking pointed out that the troops returning from the front 'were very well disciplined and that it was inconceivable that a nation like the Germans who had been brought up to respect order and discipline would suddenly get out of hand', Stinnes replied that the troops lost all discipline when they crossed the frontier and gave up their arms; in Russia too, the population 'were dominated by a small number of extremists who liked the state of unrest and wanted to go on plundering'. In his opinion, it was the duty of the victors to restore quiet and order to the world; they should announce that they would only negotiate with a stable government elected on a democratic basis, 'but that a continuance of the present state of chaos would bring with it the occupation of larger zones by the Allies, and for longer periods, and also an increase of the supply difficulties, as the Allies would not be prepared to help a nation in which anarchy and disorder exists.' If the Allies adopted such a firm policy, 'the result would be apparent very quickly and not only Germany but the Allies themselves would benefit by the firm handling of a difficult and dangerous situation.'[16] Clearly Stinnes, whose principal interests were in the Ruhr area,[17] preferred an Allied occupation to the dangers which allegedly threatened his interests. However, there was no 'present state of chaos' in Germany – only a weak government which tried to preserve law and order and for that purpose was willing to cooperate with the leaders of the old army and the old bureaucracy. From the national point of view it clearly was Stinnes' duty to support these efforts, and not to weaken the government still further by suggesting the occupation of more German territory (apart from the left bank of the Rhine which was occupied by the Allied armies under the terms of the armistice). We will see later that the occupation of the Ruhr valley, Germany's industrial heart, was an ever-present threat used by the French government to achieve German compliance with Allied demands (see pages 42, 68, 123–4).

In general, the fear of Bolshevism was widespread during the last weeks of 1918, and not only used as a bogey to frighten the Allies. The Canadian engineer quoted earlier reported that 'the better classes and the more serious among the working people and soldiers themselves are in genuine terror of such a Bolshevist attempt. Two of my informants, whom I considered best able to judge the general feeling, fully expected such an attempt to be made before the convening of the National Assembly. Both believed that the attempt would be unsuccessful, unless in the meantime the demobilization and a failure of provisioning the big cities had demoralized the present organization of the Soldiers' Councils.'[18] A British officer who went to Berlin at the beginning of December stated succinctly: 'The supreme danger – if one may judge from feeling in Berlin – is Bolshevism', and 'the atmosphere is tense, Berlin is in terror of Bolshevism.' On Sunday, 8 December, he attended an open air meeting of the Independent Social Democrats in front of the Reichstag, which in spite of slight rain (and the cold) was attended by about 2,000 people. The first speaker, the Independent deputy Heinrich Ströbel, defended his party's compromise with the moderate SPD (by the formation of the coalition government) and repudiated Bolshevism: 'You cannot introduce Russian methods into Germany; you cannot socialize in half an hour or half a year.' He was followed by a Spartacist, Friedrich Rück from Stuttgart, who 'made it clear that the policy of the Spartacus Bund is the policy of Bolshevism, *pure et simple*' and exclaimed: 'We want democracy, but true democracy, the democracy of the working classes, which is far better represented by the organized workmen's and soldiers' councils than in any constituent assembly.' There was a fair amount of interruption and, as far as the officer could judge, only 'about one-fifth to one-quarter of those present' supported the Spartacus speaker.[19] One of the German officers on the Armistice Commission even told the British that the Spartacists intended to take all the officers of the Prussian Ministry of War and their wives hostages: of this the German

8

delegation had been officially informed, and the wife of one officer had thereupon put herself under the protection of the Berlin soldiers' council. This was after the failure of an alleged Spartacus coup in Berlin on 6 December, when a radical demonstration was fired upon by a Guards' unit and was dispersed 'with considerable bloodshed'.[20]

A British secret agent who left Berlin on 21 December sent in a report which was considerably more reassuring. This was immediately after the meeting of the national congress of the workers' and soldiers' councils which decided by a large majority in favour of holding the elections to the National Assembly as early as 19 January 1919, a considerable victory for the moderate Social Democrats. The agent stated that 'position [was] now thoroughly satisfactory. Government established beyond reasonable possibility of disturbances pending meeting of National Assembly. . . . Spartacus group utterly discredited and powerless in Berlin which is only place where it even pretends to have any strength. Its failure at Congress [of workers' and soldiers' councils] was complete and its demonstrations outside quite lifeless and ineffective, it grew obviously weaker every day.' The position of Ebert, the chairman of the provisional government, was 'extremely strong' and he was generally trusted; the leaders of the USPD who had first tried to sit on the fence, 'have been driven steadily to the Right by force of events of past week. . . . Further disturbances are conceivable but highly improbable' because the troops returning to Berlin 'are anti-Spartacus to a man . . . and are only too eager to use their weapons against them.' Yet he added a severe warning that the economic situation was 'far more serious not so much regarding food as regarding raw materials and the physical difficulties of demobilisation. Food rations are being maintained at quite sufficient level and supplies will last till about second week in February when there will be no shortage but complete famine.' In his opinion, the government was 'worried to point of panic' not by this danger, 'but by immediate dangers due to shortage of coal, unorganised spontaneous demobilisation and universal unemployment.' He felt it was 'impossible to overestimate the necessity for extreme care and fullest possible understanding on our side of economic situation in Germany which failing economic supplies is literally desperate'; the continuation of the blockade would 'create a fatalistic spirit of helpless fear', an 'increasing possibility of irrevocable disaster only slightly less

9

damaging to us than to the Germans'; their ingrained habits of discipline would let the machine run as long as possible, 'but if it becomes impossible there exists no force which could control situation and Anarchy seems unavoidable.'[21]

This report was taken very seriously in London and forwarded by the Intelligence Department to the Foreign Office as coming 'from a very reliable source', 'the first really trustworthy account of events in Berlin', written by 'an intellectual Socialist who has been in touch with the German Socialists, especially the Minority, throughout the war'. The Intelligence assessment was 'that there is an enormous preponderance of opinion in Germany for a stable regime under the Socialists and Left and that the Spartacus Group are in reality a very small minority who will eventually be overthrown.' Only the economic situation, if it got worse, would increase the elements of disorder, 'and if this happened, the forces of anarchy will prevail.'[22] The fear of 'anarchy' or 'chaos' in Germany, with serious repercussions in other countries, was to reappear in the British records of 1919 and eventually caused the lifting of the blockade, yet this was to take a considerable time. The same fear was strongly present on the German side and induced the provisional government to take strong measures against internal disorders. At the beginning of 1919 the senior German representative on the Armistice Commission even informed General Haking that his government 'were most anxious to do everything possible to break down Bolshevism which had been, and might again be in the future, a serious danger to the establishment of stable government in Germany'. He went on to say that the Germans would welcome the sending of British troops to Riga and an occupation of the eastern districts of East Prussia which otherwise might be invaded by the Red Army.[23] Although Haking declined to discuss the question with the Germans he seriously considered the issue. As he informed the War Office, he was convinced 'that the German is much too stolid, possesses too much common sense, and is too accustomed to order and discipline to wish for anything but a firm government and will do what he can to get it.' But the Germans were 'worn out mind and body by the war' and likely 'to adopt the line of least resistance, at least temporarily', and this might cause a Bolshevist success, if only for the moment. He therefore suggested that plans should be prepared 'for an immediate and rapid occupation of certain important cities in Germany directly the necessity arises'; the knowledge

that the Allies were prepared to take such a step would considerably 'strengthen the hands of the German Government which
desires order and might even stave off disaster'.[24]

These lines were written after the outbreak of the so-called
Spartacus Rising in Berlin in the early days of January 1919, an
ill-coordinated and amateurish attempt by the extreme Left to
seize power, which was only supported by a tiny minority of the
workers of Berlin. On 9 January Haking was informed by the
Germans that the government was still functioning, that the
situation was improving, that the government 'were now in a
stronger position and were prepared to put down disorder by
force of arms', but that there was no electric light and the trams
were not running.[25] A much more detailed report reached
London from the British Red Cross Commissioner in Berlin, who
was an eye-witness, observing events from the vantage point of
the British embassy in the Wilhelmstrasse close to the
Brandenburg Gate. On 6 January, he wrote, 'the situation was
very critical'; severe fighting erupted in the Wilhelmstrasse and
at the Brandenburg Gate the top of which was in the hands of
government troops in the early morning but fell to the Spartacists about 11 a.m., to be retaken by government forces in the
evening. The Spartacists also occupied the police headquarters,
some railway stations and newspaper buildings, but their
attacks on the Chancellery in the Wilhelmstrasse were repulsed
with heavy losses. On 7 January the British personnel were
unable to reach the square facing the gate on account of machine
gun fire from it; there was severe fighting in the whole area and
they had to close the office about noon. The Commissioner did
not believe that the Spartacists (whom he estimated at about
4,000 to 5,000) were 'a very large group of fighters' and thought
that the government would soon gain the upper hand, as troops
had been ordered into Berlin. But he added: 'The Spartacus
group can be subdued but it cannot be exterminated unless the
German people see that the Government party can bring more
definite improvement in the shape of food supplies. . . . Even if
food does not come into the country at once, definite assurance
that something is being done would be some good and any relief
however small for the children and perhaps also for the women
would be of vital importance.'[26]

A few days later Major-General Ewart, who was another eye-
witness in Berlin, saw the German Foreign Minister, Count
Brockdorff-Rantzau, and asked what he thought of the situation.

The reply was that the government 'were getting it into hand and that they were determined to suppress the Spartacus movement'. Ewart's report included a detailed description of the storming of the *Vorwärts* building by government troops on 11 January; it also stated: 'there is a serious shortage of food in the country. The rich can still procure what they want but at most prohibitive prices, while the middle and lower classes cannot afford to pay the prices charged, and their ration is only a subsistence one.' The German officials he had seen in Berlin had shown 'a feverish anxiety to avoid anything to give offence to Great Britain'[27] – probably on account of German hopes that the blockade would be lifted, although Ewart did not say so expressly. The Political Intelligence Department of the Foreign Office commented on 'The Fight for Order in Berlin' that the Spartacists had obtained their weapons from the armament factories at Spandau through the good services of the Director of the Berlin police, Eichhorn, who sympathized with them, and that the police headquarters at the Alexanderplatz had 'for weeks past been converted into a Spartacus arsenal from which arms were distributed to Liebknecht's mob whenever disturbances broke out':[28] an account which seems to have been taken from the more sensational reports of the German press. An Intelligence report stated more accurately soon after that the Spartacist attempt had 'ended in complete disaster' because the government could rely on certain disciplined units and at least one of its members, Gustav Noske, 'was not afraid to use them', so that 'the situation was got in hand without any great difficulty or bloodshed'.[29] In reality the suppression was quite ruthless, but the fighting did not spread outside Berlin. Nothing was said about the murder of the Spartacus leaders, Liebknecht and Luxemburg, by government troops.

The same report mentioned that the centre of resistance to the government forces had meanwhile shifted to Brunswick, a small state with a long radical tradition and a radical socialist government. Allegedly, the radicals intended to bring about 'the establishment of a Bolshevik North German Republic, which is to be ruled by the Workmen's and Soldiers' Councils, and to separate from the rest of Germany', and if possible to obtain a separate peace treaty. The movement, however, was only supported by a small minority, yet it was considered symptomatic of the difficulties confronting the government 'once the authorities appointed by the Constituent Assembly have to take over the powers which are nominally exercised by the Workmen's and Soldiers' Councils which will not yield without a struggle.'[30] Yet this struggle remained limited to a few towns, such as Bremen, Brunswick and Munich where left-wing influence was particularly strong, and the large majority of the councils yielded without any fight or dissolved themselves. A British officer who visited Leipzig – another city with a strong left-wing council – in mid-January found the city 'extremely quiet and orderly': 'In the expensive lounge of the Astoria Hotel there was no reflection of the Bolshevist menace. Fish, poultry and coffee, luxuries denied to the ordinary populace, were here obtainable by those who could afford to pay the price.' But beer, sugar, butter and fats were unobtainable. The officer saw the Saxon corps commander, General Franke, by whom he was introduced to a member of the local soldiers' council. The latter said immediately, 'We must speed up this demobilisation', to which the general assented and explained that it was proceeding as speedily as possible. According to his visitor, 'it was really pathetic to see the unfortunate General who was a powerless puppet in his own headquarters, not saluted by his own sentries and having to stand up to a private soldier. No wonder he preferred to dress as a civilian.'[31] But it may well have been that the general did not want to offer a chair to a member of the soldiers' council and thus chose to stand himself. The British officer's sympathy went to a member of his own caste.

In February two British officers went to Hanover to inspect the barracks. There the officers were always saluted by the men, and a major told the visitors that the soldiers' council 'were quite well behaved and never interfered with him'. This was confirmed by a cavalry captain who stated that discipline in his Uhlan Regiment was very good and that he was in charge of demobilization at the request of the soldiers' council.[32] In Hamburg in the same month an officer found that the workers' and soldiers' council – 'a body of men whose knowledge and antecedents in no way entitles them to rule' – still exercized political power but was on the whole moderate in its politics; when the provisional government sent troops against Bremen, a far more radical city, the Hamburg left-wingers urged that Bremen must be supported by military force and the workers be armed; but the garrison of Hamburg refused to march to Bremen and the Hamburg council assured the central government of its support.[33] During the same month three British officers also reported on the political situation in Bavaria. There the revolution had 'passed fairly quietly'; the peasants were good Catholics and not influenced by the radical opinions prevailing in the larger towns, but power was in the hands of the workers' and soldiers' councils; in military matters 'they issue orders which are only endorsed by Officers as a matter of form'. A German captain whom they interviewed at Garmisch told them that the soldiers' councils 'had done very excellent work in organizing demobilization; but for them the men would have deserted their posts everywhere and chaos would have resulted.' The British officers found that in Bavaria the councils were trying hard to consolidate their power.[34] What emerges from these reports is that political conditions varied greatly in the different areas of Germany, as did the attitude of the local workers' and soldiers' councils, only a small minority of which were controlled by left-wing extremists.

In March 1919 two British officers visited the 5th Division at Frankfurt-on-Oder and found its discipline 'better than in the majority of German Divisions to-day', but in reality not all that good. 'Officers and non-commissioned officers have little authority, and are afraid to give orders. Red flags are flown over all barracks. The men are fairly smartly turned out. . . . The men do not salute their officers, and their manner towards them is friendly rather than respectful. . . . Officers do not wear swords.' The two officers also commented on the poor quality of the volunteer units raised by the government against the Poles: 'So far the results have been disappointing to the Government. The majority of the men enlisting in the Volunteer Army do so because they have no other means of employment. Their *moral* (sic) is not good, and they apparently have no intention of taking part in any real fighting. The officers have a poor opinion of the capabilities of the Volunteers.'[35] This was confirmed by a British major who wrote from Berlin in the same month that most of the volunteers enlisted because they wanted food and clothing 'and are not worth much when it comes to the point. The danger to the Entente from the mobile army is nil.' He further believed that, if Bolshevism was to be stopped, supplies must be sent to Germany: 'There is *real* want. Feeling is that we are murdering women and children unnecessarily.'[36] In March there was renewed fighting in Berlin between government forces and radical sailors and soldiers, as well as a general strike. In General Ewart's opinion, the fighting would only last a few days as the government troops were better armed and possessed four to five times the strength of the radicals. He distinguished three factions, each fighting the other two: the volunteer units, the Berlin garrison under the orders of the soldiers' council, and the Spartacists. Count Brockdorff-Rantzau had informed him that 'the Government troops were holding their own satisfactorily' against the red sailors.[37]

What military matters looked like in a large city of the German east was vividly described by another British officer, reporting from Danzig in February 1919. The commanding general, Otto von Below, lived in the house in which Field-Marshal von Mackensen had once resided and possessed considerable power, 'for all the red flags' and the armed pickets of the local workers' and soldiers' council. When the 1st Regiment of the Death's Head Hussars (Mackensen's old regiment) made their 'triumphal entry, with a full dress mounted band, numerous laurel and bay wreaths, and thousands of people to accompany and cheer them', the red flags disappeared from military headquarters, not to be seen again. Generally, however, not much notice was taken of the officers and the men were slovenly; only in the Hussar Regiment the discipline was 'distinctly good'. On the night of the ex-Kaiser's birthday – 27 January – a dinner took place at the town's leading hotel, and 'one man who did not stand to attention when the anthem was played for the toast was hove out with unmistakable emphasis'; most of the military were royalist, and references to 'mein Kaiser' or 'unser Kaiser' were often heard among men in uniform.[38] General Ewart too observed in Berlin signs 'of increasing power amongst the officer class' and even thought it might become predominant 'to the extent of carrying out a coup de main and establishing a monarchy'. General Haking, however, rightly believed that such a coup 'would be immediately followed by definite civil war' because a complete cleavage would occur between the opposing sides.[39]

That these reports were not based on rumours was proved by a visit of Colonel Max Bauer, Ludendorff's former adjutant, to Major-General Malcolm in Berlin in July 1919. He wanted to establish what the attitude of the British government would be if certain people, 'principally influential industrialists and other men with practical experience of public life', as he put it, turned out the coalition government. Other German officers had contacted General Malcolm previously, but Bauer was more explicit and mentioned that the attempt might be made within a few weeks: the govenment would be informed that they had lost the confidence of the country and that the army could no longer support them. General Malcolm expressed strong doubts 'whether the men would follow their officers in a political enterprise of this sort' and feared that its outcome would be to bring the extreme Left to power; in any case it would delay the establishment of a stable government and economic recovery.[40] Nine months later the attempt was made, but it failed miserably, and the result was civil war (see pages 34–41).

In 1919 the German civil war reached its zenith with the proclamation of the so-called 'Soviet Republic' in Munich in April, and its overthrow after severe fighting by government troops at the end of the month. Even earlier developments in Munich took a much more radical turn after the murder of Kurt Eisner, the left-wing socialist prime minister of Bavaria, by a right-wing student on 21 February. Eisner's plan had been to preserve the influence of the workers', peasants' and soldiers' councils side by side with an elected parliament, and in Munich these councils retained much of their power when they were losing it elsewhere in Germany. Eisner's death caused them to claim still greater powers and to dispute the claims of the elected Diet in which the extreme Left was only very weakly represented. A few days after the death of Eisner, Dr Johann Wilhelm Muehlon, a well known German pacifist who had found asylum in Switzerland during the war,[41] was invited by the Central Committee of the Bavarian councils to become Bavaria's Minister of Foreign Affairs, and accordingly left Switzerland for Munich. But some days later, as the British minister reported from Bern, Muehlon hurriedly returned there. Apparently he had expected to find the old, rather moderate councils in power, as they had existed at the time of Eisner. When Muehlon met the Central Committee he therefore explained to them 'his policy of working with and through parliamentary institutions while at the same time cooperating with Soldiers', Workmen's and Peasants' Councils as long as they confined themselves to technical questions'. Thereupon he was pronounced a dangerous reactionary and promptly left Munich. In his opinion, the Central Committee, the leading organ of government, was 'entirely dominated by a small board of Bolsheviks' and supported by demobilized soldiers and the unemployed and hungry; they had proclaimed 'a "provisional" dictatorship of the proletariat which will become permanent as there is no force to overthrow it'; the officials and the people in general 'display complete helplessness, hopelessness and apathy', while real power was in the hands of Max Levien, a Communist of Russian origin, whose only aim was 'to save [the] Russian revolution by spreading Bolshevism abroad'. Muehlon feared that Bolshevism, once established in Bavaria, would infect the whole of Germany unless the Entente took immediate steps to support the more sober elements in the north. The British Minister in Bern, Sir Horace Rumbold, thought the picture painted by Muehlon rather gloomy as he did not know the conditions in other parts of Bavaria. But Rumbold too believed 'that there seems little doubt that a purely Bolshevik Government has for the first time been set up in Germany, that it is controlled by a Russian who is no doubt in touch with Moscow, and that all conditions are favourable to [the] spread of Bolshevism to [the] rest of Germany once an organising centre has been set up in [the] country.'[42]

On 7 April, some weeks after Muehlon's departure, the Bavarian 'Soviet Republic' was officially proclaimed, not by the Communists, but by radical socialists and anarchists, and from the outset the strong working-class organizations of northern Bavaria were opposed to the venture. On 5 April a British officer reported from Berlin that the proclamation was imminent and that the situation was complicated because in Bavaria there were no organized troops which could be used; the nearest force was in Thuringia under Colonel von Epp, but it consisted of barely two battalions. This force, together with Prussian and Württemberg units, was eventually used to subdue Munich. The officer also suggested that 'it is extremely desirable that the Entente should publish a Note, in which it is clearly and emphatically stated that no food will be sent to Munich as long as it is in the hands of a Soviet', but that considerable quantities should be sent to other parts of Germany.[43] Another British officer reported that in Nuremberg there was great anxiety in official circles whether the town would follow Munich's example, but that the situation eased when the local workers' and soldiers' council rejected a resolution in favour of a 'Soviet Republic' by a two to one majority. Nevertheless martial law was proclaimed, cavalry was patrolling the streets, and the town hall was closed and strongly guarded. This officer too was convinced that 'the arrival of adequate food supplies will check the wave of unrest and the movement towards Bolshivist (*sic*) chaos which is undoubtedly making great strides at the moment', but it might already be too late. In his opinion, 'the greatest danger lies in the fact that the nerves of the German people appear to have broken down. A people of little political understanding, they imagined, when the Armistice was signed, that peace was immediately at hand, and that the privations of four and a half years were over.' These hopes were disappointed, and 'from the heights of hope of last November . . . they were plunged into the depths of despair. And it is this despair which has given Bolshevism its chance'; the German Communists were promising ample food supplies from the East, and 'the Germans, despairing of help from the West, are turning their eyes to the East.'[44]

One British junior officer even ventured into the turmoil of Munich, where his room was promptly searched, his papers were taken away and he himself was arrested by a red sailor. But he told his captors that he was entitled to associate with anyone he liked and that his revolver was part of his uniform. They held council and then one of them informed him: 'A British officer must have complete freedom, and this one appears to be honest and good tempered. Moreover, he is not a bourgeois and may be trusted with his revolver.' Finally, they voted unanimously for his release and apologized to him; even his gun would be given back to him. When he returned to his room he found his papers there, and none were missing.[45]

When the 'Soviet Republic' had been overthrown by the combined forces of Prussia and other German states and 'order' had been restored ruthlessly, the Political Intelligence Department of the Foreign Office stated: 'When the Soviet Government was not indulging in buffoonery or brutality its time was occupied with endless internal wranglings. In Munich experiments in Communism could for a few weeks be attempted. But no satisfactory answer was discovered to the question which Lenin asked by wireless from Moscow – How the Soviet Government intended to carry out the socialization of agriculture in Bavaria?' Only that the brutality used by the 'white' troops during the conquest was considerably greater than that of the 'red' defenders – a point which seems to have escaped the Intelligence Department. It was on safer ground, however, when it found that the result of the whole affair was 'to strengthen the cause of law and order throughout Germany, and to discredit Bolshevism and Spartacism with the masses.'[46] Yet the principal result was a swing of the political pendulum to the Right, especially in Bavaria. As far as Bavaria was concerned the hope expressed in the memorandum that the help rendered to Bavaria by the other states would bring about an 'intimate cooperation' with the central government was not fulfilled. A minute written by a Foreign Office official at that time also considered the joint military action against Munich 'a hopeful symptom . . . because it shows that the dangerous particularism of Bavaria, both Catholic and Spartacist, . . . is being overcome'.[47] This hope was fulfilled only with regard to the danger threatening from the Left; as we shall see, the right-wing particularism of Bavaria received a lasting impetus from the events of April 1919, and it was directed against the government in Berlin whose forces had 'liberated' Munich.

When a British officer visited Munich in August 1919 a high government official informed him that 'the state of the province has improved very considerably. Bolshevism has disappeared.' No separatist tendency existed, and the Bavarian government would 'strive for the widest possible autonomy within the Empire.' The head of the Dominican Order in Bavaria confirmed, on the basis of reports on left-wing extremism from all parts of the country, that Bolshevism was 'no longer dangerous'. He added that he had received many reports of a considerable increase in anti-Semitism: 'The people attributed the political agitation and consequent bloodshed to the Jews, and Jewish funds were always available to support Socialist and Communist organizations.' Meanwhile three Bavarian Reichswehr brigades had been formed with a total strength of 35,000 men, so that the military position was 'quite satisfactory', and apart from that the government as a safeguard retained the Prussian Marine (Ehrhardt) Brigade which had taken part in the conquest of Munich.[48] Soon, under the protective wing of the Bavarian Reichswehr, the extreme right-wing and anti-semitic movement was to assume formidable proportions.

For the time being, in spite of the suppression of the council movement and of the 'Soviet Republic', certain accounts still stressed the danger of Bolshevism spreading to Germany and other countries. In April General Haking reported that, in the opinion of the French delegates to the Armistice Commission, 'the Germans exaggerate Bolshevism in their country and that there is no more chance of a bolshevist Government being established in Germany than there is in France'. He thought it possible 'that the Germans were exaggerating the danger of Bolshevism in order to reduce the severity of the Armistice terms, especially the blockade', but admitted at the same time that a serious danger existed which the Allies could not neglect.[49] Some days later Haking approached his German counterpart, General von Hammerstein, and told him 'that the Germans were exaggerating the danger of Bolshevism in order to obtain relief', but the latter denied this and declared that they did not have enough reliable troops to defend the eastern frontiers and to keep down Bolshevism at home. Haking still believed in 'the imminent danger of the destruction of the German Government by Bolshevism'.[50] At the beginning of May, however, General von Hammerstein informed him that now the German government was stronger than it had ever been and that no Soviet government would be able to establish itself. The danger that still existed, on the other hand, was 'Bolshevism, pure and simple, not a Bolshevik government, but irresponsible Bolshevism, including murders, robbery, etc., throughout part or the whole of the country'.[51] Apparently he no longer feared a Communist seizure of power, but something rather different, the spread of lawlessness or anarchy – a rather unlikely development considering the German love of order and discipline noticed in so many of the reports. At about the same time a minute by a Foreign Office official stated quite clearly: 'As for organized Bolshevism, all the evidence is against the possibility of its success (even temporary) in Germany. . . . The moment peace is concluded, the imperial Government will no longer have any reason for employing the dread of Bolshevism among the Allies as a diplomatic weapon, and the suppression of Spartacist disorder will be more rapid and thorough. What is wanted above all, however, is raw materials and credit in order to facilitate the revival of industrial activity.'[52] By 'organized' Bolshevism he obviously meant the attempts of the German Spartacists to seize power which were defeated in the early months of 1919, and the other danger – that of 'anarchy' or 'chaos' – could best be combatted by economic means.

In the spring of 1919 not only individual officers, but also the British General Staff and by implication Winston Churchill, the Secretary of State for War, were urging that the blockade should be lifted and the way be opened to German economic recovery. In February a British agent, after visits to Berlin, Cassel, Frankfurt, Munich and other towns in the south, sent an urgent secret report 'that three things are necessary for the suppression of Bolshevism in Germany, first food, second food, and third food, and the most important kind of food is fat.' It was essential that the German government should be given definite support: 'It must be made clear that it is with them and with them only that the Entente will treat and [that it is] into their hands alone that food will be delivered. . . . It cannot be insisted too strongly that large quantities are necessary and still more, that a constant supply for the next three or four months must be promised if the ravages of the disease of Bolshevism are to be checked.[53] In April Churchill circulated to the Cabinet a note by an officer who had recently returned from Berlin that among the poorer classes, the small shopkeepers and small officials whose earnings had remained stationary, there existed 'a feeling of apathetic despair' and many were literally starving; it was essential 'to give the German people some hope of future security and of at least a partial recovery'.[54] A few days later the General Staff composed a memorandum on the 'Relaxation of the Blockade of Germany' which Churchill again circulated to the Cabinet. It stated that 'the national spirit of Germany seems to be completely crushed and the existing Government is extremely unlikely to contest the will of the Allies by force of arms. The maintenance of this Government is consequently a primary interest of the Allies, but its position is weak, and unless it can alleviate the terrible conditions existing in large parts of Germany, its fall is practically certain. This would be disastrous from every point of view', for any succeeding government would be unable and most probably also unwilling to carry out the Allied terms.[55] Prime Minister Lloyd George was told by Churchill that his policy was a simple one: 'Feed Germany; fight Bolshevism; make Germany fight Bolshevism.'[56] In truth, however, it was not all that simple because Britain also had to take into account the wishes of its Allies, especially of France.

In August 1919 General Malcolm, the head of the British Military Mission, wrote from Berlin that violent revolution was no longer feared as much as 'a gradual dissolution of the central authority until the country sinks into passive anarchy'; the expression was current in Berlin: 'Things have got to get much worse before they get any better.'[57] At the end of the year Churchill circulated yet another report, written by a colonel of the General Staff, which stated bluntly: 'Germany should be strengthened, politically and economically, in order to enable

21

the people to settle down and to make it possible for them to pay us. A loan is required in order to stabilize the German exchange and to provide raw material to keep the factories going'; the German government should receive some recognition for their comparative honesty and good faith; any alternative government would be either reactionary or extreme left-wing, and either would be disadvantageous for Britain, for the strongest members of the present government were genuinely anxious to carry out the terms of the Peace Treaty.[58] It was no doubt largely due to these alarming reports by British officers and the fear of Bolshevism spreading westwards that the Allied Supreme Council in March 1919 gave way to the urging of the British government and permitted large shipments of food to be sent to Germany. Although the blockade remained formally in force, it was slowly relaxed, even before the signing of the Peace of Versailles.[59]

Yet the political and economic situation of Germany remained very precarious. At the end of June General Malcolm reported that, in spite of the German acceptance of the treaty, the government was far from secure and that the two principal coalition partners, the Centre and the Social Democrats, had little in common; attacks on the government were being mounted 'both by the Reactionaries of the Right and the Independents of the Left. . . . It is, therefore, most important that the present Government, or something resembling it, should be kept in power, and I would urge that the Allied Governments should do whatever they can to support it.'[60] A few weeks later he added: 'Notwithstanding all the criticism, I adhere to my opinion that the Government has done well in circumstances of extraordinary difficulty. I recall the prophecies which used to be made so frequently that whether the peace was signed or not, the country would certainly be in revolution by the end of June, that war with Poland was inevitable, that the Army would certainly dissolve, and that other disasters were imminent'; yet the worst had been avoided and the government deserved a share of the credit, although the very general wish for peace and quiet had helped matters.[61] At the end of July Malcolm once more stated that the government was labouring under extraordinary difficulties and was attacked from both flanks; it had to surrender territory, to suppress disorders and to find vast sums of money; no government could be popular in such circumstances, but there was no real alternative: 'if we want to see stable conditions in Central

Europe, we should give Ebert and Bauer [the President and the Chancellor] all the support we can. . . . They are not men of genius, and they are without training and experience, nevertheless, in many ways they have done well in face of tremendous difficulties.'[62] A week later he reported that nationalist attacks on the government in the National Assembly at Weimar had been vigorously repudiated by the Finance Minister, Matthias Erzberger, who threw 'the guilt of commencing the war, and of continuing it, on the Conservative Party'; the result had been 'to strengthen the present Government considerably and to discredit the parties of the Right and the old regime'. A motion of no confidence in the government had been rejected by the large majority of 243 to 53.[63]

In spite of Allied shipments and food imports the situation remained critical. In July a British colonel commented on the conditions in the towns of the Ruhr, the health of the children as well as the miners. According to him, all the children were suffering from anaemia and were at least two years behind in their growth; owing to brain fatigue they were unable to carry out their work at school so that the teaching hours had to be shortened and longer intervals given; their clothing was totally inadequate – 40 per cent had no shoes or stockings, and about the same percentage no shirts. The miners of the mine he visited could not do their work on account of undernourishment; for breakfast they had one slice of bread, sometimes with a little margarine, and a cup of substitute coffee; they took one slice of dry bread into the mine, and on their return home they got some soup; in the evening they had another cup of soup and some bread with jam; once a week they received a small quantity of meat. Prior to the armistice, the mine owners obtained supplies of meat, butter and other food which they sold to the miners at low prices, but since the armistice this had come to an end; all the miners declared that they could not continue to work much longer under these conditions.[64]

In November a British businessman wrote to the Foreign Office that Germany must obtain coal and some raw materials if Britain wanted to get any reparation payments from the country: 'Germany is for many years to come down and out.' An official of the Foreign Office minuted that all reports confirmed his assessment: 'something ought to be done at once to enable Germany to obtain sufficient coal and raw material to resume her industries. . . . To oppose international relief action is to prepare the way for anarchy which some of the Reactionaries want as the preliminary condition for a *coup d'état*.'[65] And once more at the beginning of November: the economic outlook for Germany was 'hopeless', but it 'would repay the whole world from every point of view to make any measures that are practicable for securing remunerative work and sufficient food for the German people a matter of the first urgency'.[66] In General Malcolm's opinion, the one redeeming feature was that the German people were 'really ready to work if they could get the chance'; but there was general despondency and the 'growing conviction that the complete economic destruction of Germany is the deliberate policy of both England and France'; the loss of 400,000 tons of docks (by way of reparations) had caused particularly bitter feeling and 'is looked upon as a devilish device to ruin Germany's last chance of recovery'.[67]

The 'strong man' who emerged on the side of the government, not afraid to use military force if he thought this necessary, was Gustav Noske, the Minister of Defence. According to a sketch by General Malcolm, he was blunt and straightforward, wasting no time, talking to the point with self-confidence, acting at times without any instruction from the government. 'When Ebert, Scheidemann and Brockdorff-Rantzau were discussing their attitude towards Russian Bolshevist agitation in Berlin, Noske boldly arrested Radek, though German law contains no clause to ensure Radek's conviction.' Apart from this Russian emissary Noske also arrested certain leaders of the Independent Social Democrats: 'The country approved of Noske's action. He has since suppressed all Spartacist riotings in Germany.' Malcolm expressly denied that Noske was unduly influenced by the regular army officers or General von Lüttwitz, the general commanding in the district of Berlin. But he admitted that Noske had taken advantage of the hopeless situation of the young Prussian officers who were unfit for any civilian post to organize the Reichswehr: 'serving as mercenaries in their own class interests, they are the backbone of the new army.'[68] A British colonel who saw Noske at the end of 1919 wrote that he was a big man, of the warrant officer type, with a large appetite, energetic and strong-willed; he bitterly complained that the harsh demands of the Allied Supreme Council during the past months were driving many Germans towards the right-wing parties which were fostering among the people a spirit of nationalism and revenge and undermining the prestige of the German government.

General von Lüttwitz, on the other hand, so the officer reported, did not conceal his low opinion of the members of the government and did not consider them fit to rule Germany.[69] Before the Treaty of Versailles was accepted under Allied pressure by the National Assembly at Weimar Noske told General Malcolm that he would resign – a threat he repeated some months later – if the Allies should insist on the handing over of the German war criminals from the Emperor downwards, and then 'chaos would result leading to civil war'.[70] Noske's forceful actions against 'Bolshevik agents' were certainly approved by the Foreign Office. When the War Office suggested in December 1919 that pressure should be put on the German government to expel such agents, the Foreign Office considered any such step unnecessary and undesirable because 'Herr Noske himself is always ready to take any public action against agents of the Russian Soviet Government'.[71]

As to other members of the government, its leading personality was no doubt Friedrich Ebert, first the chairman of the provisional government and since February 1919 the elected President of the German Republic. In the same month the Political Intelligence Department of the Foreign Office described him as 'a solid sensible man, and the way in which his Government since the revolution has contended with a situation of desperate difficulty will perhaps some day be recognised as a very fine performance.' Ebert's government was attacked from the Left as 'being bloody and tyrannical', and from the Right as weak and being afraid of using armed force, but mistakes would seem almost inevitable in a situation as dangerous and difficult as that which the government had to face. In any case, the hope of Germany 'becoming an orderly state of democratic character with decent principles of international behaviour' rested on the success of the forces supporting the Ebert-Scheidemann government.[72] In 1920 Lady D'Abernon, the wife of the British ambassador, met Ebert and found him 'a rough diamond, coarse and heavy, but one feels at once that he is a strong personality and is no mere figurehead', possessing 'a certain simplicity and directness that is akin to natural dignity'.[73] In February 1920 the General Staff commented that the political situation in Germany had improved since the early months of 1919, in spite of the severe crisis of May and June which had been 'caused by the unexpectedly hard nature of the peace terms'. 'The German Government', the assessment continued, 'has had to contend with great difficulties, and has held its own in a way which seemed almost impossible six to nine months ago. It is by no means an ideal Government, but the General Staff believe its alternative is either the return to a reactionary rule under the Military Party and Military Junker Class, or the dominance of the Extreme Left, who have identified themselves with Russian Bolshevism.' The gradual improvement in the situation was due partly to the supply of food – 'mainly at the instance of the British' – partly to the firmness of Noske.[74]

When the terms of the Treaty of Versailles became known in Germany there was not only a severe political crisis, but a national outcry which only the Independent Social Democrats did not join. Their leader, Hugo Haase, thought the workers would accept the peace terms provided they got work,[75] and the USPD consistently campaigned for acceptance of the treaty. In late May a British officer reported that the German government was determined to prevent the signature, if the terms were not modified, by the creation of a dictatorship based on the army and the free corps which would try to maintain order and to prevent a left-wing government from signing; an expected Allied advance across the Rhine would not be resisted but it was intended to turn against the Poles or at least to oppose any further Polish encroachments in the east. (As we know from other sources, this plan coincided with that of many generals who wanted to proclaim Noske a military dictator and to start an offensive against the Poles.) In the opinion of the writer, three possibilities existed: either a government of the extreme Left which 'would not last more than a few weeks'; or the dictatorship which would offer passive resistance and would not sign; or anarchy with which the Allies could probably cope, but this might become worse if the Allies stepped up the strictness of their economic measures.[76] Another military report of the same month stressed that the principal demands for rejection came from the wealthy and the followers of the old regime; they were embittered because they had not only lost the war for which they had been so largely responsible, but also their powerful positions; they could not reconcile themselves to the power gained by their political opponents, and now they protested that Germany was kept weak by continuing starvation and was being dismembered in violation of every Allied undertaking. It was curious, the writer thought, that the specific clauses of the treaty were so little examined; for example, the reduction of the army

26

was hardly mentioned, 'although it is difficult to see how internal order is to be maintained with an army of one hundred thousand men', while at the moment around Berlin alone there were more than 50,000.[77]

With regard to another clause of the treaty, the separation of the city of Danzig from Germany, an official of the Foreign Office predicted correctly that 'the whole *bourgeois* democracy of Germany' would protest; 'it would be like handing over a Scottish town to its Irish population.'[78] Indeed, throughout the 1920s and beyond the creation of the 'Polish Corridor' down to the sea was to remain one of the major German grievances. The British delegation at Versailles was highly critical of the terms of the draft treaty but their criticism did not achieve much. Lloyd George was able to achieve a minor success in that the important district of Upper Silesia was not ceded outright to Poland and was put under Allied administration pending a decision by a plebiscite. But he was unable to prevent the occupation of the left bank of the Rhine by the Allied armies, which was desired by the General Staff as well as by the French. The occupation could be justified, as one Foreign Office official minuted, 'only on the assumption that Germany will remain a strong, vigorous and aggressive military power, but that France will remain peaceful and unambitious; this is an assumption that it will be difficult to justify.' He was convinced that Germany was now a liberal and constitutional republic and that the powers should take this into account, but other leading Foreign Office officials were more sceptical.[79]

It was above all the Union of Democratic Control and the Labour Party who denounced the terms of the Peace Treaty. Early in June the Labour Party issued a manifesto strongly condemning the terms as 'fundamentally defective' and 'based upon the very political principles which were the ultimate cause of the war'; this was endorsed by a party conference later in the same month. *The Labour Leader* called the treaty 'a document of barefaced brigandage, which is justified by canting hypocrisy': 'The Treaty itself is based upon a lie, and is justified by lies. It is an insult to the intelligence of every intelligent person to contend that the terms of the treaty conform to the conditions of the Armistice on which Germany agreed to stop the fighting. These terms violate in every particular Wilson's Fourteen Points and the terms he set forth in his speeches.'[80] In the same paper Ramsay MacDonald wrote: 'We are beholding an act of madness unparalleled in history. . . . It is not Germany that is involved. The humiliation of that nation, the starvation of its people, are nothing compared to the evil which is being done to mankind by this settlement of injustice – this awakening of every passion that has blown through the hearts of men and nations and driven them upon war and destruction. . . . Under such conditions even a League of Nations would be an instrument for evil.' In another article, published in November, MacDonald objected in particular to the financial clauses of the treaty which would 'prevent any order being established in Germany. . . . In this way a perfect plague spot is being maintained in Central Europe.'[81] But these protests exercised no influence on official policy. In the 'Khaki election' of December 1918 MacDonald and many other left-wingers had even lost their parliamentary seats.

Apart from the issue of the war criminals which will be discussed later, German national indignation was especially aroused by Polish claims to what the Germans rightly or wrongly considered old German territory, the lands on the lower reaches of the Vistula which were to form the 'Polish Corridor' – actually lands that had belonged to Poland between 1466 and 1772 and only became Prussian through the first partition of Poland, with a very mixed population. As early as December 1918 a British officer who had been a prisoner of war in Germany warned: 'there is one claim which is repudiated by every party with equal indigation, and that is the Polish claim to West Prussia [in Prussia the province in question was called West Prussia, to distinguish it from East Prussia still further to the east] or part of it, and Danzig. The Polish claims, whether based on history or nationality, are equally denied. Passion is likely to run higher on this than on any other question'; if the Polish claims were to be granted by the peace conference, the Allies should be prepared for the possibility of armed resistance; the writer added that the impressions of General Rees coincided with his own.[82] In the following month another officer reported that the feeling against the Poles was very bitter; German opinion of them could best be summarized by the word *Lausevolk* (literally 'lice people' but generally used in a pejorative sense) which was usually applied to them; the Germans seemed prepared to cede the districts with a predominant Polish element, but even that would cause great indignation in Saxony which depended on supplies of grain and potatoes from Poznania.[83] In December 1918 there was a sharp German protest when Ignacy Paderewski, the future president of

Poland, landed at Danzig and declared that, if he were elected president, he would see to it that Danzig became Polish and appealed to the inhabitants to opt for Poland. There were further incidents at Posen (Poznań) when Paderewski, accompanied by a British colonel, proceeded there, and a strong German request was made that both should be ordered to continue their journey to Warsaw and to leave German territory by the shortest route.[84] Soon bitter fighting erupted between German and Polish volunteer units for the contested areas, and a Polish uprising threatened the rear communications of the German armies which still occupied large parts of the former Russian Empire.

As General von Winterfeldt, the German military represent-ative, explained to the International Armistice Commission, when the German revolution broke out discipline in the eastern armies was much more seriously affected than it was in the west and soldiers' councils acquired much greater influence; they were successful in curtailing the authority of the officers but not in establishing order among the troops; these were forcing their way home without obeying orders and were refusing to fight the Soviet troops which followed on their heels. The German government thus called for volunteers to defend the eastern frontier and appealed to the Allies for help against the Bolshevists.[85] German volunteer units were also sent to the Baltic provinces of the former Russian Empire where they fought the advancing Red Army in alliance with local forces and occupied Riga, but were soon engaged in fighting the local Latvian units raised by the new national government. 'When the men heard of the bad conditions at home', commented the Political Intelligence Department, 'many of them shewed no desire to return and pinned their faith to promises of land which were made to them by the Baltic landowners ("Baltic Barons") of German race, or by the Letts themselves . . . and certainly by their own officers.' In their turn the officers would 'regard it as their mission, first to maintain in the Baltic lands a force which could ultimately intervene in Germany and restore the Monarchy, and, secondly, to restore something like the old regime in Russia with a view ultimately to a Russo-German political, military and economic alliance.' Under strong Allied pressure the German government agreed to recall the German volunteer units from the Baltic but met with the passive resistance of General Rüdiger von der Goltz, their commanding officer, who had 'the sympathy of the military and reactionary classes in Germany'. Even recruiting for these units continued more or less openly; the reserve section of one of these free corps in the autumn of 1919 was still quartered in an army camp near Berlin and was able almost every week to send reinforcements and war material to Courland. In the British view, the German government also hesitated to take more decisive steps to compel the free corps to withdraw from the Baltic because they feared that the soldiers 'being disappointed of the land which was promised them in the Baltic Provinces would form an element of dangerous disorder' at home and that strong measures against von der Goltz would alienate the officers of the new army many of whom strongly sympathized with him.[86] Both fears were only too justified.

In August 1919 General Malcolm reported that General von der Goltz had returned to Courland, in defiance of a government order not to leave Germany: 'so weak is its authority over the army in great things as in small, it is quite likely that the statement is true'; the so-called 'Iron Division' (one of the German free corps) had refused the order to withdraw from the Baltic.[87] In September Malcolm added significantly that from certain remarks made to him he gathered that the example of Fiume might increase the antagonism between the government and the army, especially with regard to the Baltic. For in the same month Gabriele D'Annunzio flouted the authority of the Italian government and with his volunteer units occupied the disputed city of Fiume on the eastern side of the Adriatic – a dress rehearsal for Mussolini's march on Rome three years later.[88] Although many Germans said 'look at Fiume', General Malcolm did not believe that the parallel would work because an 'adventure in the Baltic provinces would have no support from the mass of the German people'. But he was convinced that the German government was powerless to enforce its will upon the troops in Courland, or even upon some very senior officers in Germany who actively supported von der Goltz.[89]

The Allies tried to force the Germans to withdraw by imposing a blockade in the Baltic, a measure which, according to Malcolm, caused 'great anxiety'. He also reported that General Hans von Seeckt had been sent to East Prussia 'to try and bring the people there to reason and to stop the traffic across the frontier' into Courland, the vital supply lines of the German free corps. The German government, Malcolm found, was 'extraordinarily ill informed as to what is going on'; he had furnished Noske with two reports which were almost common knowledge, and the British Military Mission knew many facts which were apparently unknown to the Minister of Defence – from which he must conclude that information was deliberately withheld from Noske and the government.[90] In the end, however, the free corps were withdrawn – after an Allied Commission had been sent to the Baltic to supervise their evacuation and to control the illicit traffic across the frontier. Yet installed on the big estates of eastern Germany the volunteers were to become a source of grave worry to the government, and a danger to the republican order.

As to the character of the German army at home, British Intelligence began to notice that Noske was unable to find reliable republican officers. According to a report of October 1919, 'certain commanders of Reichswehr Brigades are striving to eliminate republican or democratic officers so as to retain only conservatives', and Noske's chief collaborator was General Georg Maercker, commander of the *Landesjägerkorps*, who had pronounced monarchical views. One Reichswehr battalion had marched through a town in Holstein preceded by the black-white-red flag of the Empire, and the officers had jeered at a bystander who had dared to remark that the army had after all sworn fidelity to the Constitution.[91] The military also reported the acquittal of Captain Marloh who was tried in December 1919 by court-martial on a charge of manslaughter. When the fighting between red sailors and government troops in Berlin was over, some 300 sailors went to the Divisional Office of the Reinhard Brigade to draw their pay and were promptly arrested there by Marloh. He then telephoned to the brigade headquarters for help and was given a verbal order to shoot half of them or as many as he could. Thereupon he selected 29 or 30 of them 'who appeared to be in possession of stolen property obtained by looting' (as it seems because they possessed some valuables) and ordered them to be shot, and this was done. Colonel Reinhard was heard as a witness in the trial and declared he could not remember the exact form of words of his verbal order, but the situation in Berlin was so critical at the time 'that he believed the most rigorous measures were absolutely necessary'. Marloh was acquitted on the principal charge but sentenced to three months of imprisonment (detention in a fortress) for being absent without leave as he had fled with the help of false papers.[92] Soon after, Reinhard, 'a strong man of the old Prussian stamp', who without any authority had furnished a guard of honour for the reception of Field-Marshal von Hindenburg in Berlin, was put on the half-pay list with immediate effect, either on account of this action or as a result of the Marloh case, as General Malcolm reported.[93] Yet the new army of the Republic continued to be officered by men 'of the old Prussian stamp' – a source of never-ending difficulties for the republican government.

Hindenburg had come to Berlin to testify before the committee appointed by the National Assembly to investigate the causes of the German collapse of November 1918. To welcome him large crowds assembled in the streets – as General Malcolm put it, he after all 'was, and is, Germany's greatest living hero'. There were shouts of 'Come back as President' and, more ominously, 'Down with Erzberger and the Jews'. *The Times* and other British papers carried alarming accounts of the demonstrations and the dangers indicated by them. General Malcolm, however, entered 'the strongest possible protest' against the articles 'which have been little short of scandalous'. He stressed, clearly from his own observations, that the largest of the Hindenburg crowds could not be compared with those which marched for two hours in the funeral procession in honour of Hugo Haase, the leader of the USPD. He added: 'If the danger of a "putsch" from the right were the greatest which threatens this country, it would be in a much happier state than is actually the case.'[94] The general felt a great deal of sympathy with the German field-marshal, but he also had some sympathy with Haase whom he had earlier described as 'an idealist, champion of the most oppressed class, he has no ambition; neither money nor office appeal to him in his unselfish struggle for what he considers the best solution of the social problem.'[95] Yet Malcolm's general assessment was proved wrong within about three months, for in March 1920 there was a 'Putsch' from the Right, and the 'Putsch' from the Left only took place 12 months later. Confronted by the challenge of the two extremist parties the governments of the Weimar Republic tried to steer a middle course, a course beset by grave perils ever since the birth of the republic. The revolution of 1918–1919 brought Germany neither political nor social stability and vastly increased social antagonisms and political passions. If the British officers serving in Germany overestimated the danger from the Left and underestimated that from the Right, their misjudgement – natural in the circumstances of the time – was shared by most Germans. What the officers did not see was that the German revolution had failed to change the social structure of the country, and that without such a change the forces of the old order were bound to reassert their influence sooner or later, in domestic affairs as well as in foreign policy.

II

YEARS OF TURMOIL 1920–1922

In July 1919 Colonel Bauer mentioned to General Malcolm that people with whom he cooperated, such as 'influential industrialists' and 'men with practical experience of public life', were planning a *coup d'état* to oust the government. On 8 March 1920 the colonel again saw the British general but did not mention a 'Putsch'; yet Malcolm 'took the opportunity to say that England would not stand anything of the kind and that any unconstitutional action . . . would be sheer madness' and would only harm German interests, while Bauer talked vaguely of 'the danger of Bolshevism and the need for stronger Government in Germany'.[1] Three days later, on 11 March, the government ordered the arrest of four men who were suspected of planning unconstitutional action, and one of the four was Colonel Bauer. Only one of them was actually arrested. On 13 March the British chargé d'affaires in Berlin, Lord Kilmarnock, was told by the German Undersecretary of State for Foreign Affairs that his goverment felt no anxiety and did not consider the matter all that serious, although rumours of an impending coup had circulated for some days.[2] On the same day the Ehrhardt Brigade, to a large extent recruited from personnel of the Imperial navy, marched into Berlin from its camp near the capital without meeting any resistance, for the assembled generals were convinced that their troops would not fight against other Reichswehr units; the coup was bloodless and Berlin was in the hands of the mutineers. The government fled, first to Dresden, then to Stuttgart, and in Berlin a new government was formed by Wolfgang Kapp, an East Prussian official, and General Freiherr von Lüttwitz, the commanding general of the district, whom Kapp appointed his

Minister of Defence.[3]

The Undersecretary of State for Foreign Affairs, von Haniel, suggested that the Allied representatives in Berlin should make a joint protest and inform the new 'government' that their action might cause disaster; but the diplomats felt that any such step might be interpreted as recognition and decided to hold no communication with Kapp and his associates. The government which had fled from Berlin equally refused to negotiate. It considered itself the only legitimate government of the republic and received assurances of support from the state governments of Bavaria, Saxony and Württemberg. It had strong support in the south and west of the country, while East Prussia and Pomerania declared for Kapp, as did many Reichswehr units in the north and east. The Kapp 'government' claimed that they were not monarchists and merely wished to rid the country of the old 'corrupt' government and to hold a general election.[4] As Lord Kilmarnock described the Berlin scene later, 'numerous ex-officers reappeared in uniform and swaggered about the streets apparently imbued with the idea that the good old times had returned. . . . Pathetic attempts were made to arouse the enthusiasm of the populace by marching military bands through the streets playing "Deutschland über Alles" and other patriotic airs.' But the whole enterprise was 'unsupported by money, organisation, or even an effective propaganda' and was characterized 'by the mentality which strove to prop up a half-baked revolution by a few thousand soldiers and a brass band'. From Stuttgart the government proclaimed a general strike which became effective within two days. In Berlin, the Technical Emergency Corps to a certain extent managed to keep the water and electricity works going, but even the senior civil servants refused to carry out Kapp's orders, and the treasury and the banks declined to provide him with funds.[5]

On 14 March Lord Kilmarnock wired to London from Berlin that in his opinion 'our policy must be to avoid any semblance of support to a Government which has come into power by purely militarist *coup d'état*' and suggested that the Allied representatives should at once leave Berlin and join the government to which they were accredited at Stuttgart. This, however, was not done, and instead the British government instructed Sir Harold Stuart, the British High Commissioner in the Rhineland, to send a member of his staff, Arnold Robertson, to Stuttgart, where the French too sent their Consul-General from Mainz.[6] On his arrival

35

Robertson saw Noske who had just received news from Berlin that the Kapp 'government' had fallen on 17 March. Noske forcefully expressed his contempt of the whole 'adventure'; he intended to cashier all officers implicated in the 'Putsch' and, if necessary, to 'start a war of extermination against monarchists East of the Elbe'; the general strike would be called off at once, but Noske feared that all the good work he had done against the extreme Left in 1919 would be undone by the Kapp venture.[7] He had trusted the generals and cooperated with them: now his achievements – and his own career – were in ruins.

In Berlin, meanwhile, Lord Kilmarnock proposed to the Allied representatives that they should together approach Kapp and tell him that he must resign and entrust the maintenance of order to a military governor, pending the return of the old government; for this post the United States Commissioner suggested the name of General Wilhelm Groener, Ludendorff's successor as First Quartermaster-General of the Imperial army; the Security Police should preserve law and order. In the end General Malcolm went to see General von Lüttwitz and told him that he must accept the terms of the old government. Lüttwitz replied that then the troops would refuse to fight the Spartacists who he believed were planning to attack: Kapp was willing to go if assured of his personal safety; allegedly he was in a 'blue funk' and willing to comply with the Allied request.[8] On the evening of 18 March Kilmarnock was able to report that the Ehrhardt Brigade, which had occupied the government district since the 13th, 'have just marched out being replaced by Reichswehr troops believed to be faithful to the old Government'. But when the Brigade passed through the Brandenburg Gate the first unit turned and fired into the crowd which accompanied its departure by hooting. There was more shooting when the second unit departed as well as 'some promiscuous shooting in front of Embassy windows', and several people were killed or wounded in its immediate neighbourhood.[9] Thus the Brigade took revenge for its humiliating defeat at the hands of the working class which had saved the government by the general strike. On the next day the situation in Berlin, according to Lord Kilmarnock, was 'very threatening owing to uncompromising attitude of Independents and Communists' who intended to continue the general strike. He had an interview with Eugen Schiffer, the Vice-Chancellor who had remained in Berlin, and told him that no food, raw materials or credits would be allowed to Germany if law and order were further disturbed from any quarter and the constitutional regime interfered with. Schiffer thanked him cordially and was authorized to publish the declaration which 'would have a most salutary effect on Extremists', and Kilmarnock spoke to a moderate leader of the USPD 'strongly in the same sense'.[10]

On the receipt of this telegram Lord Curzon, the Foreign Secretary, queried the words 'constitutional regime' because, according to his information, the German government was accepting 'an extreme Socialist programme' to maintain itself in power. A Foreign Office official, however, minuted that in his opinion the regime was constitutional: 'I read what is happening as a violent and determined revulsion against the designs of the militarist elements, a revulsion which necessarily involves a marked "leftward" movement of the Government. The cabinet, as now announced to be composed, includes trade union leaders, but there is no evidence that the wilder spirits have any influence. It is all to our interest to strengthen their hands.'[11] Although the formation of a 'workers' government' including union leaders was discussed it did not materialize, and in the end the government of the 'Weimar coalition' (from the Centre of the SPD) returned to power – only without Noske, whose place as Minister of Defence was taken by the mayor of Nuremberg, Dr Otto Gessler. At Stuttgart meanwhile Robertson had reached the conclusion, against his previous conviction, that the Ebert government 'supported by majority of National Assembly, is genuinely democratic, intends to carry out Treaty of Peace to best of its ability, and is deserving frank support from Allies'; if this were withheld, if no hope were held out of any financial assistance, Germany 'will inevitably gravitate towards Bolshevism now and ultimately perhaps to absolute monarchism again'; in any case, the next general election was likely to return many more extremists of the Left and of the Right – a forecast which was to prove only too correct.[12] Robertson also advocated negotiations with the Germans about the economic terms of the Peace Treaty. But in London such a course was considered impossible on account of public opinion in France as well as 'highly undesirable in itself', and there were after all many other ways of strengthening the German government.[13] Some weeks later Lord Kilmarnock with the approval of his government repeated his declaration 'that a fresh military Putsch would arouse greatest indignation in England and that His Majesty's

Government would view it with gravest disapproval'; any such attempt would destroy the possibility of material help in the form of food, raw materials or credits.[14]

The attention of the Allies now focused on a spontaneous left-wing uprising in the valley of the Ruhr, which was a direct sequel to the Kapp Putsch. For there several Reichswehr units and free corps had declared for the Kapp 'government', hoisted the black-white-red Imperial colours, and were soon besieged by infuriated armed workers who finally drove them out of the industrial area. According to a memorandum by a British colonel, at least 80 per cent of their officers were reactionaries and therefore ready to approve of the Kapp enterprise; even more important, he considered it 'almost certain that General von Watter [the commanding general of the area] had previous knowledge of the planned *coup d'état* and that he was prepared to support it.' In his opinion, the claims of the workmen were 'well founded', and their movement 'was directed against reaction in general, and against the Reichswehr in particular'. In the course of this movement the workers spontaneously formed a 'Red Army'; most of them were trained soldiers and they took their weapons from the depots which fell into their hands and from the units which surrendered to them. As the colonel averred, the movement was not in itself Bolshevist although the local Communists supported it; the preponderant influence lay with local leaders of the USPD. 'Visits by British personnel to the Ruhr had shown that the situation was normal, and, though the bourgeois parties were apprehensive, no excesses had yet taken place', and there was no urgent need for an advance of the Reichswehr. Reports published in many German papers 'were wildly exaggerated, and in many cases absolutely untrue'. But General von Watter and the Reichswehr strongly favoured a complete reoccupation of the Ruhr; 'the whole tone of the official reports emanating from Münster was tendentious and directed towards making a further advance of the Reichswehr appear inevitable.'[15]

From Coblenz Robertson confirmed that the rising in the Ruhr was not Spartacist but led by the combined socialist parties and the trade unions, with the cooperation of the municipal authorities; the Communists were a small minority, and were allowed to participate so as to prevent them from going into opposition; the movement was directed against militarism and reaction, inspired by 'the desire to maintain republicanism and democracy'. When the Reichswehr troops were cleared from an area peace and order were rapidly restored, executive councils assumed power, and under them committees supervized the local authorities which were permitted to continue their work so as to avoid any dislocation of the municipal machinery; no Soviets were proclaimed, but the workers demanded the dissolution of the Reichswehr and the formation of workmen's battalions. A minute by a Foreign Office official also stated that there was plenty of evidence of the anti-militarist and non-Communist character of the movement – contrary to the stories of a ' "Red" outbreak' published by *The Times*.[16]

At the beginning of April Robertson again wrote that all the information at his disposal confirmed the view that, if Reichswehr troops re-entered the industrial area, further bloodshed and sabotage would be the result, for the workers were not convinced that the government had been purged of right-wing elements and profoundly distrusted General von Watter and the Reichswehr. In his opinion, a grave danger existed that the leaders of the 'Red Army' would be carried off their feet by the hope of further success and might swing the rebellion on to more radical lines.[17] At a conference held at Bielefeld on 23 March under the chairmanship of a delegate of the central government a kind of armistice was concluded, but this was not recognized by all the combatants, and the Reichswehr leaders soon claimed that its terms had been broken by their enemies. They thus felt entitled to advance after large reinforcements had arrived from other parts of Germany, including certain free corps which had sided with Kapp: precisely the danger Robertson had foreseen; and the result was renewed heavy fighting. As the British Department of the Inter-Allied Rhineland High Commission reported in April, the 'evidence shows that there was great discontent amongst the Reichswehr in the neutral zone at being restrained from taking action, and some officers had threatened to resign. How far von Watter used this discontent to influence the Government is not known, but it is certain that the news sent from the General's propaganda and press Bureau reporting acts of sabotage, plundering and atrocities by the Red Army and the disturbed condition of the district were greatly exaggerated.' As a result of the army's advance into the Ruhr towns and country 'were filled with bands of hungry and homeless men, and a further advance, politically an error, was rendered necessary.' The Department was convinced that, if the German government had recognized the legitimate grounds of the workers' distrust of the Reichswehr and had effectively removed the grounds of their suspicions, its authority in the Ruhr could 'probably have been restored without the necessity of military intervention'.[18]

At Gevelsberg near Wuppertal a British captain interviewed one of the Communists who had organized the first outbreak in the area. He declared that not a single pane of glass had been broken in his district and the well-to-do had not been molested; that the disarmament of the 'Reds' was practically complete, and that a local force to maintain order was being formed from members of all political parties; the Reichswehr had broken the terms of the Bielefeld agreement and had broken up the Red units into bands which were forced to plunder in order to live; if they had been given a little more time they could have withdrawn and disbanded in an orderly fashion. In the towns visited by the captain uniformed police were on duty, except in Wuppertal where organized workers were keeping order until the police could be reorganized; 'maintenance of order seems to be very good. No outward sign of damage anywhere – shops well stocked, and many well-dressed people walking about. . . . The working classes would prefer an occupation by the Entente to that of the Reichswehr.'[19] Robertson reported that the great majority of the workers had handed in their arms; 'there can be no excuse for further advance into territory where work has been proceeding in quiet and orderly manner.'[20] General von Watter, however, declared that arms had not been surrendered in sufficient quantities and therefore ordered his units to resume the advance. He even suggested that the British army should close the frontier (into the occupied area of Cologne) and prevent any refugees from escaping: 'this has of course been refused'.[21]

Thus on 6 April about 5,000 former Red Army soldiers crossed into the British zone, and many more were expected on the next day. They declared that they were seeking refuge because they feared a massacre or execution without trial by the government troops – and their fears were fully justified.[22] The French chargé d'affaires in Berlin was instructed to make representations to the German government to obtain a guarantee of security for the refugees if they returned home, and the British chargé d'affaires was ordered to do the same.[23] Three leaders of the Ruhr workers, all members of the USPD, approached the Rhineland High Commission to express their sincere hope that the Allies would insist on a strict execution of the Peace Treaty and on a definite reduction of the German army, otherwise there would be no guarantee of future peàce. They also welcomed the French sanctions which had been taken because Reichswehr units had advanced into the 'neutral' zone of the Rhineland without obtaining the permission of the Allies, and they hoped this would prevent any further advance of the Reichswehr.[24] Quite clearly, it was distrust and hatred of the Reichswehr which had driven the workers into revolt and had made thousands seek refuge in the British zone – a fear that had by no means been assuaged by the defeat of Kapp and his military backers, for the Reichswehr survived the failure of the Putsch unscathed.

At the time of the Kapp Putsch the German government requested the permission of the Allies to reinforce its troops in the 'neutral' zone of the Ruhr because of the disturbances, and the matter was discussed at the Ambassadors' Conference in Paris under the presidency of the French Prime Minister, Alexandre Millerand. He made a long and impassioned speech 'appealing for unity in the face of grave danger' and emphasized that the issue was between revision and enforcement of the Peace Treaty, and that the French government was firmly for enforcement; the moment had passed for simply recording violations of the treaty on paper; he proposed to inform the German government that its troops must not enter the Ruhr valley but that the Allies would send in troops to maintain order. The British ambassador, Lord Derby, commented that it was evident that the French wished to occupy the Ruhr, a course urged by Marshal Foch, and the question was whether the British government would give its consent.[25] A few days later Sir Eyre Crowe, the permanent Undersecretary at the Foreign Office, noted: 'if the Spartacist movement is not cut down in the Ruhr district, and elsewhere, the treaty rights of the Allies are likely to suffer serious diminution'; the British interest was the rapid restoration of order in Germany and the encouragement of measures to achieve this. 'Do the French seriously believe that the interference of Allied troops with German strikers and communists is likely to bring about a rapid pacification?' In his opinion, there was 'a real danger that all German parties may combine against the foreigner'; before the Allies went in at least one German party must be won over to their side.[26]

On 22 March the subject was discussed at an Allied conference in London presided over by Lloyd George. The rebellion in the Ruhr, he declared, 'was spreading every day, would extend into Belgium and possibly into France', unless the German government were immediately allowed to send in a sufficient force to crush it; at first a small force had seemed sufficient, but owing to the delay a considerably larger one would now be required. He understood that the French were willing to grant the German request only on condition that Allied troops marched into Germany and occupied certain towns, but in his opinion 'this was a course of doubtful wisdom'; for 'there was always the danger of stimulating and welding German national-ist sentiment by outside interference, the effect of which would be to rally the moderate elements to the Spartacist side, as had been the case in Russia'; the Germans should be allowed to send in as many troops as were necessary to suppress the rebellion.[27] The conference agreed to suggest to the Allied governments that the German request should be granted, provided that the units were withdrawn within a given period and Allied officers were permitted to accompany them. But this was not accepted by the French who proposed to occupy Frankfurt, Darmstadt and some other towns as a guarantee for the timely withdrawal of the troops from the Ruhr and for some other claims on Germany. This plan in its turn was opposed by the British government. Lord Curzon declared that, according to his information from the Rhineland, the Spartacist movement might be stopped if sufficient food was allowed into Germany, and that it was the policy of the Allies 'to support the Ebert-Bauer Government, and not to threaten them.'[28]

A few days later, however, the French made good their threat and gave orders for the occupation of Frankfurt and Darmstadt without notifying London, so that the British only heard of it through the press. Curzon was incensed and told the French ambassador that this 'was an impossible state of affairs . . . either the Allies should act as they had hitherto acted, in combination; or they might act separately. The former was the only sound and practical policy.' If the French acted independently, the British might have 'to consider very seriously whether we should not withdraw altogether from the occupied area, and decline to share the responsibility for action concerning which we were not even consulted.'[29] Bonar Law, the Lord Privy Seal, added with the express approval of Lloyd George that, in the British view, the German government had to maintain order; if the Allies refused Germany the means to do so they would be morally bound to become themselves responsible for its maintenance; it was therefore only right and proper to let the Germans take the necessary measures and to stipulate a time within which the troops were to be withdrawn.[30] But the French government were apparently convinced that in the Ruhr a situation existed 'which constituted a grave violation of the treaty, and a serious menace to France', so that they must obtain material guarantees for the withdrawal from the neutral zone.[31] A British diplomat informed Millerand 'that it was scarcely credible that he should think [the] advance of supplementary troops into the Ruhr district constituted [a] pressing military danger for France'. Yet the reply was: France had been defied and public opinion expected him to act; according to the report, action was probably taken on the advice of Marshal Foch whose name was frequently mentioned.[32]

On 6 and 7 April Darmstadt, Frankfurt, Hanau and Homburg were occupied by the French. On the next day the British government protested against the action taken 'in spite of the emphatic opposition of His Majesty's Government and of the Allies'; if this were repeated 'it may have the gravest results for the peace of Europe'. The British ambassador in Paris was instructed not to take part in any discussions arising from the execution of the Treaty of Versailles, until the French gave a definite assurance 'that in no circumstances would one of the Allies act on such important matters except with the knowledge and concurrence of the remainder.' On 11 April Millerand gave the assurance requested, and the incident was closed, at least for the time being.[33] The rift which had opened between the wartime Allies on the attitude to be taken towards Germany was to reopen in 1923, again on the issue of the Ruhr. Retrospectively it is easy to see that the British fear of Bolshevism, and particularly of its spread westwards, was very much exaggerated, and that the Reichswehr over-reacted to the rebellion in the Ruhr because it was only too eager to take strong measures against the Left – so as to heal the fissures in its own ranks which had been split wide open by the events of the Kapp Putsch. The best policy might have been to refuse the German request and to give the Bielefeld agreement a chance to achieve a peaceful solution of the conflict – without invoking the sanctions urged by France. Neither of the Allied powers was in favour of such a course, for both desired action, only of a different kind.

Early in 1920 General Malcolm stated that the Reichswehr and the militarized Security Police (a mobile force living in barracks) were reliable, well armed and 'too well organized for any violent outbreak to have a chance of success'. The same opinion was expressed by the Political Intelligence Department on the occasion of a violent demonstration in Berlin against a bill introducing 'factory councils' (instead of the previous workers' councils) during which about 50 people were killed by the police. But the department warned that, if the terms of the Peace Treaty were enforced and Germany's armed forces reduced to the prescribed 100,000 men, 'the prospects of anarchy will become very menacing', for the Communist movement would grow 'in consequence of the general distress' and the recent military successes of the Bolshevists.[34] After the violent events of the Kapp Putsch and the rising in the Ruhr the War Office considered 'that Germany should be permitted to retain an Army of 150,000–200,000' in addition to a Security Police of some 50,000 to 70,000. If the German armed forces were reduced below the minimum requirements, 'the resulting feeling of insecurity amongst the population will militate very strongly against settled economic conditions and a steady resumption of work', and little improvement could be expected in the supply of coal to France which was of vital importance to her.[35] Gessler, the new German Minister of Defence, wholeheartedly concurred. In his opinion, the Allied demands for a reduction of the Reichswehr to the size prescribed by the Peace Treaty had created 'a very serious situation'; he would make one last appeal for reconsideration at the conference to be held at Spa in July, but if this failed he would resign, for 'a Communist rising will be the inevitable result' and a second revolution would occur.[36] At the conference, in spite of all German pleading, the government was given until October to reduce the army from 200,000 to 150,000 men, and by the beginning of 1921 to 100,000, and this was finally accepted by the German delegation – without provoking Gessler's resignation.[37]

Curiously enough, the man who immediately expressed dissatisfaction with the long-service character of the army laid down in the Peace Treaty was Marshal Foch, who was convinced that this would 'make it a powerful Praetorian Guard and give it complete control of the political life of the country. Such an Army was bound to be monarchical and reactionary in sentiment and would aim at a war of revenge.' But the British High Commissioner in the Rhineland replied to him that, after all, the new German army would be recruited from all parts of Germany and not only from Prussia, that he hoped that it would be influenced by the democratic spirit now growing in Germany, that the long-service British army had never assumed a Praetorian character and that Germany would be unable 'to enter a new war for some considerable time'. Foch's answer was that Britain was a democratic country, and he was rather reluctant to accept the British plea that the growth of the democratic spirit and of democratic institutions in Germany ought to be encouraged.[38] In Berlin Lord Kilmarnock found such encouragement in an official statement of the Reichswehr headquarters for Pomerania that all officers and other ranks were determined to protect the Weimar Constitution and the constitutional government against all attacks, whether from the Right or from the Left. But when he drew the attention of a left-wing socialist to 'these reassuring statements' the latter told him that the declaration of loyalty was to the Constitution, not to the republic: this point had been discussed by a meeting of the officers, and they had decided not to mention the republic – leaving the way open to 'change the Constitution into a monarchy' without violating the letter of their assurances.[39] A report by Brigadier-General Morgan of the Inter-Allied Military Commission of Control of May 1920 also emphasized that all the higher commands were in the hands of officers of the old regime and that the army's treatment of the population during the Kapp Putsch had made it 'still more unpopular'; 'as at present constituted and commanded, the Reichswehr is more calculated to provoke disorder than to suppress it'; it was a 'potent instrument in the hands of reactionaries'. In Morgan's opinion, the German army had conceived 'a highly ingenious and elaborate plan to defeat the execution of the military clauses of the Treaty of Versailles', and the best way to counter this was to insist on the reduction to 100,000 men and on their enlistment for not less than 12 years.[40] In another report Morgan pointed to the behaviour of Reichswehr units during the recent civil disorders. 'Firing on innocent bystanders without the slightest provocation or display of hostility was common. The attitude of the troops and their officers was in this respect the very opposite of that traditionally adopted by the military in case of civil troubles in England'; the peculiar conception of the German government of what constituted disorder must be borne in mind; he admitted on the other hand that in the Ruhr and elewhere the army 'had to encounter mobs of fully armed men' and was faced by a rebellion.[41]

As to the free corps which had launched the Kapp Putsch by their mutiny, a British member of the Inter-Allied Military Control Commission found on a visit to a military training ground in July that the Ehrhardt Brigade had been renamed, on its transfer to the navy, '*Schiffs Stamm Division Nordsee*' and was still kept in readiness in case of a Putsch from the Left; while the third naval brigade was renamed '*Schiffs Stamm Division Ostsee*' and was kept in another camp against the same contingency. When the Allied officers emerged from the camp office they found soldiers surrounding their car, painting swastikas and pasting anti-Bolshevist leaflets on it, and another soldier was waving a German naval ensign; the Allied officers then left to the strains of 'Deutschland über Alles'.[42] In January 1921 the British army reported that the third naval brigade should long have been dissolved and its personnel transferred to the '*Schiffs Stamm Division Ostsee*'; in reality, many of its members had moved to Pomerania where they came under the jurisdiction of the Agrarian League (and thus no longer that of the Reichswehr) and were settled on the big estates under their own officers and NCO's in military units, numbering 3,200 men in all.[43] In East Prussia, an Allied committee of inspection found a similar state of affairs. Men of the dissolved free corps were settled in units under one of their officers; through him the local groups contracted with the landlords to supply the estates with labour, and were paid by the landlords, and not by the army; the whole organization was funded by the *Heimatbund*, 'a militant Junker organization'; this evidence was discovered by the Allied officers during a 'raid' on the offices of the Effective District Committee in Königsberg during which the officers 'suddenly scattered and each made for a different bureau', while the German captain in charge was held back by a conversation. But the Military Control Commission had to admit that the military character of the organization was 'elusive' so that it would be difficult to suppress it.[44]

One former free corps officer was tried in 1921 by a military tribunal on a charge of forming a secret organization, the *Frontbund*, which traded in arms and was preparing for a new Putsch. The evidence consisted mainly of documents published by the USPD paper *Freiheit*; and the officer was acquitted because the court found 'that the organization was solely intended to procure work for demobilized soldiers of Freikorps and had no military character'. The court also used the opportunity to launch an attack on the left-wing press, and during the whole proceedings showed a marked tendency to discuss its publications, especially the *Freiheit*, rather than the case itself.[45] Thus the officially dissolved free corps continued to exist in one form or another, either within the German navy, to which large sections of the Ehrhardt Brigade and another naval brigade were transferred, or in semi-military units settled on the estates of the nobility to the east of the Elbe, waiting for 'the day' when they would be summoned to fight 'Bolshevism' at home or France and Poland abroad, and forming an illicit cadre to replenish the ranks of the army in case of mobilization.

By 1921 the Reichswehr was indeed reduced to the prescribed strength of 100,000 men under the watchful eye of the Military Control Commission, but Brigadier Morgan still found several grounds for criticism. In his opinion, very few soldiers had been enlisted for the 12-year term; the army was 'nothing but a cadre for expansion', and all the evidence pointed to a plan of passing large numbers of men through the ranks for short periods, as Scharnhorst had done after the Peace of Tilsit (1807) to be able to defeat Napoleon; the technical means for a rapid expansion of the army were available in the nominal rolls of the provisional Reichswehr and the self-defence forces, and the armed police too would provide 'excellent fighting material'. 'In any case', he concluded, 'it is not to be expected that a Nation which has been organised for war for over 50 years by the most searching form of conscription known to history . . . and whose Civil Service, Police and Education have all been tempered to that end, can be completely "demilitarised" in two years', and he therefore pleaded for a continuation of military control by the Allies.[46]

'The real master of the German army', Lord Kilmarnock reported from Berlin, was General von Seeckt who had been appointed Chief of the Army Command as a sequel to the Kapp Putsch (during which he donned mufti and retired to his private quarters). 'General von Seeckt is at no pains to conceal the fact that he desires the new army to model itself sedulously on the old', and as proof Kilmarnock sent a copy of Seeckt's New Year message to London. This expressed the expectation that the new army would compete with the old 'in martial achievement' and would keep 'the sword sharp and the shield shining', and strongly emphasized the importance of education and training. As the army and the officer corps were often criticized from the Left and were permeated by monarchist sentiment, the new

Minister of Defence, Dr Gessler, had to defend them; but, in Kilmarnock's opinion, he was rather unsuccessful in doing so: 'his latest apologia . . . is not much more convincing than its predecessors.'[47] In parliament Gessler claimed that, if he gave an order to General von Seeckt, he knew the order would be carried out. But a Communist deputy interrupted him: 'That is not the point. The point is that you never get as far as daring to give General von Seeckt an order.' Gessler also stressed his efforts 'to remove class and caste differences' from the army and to increase the number of promotions from the ranks, but he clearly met with a sceptical audience.[48]

The real issue, however, was not whether a few carefully selected NCO's would be permitted to join the officer corps, but what kind of army would develop under General von Seeckt who certainly was an officer of the old Prussian school. According to a description provided by his aide-de-camp, Captain von Goldammer, to a British officer, Seeckt 'was not personally immensely popular with the troops, who were seldom able to penetrate sufficiently far through his dry and abrupt manner and insistence on rigid discipline to enable them to obtain a glimpse of his real character, which was a very fine one'. It is somewhat ironical that the aide-de-camp went on to suggest that 'Seeckt held very progressive opinions', was 'considered to be extremely pro-English' and largely responsible for the introduction of sports in the army on English lines.[49] As the British officer did not comment on these rather surprising views, we are left to guess whether they were made to impress the gullible British or were without an ulterior motive. The British certainly would not have been amused to hear that Seeckt's nickname among the Bavarian troops was 'the Bolshevik', as Seeckt's aide-de-camp claimed.

Closely connected with the army and its prescribed strength were two other controversial issues – that of the militarized Security Police and that of the *Einwohnerwehren*, a kind of Home Guard which flourished in particular in Bavaria and East Prussia – because in the opinion of the Allies both forces would serve as reinforcements of the army in case of need. The Security Police nominally came under the Ministry of the Interior of Prussia, Bavaria, Saxony, etc., but, according to the British Army of the Rhine, it constituted 'a highly trained body of picked troops, forming the cadre of a first-class reserve'.[50] They, rather than the army, were meant to cope with any disorders, whether from the Left or from the Right. As Carl Severing, the Prussian Minister of the Interior, stated in 1920, as long as rioters were well armed, 'the *Sicherheitspolizei* could not be armed simply with rubber-truncheons and swords'; he added that about 45 per cent of its members were workers who belonged to a trade union,[51] thus reflecting the great efforts of the Social Democratic government of Prussia to create a democratic police force, very different in composition from the army. In Württemberg too, the energetic Director of Police, Paul Hahn, who was also responsible for the *Einwohnerwehr*, used methods in dealing with strikes which were highly recommended by a visiting British officer, especially when 'compared with the methods employed by the Reichswehr in the Ruhr during last March'; Hahn's office work and intelligence service were 'equally well organized' and he took pride in showing the visitors from the Military Control Commission over his establishment.[52] In London the efforts of the French government to classify the Security Police as a military force and to have it banned caused considerable irritation. At the end of 1920 a Foreign Office official minuted that 'the position is becoming intolerable'; the internal position of the French government was 'exceedingly shaky' and would become more and more critical on account of its financial difficulties and the impossibility of extracting money from Germany which increased the clamour to take drastic action against her: 'That this is a hopeful way of dealing with Germany, given her present temper and the economic prostration of Europe, can hardly be maintained.'[53] As such, however, the French demands for the reorganization of the militarized police were quite justified: many years later its units were simply used as reinforcements for the expanding army.

More serious was the question of the *Einwohnerwehren*, which had sprung up in many different parts of Germany as a response to the 'Bolshevist danger'; they were an armed force and supposed to assist the army and police to maintain 'law and order'. Politically, they stood clearly on the Right and aroused strong working-class hostility. This applied even more strongly to a very similar Bavarian organization, the *Orgesch* (Organization Escherich, named after its leader, a Bavarian forestry official). Escherich's attempts to extend the *Orgesch* to other German states were resisted by the governments of Prussia, Saxony and Württemberg and prohibited by them – which in turn aroused bitter resentment among the conservatives of

Bavaria.[54] In spite of the prohibition, Escherich's activities continued outside Bavaria. According to the British Army of the Rhine, he enjoyed the support of the Catholic Church and was successful in persuading the provincial authorities of East Prussia to disregard the government order prohibiting the *Orgesch*.[55] According to another military report, it was rather doubtful whether its existence would discourage revolutionary outbreaks; for the masses were convinced that it 'intended to carry out a reactionary movement at the expense of the proletariat' and its existence greatly provoked the Communists, so that its dissolution would reduce the risk of armed conflict.[56] Lord D'Abernon, the new British ambassador, also was doubtful 'whether these organisations make rather for order or for future trouble. They are at bottom monarchical and military, although they deny it.' Yet in the event of a Communist outbreak they 'would powerfully serve the cause of order'. In his opinion, the danger from the Left far exceeded that from the Right, and he was 'inclined to risk whatever danger there may be of the *Einwohnerwehr* and *Orgesch* giving undue assistance to a reactionary outbreak, which would hardly threaten any permanent danger', so that their support would be available 'in the more probable event' of a Communist rising.[57] In his diary the ambassador noted: 'I consider the French demand for the total disarmament of all *Einwohnerwehr* and similar organisations almost insane. It is like cutting the branch of the tree on which you are sitting.'[58] Yet in view of the very one-sided political composition of both organizations (they largely overlapped) the French demand was only too understandable.

The War Office in London took a somewhat different view. The Army Council admitted that the *Einwohnerwehren* contained 'the nucleus of a future national army, and therefore they are a danger to the future peace of Europe,' but as 'neither life nor property are reasonably secure' in Germany, their dissolution 'would be impracticable'. Even if they were officially dissolved, 'they would continue as secret organisations owing to the demand for security by the general public.'[59] In December 1920 the Army Council strongly favoured the decentralization and gradual reduction of these forces; they should be placed under the ordinary civil authorities, instead of continuing as more or less private organizations as was the case with the *Orgesch* (at least outside Bavaria); the disarmament of the civil population should not be pressed 'in too peremptory a manner', and the German government should be given time to use its influence with the difficult local authorities. 'A stable Germany is essential to the peace of Europe, and it must be recognised that the *Orgesch* and *Einwohnerwehr* constitute a strong force on the side of law and order'; but as they constituted an aid to possible mobilization, a time limit ought to be fixed for their disbandment.[60] A few weeks later the General Staff, commenting on the execution of the military clauses of the Peace Treaty, stated that on the whole the German government had carried out these clauses 'so far as lay in its power, and has worked loyally with the Commission of Control', in spite of some obstruction by the military. The only real violation of the military clauses was 'the failure to disband and disarm the *Orgesch* and the ... *Einwohnerwehren*'; but the General Staff believed that the German government was not strong enough to do this against local opposition; in general, therefore, the execution of the military clauses was 'satisfactory, and the main object of these clauses has been attained, *i.e.* the removal of the menace of German aggression, at all events for a considerable period'. In Bavaria, however, the *Einwohnerwehr* 'contains all the law-abiding and best elements of the Bavarian population.... The Bavarian Government is dependent on the *Einwohnerwehr*, and could not exist in opposition to it'; and in East Prussia the strong local forces 'are supported by the bulk of the population'.[61]

In December 1920 the French demanded the immediate disarmament of the *Einwohnerwehr*, to the irritation of the Foreign Office. The German government had little option but to give way. According to a British Intelligence report, the issue was discussed at a meeting of the central and the state governments which agreed that any further opposition was impossible because 'such an attitude would find no sympathy abroad nor any unanimous support from the German people'. The only dissent came from the Bavarian government which bluntly stated 'that neither by fair means nor foul would Bavaria allow herself to be deprived of this means of self-defence'. But this attitude evoked general opposition from those present, and Chancellor Fehrenbach rightly pointed out that 'owing to the events which took place during the Soviet regime, Bavaria was much more securely safeguarded from the Communist menace than other States'.[62] Outside Bavaria – which will be discussed later – these semi-military forces were in fact officially disbanded or at least disarmed. Yet in June 1921 Brigadier Morgan stated it was very unlikely that they would disappear altogether; they would retain their nominal rolls and thus provide lists of men available for training with the army, and in East Prussia this had already been done with the local defence forces (which became known as the *Grenzschutz* or Frontier Defence units).[63]

The issues of the army, the police and the self-defence forces were part of the larger problem of German disarmament which came under the auspices of the Inter-Allied Military Commission of Control, which was installed in Berlin and carried out regular inspections in all parts of Germany. In the view of the War Office, the vital military clauses of the treaty had been more or less carried out by the spring of 1921, with the exception of those 'which provided for the disbandment and disarmament of the *Einwohnerwehr* and of the self-defence associations, and for the delivery of certain surplus war material': these issues should be settled by a compromise. Summing up the controversy, the Foreign Office stated in April 1921 that technically Germany was in default; but it was 'difficult, except upon the theory that Germany must pose and act as a repentant sinner, to establish a charge of bad faith', for the aim of the treaty 'was not to destroy Germany, but, in the interests of the peaceful settlement of Europe, to ensure her disarmament and the payment of reparation'.[64] In May the Allies issued an ultimatum on disarmament, reparations and other issues to Germany, and the Fehrenbach government resigned. A new government was formed by Joseph Wirth which accepted the ultimatum backed by a majority vote of the Reichstag, and on the basis of a 'policy of fulfilment'. A few weeks later Lord Kilmarnock was able to report that the work of the Control Commission was 'going on more smoothly as a result of the change in the political situation', that the instructions of the central authorities 'to facilitate Control instead of to obstruct it, appear to have fallen on less deaf ears than formerly', and that 'the Government is anxious to understand and meet the objections' of the Control Commission in the matter of the self-defence forces and the police.[65]

In August it was reported even from East Prussia that the work of control 'is now running smoothly and is in fact easier than it has ever been'. In Bavaria too, large quantities of arms were surrendered; 'having lost the bulk of their arms, the Germans are anxious to satisfy outstanding demands as soon as possible in order to put an end to the Control.'[66] But during the autumn and winter of 1921 obstruction again increased, and in the early months of 1922 the Control Commission met considerable opposition, which the General Staff ascribed to 'a genuine revival of national sentiment in Germany'.[67] Yet the General Staff believed 'that Germany has been effectively disarmed as far as material is concerned' and was 'quite powerless to fight a war with any fully organised great military power', that the armaments and material needed for a major war had been surrendered and destroyed and could not be reproduced quickly; the Control Commission had made great progress and had 'accomplished far more than the members of the commission at the outset considered would ever be possible', so that its personnel could be progressively reduced.[68] Early in 1922 Lord D'Abernon added his voice to this request by stating that, if the views of the Armaments Subcommission of the Control Commission were adopted, the commission 'will remain in Germany until the Day of Judgment'. In his opinion, the minute examination of the organization of man-power and the never-ending visits to every military centre were methods unsuitable to guarantee peace; instead reliance should be placed on the destruction of heavy war material and on supervision to prevent its replacement – a view which found the general agreement of the British representative on the Control Commission, General Bingham.[69]

Brigadier Morgan, however, disagreed, and in June sent another report to the War Office which was 'to prove that there is on the part of the German military authorities a deliberate design to use the army allowed to them by the treaty as the nucleus and the skeleton of a new army organised for a war of revenge'. As evidence he pointed to the army estimates, the police, the army administrative services and the para-military organizations. He therefore pleaded for continuing the work of the Control Commission. This was queried by the Foreign Office as not in agreement with the terms of the Peace Treaty; it was further emphasized there that Morgan's opinions were not shared by General Bingham and the War Office. Another official added that surely other men were better qualified to give an authoritative opinion, for Morgan was not even a professional soldier but in civil life a professor of constitutional law. Sir Eyre Crowe considered him 'an inveterate intriguer and self-seeker', but was nevertheless 'much impressed by the force of his arguments', while he thought General Bingham's judgment biased as he 'sees everything rosy through intensely pro-German spectacles'. Crowe thus held that Morgan's views were basically right but exaggerated.[70] British views on this crucial issue differed widely, and no consensus was reached, while the French, broadly speaking, shared the opinion of Brigadier Morgan; the Control Commission continued its work, for the French were convinced that the Germans, by accepting the Allied ultimatum, had consented to the continuation of military control.[71]

During its work the Control Commission often discovered small infringements of the disarmament provisions and raised points of detail which the German government had to answer as best it could. In the spring of 1922 Walther Rathenau, the Foreign Minister, complained to Lord D'Abernon that his position was made impossible, if his entire time was occupied with answering notes on such minor details. D'Abernon's advice to Rathenau was on several occasions that Germany should not only carry out disarmament on broad lines, but should try to remove the grounds of complaint; in his opinion, 'disarmament has been carried out, and has been carried out very effectively, but Germany gets little credit for this because shreds and remnants are left which . . . are profoundly irritating to those who desire to clean up the situation and to prove that it has been cleaned up.'[72] A Foreign Office official who was preparing notes for a discussion between Lloyd George and Wirth at the Genoa Conference of May 1922 felt that the Germans 'have not been without blame', but that the constant complaints of the Control Commission 'are not a wise policy if it is desired to strengthen the hands of the Wirth Government'; these complaints 'add fuel to the flames of Nationalist criticism' of the government and made it increasingly 'difficult for the Government to pursue a wise policy towards the Allies'. The wisest policy would be to withdraw the Control Commission and to replace it by a small military supervisory committee: 'the Allies would then have all the safeguards they really require', and the moderate political parties in Germany would be strengthened. But Crowe underlined the words 'all the safeguards they really require' and wrote in the margin: 'i.e. Nil!'[73] Some of the complaints of the Control Commission concerned the sale of German arms, for example to Turkey or Afghanistan, which were carefully listed in London. Another one was caused by the sale of ten hydroplanes by a German firm to Soviet Russia, which in the opinion of the Army Council constituted 'a glaring instance of a breach of the Treaty of Versailles', Article 170 of which forbade Germany to manufacture and export arms, munitions and war material of any

kind.[74] Incidents such as these seemed to justify Lord
D'Abernon's advice to Rathenau that Germany ought to try to
remove the grounds of such minor complaints.

More serious incidents occurred when members of the
Control Commission attempted to carry out local inspections. A
very serious incident took place at Passau in October 1922 when
a group of Allied officers inspected a battalion of the 20th
Infantry Regiment. Its commanding officer, who was also the
leader of the local 'Oberland' free corps, was allegedly on leave
and so his deputy produced the books required by the visitors.
The German officers gave all the information asked for but their
attitude was hostile. Abusive notices referring to *Franzosen-
hunde* (dogs of Frenchmen) were found posted on the walls of
the corridors. Meanwhile a crowd of several hundred had col-
lected in front of the barracks waiting for the Allied officers,
shouting abuse and threats and singing patriotic songs. When
they left their car was pelted with sticks, stones and pieces of
iron, the windows of the car were smashed, revolver shots were
fired, a French officer was struck in the face and his nose cut.
There were shouts of 'Get the Frenchmen out!' and 'Pigs!' Once
the car was clear of the barrack square there was no more
trouble.[75] There was a similar incident at Ingolstadt, also in
Bavaria, where Allied officers were forcibly prevented from
entering a munitions depot. In November the Conference of
Ambassadors in Paris decided to levy a fine of 500,000 gold
marks on each of the two towns; if the fine was not paid within
ten days it would be levied on the resources of the Bavarian
government in the occupied Palatinate, otherwise on German
state revenue in the Rhineland. The Allies also demanded
apologies from the Prime Minister of Bavaria and the local
authorities and the dismissal of the police officials considered
responsible for the incidents.[76]

When the Allied demands became known in Munich there
was an outburst of fierce nationalist sentiment. The Prime
Minister, Eugen von Knilling, addressed a crowded meeting in a
beer cellar, exclaimed among storms of applause that the
Entente was above all responsible for the incidents and casti-
gated 'French sadism'. According to the British consul in
Munich, people thought it 'quite natural that some hotheads
should, as usual, have translated into action the feeling to which
the vast majority of the population only give expression in
words: the attacks were regrettable but inevitable. . . . In the eyes

of those Bavarians who have overcome their first stupefaction, France, and France alone, is the aggressor. . . . France . . . has now seized an excuse to crush the last stronghold of patriotism in Germany.' The consul added significantly that the eyes of most people would turn towards 'Hitler whose fame has now risen so high' that he was able to address in turn five meetings held simultaneously which could not hold 'all his disciples'.[77]

The Bavarian government refused to apologize to the Allies, and the town of Ingolstadt equally refused to retire the police official whose dismissal was demanded by the Allies. It took the view that, as he had been elected to his post, he could not be discharged and that the town could not be blamed for the incident. Finally, the German government undertook to apologize on behalf of the Bavarian government and to pay the fines demanded. The French government urged 'that some notice must be taken of the Bavarian Prime Minister's action which nullified the apology made on his behalf by the German government'. But Lord Hardinge, the British ambassador in Paris, argued that 'it is well known that the Central German government was powerless to call the Bavarian Prime Minister to order', and was finally successful in persuading the French government not to reopen the issue and to be satisfied with calling attention to the language used by von Knilling without asking him for yet another apology.[78] It took three months to settle these incidents, and they were only settled because the German government took the blame and paid the fines – for events which were completely outside its control.

Another highly controversial issue, which equally inflamed German nationalist feeling, was that of the trial of the alleged war criminals who, from the Kaiser downwards, were to be handed over to the Allies for trial according to the Treaty of Versailles. When the long lists of German officers and others who were to be extradited were published in February 1920 there was an outcry. From Berlin General Bingham reported that 'the inclusion of the names of Hindenburg, Ludendorff and other Army commanders has raised the feeling to such an extent that it is impossible to say what may happen in the next few days'; the German government would not dare to hand them over and, even if they wanted to comply, had no means of doing so; the lists included the names of six or seven men who were dead; if the Allies insisted on surrender 'the work of disarmament of Germany and the reduction of the army will become an impossibility.'[79] Another British officer saw Noske, the Minister of Defence, who declared that 'this thing which I am asked to do is beyond me – beyond my Government.' The officer added: 'You will never get a single Officer out of Germany except such as might take it into his head to give himself up'; if a man were tried in Britain the German government would fall, 'for the people would rise up against a Government who were too weak to prevent this'; but in his opinion '*This Government must be retained and supported* – not only morally supported but practically.'[80]

The British General Staff then suggested that the terms of the Peace Treaty should be modified and the trials should be conducted either by German courts with Allied prosecutors or by neutral courts; if it were considered absolutely essential to demand the surrender of certain war criminals, 'to act as a precedent and deterring factor in future wars', then the number should be limited to about six or twelve men who were guilty of appalling crimes against prisoners of war, women or children or had fired on people trying to escape from sinking ships. It was virtually certain that German soldiers and policemen would refuse to carry out the arrests, especially if the list was long and included distinguished soldiers or sailors. 'The result will almost inevitably be the fall of the present Government and its replacement by a régime which is hardly likely to be satisfactory to us.'[81] The German Peace Delegation added its share to the difficulties by asking for the evidence in support of the accusation in several cases, claiming that at least in one case, the accused, Count Nikolaus von Bismarck, was still at school at the time in question, and in another that a woman's death in hospital was not due to 'inhuman treatment' but to cancer of the breast.[82]

In the end the Allied powers agreed not to insist on surrender but to have the cases tried by the Supreme Court at Leipzig, which meant that the evidence had to be handed over to German legal experts, that the witnesses had to appear there and that British barristers and legal officers attended the proceedings at Leipzig. Soon the Germans claimed that some of the accused could not be found or had gone abroad (as indeed had William II whom the Dutch government refused to hand over). The Attorney General found himself involved in lengthy discussions with German lawyers which, according to Lord Curzon, were continuing in a 'leisurely way'. In March 1921 Sir Eyre Crowe minuted: 'It seems to me that if we want to take our stand on the ground that the failure of the German government so far to bring any of the criminals to justice is a gross breach of their obligations then the discussion between the Attorney General and the German experts ought to be carried on in a somewhat different tone.' As early as December he had written: 'I do not think there is any chance of justice being done by the German Court.'[83] As it turned out his apprehension was only partly justified.

The cases concerning war crimes against British subjects were heard at Leipzig from May to July 1921 and were attended by British law officers. On his return the Solicitor General rather surprisingly informed Curzon: 'I was much impressed by the Supreme Court of Leipzig – the trials were conducted very impartially with every desire to get at the truth.' Another law officer made much more detailed reports on the trial of German soldiers accused of maltreating British prisoners of war. When the technical military adviser to the court, General Fransecky, remarked that in a mutinous camp the accused was entitled to give a box on the ears, the president interrupted him to say that in his opinion the blow inflicted on Jones could not be justified by any military or other law; it had been established that the camp was not in a state of mutiny, and he asked rather pointedly whether the general considered it was mutiny when men reported sick and whether knocking them about was the best way to treat them even if they were not ill. In summing up a few days later the president 'unequivocally condemned the course of conduct of the accused, which he described as besmirching the good name of the German Army' and paid tribute to the testimony of the British witnesses. The accused was sentenced to ten months' imprisonment, while the public prosecutor had demanded two years.[84] Two other German soldiers were sentenced to six months each for a similar offence. Two British barristers present at the trials considered that they were conducted fairly but that the sentences were too light. Lady D'Abernon thought this could be explained by the fact that the accused 'were merely the tools of others more highly placed', which made it difficult to inflict adequate sentences.[85] In July two U-Boat officers were tried for firing on the survivors of a sinking hospital ship and sinking open boats full of nurses and wounded soldiers. They were found guilty of being accessories to attempted murder and sentenced to four years' imprisonment. For the first time a German court acknowledged that war crimes had really been committed, and only the right-wing papers found excuses for the crimes and described the sentences as too severe.[86] One U-Boat commander was acquitted on the plea of acting on superior orders, and three others whom the British wanted apprehended escaped from Germany. The French government protested against the 'derisory' sentences inflicted by the Leipzig court and withdrew its representatives from it after they had been insulted in the streets; but this course was not followed by the British.[87]

What aroused British ire, however, was the treatment of the condemned prisoners and the ease with which they made their escape. Two of them were soon released, one on the ground of ill-health on the strength of a medical certificate, the other for 'the extraordinary reason' that his family should not be deprived of their means of support and that his employer should be enabled to keep his post for him. These were men serving short sentences for cruelty to prisoners of war. The two U-Boat officers escaped (with the help of former comrades from the navy). One of them, while serving his sentences, was able to carry on his business, wear his own clothes and provide his own food. Sir Eyre Crowe informed the German ambassador: 'That officers guilty of sinking defenceless open boats full of nurses and wounded should be considered sufficiently punished by living like private gentlemen at their ease within the precincts of the prison, . . . was, I thought, a matter which we had every reason to resent as outrageous. After that it was really hardly surprising that the officers should find their way out.' All this 'would have the most unfortunate repercussions on the sentiments of this country towards the German people' who had sided with convicted war criminals.[88] Lord D'Abernon addressed a strong protest to the German government: the escape of the two officers was bound to raise 'grave doubts respecting the sincerity of the German Authorities in dealing with those prisoners.'[89] More than 12 months later the British consul at Leipzig reported that an officer of the former Ehrhardt Brigade who was serving a sentence for complicity in the murder of the German Foreign Minister Rathenau was sentenced to an additional month of imprisonment for attempting to free the two U-Boat officers; two other accused were acquitted, and one was fined a small sum. The court accepted the curious plea that the accused had made the attempt entirely on their own initiative, without any involvement of 'Organization C' (the clandestine successor to the Ehrhardt Brigade) and for purely 'patriotic motives'.[90] There was no comment. Thus ended the attempt to bring the German war criminals to trial.

Members of the Ehrhardt Brigade or of 'Organization C' were also responsible for a series of political murders, as they had first been practised against the leaders of the Spartacus League and later against many others. The first such case reported to the Foreign Office concerned a former naval officer, Lieutenant-Commander Hans Paasche, who had become a prominent pacifist. In May 1920 about 60 soldiers of the Brigade descended on his country house, cordoned it off and found him bathing in a near-by lake. No weapons were discovered during the search (as he was bathing he was obviously not armed), and it was not clear whether he was shot at sight or whether he had tried to escape.[91] This clearly was a case of revenge on a former officer who had joined 'the enemy'. Fifteen months later the former Minister of Finance, Matthias Erzberger, one of the signatories of the Peace Treaty, was murdered by members of 'Organization C'. The murder caused 'a violent storm' in the left-wing press which urged the government to take the strongest measures 'against any recurrence of such disgraceful lawlessness which imperils Germany's position in the eyes of the civilised world'. Lord D'Abernon described the murdered man as 'aggressive, ingenious, bold almost to recklessness and an indefatigable worker', but lacking moral scruples.[92] From Munich the British consul reported that there 'conservatives and bourgeois were unanimous in saying that the man who had smilingly signed the humiliating conditions of the peace was a good riddance'; their satisfaction was only moderated by the fear that the socialists would be able to profit from the outcry the murder was bound to cause.[93]

In June 1922 Walther Rathenau, the Foreign Minister, was murdered by members of the same organization; he was a leading industrialist and he was a Jew. From Berlin the British embassy commented that the extreme Right was morally responsible for these murders, for it held up those attempting to govern Germany not only to ridicule but 'branded [them] as traitors, murderers, valets of the Entente and undesirables who ought not to be allowed to exist', while the respect for human life 'has been largely lessened by four years of war succeeded by a revolution'.[94] The British consuls at Frankfurt and Munich reported on the impressive counter-demonstrations of the Left. In Frankfurt, work ceased in all factories, shops and business houses and some 100,000 people assembled; 'there is no doubt that it was a genuine labour demonstration'. In Munich, 'the enormous and orderly crowd was a unique sight', according to the consul; 'today's meeting was a revelation.' It showed that 'a spirit has been aroused among the workmen which the Nationalists would do well not to disregard.'[95] Both consuls noticed that these were demonstrations by the socialist workers; the middle class stayed at home.

When the Ehrhardt Brigade marched into Berlin during the Kapp Putsch its emblem was the swastika and its ideology was strongly anti-semitic. A few weeks after the Putsch an Intelligence report from Rotterdam pointed to the growth of anti-Semitism in Germany, and a Foreign Office official minuted: 'it was easy to foresee that an agitation of this kind would arise,' because the ordinary German refused to believe that the army was defeated and attributed the defeat to the revolution and the secret agitation of the Independent Socialists and Communists, among whom 'many Jews have taken a prominent part'; many Jews, too, were among the Bolshevist agents in Germany; 'all this . . . in a country in the condition in which Germany now is, will inevitably take exaggerated and brutal forms.'[96] In June 1920 a report by the British Army of the Rhine pointed to the anti-semitic campaign organized by the Nationalist Party for electoral purposes; in trains, stations, public urinals etc. small bills could be found denouncing the Jews as the authors of the war and for causing the rise in prices by their black-market activities; in spite of their small numbers, Jews 'are in possession of the greater part of the country's present capital'.[97] In September another report from Rotterdam emphasized the growth of anti-semitic propaganda in North Germany and for the first time linked it with the nascent *völkisch* movement. 'The anti-Semites are now pushing the "völkisch" or racial element right into the forefront of their campaign, and they christen it everywhere as the "Deutsch-Völkische Bewegung". . . . More than fifty per cent of all this literature is devoted to the question of the Jews' participation in the war.' The report listed 14 newspapers carrying this kind of propaganda.[98]

In the occupied Rhineland the British authorities soon noticed *völkisch* activities. In 1921 the British High Commissioner drew the attention of the Rhineland High Commission to the case of a Cologne bookseller who for some months had been selling anti-semitic and anti-Allied literature, among them a 'Swastika Yearbook' showing 'pictures of Indians being tied to the mouth of cannons by British troops' and well known *völkisch* journals, such as *Der Hammer*. The man had been warned and his shop had been raided by the military, but he continued to sell 'literature of the most pernicious kind', and should therefore be deported from the occupied area.[99] In March 1922 the *Deutsch-Völkischer Schutz- und Trutzbund* held a meeting in Cologne which was stopped by the representative of the Rhineland High Commission on account of anti-semitic invectives, and the chairman was forced to clear the hall.[100] When the *Schutz- und Trutzbund* was dissolved by order of President Ebert in July 1922 the British Commissioner at Cologne thought that this would only drive the members underground: 'that these people will continue in secret to meet and scheme for their ideals is certain.'[101]

In general, however, far more attention was paid to the traditional monarchist and nationalist forces than to the comparatively small racialist and *völkisch* movement, for there always was the possibility of a monarchist restoration with its inherent threat to the peace and the Allied position in Germany. In March 1920 a British official sent to supervise the plebiscite in the district of Marienwerder, close to the Vistula, observed that the great landowners of East Prussia – such as the Counts Dohna and Finckenstein and Baron von Oldenburg-Januschau – had been busy recruiting to support the Kapp Putschists if they should succeed; they and their friends did not conceal 'their detestation of the democratic rule of Herr Ebert', and most of the local officials too would welcome 'a return to the old order'.[102] In June the British consul reported from Frankfurt 'that a great majority of upper classes and the bourgeoisie aim at an eventual restoration of a Monarchy' and that the monarchist spirit was fostered in the secondary schools and universities where teachers as well as students were imbued with it; they firmly believed in the greatness of the German Empire and the essential superiority of the Germans over other nations, and they dreamt of taking revenge on France. Recently the consul had stopped to watch pupils being drilled by an instructor who 'was unmistakably a former drill sergeant'; they drilled 'surprisingly well with much of the old Prussian spirit', and the instructor did not hesitate to use his cane on the children when he considered this necessary.[103] In August Lord Kilmarnock remarked on the strong nationalism permeating the universities, 'generally accompanied by anti-semitism'. But he found the Left too inspired by the 'national idea', especially on the issues of the Saar, the right bank of the Vistula and Upper Silesia (the plebiscite areas); in the latter the Social Democrats had threatened a general strike to protest against Polish activities; a prominent Social Democrat lecturing to a radical audience on German neutrality had asked them recently the rhetorical question whether they wanted to fight the Poles and had received the reply: 'No: but against France.'[104]

In October 1920 a British officer serving in the Rhineland reported that, during the past months, German bitterness against the French had considerably grown; more and more often Germans declared that there must be a war of revenge against France within a few years; this feeling was shared by all classes and parties except only the extreme Left, and every difference between France and England was hailed with delight. In comparison, the correct behaviour of the British was extolled, but probably 'this flattery of the British is merely cupboard love' and aimed at separating Britain from France.[105] Early in 1921 Lord Kilmarnock found that 'there is at present lamentable little evidence' of 'a change in the spirit of Germany'; the propaganda in the schools favoured a war of revenge; this tendency had been intensified by the occupation of Frankfurt by the French and the use of coloured troops for the purpose; the real danger was that all social classes would unite 'in a common feeling of undying hatred'.[106] A few months later a British official of the Rhineland High Commission also spoke of 'hatred of the French increasing amongst all classes of the population', especially in the Palatinate and the French zone of occupation; this was caused by the local French officials, petty interference with appointments of teachers, the requisitioning of schools, the use of coloured troops 'and other annoyances small and great'; and now a fear existed that the French government deliberately intended 'to crush Germany out of all power of recovery'.[107]

The use of coloured troops in the Rhineland was also raised in London. Early in 1922 a member of parliament wrote to the Foreign Office that, as he had heard on good authority, the French had sent black troops into Frankfurt; could it not be intimated to the French in some form that this was contrary to British feelings and that these units should be withdrawn? It was 'adding insult to injury for the French to still persist in

making things as unpleasant as possible in such an objection-
able manner as by employing coloured troops.' But the Foreign
Office gave a very non-committal answer and minuted that it
surely was up to the French government to decide what troops to
employ and that the press reports of outrages by coloured troops
'have been greatly exaggerated'; in spite of parliamentary pressure this view was constantly adhered to.[108] Another Foreign
Office official minuted that in his opinion the use of coloured
troops by the French 'is a great scandal'. He felt above all concerned with the effect service in Germany would have on the
black soldiers. 'The prestige of the white man in Africa will be
adversely affected as a result of the black having seen too much
of the sordid side of European life'; but he did not think that the
British could interfere or advise on this issue. His minute was
followed by another which suggested 'that he shares the popular
delusion that these barbarians are "sexually ungovernable".
Nothing could be less true of them under their national conditions.'[109] As the French saw no reason to change their policy,
German propaganda against 'the black shame' had a free field.

The decisions of the Allied conference in Paris, taken early in
1921, to demand from Germany the payment of two to six
million gold marks during a period of 42 years plus a fixed
percentage of German exports provoked another storm of
national indignation. According to the British Army of the
Rhine, there was at first silence, followed by 'hot protests', so
that 'at the present moment almost everybody in Germany is
"national".' From Frankfurt the British consul reported that the
political result of the Paris decisions would be 'a sharp movement to the Right'; such a tendency had been very marked
during the past months and would produce a growing desire for
revenge 'and reinforce the ideas of a monarchist and military
State'.[110] From Munich the British consul wrote that the gentlemen of the Right had learnt nothing as a result of the war; their
arguments to a large extent were an elaboration of a statement
made recently in Munich by Dr Karl Helfferich, a leading
German Nationalist, 'Reparation! I hate that word, for Germany
has nothing to repair!' In the Bavarian Diet the president
declared that the demands of Paris had nothing to do with peace
but were a continuation and aggravation of the blockade.[111] The
German papers described the Allied demands as 'impossible
nonsense' and Allied policy as 'strangulation' of Germany, and
urged the government to say an emphatic 'No'.[112] Summarizing

the trend of German ideas the British consul at Frankfurt stated: 'The German is not by nature revengeful but now a desire for revenge has been fostered and must be counted as a force to be reckoned with in the future unless France has the wisdom to fundamentally alter her policy before it is too late.'[113]

In April 1921 the funeral of the former Empress Augusta was the occasion for a vivid demonstration of monarchist sentiment. As Lord D'Abernon noticed, in Berlin many people were wearing mourning, and the old Imperial flag flying half-mast was 'conspicuous throughout the city'. Her funeral at Potsdam was attended by about 200,000 people, many of whom had to spend the previous night wherever they could; also present were Hindenburg, Ludendorff, Mackensen and Tirpitz. The police were able to cope with the crowds until the funeral procession had passed but were then overwhelmed by the multitude.[114] In the same month a Swiss student, who during the past year had read economics at Berlin and Freiburg, found that at the universities about 95 per cent of the professors held reactionary views; if a professor ventured to express an opinion which sounded democratic he would be unable to continue owing to noisy demonstrations by his audience; the large majority of the students belonged to reactionary clubs and societies; students with democratic or socialist convictions hardly dared to participate in discussions because the outcome usually was an assault by a superior number of reactionary students; only in Berlin were the republican elements strong enough to make themselves heard, if only ocasionally.[115] A British woman engaged in relief work among students also noticed that 'all the professions are full to overflowing, how are the young men and women of the middle classes to get a living? They feel bitterly the loss of their colonies, the British Dominions are shut to them, and there is no world outlet for their surplus young population.' 'An increasingly bitter and hostile attitude' was spreading among old and young, 'and the seeds of revenge are being sown which will blossom into a fierce war of retribution far more terrible than the last.' These words were written in May 1922 and they sound prophetic. She felt that 'working amongst these people is rather like living on the slopes of Etna, one feels there is a spirit, which if provoked too far will erupt and engulf civilization.'[116]

German nationalism was also stirred by the clause of the Peace Treaty which attributed the responsibility for the outbreak of the war to Germany and her allies and therefore imposed on Germany the duty to pay reparations. Soon a vigorous propaganda campaign was launched to absolve Germany of 'war guilt' and 'to throw the responsibility for the war on the shoulders of Russia and Austria'.[117] In 1921 Lord D'Abernon wrote that articles were constantly appearing in the press stressing 'the necessity of removing from the minds of the world this impression of Germany's war guilt', asserting Germany's innocence and repeating the old accusations against the Allies.[118] When Lloyd George declared in a speech that the serious war damages in Belgium and Northern France were 'mainly due to a deliberate scheme of destruction' by the Germans the German Officers' Union published an appeal for photographs to disprove the allegation, for the Allies possessed far superior artillery and launched totally unnecessary air raids on peaceful Belgian and French villages and towns; all former soldiers were urgently requested to collect and forward this material 'to frustrate the monstrous assertions of our enemies'.[119] In September an Intelligence report stated that the number of individuals and societies engaged in anti-Peace Treaty propaganda was 'innumerable'; a fulfilment of the treaty was always painted as amounting to 'national suicide'.[120] More dramatically the woman engaged in relief work among the students, who has already been quoted, wrote: 'the clause stating that Germany had the whole guilt in starting the war . . . is to each one of them a personal unhealed wound. They feel that Germany, at the moment when she was beaten and down, was forced to acknowledge herself a criminal, before the whole world, and in consequence the world passed judgment on her, without her being allowed to stand on her defence, a privilege which is regarded as the right of a common criminal before sentence is passed.'[121] Two leaders of the Independent Labour Party, on their return from an international meeting in Vienna, stopped in Munich in 1921 and addressed a meeting of the USPD. There Ben Riley and Emanuel Shinwell declared that their party would continue the fight against imperialism and the Allied decisions taken in Paris in 1919.[122]

In 1921 yet another issue violently inflamed German nationalism, perhaps more so than any other cause: that of Upper Silesia, where according to the Peace Treaty the inhabitants had to vote whether they wanted to belong to Germany or to Poland. This was to be done under the supervision of an International Commission and under the protection of Allied troops who were to guarantee a free vote, in a district with a very mixed population where national passions ran extremely high. The Commission as well as the troops consisted of British, French and Italian contingents. The French chairman, General Le Rond, and the French military tended to favour the Polish side and more or less openly sided with the Poles, especially after the outbreak of a Polish insurrection in August 1920, while the British and the Italians tried to preserve an uneasy balance. Early in September the British Commissioner, Colonel Percival, informed London from Oppeln (Opole) that, on account of the failure of the French troops to suppress the Polish bands infesting Upper Silesia, 'the chances for the conduct of a really impartial plebiscite are small'; he and the Italian Commissioner were convinced that they could no longer rely on General Le Rond to conduct it 'in strict impartiality'.[123] A few days later Percival wrote that, outside the big towns, 'the Poles have been allowed to intimidate German sympathizers throughout the industrial area'; often the French troops were in contact with the Polish insurgents and 'fraternized' with them, and only in a very few cases had they succeeded in disarming them; on their arrival the French troops had been welcomed by the Polish inhabitants and disliked or hated by the Germans; from that moment they associated with Polish sympathizers, went to Polish shops and places of entertainment and were invited by Poles; the higher French authorities and the French President of the Commission must be held responsible 'for the ease with which the insurrection started and spread'.[124]

In Warsaw, Sir Horace Rumbold went to see the Vice-Minister for Foreign Affairs and told him bluntly that, in spite of their experiences in the earlier plebiscites (in Allenstein and Marienwerder where the Germans gained overwhelming victories), the Poles 'were continuing the same foolish methods in Upper Silesia. These methods were bound to alienate the sympathies of doubtful voters and of every reasonable person.' It had definitely been established that large quantities of arms had been supplied to the Polish bands in Upper Silesia, and the Polish government should 'induce its agents to keep quiet'.[125] The Foreign Office wired to the British ambassador in Paris, Lord Derby, that it seemed clear that General Le Rond 'cannot be trusted to carry out the disarmament, or to keep peace impartially between contending factions'; it was of vital importance to restore the prestige of the Commission, so as to reestablish peaceful conditions and to avoid a breakdown in the production of coal, which would have far-reaching political results.'[126]

At the end of 1920 Lord Hardinge, the new British ambassador in Paris, informed Lord Curzon that the French government did 'not in the least share the apprehension felt by His Majesty's Government as regards the freedom and fairness of the plebiscite'; their dominating fear was that it would result in a German victory; this would leave Germany in the possession of the vital coal-field and thus make her less dependent on Ruhr coal; but the more dependent Germany became on this 'the more potent will be their favourite threat of a French occupation of the Ruhr basin'; this consideration influenced their whole outlook and therefore they would not accede to the British demand for the expulsion of Wojciech Korfanty, the leader of the Polish nationalists, from Upper Silesia; if the British demands were not met Britain should consider withdrawing from the Plebiscite Commission. But Sir Eyre Crowe disagreed, for this 'would mean not only an open rupture with France but an open encouragement of German resistance to the plebiscite decision if adverse to Germany'.[127] Early in 1921 a British officer serving with the Commission stated that things were moving very slowly; trying to get a move on was like trying to push a steam roller; most of the trouble was caused by the partial behaviour of the senior French officials, 'not to mention the President himself', and the constitution of the Commission gave the French far too much power in its different departments; 'it has been a great lesson to most of us here.'[128]

The plebiscite was finally held in March 1921; it gave the Poles just over 40 per cent, and the Germans just under 60 per cent of the vote, but produced large Polish majorities in a few districts, such as Pless and Rybnik. Lord Curzon's view, expressed in a private letter to Colonel Percival, was that 'in view of the overwhelming German majority,' the German claim to the whole of Upper Silesia should be recognized. The difficulty of any other solution – such as drawing an arbitary frontier line, or creating Polish enclaves in Germany, and German ones in Poland – was described as 'overwhelming' by the Foreign Office; yet the recognition of Germany's claim would inevitably meet with French opposition while it might be supported by the Italians.[129] Two days later, however, a Foreign Office official minuted that, according to the fuller information received meanwhile, it would be difficult to allot the whole area to

Germany; the French and Poles were bound to contest the suggestion that the important industrial districts which showed a German majority must not be separated from Germany; it thus looked as if Britain would have to compromise by giving the district of Pless and 'as much of the rural districts . . . as can be conveniently managed' to Poland, while allocating 'the urban and industrial plums' to Germany. Crowe added the Poles and French would argue that the large German majorities in the towns were obtained by the influx of the 'outvoters' (who came from Upper Silesia but no longer lived there) who had no real stake in the country.[130]

The decision of the Allies thus went in favour of partition. But in May 1921 there was another Polish insurrection led by Korfanty and supported from Poland. Colonel Percival wired from Oppeln that the German population was rapidly losing patience; during the last days he had done his utmost to persuade their leaders not to take up arms, which would have catastrophic results for the area; so far they had restrained their people, but they had now told him they were losing control over the masses; they demanded that British troops must be sent and the Reichswehr must restore order; the situation was deteriorating rapidly. Percival also told Le Rond that they must reckon with a German offensive and that he could not keep the Germans back any longer; it was useless to tell them to rely on the Commission because it was clear that it was powerless.[131] The British minister in Warsaw wired that the Poles had good reason to believe in the doctrine of might and any yielding to their *fait accompli* would only confirm them in this belief and make them 'a perpetual menace to stability of present order of things in Central and Eastern Europe.'[132] In Paris Lord Hardinge handed to Briand a British memorandum that the gravity of the situation in Silesia seemed to be insufficiently appreciated by the French government; with the connivance of the Polish government a rebellious Polish leader had overrun large parts of the area and flouted the Plebiscite Commission; the French troops had acquiesced in this and in some cases shown active sympathy with the insurgents who had committed 'an act of unlawful and predatory violence'; if the French government was determined to insist on the cession of the whole industrial area to Poland, the British government 'must inform them that they cannot possibly acquiesce in any such development', nor would they continue to exercise pressure on the Germans to refrain from counter-measures, 'for which they can already find ample excuse'.[133]

From Oppeln Colonel Percival reported that the French allowed the armed insurgents to move about unhindered and to occupy unmolested large parts of the country; they justified this by the argument that the troops were far too weak to do much against the insurgents and that any action on their side would cause serious reprisals by the insurgents against the German population. The Commission, he continued, had lamentably failed to fulfil its promise of putting down the insurrection and therefore he had suggested the withdrawal of the entire British section, but this 'would be regarded by the German section of the population as leaving them in the lurch'; surprisingly, they had so far abstained from taking counter-measures, but it was more than could be expected from them 'to see their country overrun by an army of bandits . . . who are there with the single object of taking from the Germans by foul means what they cannot obtain by fair'; inevitably the Germans now took matters into their own hands and were collecting their forces.[134] As Lord D'Abernon reported from Berlin the men of the (officially dissolved) free corps, not only from Silesia but also form Berlin and Bavaria, were assembling in the neighbourhood of Neustadt in Upper Silesia and the Military Control Commission demanded their disbandment.[135] Soon heavy fighting broke out between the Polish insurgents and the German self-defence units, recruited to a large extent by the free corps, which lasted until mid-June.

At the end of May a British officer reported from Upper Silesia that there was an 'essential difference' between the German and the Polish contestants: the Germans cooperated with the Commission to restore order, and the Poles worked against the Commission 'for the creation of disorder'; and the leaders of the German forces 'may be trusted as hitherto to adopt British advice in any event'.[136] British reinforcements were quickly sent from Cologne, but their commanding officer bitterly complained about total lack of cooperation from the French side; almost every promise made to him or to the British High Commissioner by the French was broken.[137] The British Food Commissioner on the other hand related that the Germans would not allow food supplies into the contested areas and were starving their own people in the towns; it should not be forgotten that the miners had real grievances: they had been exploited by German capitalists who made huge fortunes out of their labour while they could not buy enough food for themelves and their children. 'These men have been sweated. They have a grievance. Let this be remedied.'[138] At the beginning of July the new British High Commissioner, Sir Harold Stuart, informed Curzon somewhat optimistically that relations between the British and the French were improving. He had given a large garden party for the Allied officers and their families, and 'this demonstration of Allied friendship and cordiality' had convinced both Poles and Germans of 'the solidarity of the Entente in Upper Silesia'; the Commission had ordered the Polish insurgents and the German irregulars to withdraw from their positions and to disband and announced that it was resuming the government of the province.[139] But two weeks later Sir Harold had to admit that the authority of the Commission 'is only a very thin veneer and in villages hardly exists at all'; for it was unable to protect Poles or Germans who lived in a place where the other nationality predominated.[140]

Meanwhile Anglo-French friction continued unabated. In July even Crowe had to admit that the British government would be justified to declare, if further disturbances broke out, that the French themselves were principally to blame; the British might go further and say that, if France continued her present policy, the British government 'cannot remain associated with it, and will feel compelled to make this clear to the whole world by withdrawing all British troops not only from Upper Silesia but also from the Rhine.'[141] At the same time Sir Harold wired from Oppeln that the French military authorities were adopting provocative measures; they intended to employ a new French division in the German districts so as to overawe the people; this would cause German reprisals and the consequences would be disastrous; it was vital to stop the despatch of the new French division.[142] The British commanding officer, Major-General Heneker, drew attention to the tendentious reports in the French press which grossly exaggerated the German activities, 'often without foundation', but never mentioned those of the Poles; the 'calculated restraint of German population under considerable provocation is very marked.'[143]

In October rumours began to reach Germany that the decision on the partition of Upper Silesia would be unfavourable to Germany, that the industrial area would be divided and that Kattowitz and other towns would be allocated to Poland. The president of the Reichstag, Paul Loebe, at the suggestion of President Ebert went to see Lord D'Abernon and told him that such a decision would destroy the government of Chancellor

Wirth as well as all German confidence in Britain; this German confidence was so strong 'that we all feel impelled to appeal to her for protection against the bitter and unjustified suspicion of the French'; even the leaders of the Nationalist and People's parties, Helfferich and Stresemann, had recently declared: 'do nothing to alienate England – our policy must conform to hers – that is the only path to safety.'[144] The German Foreign Minister, Friedrich Rosen, addressed by hand a personal appeal to Curzon: 'the loss of . . . two fifths of Upper Silesia, and those the most valuable districts of the whole country, including a number of important German towns, three years after the war has ended, would create an extremely difficult situation for Germany as a whole, and for all supporters of a better understanding with England in particular.'[145] The British Cabinet expressed its concern that the industrial area of Upper Silesia should be divided and that districts with a considerable German majority should be handed over to Poland.[146] In Berlin, Lord D'Abernon reported, excitement continued to increase, the government was 'in something like a panic', and there was talk of resigning.[147] In the Reichstag Chancellor Wirth spoke strongly against partition. But the Council of the League of Nations and the Supreme Council of the Allies approved it and it was carried out.

In December 72 British intellectuals and politicians sent a letter protesting against the partition, 'a departure from justice, a disregard of history, and a defiance of the verdict given by the recent plebiscite'; it would 'intensify afresh the unrest of Europe, the danger of a future war, and the disorganization and impoverishment of society, not only on the Continent, but in this country'. Among the signatories were Professor Raymon Beazley, R.H. Tawney, George Lansbury, E.D. Morel from the Union of Democratic Control and the Leaders of the ILP. A Foreign Office official thought that the list 'includes names of men so intelligent and sincere that I always wonder how they can join with the busybodies and humbugs to lay down the law on matters of which they can only have the most superficial knowledge. Mr Keynes is absent.' But Crowe went one further and wrote: 'I do not notice the "intelligent" members of the congregation, except the writer of the covering letter', Professor Beazley.[148] In his opinion, 'intelligence' only existed on the other side of the political spectrum.

This was not yet the end of the matter. In July 1922 General

Heneker reported that large numbers of the former German self-defence forces had got out of hand and were attacking the French at every opportunity; heavy fire had been directed at a train evacuating French troops from Upper Silesia and arms surrendered for destruction had been captured by the Germans; the bands of armed young Germans 'are a menace to the peace of the country.'[149] A British report of the same year gave the strength of the German self-defence forces as between 69,000 and 77,000 men, with arms sufficient for 59,000 and headquarters at Breslau in Lower Silesia. There were also 'undesirable elements', expelled from the central organization, whose 'chief occupations are acts of terrorism, robbery with violence and in many cases murder'.[150] But on the economic side there was progress. In February 1922 Lord D'Abernon reported that the negotiations between Germans and Poles were 'proceeding more satisfactorily than anyone in Berlin anticipated'. Two months later he added that the gloomy German prophecies as to the ruin of Upper Silesian industry had not been fulfilled; the Germans had feared serious Polish interference with the working of the industrial enterprises, but these fears were unfounded, and on the whole Poles and Germans were now 'working very well together'.[151] In early June 1922 the German and Polish representatives exchanged the ratifications of the main convention, which had been ratified by the German and Polish parliaments; it protected to a large extent the interests of the German industrialists and landowners whose property was situated in Poland, but in Germany national indignation prevailed.[152] The issue of Upper Silesia had caused fundamental differences between Britain and France and almost led to an open rupture. The Germans were looking to Britain for protection and help which was rendered somewhat tardily, for Britain was determined to save the alliance with France.

Yet Anglo-German relations had improved and the German government could rely on British advice and a certain amount of support. At the beginning of 1920 General Malcolm reported from Berlin that 'a considerable amount of credit is due to the German Government for the way in which they have so far kept the country together. Men with little experience of Government and almost without tradition found themselves suddenly confronted by a stupendous task'; a new constitution had to be drafted, industry was at a standstill, communications were disorganized, disorders broke out, 'and the armed forces, such as

73

there were, anything but reliable'; the government had loyally carried out the terms of Versailles and its position 'is certainly stronger than it was when peace was signed'; in June 1919 no one expected it to last three weeks, but it was still in power.[153] In February the General Staff stated that it was 'of great importance to maintain the present Government in office and to strengthen its position'; the situation in Germany had improved since the early months of 1919, but 'elements of serious danger remain' due above all to the rising commodity prices and the alarming decline of the German currency.[154] Yet this was only the beginning of the German inflation which was to continue at an ever accelerating pace until the autumn of 1923 and to bring with it ever growing dangers to the existing order.

From June 1920 to November 1922 the German Chancellor was a leader of the Catholic Centre Party, first Konstantin Fehrenbach, and after him Joseph Wirth. Both received very favourable notices in the diplomatic reports. Lord D'Abernon saw Fehrenbach soon after his appointment and wrote: 'Chancellor made excellent impression on me as to honesty and goodwill.' His motto was 'plenty of food and plenty of work'; all he wanted was to increase productivity and to restore Germany's economic strength; any idea of *revanche* he considered 'ridiculous with a people as beaten as we have been.'[155] In an Intelligence report Fehrenbach was described as 'fearless, just and strong, . . . one of the bigger men of Germany today'; he was of massive build, 'dresses badly in an ill-fitting frock coat, a collar several times too large, even for his thick neck, and a tie that is never in place'; he had a charming sense of humour, so that 'in the heat of debate his witty words have at the right moment been as oil upon troubled waters.'[156] As to Fehrenbach's successor, in June 1921 D'Abernon wrote: 'Wirth is showing great courage and determination. He is loathed by the Nationalists', and 'the Chancellor continued to make on me the impression of a very sincere man of great courage, faced by an almost impossible task in which he both requires and deserves assistance.'[157]

At the height of the Upper Silesian crisis the British Army of the Rhine stated that the fate of the Wirth government depended on the decision to be reached by the Allies. 'One can say without favour or prejudice that the fall of Dr Wirth would constitute a considerable set-back for the Entente, his being the first Government that has shown any signs of attempting to fulfil the country's obligations.'[158] To Lord D'Abernon Wirth explained that the Allies made a big mistake in speaking of their policy 'towards Germany', for there was not one Germany but two, 'a democratic Germany which sincerely desired peace and work and reconciliation', and a Germany of the reactionaries and Communists who seemed to prefer catastrophe to commerce; now the democratic Germany was in the saddle and he hoped that the good intentions of his government would be sustained by friendly help; if the German public saw that a democratic policy brought about an easier fate all would be well.[159] Retrospectively it is interesting that, before Wirth was appointed Chancellor, the post was offered to Dr Adenauer. But he put forward several conditions, such as the replacement of the eight-hour day by a nine-hour day if this were necessary, and complete freedom for him to select ministers from any party, and his appointment fell through. The British Commissioner at Cologne in reporting this added that Dr Adenauer's 'intense personal ambition' was well known and that the idea of a 'dictatorial government, with himself as Dictator, no doubt appeals to his imagination.'[160] As to other members of the government, British interest naturally centred on the person of the Foreign Minister, and in March 1920 the Foreign Office even took the curious step of vetoing three candidates for the post, Counts Bernstorff and Brockdorff-Rantzau and Friedrich Rosen, all diplomats of the old school. Crowe minuted: 'These are the most notorious agents of the government in organizing outrages in neutral countries directed against the Allies [during the war].' The British government 'would have to regard such a choice as convincing evidence that German foreign policy remains inspired by all the ideas which brought about the war and directed by all the old methods which have produced the bitterness in the feelings of the allied nations against Germany.' The British chargé d'affaires in Berlin was instructed to point out that, if a man of that type was appointed, 'it will be quite impossible for His Majesty's Government to have any confidence whatever in the German Government.'[161]

Yet 14 months later, in another government, Rosen nevertheless became the Foreign Minister, and it does not seem that the British objections were sustained. But he only remained so for eight months. He was followed in office by Walther Rathenau, a much more powerful figure and a strong proponent of the policy of 'fulfilment'. Lord D'Abernon thought that, before taking office, Rathenau favoured a continental or pro-French

policy; but once in office he 'found the French attitude of incessant nagging and complaint so intolerable' that he-revised his
opinion and became impressed 'by the broad-minded and toler-
ant attitude assumed by English Ministers'.[162] Lord Kilmarnock
too found Rathenau 'distinctly bitter against the French'. He
complained about French propaganda in the Rhineland, especially in the schools, and about the whole policy of the Inter-
Allied Rhineland High Commission which in his opinion trans-
gressed its competence. He also asked for an increase in the
number of British troops in the Rhineland – 'an awful thing for a
German Minister to have to ask for' – to counterbalance French
power on the Rhine.[163] As Rathenau was responsible for the
conclusion, in May 1922, of the controversial Treaty of Rapallo
with Soviet Russia, which inaugurated a policy of cooperation
between the two countries, he met growing opposition in
Germany, even inside the Wirth government, and great personal
animosity. As the British embassy reported, the right-wing
parties were opposed to Rapallo for obvious reasons, and equally
the conservative People's Party which for business reasons had
at first been inclined to approve. Wirth's party, the Centre, was
divided, supporting the treaty out of personal loyalty to the
Chancellor but, 'if left to itself, would be unqualified in disapproval'. The largest party, the SPD, 'dislike Bolshevism as
much as, if not more than, any other Party' and followed the lead
of President Ebert.[164] Indeed, Ebert was very hostile to Rapallo
and said that Rathenau as well as the Undersecretary of State in
the German Foreign Office ought to be dismissed; but, according
to D'Abernon, 'Ebert cannot afford to do without him'. In May
1922 the ambassador wrote: 'Rathenau has to face the undying
hatred of the Right and he receives continually threatening
letters from members of the extreme Nationalist organisations';
but he was so contemptuous of danger that he refused all police
protection.[165]

Six weeks later Rathenau was murdered by members of
'Organization C'. D'Abernon described the general feeling in
Berlin as 'one of profound horror'; even anti-semitic circles
expressed indignation; but he also mentioned the 'violent
animosity of Nationalist circles' to the dead man. 'Conversant
with all the doctrines of socialism, communism, and every other
ism, a bold enquirer into new theories – such a man was not
limited or confined by any arbitrary geographical frontier. He
belonged to the Universe.'[166] By contrast the President of the

Republic, Friedrich Ebert, was a more pedestrian figure; but he had his strong points and certainly strong opinions of his own. In 1921 Lord Kilmarnock wrote: 'Ebert's tact, impartiality and moderation have been generally acknowledged by the bourgeois parties, including even the German People's Party. He cannot, however, be described as an imposing or popular figure; he is constantly held up to ridicule by the extremists both of the Right and of the Left'; it thus seemed very unlikely that the bourgeois parties would agree to an extension of Ebert's term of office beyond 1922, unless they could not discover a suitable candidate of their own. The growing nationalist trend of public opinion would almost certainly cause the right-wing parties to put forward a candidate 'to impersonate the national idea', such as Field-Marshal von Hindenburg or Prince Bülow for whom a vigorous propaganda campaign was carried on.[167]

Among other leading politicians Gustav Stresemann, the leader of the People's Party, was singled out for praise by Lord D'Abernon. During the crisis over Upper Silesia he 'appeared to have behaved with great good sense and patriotism. Instead of attacking the Wirth Government as he could have done with a good chance of success – since they have or had temporarily lost their nerve – he has maintained a very reserved attitude, and has not withdrawn his offers of support in a projected coalition.'[168] It was this issue which brought down the Wirth government in November 1922 because the SPD refused to agree to a widening of the coalition government to include the People's Party, unless it consented to specific demands, such as the preservation of the eight-hour day and the stabilization of the currency. These were rejected by the People's Party on the ground that its attitude was sufficiently well known. Wirth then requested the Social Democrats to accept the principle of a broad coalition once and for all, assuming that their support 'was his whatever course he might choose to pursue'. But he forgot that a few months earlier the Independent Social Democrats had rejoined the SPD and now exercized strong influence within the united party. Where he 'expected to find tame and sympathetic adherents, he found instead resentful opponents who reproached him for having given way to capitalism' and taking the leaders of the People's Party into the government without previous consultation.[169] With regard to the extension of Ebert's term of office Stresemann told Lord D'Abernon that 'the Party Leaders know how wise Ebert was; what services he had rendered'; but if Ebert insisted on election by the people the People's Party 'would not and could not vote for Ebert; they wanted . . . someone less a mere child of the Revolution', and the leaders would be unable to persuade the masses to vote for him.[170] There was no election by the people, and a law of October 1922 extended Ebert's term of office to 1925.

Wirth's successor was Wilhelm Cuno, a director of a leading Hamburg shipping line. Lord D'Abernon described him as 'distinctly Western and not Eastern' and as 'an intimate friend of President Ebert' who was strongly anti-Soviet; Cuno would rely more on British and American assistance than on any aid from the East.[171] The Financial Secretary of the embassy, Joseph Addison, added that Cuno was chosen because, to extricate Germany from her financial difficulties, a man with business experience was required and no such man could be found in parliamentary circles. Yet it was disappointing that on the subject of reparations 'Cuno could apparently find nothing more original to say than to make once more the well worn comparison of Germany to a bankrupt debtor pressed by his creditors'; what he forgot to say was that the analogy was not complete, because 'what the German Government has done is, by an insane policy of inflation, to lower the expression in money terms of all German values and then to declare that owing to these fictitious values the country is in a state of bankruptcy.' In Addison's opinion, there were two alternatives, 'each equally disagreeable': either to deflate and to go through a period of convalescence, probably accompanied by disturbances, or to trust to 'something to turn up' to make the inflation less disagreeable. The position of the government was like that of a man who had to undergo either ordeal by fire or ordeal by water and who put off the day of trial in the hope that it could be postponed indefinitely.[172]

As early as December 1920 Addison wrote in a private letter from the Brussels Reparations Conference that in Lord D'Abernon's view Germany was practically bankrupt and that any idea of obtaining from her large payments over and above what she was paying was 'fantastic'; but this fact could not suddenly be brought to the notice of the public in the Allied countries, and therefore something ought to be done to make it appear that Germany was giving value to the Allies. This would enable the Allied governments 'to accustom the public to the idea that our original claims are impossible of realisation'. In short, the best policy would be to drag the matter out and to make use of the press 'to bring home to the public what Germany was doing, and how unlikely it is that she can do much more.' He suggested fixing the total German indemnity at an arbitrary figure of perhaps five or six milliard pre-1914 pounds sterling, 'so as to give the public the idea that something has been done', and to fix the annual payments at something like 100 or 150 million of the same pounds; but he thought that French public opinion 'will be a great stumbling block'.[173] In 1922 Lord D'Abernon wrote that hitherto the system of reparations 'has been to demand large immediate payments or, in default, large deliveries in kind – an alternative hardly less burdensome to the German Government than payments in cash', but this system 'has irretrievably broken down'; the payments and deliveries were met by printing paper money, and inflation had now reached such a level that a continuation of the method no longer produced adequate results in foreign currency.[174] During the following year the inflation was to reach truly astronomical proportions, but the seeds of the trouble went back over many years. In April 1922 D'Abernon attributed the responsibility 'in about equal proportion to the German Government and to the Reparation Commission. . . . Neither party appears in the least to realize that the continuation of the present course, for a short time, must lead to a financial catastrophe'; for the Germans made no serious effort to stabilize their currency, and the Reparation Commission made demands for payment and for deliveries in kind without taking into account the effect which such demands must have on the financial situation of the country.[175]

There was another form of 'reparation' to which the German government objected. Under clause 172 of the Peace Treaty they were obliged to hand over information on all chemical processes used in the war or in preparation for such use. The Military Control Commission then tried to extract from the German chemical industry certain information useful to British industry and used by it which was of commercial, and not military value. In 1921 Rathenau complained about this practice to D'Abernon, adding that the chemical industry was threatening to sue the government for compensation. The Foreign Office minuted that it was perfectly true that the Control Commission employed representatives of Allied firms for purposes of control and that the information they acquired was used by their firms; the name of Brunner Mond had been mentioned in this connection: 'this is an old and not very pleasant story.' But the War Office was adamant and maintained that the clause in question was framed to safeguard national defence in a future war; information which in peace time was purely commercial but in war time essential for the mobilization of industry 'must obviously be supplied by the British Government to the interested firms'; the German government was merely trying to evade the execution of the relevant clause of the Peace Treaty. And the Foreign Office eventually expressed its agreement.[176]

Early in 1922 Lord D'Abernon thought that the internal political situation in Germany was entirely dominated by continuous Allied pressure to comply with the terms of the Treaty of Versailles; in consequence the German government remained weak, and the main source of its weakness was the financial position; already during the war loans were piled upon loans in the hope that the defeated Allies would have to pay the bill. Ever since the revolution the government was prevented from taking strong measures to balance the budget; 'the reparation payments on the top of this confusion have prevented any recovery and brought the Government ... to the verge of bankruptcy.'[177] Already at the beginning of 1920 the British minister in Berlin had asked 'whether we can, without sacrificing our vital interests, do anything to increase the stability of the present Government'; if anything tangible could be done to restore tolerable conditions in Germany, 'I believe that we should in the long run be the gainers'; it should be seriously considered whether the best policy was not to strengthen the hands of the German government. Some weeks later he added that the alternative policy of crushing Germany, so as to render any chance of recovery impossible for a long time, would have repercussions for Europe as a whole and all chances of creating a stable equilibrium would vanish.[178]

In March 1920 General Haking went further and suggested that the only course open to the Allies was 'to back, in every way possible, a Democratic Government in Germany' and to ameliorate the conditions of the Peace Treaty. In the Foreign Office it was then minuted: 'General Haking ought by this time to be fully aware that it is not part of our policy to "crush" Germany as he calls it.' Crowe wrote more sharply: 'Our generals, like the officers in the War Office who lay down the law about foreign policy, are a terror. But as there is no real discipline in the upper ranks of the army, and as every general, whether serving or retired, freely expresses his views about the policy of HMG, we should gain nothing by complaining to the War Office, who rather like this state of things.'[179] In the same month Churchill suggested to Lloyd George Britain should conclude a defence alliance with France against Germany 'if *and only if* she entirely alters her treatment of Germany and loyally accepts a British policy of help and friendship towards Germany': the Peace Treaty should be revised and Germany should be invited 'as an equal partner in the rebuilding of Europe'.[180] In August 1920 the General Staff, in a memorandum on the situation in Germany which was circulated to the Cabinet by Churchill, proposed a clear revision of policy towards Germany: 'We should treat Germany, as long as she has a moderate Government like the present one, . . . as a Sovereign Great Power, though as a debtor to the Entente. We should abandon all idea of hatred and vengeance and cease treating the German people as outcasts and pariahs. We should help her economically and, in fact, readmit her to the European family of nations.' It should be recognized that a German military danger might still exist, but it was not a present danger; 'the Bolshevik is a present one and far greater, and we must deal with it first, or we shall go under.'[181] How much did this memorandum owe to the ideas of Churchill?

At the beginning of 1921 a Foreign Office official submitted that the time had come to bring pressure on the French government to reverse its policy towards Germany; the French 'are incapable of adopting any other method than that of threats and blows'; but this could not produce any good results, as little as 'if applied to a bad-tempered, sulky and malignant child'; it was 'vital to the peace and recovery of Europe that the penal method should be, if not replaced, at least modified by some system of good-conduct prizes'; Lords D'Abernon and Kilmarnock held the same view; obviously, it would be difficult to impose such a policy on the French, but 'the dangers involved in continuing the drift at the heels of the French are very great.'[182] In November 1922 the British Commissioner at Cologne warned: 'We can't sit still and see Germany dissolve into fragments, which is what will happen sooner or later if the French have a free hand'; Britain's 'future prosperity lies in a healthy Germany, if possible, well disposed towards us – not in a chaotic Europe with a bankrupt France marching a huge army about.'[183] In the Foreign Office too it was recognized that 'our need to trade implies a prosperous Germany; a prosperous Germany implies, in its turn, a politically stable and independent Germany'; the creation of a stable German government was 'the essential and central requirement of British policy, the first condition to which our national recovery is subject': to pursue any other aim in Europe was 'to pursue a mirage'.[184] Yet little was done along these lines. It needed the severe crisis of 1923 before this policy was put into practice in earnest and before the French could be persuaded to follow it, and that crisis very nearly led to the overthrow of democracy in Germany.

The creeping inflation of the early 1920s had disastrous social consequences but did not hit all social classes equally – a fact noticed in the reports. Early in 1920 General Malcolm reported from Berlin that prices were rising daily and the poor were unable to buy 'the barest necessities of life'; members of the middle classes had to sell their furniture and were 'down to their last suit of clothes' and could not replace them on account of the prices; a woman from the Society of Friends working in the poorer quarters of the city related that underclothes were almost unknown there; as to food, 'the tragedy of Vienna is likely to be repeated, only on an infinitely greater scale.'[185] According to a British official sent to East Prussia in 1920 to supervise the local plebiscite, Berlin had 'sunk to the level of a large provincial town'; the few people seen in the streets appeared underfed; the streets had apparently not been cleaned for weeks and houses were unpainted and unrepaired; with few exceptions the shops were empty and the prices high, such as 3,000 marks for a suit and 300 marks for a pair of boots; milk and sugar were almost unobtainable, and the bread ration was down to 1,900 grams and that of potatoes to two pounds a week. A cab driver told him that he was earning only 150 marks a month, that he was still wearing his pre-war clothes and shoes and could not possibly replace them although they were completely worn out.[186] In November 1920 the ambassador wrote that the lot of the lower classes and of those living on fixed incomes or salaries was extremely hard; for the cost of living was eight to ten times what it had been; the 'middle classes are infinitely worse off than labour, and if they had not been found so strangely speechless in all countries it would be a cause for surprise that their discontent with the present conditions had not found louder voice in Germany'; the conditions of the working class were 'certainly not good', but its discontent was less marked than it had been earlier in the year.[187]

The commercial secretary to the British embassy remarked

that, owing to the high prices, Germany during the greater part of 1920 suffered from severe stagnation; this kept back foreign as well as domestic buyers, the effect of the crisis had not yet been overcome, and the level of unemployment caused concern.[188] When bread and meat were decontrolled in the autumn of 1920 he thought that the maintenance of bread supplies would 'cause considerable difficulty in view of the unexpectedly bad rye harvest'. But now plenty of meat had appeared in the shops although prices were 'higher than the controlled figure', but not higher than those paid surreptitiously during control. He believed that the working class 'with their high wages' would benefit, but the lower middle classes and people with fixed incomes would not because they would no longer be able to obtain the small meat ration at controlled prices.[189] Lady D'Abernon was told by her German teacher that the working classes did not suffer any actual want, were far better off than her own class and getting 'much more than a living wage', but small rentiers, teachers, artists and academics had 'less and less to live upon' and had fewer and fewer pupils, while the black-marketeers 'live like fighting-cocks' and their women folk were wearing fur coats with pearls and jewellery on top of them, as well as high yellow boots.[190]

That the middle-class complaints about high working-class wages were only very partly justified was recognized by Lord D'Abernon. In November 1922 he wrote that the cost of living 'has risen, is rising, and will continue to rise in consonance with the fall of the mark. Wages follow but only tardily and for the most part inadequately.'[191] In the spring of the same year a woman doing relief work in Berlin was shocked 'to see how the middle class lives, what poverty there is to be found behind closed doors'. She knew families which kept two servants before the war and now they did their own house work and instead of dinner they had brown bread and weak tea; in well-furnished houses there were chairs without leather which had been used for shoes, and curtains without lining which had been turned into children's clothes: 'this sort of thing is not the exception but the rule.'[192] The ambassador saw the only hope of financial recovery in a stabilization of the mark, a need that was 'admitted theoretically by English authorities' but 'flouted by everyone else'; the Germans were printing notes as hard as they could for their own supposed requirements and hoped soon to be able to turn our four milliards of new notes per day; France and Belgium threatened to take hostile action unless Germany made payments, 'which – in effect if not in intention – compel Germany to print faster still.'[193] The commercial secretary reported that there was enormous speculation in foreign currencies which were hoarded by large numbers; 'so far as my own experience goes, I hardly know a single German of either sex who is not speculating in foreign currencies, such as Austrian Crowns, Polish Marks, or even Kerensky Roubles.'[194]

That not all social classes were suffering from inflation was clearly seen. Early in 1921 Kilmarnock reported that there was unemployment but not to the same extent as in England and elsewhere; owing to the low value of the mark considerable trade with other countries went on and in spite of the coal shortage, 'German industry is showing signs of getting on its legs, and the employers are able to make considerable profits in spite of the high wages in marks which have to be paid to the workmen'; the will to work seemed to have revived more strongly than in many other countries.[195] Another member of the British embassy noticed that inflation had 'given ample scope for juggling in balance sheets', and firms could salt away profits without payment of taxes; some years ago a machine had been bought for 100,000 marks, ten per cent of which was written off annually; now the same machine cost at least a million marks and thus 100,000 had to be written off annually, and the same sum had to be allowed retrospectively for the intervening years.[196] At the end of 1922 the embassy reported that the enormous profits made in paper marks by the industrialists were daily used by them to extend their possessions and their influence 'beyond what would have been possible under stable conditions'; while the prices of all essentials soared with the fall of the mark, those of land, houses, factories etc. did not do so and thus the industrialists 'consider that they are gaining more at one end than they are losing at another'. The captains of industry tried to persuade the workers that the low wages and impossible conditions of life were not due 'to faults committed at home but entirely to the demands of the Entente'; as far as they personally were concerned 'they could exist for a long time on the excessive profits already made and on their bank balances abroad.'[197] Apart from the industrialists, there were, in Lord Kilmarnock's words, 'a large class of war profiteers and people who were living recklessly on their capital on the principle that it is better to get what enjoyment they can . . . filling the restaurants and the dancing halls, crowding the theatres where new plays of abysmal decadence compete in obscenity with revivals of the medieval dramas. . .'[198] Unfortunately, he did not say what were the new plays 'of abysmal decadence', but it seems very doubtful whether there really was such 'a large class' of war profiteers.

There is no doubt, however, that social distress remained very acute. In 1920 the British High Commissioner at Coblenz reported that even in the rural districts of the Rhineland the appearance of the children compared very unfavourably with that of English children; 'starvation is a fertile soil for revolution and anarchy', and unless something was done 'without delay. . . the consequences for European civilisation will be very grave.' The head of the US mission for child relief in Berlin estimated that 25 per cent of the Berlin children between the ages of one and 14 belonged to the category of 'the extremely under-nourished', and most others to the poorly nourished and under-nourished.[199] General Morland, the commanding officer of the British Rhine Army, wanted to open a soup kitchen for poor children in Cologne to supply them with soup from military surplus stores on account of 'the conditions of distress pre-vailing amongst the poorer classes'. Lord Curzon cordially approved but the War Office considered that the cost should be met from Foreign Office funds, which was rejected by the Foreign Office.[200] A British officer visiting Cassel in June 1920 found the scarcity of milk, fat and meat greater than in Berlin; only the rich could afford to buy clothes, boots or furniture; a state of near-starvation prevailed among the families of minor officials, ex-officers and pensioners; 'countless families are keeping alive by selling their jewels and furniture, and many have already sold everything they can spare.'[201] According to a memorandum of the General Staff of the same month, the middle as well as the working classes, professional men and officials 'are poorer than ever before'; many workers felt that their class had 'been cheated of the results of the November revolution and that its social conditions of life have not been bettered'; they intensely disliked the whole military policy of the government and were permeated by 'a strong anti-militarist spirit'.[202] At the end of 1920 another officer reported from Berlin that potatoes were almost unobtainable, and butter, milk and eggs in very short supply; large quantities of meat, poultry and fruit were on offer but the prices were very high. Although coal was in short supply some hotels received all they needed.[203]

As to the Ruhr miners – vital for reparation coal deliveries – a British member of the Coal Committee at Essen wrote in April 1920 that their ration per week was two pounds of potatoes and two of bread; they took bread with a little lard into the mine, but they got no meat, and the miners told the Committee that they had forgotten how to eat meat; in a certain mine recently inspected 23 per cent of the miners were absent looking for food.[204] In August the British Consul-General at Cologne reported that among the miners feeling against working extra shifts was growing every day; as yet there was no improvement in the food situation, in spite of the agreement reached at Spa; even the 'Christian' miners union had given notice that, if food supplies did not improve, no extra shifts would be worked; but if supplies came in, the mills would be unable to mill the flour on account of the coal shortage.[205] The British Army of the Rhine noted that the miners were only interested in obtaining better and cheaper food; discontent was rife because they saw the mine owners making profits of 70 to 80 per cent, 'while they are forced to live in conditions of general misery'; if occupation by a foreign army brought about better conditions, they would willingly work overtime as they intended to fulfil the obligations of Germany under the Spa agreement.[206] Indeed, early in 1921 representatives of the miners unions of Rhineland-Westphalia went to see the Minister of the Interior to tell him that they were willing to work overtime so that Germany could meet her obligations towards the Entente and an Allied occupation of the Ruhr could be avoided; they had raised output although food conditions were steadily getting worse instead of improving as the government had promised; the miners were vitally interested in avoiding a rupture over coal deliveries and the disarmament issue and pressed for a clear and precise declaration by the government on the dissolution of the various self-defence organizations such as the *Einwohnerwehren*.[207] In November 1921 a British official of the Rhineland High Commission still found that a working-class family never saw butter and only rarely milk, while the price of margarine and cooking fat had doubled or more than doubled, that of beer was to go up by 300 per cent and the industrial concerns were continuing to pay high dividends.[208]

On account of the rising prices the workers frequently demanded higher wages, but the employers often refused the demands. At Solingen in February 1920 some of the workers came out on strike, and the employers announced that they would dismiss all the workers for breach of contract. Thereupon all the metal workers of the district declared a sympathy strike, and the employers replied by a lockout affecting about 40,000 workers. The Rhineland High Commission did not intervene directly, but informed the gas, water and power workers that, if they joined the strike, they would act contrary to the Commission's ordinances, and they remained at work. The metal workers then modified their attitude and were willing to meet the employers if they granted them a general wage increase, but the latter insisted on a resumption of work and on treating not with the strike committee but only with the recognized trade unions. The High Commission learned that the strikers wanted to force the railwaymen to join the strike and warned the strike leaders of the risk they ran: they would be held responsible if its ordinances were not complied with. This had the desired effect, and the railway and transport workers remained at work.[209]

At the end of 1921, however, a partial railway strike did occur in the occupied area, and the Allied armies requisitioned some of the railway personnel. Considerable unrest existed among the men because of the rising prices and their inadequate wages which had fallen behind those in private industry, as Lord Kilmarnock reported from Coblenz. But the authorities in Berlin rejected the men's demands without discussion and the strike started. The French and Belgian High Commissioners were in favour of immediate military action, but the British High Commissioner 'pressed for a more moderate procedure in the hope that an early settlement will be reached in Berlin and that military action may be avoided'. After two days a settlement was indeed reached and the service returned to normal. According to Lord D'Abernon, it was 'a hopeful indication of the steadiness of the German working classes'; so far the strikes expected owing to the higher cost of living had not materialized.[210] Another railway strike in February 1922 also lasted but a few days. A municipal strike in Berlin, which left the city without water, gas, electricity and trams, lasted four days. There was some resistance to the resumption of work, but the Social Democrats supported the government against the Communists who supported the strikers.[211] Hunger and misery had driven the workers on to the defensive so that the number of strikes remained comparatively small – exactly as during the deep economic crisis of the early 1930s.

The British diplomats paid more attention to the growth of the extreme Left than to that of the extreme Right – not surprisingly so in view of the fear of a spread of Bolshevism. Soon after the failure of the Kapp Putsch Kilmarnock reported from Berlin that as a result the SPD has lost much of its influence and that many had transferred their allegiance to the USPD, but the latter too had to a considerable extent lost control of the workers who went over to the Communists; during the Kapp crisis some USPD leaders had practically appealed to him to help them by a statement that any hope of help from outside depended on the maintenance of law and order. The USPD and Communists seemed strong enough to exercize a direct influence on the composition of the government and had vetoed several appointments; but even on the Left there was much anxiety as to what attitude Britain would take towards a government based on workers' councils.[212] In April 1920 Kilmarnock attended an USPD meeting at which the speakers urged the abandonment of 'a purely parliamentary democracy' and the arming of the workers; but in his opinion they stood 'too much in awe of the military forces at the disposal of the Government' to risk a conflict, while the government 'can scarcely count on that force as a reliable or permanent factor'.[213] In the same month this was followed by a report on the 'Hölz revolt' in Saxony, where Max Hölz led a band on a 'plundering expedition', extorted money, took hostages and terrorized the district, all on the plea 'that this was part of the Red Army which was fighting for Communism'. The Saxon government wanted to use troops, but the local workers protested that the 'revolt' would be used as a pretext to crush them and threatened to call a general strike. Eventually the troops took the offensive, and Hölz then made for the Czech frontier and continued to pillage the countryside. Most members of his band were eventually captured, but Hölz escaped and was finally arrested across the frontier by the Czechs.[214] While serving a long prison sentence Hölz became a Communist martyr. Later he disappeared during the purges in Soviet Russia.

By contrast with these semi-anarchists, a British officer who visited the Ruhr in May 1920 wrote that the USPD leaders he had seen 'made an excellent impression: steady, honest and earnest men' who in England 'would be considered moderate members of the Labour Party'. Another visiting British officer compiled an extremely detailed report on what he had observed, and stated 'the U.S.P. is the only honest party because it is independent and knows and says what it wants. . . . It is impossible to run a Republic with a Monarchist Army.'[215] Before the general election of June 1920 Kilmarnock predicted a swing to the more extreme parties which would cause the government of the 'Weimar Coalition' to lose its majority so that a 'bourgeois block' might emerge. 'This would throw the whole of the Socialist working classes into violent opposition and it is more than doubtful whether they would restrict themselves to parliamentary methods.'[216] Some days after the election which bore out his forecast he stated that the working classes, dissatisfied with the meagre successes of the coalition government, 'have swung heavily to the Left'; the USPD had more than doubled its vote, and the moderate SPD, who had lost heavily, realized that any compromise with the bourgeois parties would drive 'the greater part of their remaining adherents to the Independents' and 'alienate still further the sympathies of the working class'. Their mood was that the non-socialists should show 'whether they can do any better than the opponents whom they have bespattered with opprobrium and abuse', and they expected 'that if they [the bourgeois parties] are given enough rope they will need but a short drop to hang themselves.'[217] A few days later a bourgeois government was formed under a Chancellor from the Centre Party.

The leftward trend within the USPD was clearly noticed. In July 1920 an Intelligence report on its leaders described two of them who had just been to Soviet Russia 'to study news on the spot': Arthur Crispien, who during the war had served a prison sentence for political propaganda and then been sent to the front 'but would never as a matter of principle fire a shot against the enemy'; and Ernst Däumig whose 'Germanic race and sentiments' constituted 'quite a contrast to the usual Jewish type of U.S.P. speakers who "seem to speak for nobody". . . . His voice is very powerful and fills even a big place like the Busch circus quite easily.'[218] A Foreign Office official who had attended meetings of the USPD and the KPD formed the impression that the extremists among the USPD leaders such as Däumig 'are much more dangerous than the Communist orators, who are frequently more concerned to prove themselves right in argument than to devise a practical policy of Communist revolution.' As to the still more extreme Communist Workers' Party (the KAPD) and the 'National Bolshevist' movement led by men expelled from it, he did not believe that their propaganda would have much of a result, except in places where distress and discontent were rife.[219] In spite of the prevalence of distress, this proved quite an accurate assessment.

In October 1920 the USPD split at the Halle congress and its left wing soon joined the KPD, so that for the first time a strong German Communist party came into being. A report of the British embassy of the time predicted correctly that the right wing of the USPD would gradually disappear, so that the German working-class movement would be divided into two main parties, 'the reformers by legal methods' and 'the advocates of a revolution by violence' consisting of the USPD left wing and the Communists.[220] The Halle congress was addressed by two Bolshevist emissaries, Zinoviev, the president of the Communist International, and Lozovsky, a leading Soviet trade unionist, who both excelled in violent speeches against the moderates. A few days later the embassy reported that the German government had ordered their deportation on account of their 'provocative attitude', their 'attempt to rouse the masses to extreme class war', and the violation of the conditions stipulated before their admission.[221] Early in 1921 the Directorate of Intelligence at the Home Office noted a tendency to return to the USPD among those who had left the party to join the KPD; the latter 'appears to be a house divided against itself', and Moscow was attempting to bring about a fusion of the KPD and the KAPD 'which have their own underlying difficulties'.[222] What the difficulties of the KPD were was explained by Lord D'Abernon in February: 'the Moscow Executive consider that the German Communist Party show too little enthusiasm for revolutionary action, and the German Communists are beginning to think that Moscow is too apt to interfere in matters which do not concern them and regarding which they are not qualified to judge.' The first clear difference arose when the KAPD was admitted as a 'sympathizing member' to the Communist International and stated publicly that Moscow was tired of the passivity of the KPD. The second occurred when Dr Paul Levi, the KPD leader, published an article in *Die Rote Fahne* which severely criticized the split of the Italian Socialist Party brought about at the instigation of Moscow. Levi was immediately attacked by other members of the KPD as well as 'the Berlin liaison agent of the Moscow Executive' and offered to resign as party leader. Finally, in Munich a local KPD leader had called upon the nationalist students 'to share their arms with the Communists and to form a single army which should present a united front to the Entente', a proposal greeted with great enthusiasm by the students: another case of the 'National Bolshevism' officially condemned by the KPD.[223]

At the end of February the British embassy reported that not only Dr Levi but four more members had resigned from the Central Council of the KPD on account of the Italian conflict, among them its joint secretaries, Clara Zetkin and Otto Brass; of these Zetkin 'commanded respect as a venerable ruin of the past and also in view of the uprightness and sincerity of her character', while Levi, 'without possessing any great driving force, has considerable intellectual suppleness'; another dissident, Adolf Hoffmann, was 'a master of Berlin Billingsgate'; the new leaders succeeding them could not compare with them 'so far as ability and popular influence are concerned'.[224] When the Communist uprising which Moscow pressed the KPD leaders to start broke out in the district of Halle in central Germany in March 1921 and ended in disaster after a few days, Lord D'Abernon reported that 'a certain amount of nervousness was prevalent in Government circles', but considerable progress towards the restoration of order had been made in Halle and Hamburg. In spite of minor clashes between Communists and police Berlin had generally remained quiet; an attempt to blow up the Victory Column in front of the Reichstag had failed, as had an effort to call out the gas workers. In his opinion, the most dangerous factor was the violent attacks of the right-wing press on the government for alleged weakness and the call for more rigorous measures of suppression.[225] At a Communist meeting in Wald in the Rhineland at the end of March a speaker exhorted his audience, according to the police, to 'close the factories by force' – a method used on the previous day in the whole district. After the meeting disorders broke out afresh and took a more serious form so that British troops and police had to be sent from Cologne to cope with them. As the KPD leader of Wald had been warned that he was responsible for law and order and had promised that it would be maintained, the British Commissioner at Cologne demanded the deportation of the local Communist leaders from the occupied area. This was carried out, but it was rescinded after seven months.[226]

Meanwhile the British Army of the Rhine reported that attendance at the few Communist meetings was poor and the speeches tame; local leaders in Wald has resigned from the party because 'they can no longer afford to follow in the wake of a rabid and unreasonable leadership'. In the working-class quarters of Cologne so many resigned in the spring of 1921 that the remnants of the local party cells had to be amalgamated.[227] The severe crisis in the KPD caused by the resignation or expulsion of Levi and many others was reported in very great detail, especially by the Intelligence service of the Home Office. In August 1921 it gave an account of the Jena party conference which – after the failure of the 'March Action' – 'was given to party stocktaking'. The Central Committee strongly denied any decline of the membership on account of this failure and put its strength (after amalgamation with the left wing of the USPD) 'at a little over 300,000', not counting about 50,000 unemployed who could not afford the subscription. But the discussion on tactics made it clear that the party's morale had declined. According to the report three groups existed inside the KPD: the most able consisted of the followers of Levi and 'looks with suspicion on the Executive of the Moscow International and its pretensions to govern the universe'; the second and strongest group desired a 'policy of action'; and the third was formed by the followers of Zetkin who aimed at reconciliation between the other two. These groups also differed on the method to be used 'to attain the conquest of the trade unions'.[228]

In September 1921 Lord D'Abernon wrote that the Communist vote had sharply declined and that the general threat to law and order had receded. He ascribed this to 'the failure of Communism in Russia' and the ill-success of the Communist outbreaks in different parts of Germany; only 12 months ago there had been a grave danger, but this no longer existed.[229] In October a member of the Rhineland High Commission noted that Levi and Hoffmann were forming a strong group from Communists who had been expelled or resigned from the KPD; should they found a new party, less under Russian control, they might attract radical workers who were disgusted with the cooperation of the SPD with the bourgeois parties (in the Wirth government).[230] In November 1922 D'Abernon referred to the food riots and the plundering of food shops which had occurred in several towns, such as Brunswick, Dresden and Berlin, and were allegedly fomented by the Communists, but also took on an anti-foreign slant because the papers attributed the fast rising food prices to the presence of many foreigners.[231] In December the chairman of the British Communist Party, Arthur McManus, spoke at a mass meeting in Halle and exclaimed: the Treaty of Versailles, 'concluded by a band of international thieves, must be torn up by the working classes of all lands. . . . This band of international robbers must be opposed by a single battle front of the united proletariat'; if bonds of international solidarity were forged the day would soon dawn when the rule of the capitalists would be broken for ever.[232] In the course of the great crisis of 1923 the KPD was to emerge as one of the major factors on the German political scene; but the various splinter groups which had broken away from it, such as the KAPD or the group led by Levi, became political sects.

British attention was also focused on another political movement, even before 1923: that was the Separatist movement in the Rhineland which was assiduously fostered by France in the hope of separating the Rhineland from Germany, or at least from Prussia. When a Rhenish Republic was proclaimed under French protection at Mainz, Speyer and Wiesbaden in the spring of 1919 without any popular support, an official of the Foreign Office minuted his doubts 'whether history will endorse the eulogy passed by M. Maurice Barrès in the *Echo de Paris*: "Nos poilus sont des excellents diplomats"'; fortunately, these people only represented 'a small reactionary minority in France'.[233] In September of the same year Joseph Smeets, a Separatist leader, wrote to Lloyd George requesting recognition and a freely elected local parliament. A British official in the Rhineland then informed the Foreign Office that Smeets' association, the 'Rheinlandbund', was formed in August by former members of the USPD; its paper, *Rheinische Republik*, had a circulation of about 13,000 and was full of violent attacks on the Prussian government; the party aimed at the creation of 'an entirely independent buffer State' and the destruction of Prussia. A Foreign Office minute described it 'as the Sinn Fein of the Rhenish autonomy movement', but another Separatist leader, Dr Adam Dorten, merely wanted an autonomous Rhenish Republic within the German federal system. It was decided not to reply to Smeets' letter.[234]

More important was the attitude adopted by the Rhenish Centre Party – the largest party of the Catholic Rhineland – towards the Separatists who were also to be found among its own members. As the British department of the Rhineland High Commission put it in 1921, the Centre 'had to guard itself against the accusation of disloyalty or even treason to the Reich', but it also had to preserve its strength as a Rhenish party so that it adopted a 'somewhat vacillating attitude' to the question of autonomy for the Rhineland, at least before the Prussian Constitution was passed in November 1920.[235] In September 1922 Lord Kilmarnock reported from Coblenz that the feeling against the Rhenish Republic had become stronger; some years ago the Centre had favoured a federal solution for the Rhineland, but now all the Rhenish parties were resolutely opposed to autonomy, federalism or neutralization. Dr Adenauer, the mayor of Cologne, estimated that the followers of Dorten and Smeets, the Separatist leaders, numbered perhaps three per cent of the population, while the large majority wanted to stay with Germany and would accept any solution that 'will bring profit to themselves'; if they were promised release from reparation payments 'it is more than probable that a considerable change in their views will take place.' Kilmarnock, however, thought that any such concession was so unlikely and the reparation burden was so heavy that 'this appeal to the cupidity of the peasant' would be unsuccessful.[236] He also reported that the Smeets party had split and that the dissidents had formed a new *'Rheinische Freiheitspartei'*; Smeets seemed to fear that this split as well as British and American pressure would induce the French to withdraw their support from him. In 1922 he was sentenced to four months of imprisonment for abusive language against three policemen whom he called 'Prussian hangmen', yet in court it turned out that they were 'Rhinelanders born and bred'. In any case, the Rhineland High Commission forbade the execution of any sentence passed against him.[237]

As to the general feeling of the people in occupied Rhineland, British members of the Rhineland High Commission repeatedly drew attention 'to the growing feeling of hatred of the French' which showed no sign of abating. When British units were sent from Cologne to Upper Silesia it was considered important that as few French battalions as possible should be sent to replace them. In July 1921 British officials pointed to the 'feeling of despair which appeared to be growing apace among the German population who see the French everywhere and also read with anger the provocative utterances of the French Prime Minister and the French Press'; this feeling was increased by the apparent indifference shown by the British and American governments which, when holding views opposed to those of the French, 'are unable to make those views prevail'. According to the British, the effect of French propaganda in the Rhineland was 'the exact reverse' of that intended; and the attitude of the local French officials created a bitterness against them which had not existed previously.[238]

In the Rhineland the singing of German patriotic songs in public or in a provocative manner was forbidden by ordinances of the Rhineland High Commission. In 1921 the German embassy in London complained that the owner of a house in Düsseldorf, then occupied by the French, was fined and sentenced to deportation from the Rhineland because at a wedding reception in his house the guests had sung 'a traditional wedding song' to the tune of 'The Watch on the Rhine'. The British department of the Commission replied that the song was in reality intoned to the tune of 'Deutschland über Alles' and added: 'Perhaps it would be well if the Counsellor of the German Embassy made up his mind which of these two tunes it is traditional to sing at German weddings'; in any case, the song had been repeated by passers-by with the actual text of the German national anthem, 'a very foolish demonstration'. The order of expulsion from the Rhineland was subsequently withdrawn.[239] This was but one example of the more or less constant friction existing between the French and the German inhabitants – and there was little the British government could do, except occasionally registering its own opinion and maintaining better relations in its own zone of occupation. When a new director of police was to be appointed to Cologne and the Prussian Minister of the Interior put forward the name of Karl Zörgiebel, a deputy and official of the SPD, the British Commissioner at Cologne was in favour of consenting although the candidate possessed no technical qualification for the post. He argued it would be difficult to find a man with the technical knowledge required, 'unless he has held a high position in the German Army or the German Civil Service', where he would have absorbed 'reactionary ideas, which are undesirable in a man holding a responsible position in the Occupied Territory'; in Cologne class feeling was running high, and a large section of the population were workers who in their majority supported the SPD; a strong director of police belonging to the same party would be able to carry out his duties with less friction and greater efficiency than a member of the Centre or of a right-wing party; the previous director of police had been inefficient and without force of character, and Zörgiebel should be appointed.[240] He served in this post until 1926 when he was moved to Berlin.

The years 1920 and 1922 brought no consolidation of the German Republic. This was due to economic as well as to political causes, to the demands of the Allies as well as to the growth of extremism on the Left and on the Right, to the rebirth of a virulent German nationalism as well as the decline of the German mark. The parties of the 'Weimar Coalition' lost their absolute majority as early as June 1920 and never regained it. Social distress and social conflict remained prevalent. The civil war had come to an end, but there was no real peace.

III

BAVARIA TO THE
HITLER PUTSCH

Until 1923, no other German state attracted as much attention as did Bavaria, for there the issues occupying the British diplomats in Germany crystallized: the possibility of a monarchical restoration, the danger of separatism, the refusal to disarm and dissolve the self-defence organizations, the rapid growth of right-wing extremism, the ever sharper conflicts with Berlin which in 1923 led to a complete breach between Munich and Berlin. Thanks to the voluminous reports of the British Consuls-General in Munich, political and social developments in Bavaria are documented in great detail. The consuls had close contacts with the leading Bavarian politicians, and other British officials, too, often reported on the situation in Bavaria, making use of their own contacts and providing interesting information.

In July 1919 the British minister in Bern, Lord Acton, sent a report given to him by Professor Friedrich Wilhelm Foerster, the well known Bavarian pacifist. According to Foerster, Bavaria would never accept the position which the centralists in Berlin (meaning the German government and the new Constitution, then nearly completed) tried to impose upon her, and the country was 'more hostile than ever' to Berlin and to Prussia; for the moment Bavaria was impotent owing to the presence of 40,000 Prussian troops concentrated around Munich who had been sent to 'liberate' it from the so-called 'Soviet Republic' of April 1919 (see pages 17–18), but resistance would be organized by the Catholics led by Dr Georg Heim, who had seceded from the Centre Party in protest against its approval of the draft Constitution (which was by no means centralist). Heim would work for the separation of Bavaria from Germany and Prussia in

97

their 'present form'; the *mot d'ordre* of all Bavarian Catholics and many Bavarian socialists was *'Los von Preussen'*; the anti-Prussian movement was supported by the lower clergy and many senior army officers, but did not extend to industrial and Protestant Franconia; soon Bavaria would proclaim her independence and form a nucleus around which a new Germany would arise; together with German Austria Bavaria could then become 'a vast Alpine republic, agricultural, pastoral and Catholic': the Allies should send diplomatic representatives to Munich and thus demonstrate their support for Bavarian autonomy.[1] Throughout the report no proper distinction was made between autonomy and independence.

In October 1919, at a mass meeting of Bavarian Catholics, Cardinal Michael von Faulhaber, Archbishop of Munich, launched a massive attack on the central German government which, in the opinion of a British officer, clearly showed the independence of the local parties. In their eyes, 'the present system of Government by Noske and his friends is reducing the National Assembly to a farce. Berlin is regarded as the future bridgehead of Russian Bolshevism, and Communism is considered the only future for Germany if the present régime continues.'[2] This applied in particular to the strongest Bavarian party, the Bavarian People's Party, which had split off from the Centre because it was too 'centralist'; in 1919 it polled 35 per cent of the total vote, and in 1920 nearly 40 per cent. In the Foreign Office it was discussed at the time whether to send again separate diplomatic representatives to Munich and to Dresden — a move strongly favoured by the French government. In the opinion of Headlam Morley it would be illegal under the new German Constitution for a state government to receive diplomatic representatives 'in the old way' and the central government 'would almost undoubtedly refuse permission'. If Britain took action 'showing that we do not consider them worth the ordinary obligations of courtesy, we shall do great injury to their position in their own country' and would even injure 'our own reputation'. If the Allies identified themselves with the opposition to a unified German government, it would drive patriotic Germans 'into the tendency which we oppose', but it was important to obtain good information from Bavaria and Saxony, and special instructions should be given to the British consuls there to report on political affairs. Another Foreign Office official, however, disagreed: 'to give encouragement to separatist tendencies in Bavaria would, I submit, be all to the good', and a diplomatic mission should be sent to Munich. This view was immediately contradicted: a separation of Bavaria 'would immensely increase the power of Prussia in what would remain of Germany'; it would also 'make the German Austrian question and especially the position of Vienna more desperate, if possible, than it is' because the Tyrol and Vorarlberg would then want to join Bavaria.

Headlam Morley felt that, from the point of view of the balance of power, it would be an advantage if Bavaria seceded, either alone or with the other south-German states; 'but it must be as a result of overwhelming desire of the people as a whole', and the reports from Bavaria gave no indication 'of a genuine popular movement on which it would be safe to base our policy'. Sir Eyre Crowe wound up the debate by stating: 'It ought not to be our policy to oppose the unity of the German state. . . . Any interference from outside will only strengthen the determination to remain united. This tendency is natural and in accordance with the movement of modern thought. It would be bad policy to work on lines opposed to it.' But Britain would have everything to gain from promoting particularist tendencies within Germany so as to weaken the hegemony of Prussia; 'insofar as Bavaria represents such tendencies, by all means let us encourage them where we can do so safely.' If there was no legal difficulty he was in favour of sending a diplomatic mission to Munich, only that in the present situation it would not be wise to try such an experiment. Lord Curzon, however, was opposed to it and expressed his surprise 'that it had found such warm advocates'.[3] He opted for the appointment of a Consul-General — in contrast with the French government which sent a minister. This step, taken in July 1920, caused a Foreign Office official to minute: 'Separatism means reaction and civil war, and we should be ill advised to take a step which could only be interpreted as intended to push the reactionary Bavarian Govt. into an open quarrel with the Central Govt.' That the French had done so 'affords no reason why we should associate ourselves with them.' Curzon added that he had discussed the question at Spa with the Italian Foreign Minister, Count Sforza, and had told him that he had no intention of sending a minister to Munich.[4] The issue was never revived. And the French action, taken as an encouragement to Bavarian separatism, did not earn them any good will in Bavaria.

The man who emerged as the 'strong man' of Bavaria as a result of the Kapp Putsch was Gustav Ritter von Kahr who was elected Prime Minister by the Bavarian Diet in March 1920. Two months later Lord Kilmarnock met him and three other Bavarians in a private house and was favourably impressed. Kahr would not be 'afraid to act and backed as he is by a people largely consisting of peasant proprietors who have learnt at first hand what mob rule means, he may well come to play a highly important part in the events of the near future.' Kahr told his interlocutor that, if there was a clash between bourgeoisie and working class as a result of the forthcoming election, 'Bavaria will provide the solid bulwark against the attempt to establish a dictatorship of the proletariat'. One of the other Bavarians present hinted that in such a case Bavaria might be obliged to 'cleanse' Berlin of the forces of disorder. Kahr added that Bavaria would certainly be able to suppress any disturbances with the *Einwohnerwehr* so that the army could be used elsewhere, where it might be most needed. His last words were: 'if Bavaria was disarmed and abandoned to the tender mercies of the Communists there would be nothing left for any decent person to do but to take a revolver and blow out his brains.'[5] The newly appointed British Consul-General, Robert Smallbones, however, took a less favourable view of the doings of Kahr and his friends. In April he wrote from Munich that Dr Heim 'was playing on their heartstrings when he advocates the formation of a southern confederation', apparently including the Tyrol. And in July more sharply: 'I consider the aims pursued by Dr Heim and his party a danger to the peace and order and reconstruction of Germany.' In the consul's opinion it was impossible to set the clock back and to force Germany to revert to an agricultural country, nor was this desirable in the interests of Europe; any such attempt would provoke civil war; the *Einwohnerwehr* in the hands of these men was not a voluntary police force for the maintenance of order but 'an instrument of class warfare'. He could not conceive 'that the ignorant and bigoted Bavarian peasants and their, no doubt, less ignorant but certainly equally bigoted leaders can constitute themselves the spiritual governors of Germany.'[6]

In May 1920 General Malcolm visited Munich to report on the issue of the *Einwohnerwehr* which assumed great importance in the Allied councils because of the French demand for its disarmament and disbandment. He found the explanation for 'the bitter class-hatred which exists in Bavaria to-day' in the 'months of misrule ... maintained by violence without intelligence' under the government of Kurt Eisner, his murder and the subsequent drift to the Left. In his opinion, the *Einwohnerwehr* was formed 'to prevent a return of this experience' and it was its achievement that Bavaria had remained quiet; it was therefore not surprising that the order to disarm it aroused such violent opposition; a direct order to do so would probably have no effect whatever, and how could it be enforced? A blockade would be ineffective because it would increase the misery of the unarmed workers and have little effect on the wealthy and the peasants; the alternative was occupation by the troops of the Entente to carry out the disarmament and to keep order, but the objections to this 'are many and obvious'.[7] In an interview with Lord D'Abernon Kahr described the *Einwohnerwehr* as a 'fire brigade': 'if a fire – political or otherwise – broke out, the *Einwohnerwehr* would put it out'; it was 'manned by the best elements of the population'.[8] In September 1920 its 'Rifle Meeting' in Munich became the occasion of a strong patriotic demonstration and 'much self-congratulation that Bavaria is not as other States'. A British officer who watched the parade of about 50,000 armed men felt that what they desired was law and order, farming, 'no Socialists' utopia', and no Communist riots. But in November a proposed socialist meeting in honour of the birth of the Republic was prohibited by the police.[9] In December the German Foreign Minister Dr Simons told the British minister in Berlin it would be 'physically impossible' to disarm the Bavarian peasants; if it were attempted they would resist and the army could not be trusted to take action against them; he intended to go to Munich next month to try to persuade the Bavarian government 'to do their utmost to comply with the terms of the [peace] treaty'.[10] Indeed, it was quite inconceivable that the Bavarian Reichswehr would carry out an order to disarm the *Einwohnerwehr* which they themselves had helped to create and to arm.

Early in 1921 the British consul in Munich assessed the situation: the Bavarians would certainly refuse any demand for immediate or early disarmament 'unless backed by threats or coercion'; coercion could only be military – which was out of the question – or economic; if coal supplies to Bavaria were stopped Bavaria could retort by stopping food supplies; if the Allies threatened to occupy the Ruhr, 'I fear that Bavarian Government might not necessarily be moved from their obstinate position by mere threat'; but some form of economic pressure might never-theless be tried.[11] About the same time the British General Staff stated: 'The Bavarian *Einwohnerwehr* contains all the law-abiding and best elements of the Bavarian population; the country is still obsessed with a fear and hatred of Bolshevism, due to the Soviet régime in Munich. . . . The Bavarian Govern-ment is dependent on the *Einwohnerwehr* and could not exist in opposition to it.' The strength of the whole force was estimated as about 300,000.[12] Lord Curzon told the German ambassador in plain words that 'the now familiar truisms' with regard to Bavaria 'were not good enough to dispose of the fact that, at a moment when the Communist agitation and the danger of a Communist rebellion in Bavaria were less than they had been at any time since the War, the Bavarians nevertheless persisted in maintaining a force of 300,000 men . . . and that this total had been swollen by 70,000 since the Spa Conference' at which the German government had accepted the Allied ultimatum; the Peace Treaty 'was meant not to be evaded but fulfilled', and 'it was a foolish game to try and produce dissensions among the powers'.[13] When the liberal *Frankfurter Zeitung* indirectly supported the Allied demand for the disbanding of the *Ein-wohnerwehr*, the British consul at Frankfurt added another interesting point to the discussion: even the Jews of Upper Bavaria, 'apprehensive of anti-Semitism', desired the main-tenance of an adequate armed force and were 'much concerned with the attitude of the *Frankfurter Zeitung*, itself an organ under Jewish political and financial control'.[14]

Another disturbing factor was soon noticed in Munich. In July 1920 Smallbones wrote that, according to reliable information, 40 railway trucks of five tons each with small arms had passed the Austrian frontier into the Tyrol, intended for the Tyrolese peasants. The Allied Military Commission of Control in Austria reported similar cases, not only concerning the Tyrol, but also Carinthia and Styria.[15] Indeed, the Austrian *Heimwehren* (a reactionary, anti-socialist force) received very large consign-ments of arms from Bavaria. According to the British Army of the Rhine, apart from their rifles, the Bavarian *Einwohnerwehr* possessed a 'very large' number of machine guns and more guns 'than the entire Reichswehr since the Peace Treaty'; these and even aeroplanes were concealed on the big estates; the force also had its own Intelligence service.[16] Yet speaking in the Bavarian Diet Kahr claimed that the *Einwohnerwehr* 'does not constitute an infraction of the Peace Treaty'; it would be disarmed as soon as conditions permitted, but its disarmament at the present time 'would inevitably be followed by a communistic rising'. Kahr's attitude was approved by all the Bavarian government parties, and no possibility existed of forming an alternative government. The British consul in Munich did not believe that the *Einwohnerwehr* constituted a military danger, but a waiving of the peace terms imposed on Germany would have a moral effect: 'If Bavaria, single handed, is able to defy the Allies successfully the opinion might gain ground that defiance on the part of a united Germany will reverse the decision of the Allies on any point'; and the success of 'the most reactionary Government in Germany' would make itself felt at the next election and might make the government 'dangerously self-confident'.[17]

When the British miners went on strike in the spring of 1921 and civilians were used to reinforce the army and police, members of the Bavarian government as well as the local press gleefully pointed out that now the British government too recognized the need for supplementing the regular forces. The arguments of the British consul that the Communist rising in central Germany, the 'March Action', was crushed by the police alone without calling in the army and that in Bavaria all Communist activities were stopped by the police were countered by the statement that only 'the strong, silent force of the *Einwohnerwehr*. . . had saved the country'.[18] During the second half of 1920 the consular reports from Munich centred around the figure of Georg Heim, the leader of the Bavarian People's Party and of the Catholic Peasant League. 'Dr Heim is a powerfully built man', Smallbones wrote in July, 'with rough hewn features. His oratory is homely and without grace. . . . He could certainly be Prime Minister of Bavaria if he wished but he prefers to leave that post to Herr von Kahr who in my opinion is the puppet of the *Bayerische Volkspartei*.' When the consul pointed out to him that his system of government hardly conformed to the usual parliamentary methods Kahr replied that the function of parties was to frame a programme which he would carry out according to his own head and that he would resign rather than accept interference by a party. Dr Heim told the consul that Bavaria would secede from Germany if 'the north turns Bolshevik'; as Heim was convinced, in the same breath, that 'the north will turn Bolshevik', the conclusion must be that secession was inevitable.[19]

In December 1920 the new Consul-General, William Seeds, thought it a gross exaggeration to say that Heim and his party were 'militant monarchists'; undoubtedly, they had 'a warm corner in their hearts for the Bavarian Royal Family and are obsessed by a genuine fear and hatred of anything savouring of Bolshevism; their monarchical leanings are however, for the present at any rate, only a matter of pious sentiment, not of practical politics.'[20] In an interview with the consul in May 1921 Heim claimed that by the following year 'Germany would infallibly in her despair throw herself into convulsions either of Nationalism or Bolshevism' of which the latter was the more likely; yet the Allies had 'the cynical effrontery to demand that Bavaria should give up her only protection'; but Bavaria would not commit suicide: let the German government do its worst if it dared or let the Entente use force. To him, the argument that compliance with the demands was necessary to save the Ruhr was absurd, for the French were bent on seizing it and would do so in any case; he would not lift a finger to save the Ruhr; they should occupy it, 'for that would prove the Allies' doom'. When Seeds ventured to point out that after all Germany had accepted the Allied ultimatum Heim turned violently on him: 'Germany! What Germany?'[21] An official of the Foreign Office recorded after several conversations with Heim that he was not a Separatist or only a conditional one; nor was he likely to be influenced by 'clever French diplomacy', and in any case, the French 'were ignorant of real Bavarian sentiment'.[22]

The strong anti-Prussian feeling in Munich was, according to Seeds, not due to provincialism or jealousy but 'something deeper and truer'; to arrive in Munich from Berlin was like entering 'what Germany must have been in the middle of the last century before militarism had done its worst'; in contrast with Berlin Munich was not affected by 'the demoralization of defeat and the greed of the profiteer'; to the Bavarians, 'Berlin is a cesspool of atheism and vice, a sordid market where culture is at a discount and only the money-grubber flourishes, a town without a soul, a city in Germany but not a German city'. The consul had so far not met anyone who believed an immediate restoration of the monarchy possible; leaders of the Bavarian People's Party apparently contemplated a restoration after eight or 10 years, and it would be difficult for the party to support the candidature of Prince Rupprecht (the former crown prince) with any enthusiasm because in the past it had violently calumniated him.[23] In the consul's view the most burning issue in Munich at the end of 1920 was not even the *Einwohnerwehr* but the delivery of milch cows to the Entente; no conversation was complete without a virulent complaint about it. A great protest meeting at Munich University was addressed by eminent doctors on the ravages caused by lack of milk; other speakers 'stigmatized the Entente as child murderers, declared that history could show no precedent for such an attempt to destroy a whole civilised people, and urged that not a single milch cow should be delivered to the Entente either now or later.'[24]

Yet no crisis occurred over the *Einwohnerwehr*. In the end the Bavarian government gave way and accepted its disarmament 'as far as possible'. The British consul considered its total disarmament 'an impossibility. I have not yet seen the man, whether German or foreigner, who is of the opinion that all the arms can be extracted from the peasants.' He suggested therefore that the Allies should be satisfied with the surrender of the field guns and a large number of rifles and the dissolution of its central organization; the real danger was likely to come from the leaders of the *Einwohnerwehr* units in the countryside.[25] In June the Bavarian Commissioner for Disarmament ordered compliance with the demands of the Entente: guns and machine guns should be surrendered by 10 June and other weapons by the end of the month. Even before the date Rathenau informed Lord Kilmarnock in Berlin that he was authorized by the Chancellor to say privately that the surrender was 'very satisfactory'.[26]

Before the end of 1921 an entirely different issue caused the latent conflict between Munich and Berlin to break out openly. In August Matthias Erzberger was murdered by right-wing extremists, and a few days later a presidential decree, based on Article 48 of the Constitution, empowered the authorities to suspend journals which incited people to change the Constitution by violent means and to prohibit public meetings and associations for the same reason. But the Bavarian government on legal grounds refused to carry out the decree, while all other state governments complied. A report of the British High Commission at Coblenz saw a strong probability 'that the substance of right and common-sense is to be found not on the side of the legal pedants in Bavaria but on that of the Central Government'. It added significantly that 'Pan-German extremists' who were not Bavarians had established their headquarters in Munich, that they aimed at weakening the Berlin government and were 'whipping up local feeling to the boiling point'; Bavarian officials were protecting the leaders of the Kapp Putsch, such as Colonel Bauer, Captain Ehrhardt and Captain Pabst, and the Bavarian Minister of Justice was maintaining direct relations with Ehrhardt although a writ had been issued for his arrest; in Munich it was particularly resented that Chancellor Wirth in his campaign against the Kahr regime was using a report by the Commissioner for Public Order, a high Prussian civil servant.[27] The conflict did not last long, for the steering committee of the Bavarian Diet refused to follow Kahr into an open breach and he had to resign. As the British consul put it, 'Herr von Kahr has disappeared with the *Einwohnerwehr*', and Heim had failed to carry the rejection of the Allied ultimatum and of the Allied decision on the partition of Upper Silesia.[28]

In November 1921 Lord D'Abernon received a secret message from Prince Rupprecht that the monarchical movement had made great progress in Bavaria, that an attempt at restoration or at making him president would be made shortly; he had little doubt about its success and hoped for a similar movement in Hesse and Hanover, but he was much less hopeful of the other states.[29] In June 1922 the British consul reported that at no time had 'the militarists and reactionaries displayed such activities as during the past two months'; in Munich Prince Rupprecht publicly reviewed the veterans of the First Bavarian Regiment; several thousand of them marched past 'accompanied by every conceivable military and police band' and the 'tradition companies' of the Reichswehr; similar meetings were organized in other Bavarian towns and everywhere the princes present received an ovation.[30] At a memorial service in the cathedral in honour of the late pope, which was attended by the entire Bavarian government, the members of the royal family were placed above the government and Prince Rupprecht was allocated a special place of honour. Diplomats who had known Munich since before the war told the British consul that, apart from the fewer uniforms and the smaller display of troops, the cathedral presented a picture identical with that of the days of the monarchy.[31] Yet the monarchists were far from united. According to the consul, the antipathy between Rupprecht and General Ludendorff (who had taken his residence in Munich) was 'typical of the mistrust which renders cooperation between Bavarian and Prussian reactionaries almost impossible in normal times', and the Prussians 'have lost none of their pre-war qualities of grating on other people's, in this case the Bavarians', feelings.' The conditions in the reactionary camp prevented a united effort which might lead to the overthrow of the republic, and even if such an effort were possible, it would in his opinion fail in the face of a general strike.[32]

The new Bavarian Prime Minister was Count Hugo von Lerchenfeld who was a declared conservative and not above making strongly nationalist speeches. When he referred to France as 'the enemy' and allegedly incited the population of the occupied territory to rebel against the occupation armies the French minister in Munich made an official protest. The French chairman of the Inter-Allied Rhineland High Commission threatened to have Lerchenfeld arrested and deported if he should visit the Bavarian Palatinate. Speaking to the British consul, the Prime Minister claimed that he was 'always preaching patience and submission' because he realized how defenceless Germany was; he was not the man to incite the people to revolt and they and not he would have to suffer the consequences; but French provocations in the Palatinate surpassed anything he had witnessed during the war in occupied Warsaw. He quoted certain French actions against schoolchildren and said it was extraordinary how France had managed to turn the benevolent neutrality with which she had been regarded in 1918 into hatred – a hatred that 'boded ill for the peace of Europe'. The threat that he would be arrested was 'intolerable', and in that case 'every Frenchman in Bavaria without exception would be dealt with in a similar manner'. As the chief executive of Bavaria the Prime Minister was anyhow immune from arrest by the French.[33]

The Bavarian administration of justice was as reactionary as was the government, and at least in one famous case of 1922 the purpose clearly was to seek vengeance on the protagonists of the 'red' regime of 1919. Three socialist journalists, among them Felix Fechenbach, Eisner's former secretary, were tried for attempted treason because they had published through the Transatlantic News Agency details of the secret military organizations in Bavaria and their weaponry and thus caused damage to Germany. The court rejected any appeal on grounds of the freedom of the press, for the revelations tried to prove that the Bavarians were evading the restrictions of the Peace Treaty (which they did). In the words of the British consul 'the fundamental fact, however, is that the proceedings were political and not judicial; the sole concern of the President of the Tribunal, and of all the authorities connected with the case, was to inflict the maximum sentence on Fechenbach and his associates as enemies of the Bavarian reaction.' The foreign press was excluded from the trial. Fechenbach was sentenced to 11 years of penal servitude, the two others to 12 and ten years respectively: 'the trial stands out self-confessed as a deliberate provocation to the Socialists.'[34] There was considerable indignation in the German press, and even some Bavarian papers intermittently pressed for an official declaration of Fechenbach's innocence. He was released in December 1924, as were the last four prisoners sentenced for their activities at the time of the Munich 'Soviet Republic' of 1919, among them the anarchist Erich Mühsam. In the following year Fechenbach's lawyer, Paul Levi, 'who is now a pillar of German Social Democracy', wanted to reopen the case to prove his client's innocence. He therefore asked for an official British statement that the Transatlantic News Agency had no connection with the British government, and the embassy forwarded his letter to the Foreign Office. There it was felt that the case was one between the German government and one of their own nationals and that the British government was unable to intervene. One official minuted: 'We are already in a sufficiently lurid lime-light in France, without gratuitously becoming the focus for Bavarian spotlights as well.' Thus no action was taken.[35] Both Fechenbach and Mühsam were later killed by the National Socialists.

In September 1920 the British consul mentioned for the first time a new party which made 'itself rather conspicuous in Munich by frequent meetings and lectures and still more by the posters announcing these. They are extremely violent in tenour [sic] and usually anti-semitic.' He thought that the new party possessed funds 'as one display of posters at a low computation costs M. 10,000'. This was the National Socialist German Workers' Party, organized by Anton Drexler and Adolf Hitler. Smallbones believed that the party was 'the socialist tail' of the Nationalists and that its socialism was 'of the negative, anti-capitalistic kind which does not frighten the present-day German millionaire'.[36] After the murder of Erzberger in August 1921 the republican organizations of Munich demonstrated en masse in protest. The consul then reported that the National Socialists staged a mass meeting as a 'counter-attraction' at which all the blame for the state of disorder and the inflation 'was put on the shoulders of the Jews'. In his opinion, the party was so far 'of little importance', but its posters, 'which exposed Erzberger's misdeeds and urged that such a man's death was not worthy of the trouble it had caused', had attracted great attention.[37] Early in 1922 Seeds commented on Hitler, 'a rabid nationalist and anti-Semite who by adroit posters and inflammatory speeches has attained a certain notoriety'; the average citizen of Munich was amused by Hitler's speeches and the scurrilous paper, the *Völkische Beobachter*, but they 'seem to anger the real Socialists beyond words'.[38]

In June 1922 a new conflict occurred over the planned visit of the President of the Republic to Munich because he insisted that the republican colours of black-red-gold (hated by all good nationalists) must be publicly shown. As a concession the Bavarian government had two such flags hoisted, one at the main station and the other at the trades fair which was the official reason for the visit. The first was promptly torn down and publicly burnt to the strains of 'Deutschland über Alles', with the police unable (or unwilling) to prevent this or to arrest any of the culprits. The other flag was 'blown down the same day by the "patriotic" wind of Bavaria but there is no doubt that the elements were assisted by human agency.' The flags were replaced and remained unmolested. When it was announced that Ebert's visit would now take place 'Dr. [sic] Hitler at once issued a proclamation declaring that the visit of the Republican President was an insult to Bavaria and threatening to use force if necessary to prevent it.' Ebert arrived and 'had the unpleasant experience of being hooted at wherever he went'; some of the hooters were arrested by the police and the few people in the streets seemed apathetic. 'There was no display of troops or bunting in the President's honour, the German Republican flags at the station and at the exhibition remained in splendid isolation.'[39] Thus the consul's report; he clearly thought that every German politician must have a Ph.D.

By the autumn of 1922 Seeds was convinced that Hitler 'has developed into something much more than a scurrilous and rather comic agitator': he had succeeded in forming 'an efficient and active organisation, composed to a very minor degree of young workers but mostly of students and the like, which has on various occasions dealt unmercifully with Communists or with any persons suspected of communistic and anti-patriotic ideas'. Hitler's indiscriminate abuse of the German and Bavarian governments, of the Entente, of the Jews and profiteers, of all politicians whether moderate or left-wing, was apparently justified in the eyes of the middle classes which 'now begin to look upon him as their Mussolini' (the despatch was written a few days after the March on Rome). The consul felt greatly impressed by the growing reliance placed by Bavarian conservative circles on Hitler's men 'as a safeguard against Communism'. He had heard discussions whether Hitler would assume the leading role in Bavaria if the politicians proved unable to find a prime minister. Hitler and his bands, travelling about the country in special trains or cavalcades of lorries, must cost his financiers a lot of money, 'but the money is efficiently spent'. Dr. Eugen von Knilling, the new Prime Minister, admitted to the consul 'that Hitler has now become a power in the land'; his followers included people of all social classes, many genuine patriots as well as 'Communists of the more ruffianly rather than the political sort'; according to von Knilling, the army and police could be relied upon to act against the National Socialists if called upon to do so; their plans envisaged action to be taken after the outbreak of working-class riots, but the workers 'were being kept well under control by the Socialists'.[40]

A memorandum composed by the British embassy in Berlin about the same time also referred to Mussolini's success in Italy: it 'could not fail to produce a certain effect in this country where people are weary, despair of good government and are seeking a saviour.' A German friend had recently mentioned as a positive fact that Italian Fascist emissaries had been to Germany to establish contacts with 'the leaders of reaction'. As to Bavaria, at least three-fourths of the population were strongly conservative and desired a return to the monarchy, but they were the people who suffered least; if disturbances should break out a 'red' revolt was more likely. It would, however, be a great mistake to underrate Hitler and 'to treat him as if he were a mere clown'; he 'must have some sort of organising ability and some power for expressing the discontent of the time in a form accessible to the average intelligence'.[41] By the end of 1922 the British diplomats were convinced that Hitler had to be taken seriously. An American officer who visited Munich in November and attended a parade of the Stormtroopers described their turnout and discipline as 'excellent'. A British officer who had also been to Munich reported that the National Socialist Party 'has gained much support from former Communists and Socialists, especially in the agricultural districts and in small factories', but that in the large factories they were still unable to make headway against 'the trade union discipline'; the party had ample funds, for allegedly 'various big German industrialists have made very large contributions' as well as Henry Ford, 'a keen Anti-Semite'.[42]

In his report on the year 1922 the British Consul-General declared the progress of the party 'one of the most remarkable features of the year'; until then, its existence was only known through enormous red placards advertising Hitler's speeches; his chief platform was anti-Semitism but he was 'anti-everything, the Entente, the Reich Government, the capitalists, the Bavarian Government at times, the Socialists and Communists, all were depicted in eloquent language as betrayers of the people'. The public was at first amused, but as political and economic conditions became worse and worse, many thought of Hitler 'as the man who was always in the right'; long before Mussolini's *coup d'état* 'Hitler's name was in everybody's mouth as that of the only possible saviour of the people.' Hitler 'is a self-educated man, lives solely for his cause, and in private conversation expresses himself with sobriety and modesty. He declares that his anti-Semitic ravings are solely for advertising purposes.' But he had no reliable deputy to take his place, and some of his sub-leaders aroused clerical apprehensions 'by lamentable sneers at the race of the founder of Christianity and by other aberrations of anti-Semitic wit'. Especially prominent among the party's followers, who came from all social classes, were students, government employees and officials, policemen and the middle classes in general, but workers were in a minority. As Hitler would not declare himself a monarchist or a militarist, the 'patriotic associations' accepted him into their general league with certain reservations, and their leaders 'worked out schemes for using Hitler as at least a pawn in their own game'; they calculated that violent disturbances would provoke 'a national demand for that strong hand which only a régime of the pre-revolutionary type can apply', but the occasion did not arise. There had also been 'displays of military uniforms, brass bands and bemedalled princes at countless assemblages of war veterans', with Prince Rupprecht and Bavarian ministers much in evidence. Whenever they had no actual grievance against the Entente, the 'war guilt lie' and Dr. Wirth's 'policy of fulfilment' always proved suitable objects for exploitation. But the blatancy of the reactionary campaign had aroused the Socialists from their apathy, some of the 'patriots' who hooted President Ebert on his visit to Munich were badly beaten by workmen, and when the Socialists 'put on the Munich streets a most business-like body of unofficial "guards" the courage of the Nationalist rowdies evaporated.' In general, however, 'the weeds of chauvinism began to flourish exceedingly', and 'Hitler's fame is so great that he was able recently to fill to overflowing no less than ten meetings held simultaneously.'⁴³

In January 1923 Seeds sent further reports on the progress of the nationalists and 'patriots'. On and after 18 January the anniversary of the foundation of the German Empire by Bismarck was celebrated and 'reactionary sentiments of the most outrageous kind were uttered'. At a meeting of the student Corporations three Bavarian ministers as well as Ludendorff, Kahr, and of course Prince Rupprecht were the guests of honour; the speakers demanded 'revenge', the reintroduction of general conscription, 'blood and iron', and the restoration of the monarchy. One of them exclaimed that 'the only weapon left in Teuton hands at present was "German hate".' At another meeting, Rupprecht entered the hall under an arch of swords and to the strains of the Bavarian royal anthem and was greeted with shouts 'Long live King Rupprecht'. Afterwards a copy of the Treaty of Versailles was burnt in a public square and the demonstrators were reviewed by Rupprecht from his palace. Simultaneously anti-French feeling rose to new heights; French officers of the Control Commission were refused food in all hotels and restaurants and the papers used inflammatory language to enforce the boycott. The consul also feared trouble from the National Socialist followers 'who are rapidly getting out of hand'; there were many indications that Hitler 'will have to take violent action at an early date'. But at the end of January he reported that for once the Bavarian government had acted and prohibited the planned open-air meetings of the National Socialists; at their recent meetings 'the numbers and enthusiasm of Hitler's followers were much less than had been expected', and 'the Hitlerites themselves consisted to a surprising extent of immature boys'; at the general meeting of the party 'the hall was only partially filled', allegedly because many members had returned home to other parts of Germany.⁴⁴

At the beginning of February Seeds quoted a paper of the Bavarian People's Party from Ratisbon which stated bluntly that

'Bavaria will not stand a Prussian Government in Munich', not even a 'Prusso-militaristic' one; if 'these Prussian-minded dictators' should overthrow the government by violence, 'they would soon learn that Bavaria is fundamentally democratic' and would have to contend with 'the opposition of the whole people'. He commented that now Hitler 'has been called a Prussian. It is hard in Bavaria to live down such a stigma.' Some weeks later he felt (as it turned out quite prophetically) that Hitler 'and the men of energy' were hampered by the Bavarian temperament, 'slow to commit itself to action, and intensely suspicious of the outsider's motives'; the Bavarians 'would keep on awaiting the "proper moment", to the despair of the Ludendorffs', who knew that a proper moment seldom came if too long postponed.[45] At a private meeting of his party Hitler had demanded the creation of a special tribunal to pronounce the death sentence against 'Socialists and traitors' and the seizure of the members of the Allied missions in Germany as hostages regardless of nationality. When the British government dissociated itself from the French march into the Ruhr, Seeds noticed 'at first a nauseous tendency to regard us as the allies of Germany', and even comparatively sensible Bavarians expected a Franco-British war. When the reaction set in there was a revival of 'the old German delusion of pre-war days that England's policy is dictated by a recognition of her own internal weakness and imminent dissolution' of the British Empire; people were arguing that France represented a danger to Britain and that an Anglo-German alliance offered 'glorious possibilities'. But the consul thought that a resurrected Germany was far more dangerous than France could ever be and that an Anglo-German understanding would be the preliminary to a war of revenge against France – after which 'the fundamental German envy of Great Britain will be free to develop itself'.[46] The embassy in Berlin meanwhile received 'disquieting' information from German sources as well as from British officers that the Bavarian division of the Reichswehr 'had taken on local colour' and could not be relied upon to cooperate with the other units of the army.[47]

When *The Times* in January published a news item headed 'Mob Rule in Munich' its local correspondent was summoned to the Munich police and strongly abused for daring to send such a message. He was warned that he would have 'to suffer the consequences'. The consul at once protested strongly to the

Bavarian government and asked for an immediate enquiry. On the next day he received 'the startling statement' that the chief of police knew nothing of the affair and could not trace a visit of the *Times* correspondent to his department; he was assured that there was no intention of taking action against the correspondent, nor was any contemplated at any time, and a private car would be sent to take him to the chief of police 'to clear up the mystery'. When the correspondent went to the police department he was received with the greatest courtesy and expressions of regret; the official responsible had been traced and severely reprimanded; if required he would offer his personal apologies. Seeds commented that the correspondent had been the object of a vendetta on the part of 'ultra-patriotic officials', but that the higher officials were always ready to meet any of his requests.[48] It was, after all, in the German interest to try and drive a wedge between Britain and France and to exploit the strong differences of policy which came to the fore in 1923: a fact that even the Bavarians were bound to observe. So as not to be outdone in national sentiment the Bavarian People's Party, together with the para-military League *Bayern und Reich* (one of the successors to the dissolved *Einwohnerwehr*), organized on a Sunday in February 40 mass meetings along the Czech frontier to protest against 'the danger which menaced Germany'; it was claimed that a Czech invasion aiming at eastern Bavaria down to Ratisbon and Passau was part of the French programme; and that three and a half million Germans were 'living in servitude across the frontier': they were urged to remain faithful till the day when all Germans would be united.[49]

On the eve of May Day another clash between the National Socialists and the Bavarian government occurred when the former threatened they would prevent the traditional May Day demonstrations by force, claimed that the government had appealed to the para-military associations to suppress a left-wing Putsch and warned the people to keep off the streets if they wanted to avoid bloodshed. The government immediately published a communiqué that it had made no such appeal to the right-wing associations, and on 1 May the heavily armed Stormtroopers were separated from the Socialists and disarmed by troops and police. As the consul reported, 'Hitler assembled at the aerodrome some 1,000 men, with arms and even machine guns, to whom a liberal supply of military uniforms and steel helmets gave the appearance of regular troops in the Field', while the Socialists had the sole advantage of superior numbers.[50] Not to be outdone by his rivals Dr Heim two weeks later paraded his peasant followers through Munich and addressed them on 'Hitler's pernicious plans for nationalizing agricultural lands' (which figured in his original programme), while Hitler denied any such intention and claimed he would only take action 'against profiteers in land'.[51]

In September Joseph Addison from the Berlin embassy visited Bavaria 'to have a look round'. He tried to buy an egg from a chicken farm and a glass of milk from a dairy farm, but in both cases his request was refused politely by the peasants. When pressed for the reason they simply replied (at a time of rapid inflation): 'We do not want any Jewish rags *(Judenfetzen)* from Berlin.' This pronouncement was usually accompanied by a lamentation that Bavaria in 1870 had given up her own currency and the claim that things would only improve when Bavaria would 'refuse to take any orders from "the Jews in Berlin".' Addison found it impossible to find any Bavarian who did not sigh for a strong government and, if possible, the monarchy.[52] At the beginning of October he reported from Berlin that the German government had recently written to von Kahr, who had been appointed General State Commissar of Bavaria, enquiring what he meant by certain utterances, but Kahr had simply ignored the letter. He was on the best of terms with the local Reichswehr commander, General von Lossow, 'whose ambiguous attitude is also causing some anxiety'; the general was always protesting that he was doing his best to carry out the instructions sent from Berlin but something always prevented him from doing so; 'his instructions arrive too late, or he is out to lunch, or he is burying his aunt. . . . Bavaria is no longer part of the German Reich.'[53]

From Munich the new British Consul-General, R.H. Clive, wrote that the decision to appoint Kahr 'a dictator' was largely taken to combat the activity of Hitler whose meetings had once more been forbidden; as Hitler intended to hold them nevertheless a clash was feared. In Clive's opinion Kahr possessed the confidence of the majority of Bavarians 'as the man who is determined to maintain order at any price'. For the moment Kahr was 'all powerful'. His intentions were good, and no one believed that he contemplated a coup in favour of separation or monarchical restoration. He was there to maintain law and order and to make Bavaria strong; he looked upon the Socialists as responsible for half of Germany's ills and was strongly opposed to the eight-hour day. When Kahr gave an interview to the consul he told him that Hitler was a demagogue but 'a very honest fellow *(ein anständiger Mann)*'; he was a man who believed he had a mission and who had 'a loathing for Jews and Frenchmen'; as to Frenchmen, 'that was perhaps not unnatural, most Bavarians felt the same way.' The consul further reported that all the reactionaries were finding 'a safe home' in Munich; it had been 'unceasingly instilled in the young men of the patriotic associations for the past three years' that Bavaria had a great mission to fulfil 'in bringing about the rebirth of Germanism'.[54]

In the summer of 1923 the government asked the War Office and British officers in Germany for reports on the German situation, especially in view of a possible German collapse. In July the opinion was expressed in the War Office that in the south of Germany the para-military associations were so strong and their organization so perfect that the Communists had no hope of seizing power 'for more than a few days'; the Hitler-Ludendorff movement claimed it could mobilize half a million fighting men; this might be an exaggeration, but it was certain 'that the best trained military and organizing brains in Germany would be on their side in case of trouble'.[55] In September General Bingham reported that two important para-military organizations, *Reichsflagge* and *Oberland*, had agreed to recognize Hitler as their political leader so that his power and prestige had grown.[56] In October the general was given the personal impressions of the *Daily Mail* correspondent who had interviewed Hitler in Munich. In his opinion Hitler was a 'hot-air merchant' and Kahr had nothing to fear from him; but 'his gangs of hooligans and desperadoes' were pretty much out of hand and were 'capable of any act of violence, preferably the isolated murders of unarmed men'; Hitler had incited them to violence and 'lost practically all control of them'.[57] The report did not mention the Stormtroopers but only the members of the Blücher, Wiking and Rossbach para-military units which belonged to the motley crowd of the so-called patriotic associations, or rather their most extreme wing. The picture of the 'hooligans and desperadoes' was true to life, partly on account of the prevailing misery, partly on account of the past career of many of the men in the free corps – fighting desperate struggles in the Baltic or in Upper Silesia, or against 'Bolshevism' at home. They were seeking vengeance for the lean times they had experienced.

They were also seeking vengeance on the Jews whom they blamed for all the ills of Germany. As early as January 1923 the Jewish Board of Deputies and the Anglo-Jewish Association wrote to Curzon that a pogrom was being planned in Munich according to a 'most respectable and reliable source': instructions should be sent to the British consul to make representations to the Bavarian government that it must preserve order. The Foreign Office wired to the consul for his observations, but he believed that the rumours were exaggerated, although he admitted that Hitler might be forced into action by his followers. In November the Jewish organizations in London repeated their request: the violent anti-semitic agitation in Bavaria was endangering the lives and property of the Jews and in addition non-German Jews were being expelled 'in circumstances of great hardship'; British influence should be used to protect them. The expulsion orders were also mentioned by Clive, the new consul, who confirmed the assertion by a local newspaper that 'the authors of this step wanted to ingratiate themselves with the Hitler party'. He went to see a high civil servant and informed him that the expulsion orders had been brought to the attention of the British government; but when he was asked whether he was making a protest he replied no, as no British subjects were affected. He was then told that the Bavarian government was not responsible for the orders which had been issued by Kahr directly to the police 'under the dictatorial powers conferred upon him' and only concerned 'undesirable aliens', mostly Polish Jews. They were guilty of profiteering, dealing in foreign currencies and similar offences, they numbered no more than about 40 families, and a protest had only been made by the Polish Consul-General. The Jewish representatives to whom the consul spoke did not favour the idea of a protest to the League of Nations and seemed to prefer 'to let sleeping dogs lie', especially after the failure of the Hitler Putsch which had brought about a decline in anti-semitic propaganda.[58] Kahr had clearly acted against people unable to defend themselves – as a sop to popular anti-Semitism.

On the day of the Hitler Putsch, 9 November, the French government called 'for an immediate examination of the situation by the Allied governments', for they could not remain indifferent to a movement which was known to favour the repudiation of the Treaty of Versailles: they should make a joint *démarche* and demand from the German government that it must withdraw its support from the military organizations which existed contrary to the treaty. On the same day Crowe minuted that 'the threatened disruption of Germany is the direct result of French policy'; it was difficult 'not to believe that it represents an object for which they [the French] have systematically worked'; the revolutionary movement in Germany was 'the direct outcome of, or at least is closely connected with, the Separatist movement on the Rhine' which the French authorities encouraged 'and which they are even now promoting everywhere'. Crowe feared that the course proposed by the French government might develop 'into a direct armed intervention of the Allies in Germany' or might induce them 'to impose a democratic régime on Germany' – a policy with which the British government could not possibly associate itself.[59] This was written before the failure of the Putsch became known in London and the officials of the Foreign Office must have sighed with relief when they heard the news, as did the leading German politicians and officials in Berlin. During the night from 8 to 9 November, when the 'national revolution' was proclaimed in Munich and it seemed in Berlin that Kahr and Lossow had joined hands with Hitler and Ludendorff, the Undersecretary of State in the *Auswärtige Amt*, Ago von Maltzan, even called on Lord D'Abernon at two a.m. in order to hear his advice about the events in Munich: a clear proof how strongly the *Auswärtige Amt* relied on the ambassador in times of crisis.[60] Maltzan informed D'Abernon that the government was determined to defend the republic 'with all the force at their command' and to suppress the movement: it looked 'very much like the beginning of civil war'. The ambassador also heard 'authentic rumours' of strong sympathies with Hitler in Pomerania and East Prussia. At 9.30 a.m. Maltzan returned to say that the government had received news that Kahr and Lossow had given their assent under compulsion, 'had dissociated themselves altogether from Hitler and Ludendorff' and issued orders for their arrest.[60] Another high dignitary who expressed his relief at 'Germany's escape from the peril of complete disintegration' was Cardinal Gasparri, the Cardinal of State at the Vatican. Talking to the British minister on the day after the Putsch he remarked: 'What a pity it is that a stray bullet did not finish off the career of General Ludendorff', a pious sentiment which the minister cordially shared.[61] Neither seems to have mentioned Hitler, the true *spiritus rector* of the affair.

From Munich Clive gave a detailed account of the events. In the afternoon of 9 November the streets in the centre of Munich were filled with angry crowds, so dense that it took him about an hour and a half to return to his office. 'I could but admire the good temper and self-control shown by the Reichswehr and police, who were persistently booed and sometimes even spat at. It was clear that the feeling of the crowd was all for Hitler. They thought he had been badly betrayed and his followers wantonly shot down. The women were loudest with their cries of down with Kahr, and all spoke of his behaviour the night before as cowardly.' Some days later the consul still found it difficult to explain the attitude of the people of Munich: 'Hitler is an atheist, anti all religion (which means a lot in this country), and not even a Bavarian. Ludendorff is a Prussian whom no one here even pretends to like . . . and yet the whole town was against Kahr and the forces of law and order. Had Hitler been in complete possession even for one day, I don't believe there would have been a French officer alive in Munich, and we should doubtless have had the pleasure of a French occupation.' Yet Kahr and the Bavarian government must bear their share of responsibility for the events: 'If they did not actually encourage Hitler, they had more than tolerated him for the past two years. They had allowed him to carry on an intensive propaganda against every succeeding Reich Government and to train and arm bands of young men until the movement had gone so far that they feared to stop it.' The Bavarian government was 'completely bankrupt in statesmanship'.[62] In his annual report for 1923 Clive returned to the subject: while Hitler became a hero and a martyr, Kahr's popularity sank to zero and he had to live 'surrounded by detectives and barbed wire entanglements'. When Cardinal Faulhaber wrote a letter deprecating the wild anti-Semitism of the National Socialists he 'at once became the target for scurrilous abuse, and it was openly suggested that he had been bribed by wealthy Jews to write as he had.' Ludendorff and the National Socialists were adopting an openly anti-Catholic attitude.[63]

On 16 November, a week after the Putsch, Clive reported that Kahr, who had established himself in the infantry barracks on the outskirts of Munich, had retaken possession of his offices in the centre. Munich University had been reopened after its closure on account of the unruly behaviour of the students. Throughout Bavaria all Communist organizations were dissolved and all SPD papers suspended. The Reichswehr units were reinforced owing to the fear of disaffection. Ten days later he wrote that, although the National Socialist organizations were dissolved by orders from Berlin, they 'are very far from being dissolved'; and the military training and arming of young Germans 'is going steadily forward all the time', so that people lived 'in a perpetual atmosphere of Putsch rumours'; the 'patriotic associations' which were responsible for this training 'are broadly in sympathy with the aims of the National Socialists'. At the end of 1923, the consul reported, Hitler's followers still constituted 'a somewhat formidable element'; a Scottish doctor who had lived in Munich for many years and lectured at the university, told him that all his students were 'ardent admirers of Hitler' and this mood was general among the university students. Apart from them, ex-officers who had to earn a precarious living and young men who had not been to war were Hitler's principal followers. That Kahr now tried to frighten people by alarmist posters was taken as a sign of fear and would defeat the purpose 'by stiffening the backs of the Hitler adherents' and might even increase their number.[64]

In February-March 1924 Hitler, Ludendorff and eight others were tried for attempted treason. In Clive's opinion, by far the most illuminating evidence was given by General von Lossow. In the summer of 1923 he was told by friends in north Germany that 'the only road to salvation in Germany was by way of a national directory acting with dictatorial powers independent of the Reichstag and the Constitution'; he entirely approved of this plan and discussed it with Kahr and the commandant of the Bavarian state police, Colonel von Seisser, who fully agreed with him; even Stresemann when forming his cabinet had declared: 'This is the last parliamentary Cabinet.' Lossow realized all along that this plan could only be carried out with the cooperation of the army and the state police. He also knew that Hitler and Ludendorff would be useless when it came to practical matters; Hitler was simply a wild man, useful for 'stirring up the nationalist feeling'. Ludendorff was much too self-centred and self-important for practical purposes but was an 'admirable figurehead'. Kahr, on the other hand, 'persistently appeared to encourage Hitler, while all the time being half-afraid of him': he was the most responsible for the events. In the eyes of the nationalists Kahr was an 'irresolute man who needed the stimulus of a *coup d'état* to make up his mind'. If the French pointed to the spirit of nationalism disclosed by the trial to justify their fears one could hardly be surprised.[65] From Berlin Addison also reported that Lossow had admitted 'to having plotted for the establishment of a National Directory with dictatorial powers', that negotiations to that end had taken place with, among others, Admirals Scheer and von Tirpitz, that 'the more serious scheme to abolish the existing form of government' was frustrated by Hitler's ill-conceived Putsch. It was difficult to find out to what extent Prince Rupprecht was acquainted with the plot, but it seemed improbable that he 'had been wholly ignorant'. Locally, the whole trial was 'looked upon as a comedy'.[66]

These views of the British diplomats were to a large extent shared by Gustav Stresemann, the Foreign Minister. He told Lord D'Abernon: from what emerged in court it became clear that the danger in November had been 'infinitely greater' than the public realized; he had always known that Germany had been within an ace of a successful right-wing Putsch, but official circles had hitherto underrated the danger. Now it was fairly clear that Kahr 'had contemplated measures against the Republic not less subversive than the schemes of Hitler and Ludendorff'; it was equally clear that Kahr had wide assurances of support from the north. The peril had been all the more imminent because the German government possessed only doubtful means to suppress the movement as the Reichswehr soldiers were to a large extent partisans of the Right.[67] From Munich the British consul added that Ludendorff's speech at the trial had aroused a storm among the Catholics; he had accused the high clergy of protecting the Jews, and large circles of the Centre Party and big industrialists of cooperating with Jews in favour of Separatism in the Rhineland; the Catholic papers had launched a virulent attack upon Ludendorff. 'General Ludendorff has never been popular in Bavaria but in spite of everything the glamour of his name remains and no one seems to think that he will be found guilty in the present trial, whatever may happen to Hitler.' The general view was: 'The greatest living soldier cannot be sent to prison.'[68] As expected Ludendorff was acquitted; Hitler was sentenced to five years of honourable detention in a fortress and soon amnestied. The other accused were similarly sentenced; none of them served his full term.

In the early 1920s Bavaria presented a bewildering spectacle of nationalist, monarchist, catholic and extreme right-wing currents, all equally hostile to Berlin and its allegedly 'Marxist' government. If they had been united, they might have been able to carry out a successful *coup d'état* as they had numerous sympathizers in other parts of Germany. But united they were not, and their leaders for ever engaged in personal rivalries and conflicts. This fact alone may have saved the Weimar Republic in the year of its most severe crisis, for – as Stresemann correctly pointed out – it had very few reliable defenders. Among the rival leaders and para-military associations, the reports from Munich paid due attention to the person of Adolf Hitler and his party, to his oratorical and organizational qualities, to his financial resources, and to the people who fell under his spell. The special role of Bavaria in the years 1918–1923 has usually been explained by the shock effect of the proclamation of a 'Soviet Republic' on a profoundly conservative and catholic country. But its roots went back further: to the unification and conquest of Germany by Prussia and to the terrible sacrifices of the First World War. Prussianization and the war had only brought misery, defeat and 'red' revolution, and a complete rejection took place of everything connected with Prussia and 'godless' Berlin, of centralization and modernization, of liberalism and democracy. As such this had little to do with 'Fascism', but it helped to prepare the ground for it. Significantly, several of the reports mentioned the effect which the March on Rome and Mussolini's victory had on the extreme Right of Bavaria. What the Blackshirts had achieved in Italy surely could be accomplished in Germany by the 'patriotic associations'. Even Hitler's bungling in November 1923 did not break the spell cast by him: to the people of Munich not he but Kahr was the traitor and the coward, and Hitler the national hero who had been betrayed.

IV

THE GREAT CRISIS OF 1923

Ever since 1920 the threat was present that the French would occupy the Ruhr basin because Germany had, in the opinion of the French government, not fulfilled her obligations under the Peace Treaty or with regard to the payment of reparations. In July 1920 Lord D'Abernon in Berlin believed that the Germans 'regarded the occupation of the Ruhr as a fixed determination of the French'; they thought the blow would fall whatever efforts they made to ward it off, while the ambassador felt that any such action would be 'deplorable' and 'would certainly endanger the whole "Europe" position'.[1] A British officer of the Army of the Rhine also reported that among all social classes 'there is a growing conviction that the French are determined at all costs to occupy the Ruhr Gebiet'; what ever Germany did or did not do, 'the French will always find a pretext for it.' According to another officer, it was felt that a French occupation would deal German industry 'a blow from which it may never recover'.[2] In November 1920 Lord D'Abernon thought that the occupation would lead to serious labour troubles and a violent disturbance of orderly restoration, and the Army Council expressed its complete agreement with his opposition to it.[3] This view was shared by no less a person than the Belgian Prime Minister, Leon Delacroix; in September he informed the British minister that he would consider the occupation 'a cataclysmic event', 'a general catastrophe'. It would require an army of at least 100,000, the miners would stop working, and how could the Allies force them to work properly? The supply of coal would dry up; what was produced would be needed locally and the remainder taken away by the Allies; there would be no coal for the rest of

Germany, and the industrial workers would be thrown out of work; probably revolution and general disorders would break out. He felt so strongly on the subject that he would rather resign than agree to the occupation. The minister added that what Delacroix had in mind was an 'isolated action on the part of France, and not a joint allied occupation' resulting from 'some grave misdemeanour on the part of Germany'.[4]

In April 1921 there were again strong rumours that the French would occupy the Ruhr and Aristide Briand, the French Prime Minister, handed to the British a memorandum on the subject. In the Foreign Office it was minuted that this was intended to bring pressure to bear upon Germany to fulfil the articles of the Peace Treaty and especially the reparation clauses; but further deliveries of coal were not in the British interest, and it was doubtful whether Germany was in default: 'For these nebulous aims, we are compelled in the interests of allied solidarity to engage in an adventure, whose consequences are incalculable, and from which no one can foretell the issue.' The Allies would saddle themselves with the responsibility of feeding a further three to four million Germans if unoccupied Germany should refuse its help or if a general strike should break out; Germany's recovery would be set back and so would be 'the reconstruction of Central Europe and probably of Russia also', as well as the revival of British trade.[5] In August 1922 the Italian ambassador to London informed the Foreign Office that his government was perturbed by renewed rumours of French intentions to intervene in the Ruhr and suggested a joint protest to Paris. The British official whom he had approached replied that in his opinion the occupation 'would secure for Monsieur Poincaré and the Marshals of France a 20 years lease of power' – a development which neither the British nor the Italian government could desire.[6]

At the end of 1922 Poincaré, at an Allied conference in Paris, seemed to the British determined to proceed with the occupation 'whatever happened'. To the suggestion that the French reparation claims might be reduced he replied that this was impossible unless the British government agreed to reduce the French debt to Britain. Bonar Law, the British Prime Minister, declared that no British government could agree to the occupation which was intended 'to enforce demands which everyone regarded as impossible'. In the opinion of the British government the occupation would not only fail to produce the desired results, but was 'likely to have a grave and even disastrous effect upon the economic situation in Europe' and therefore it refused to participate.[7] The German government in its turn stated that the occupation must lead to closer cooperation with Soviet Russia. As Dr Frédéric von Rosenberg, the Foreign Minister, told D'Abernon, they had taken office 'to save their children's country from Bolshevism'; if a French march into the Ruhr might be regarded as the second act of the drama, the 'third act might well begin with Russian Bolshevism on the Rhine'.[8] In 1923 the fear of Bolshevism was as strong an argument as in earlier years.

A few days later the French and Belgian advance into the Ruhr began. On 11 January the Foreign Office, in answer to an enquiry by Lord Kilmarnock, the British High Commissioner at Coblenz, replied that the British government disapproved of the action but was anxious 'to minimise as far as possible adverse effect on Anglo-French relations of French independent action'; he should continue to attend the meetings of the Rhineland High Commission but not participate in any decision connected with the occupation; he should place it on record that the government would take no responsibility for any decision of the Commission with which it was not associated by his vote. The same attitude was adopted by the British representatives on the Reparations Commission and the Conference of Ambassadors in Paris.[9] From Coblenz another official of the Commission wrote to London that he was not surprised that the British and the French had to part company on the reparations issue: 'After all the real issue between us is not moratorium or pledges of Allied debts but whether Germany is to be allowed to recover.'[10]

Two weeks later Lord Kilmarnock considered that the British failure to prevent the French march into the Ruhr 'must be regarded as little short of a catastrophe'; the old British policy of trying to revive 'the shattered markets of Europe' was now invalid; the policy of passive resistance proclaimed by the German government caused an ever deeper French involvement, and any admission of failure would be fatal to the French government and to the credit and prestige of France in general. In his opinion, Britain could not possibly withdraw from the Rhineland, but the bitter resistance of the Germans to France would gradually force the British government 'to take a more definite stand by the side of France'. The Germans were 'extremely cunning in devising means of driving wedges between the Allies if they can discover any crevices in the solidarity of the latter'. On the next day he added two more arguments against a British withdrawal: it would have a serious effect on British trading interests 'which would be entirely at the mercy of our Allies', and it 'would enable the French to pursue untrammelled their policy of establishing an autonomous Rhineland Republic'. He was convinced that this movement was not based on the will of the people but only on French money and influence; 'if work were completed under French domination [the] edifice could only be sustained by aid of French bayonets', and the outcome would be a forcing ground for war.[11]

Yet a British withdrawal from the occupied Rhineland was seriously considered. In the Foreign Office a memorandum of its effects was drawn up in January by Colonel Ryan from the Rhineland High Commission. It emphasized that as a result the whole of the Rhineland would fall under French influence; the British occupation of Cologne 'has automatically placed a check on French separatist activities'; the Germans would view such a step 'with grave misgivings'; the Rhinelanders in particular 'regard our presence as safeguarding their national interests against French annexationist designs, and as tending to lighten the rigours of the occupation.'[12] In February the Central Department of the Foreign Office added its voice to the effect that nothing was to be gained by a withdrawal but much was to be lost: the retention of British troops pleased the French as well as the Germans and Britain would retain her share in the guarantees of the Peace Treaty 'for the eventual fulfilment by Germany of the pledges wrung from her as a result of the war'; a withdrawal would be justified 'only in case of absolute necessity'.[13] But when the French reacted to the German policy of passive resistance by expelling growing numbers of senior German officials from the Rhineland, the British Commissioner at Cologne felt that the expulsions and arrests placed the British in an 'impossible position'; 'during the years we have worked with these officials we have found them invariably loyal, and we have built up an atmosphere of mutual confidence on which to a great extent the safety and comfort of the Army depends'; within a few hours all this would be ruined 'and I think it would be impossible to continue our work here under those circumstances.'[14]

As the French military traffic into the Ruhr had to pass through the British zone of occupation, it was decided not to allow them more than ten trains a day, nor any increase by rail in men or material destined for the French forces in the Ruhr or for any further advance through the British zone. At a conference with high German railway officials about the problems of this French military traffic the British officers present stressed that the withdrawal of the British troops was not a bluff but a serious possibility. General Groener, the German Minister of Transport, replied that this threat would never be carried out in view of the serious consequences it would cause; to him, the situation resembled 'two dogs who had each other in such a grip that neither side would let go' so that a third party would have 'to separate them':[15] a clear appeal to Britain to act as an arbiter to which the British side did not respond. Groener was not the only German to express such a hope. In April Lord Kilmarnock wrote, quoting an article in the respected *Kölnische Zeitung*, that 'the Germans still cling to the hope that they may obtain help from British sources', although they no longer seemed to expect British assistance against France; the degree of misapprehension in German circles was quite remarkable.[16]

Britain's policy throughout remained the preservation of the Entente with France, as Curzon emphasized in the House of Lords in March: 'We are profoundly convinced that the Entente is the basis of European recovery and of European peace.' If Britain had sided with Germany, on the other hand, she would have been disloyal to her late Allies; Germany 'has shown a capacity for resistance which has surprised both her opponents and her friends'; her position was very difficult, but she 'has shown a stubborn willingness to endure loss and privation'; the cost of production had risen steeply, and there were 'amazing fluctuations in the exchange value of the mark'. Curzon had constantly advised the German government to make an overture to France or to the Allies; this would have to be made sooner or later, and 'the sooner the better'.[17] The French press, however, suspected the British – or at least Lord D'Abernon in Berlin – of encouraging the resistance of the German government to French demands. The ambassador hotly denied the suspicion: it was a complete misconception 'to suggest that a violent national revolt could have been produced at the instigation of any foreign agency'; and the German view of the British attitude was precisely the opposite; Chancellor Cuno had many a time underlined the fact that Germany stood alone and could count on no foreign support; while the German press had gone further and 'has established an analogy between the attitude of England and that of Pontius Pilate.'[18] In August D'Abernon wrote that it was vital for Britain 'to prevent the breaking up of Germany. As long as Germany is a coherent whole, there is more or less a balance of power in Europe.' If Germany broke up, France would remain 'in undisputed military and political control, based upon her army and her military alliances.'[19] Curzon's efforts of persuasion succeeded in June in producing a German offer that the whole question of the capacity to pay reparations should be submitted to an international committee of experts. But the French government insisted that first the policy of passive resistance must be terminated unconditionally – a course that was rejected by the Cuno government.

The British government, too, favoured the submission of the whole reparations issue to a committee of experts, and a British note with that suggestion was handed to the French and Belgian ambassadors in August. It pointed out that the occupation of the Ruhr, undertaken at great cost, had produced less coke and coal for the Allies than had been delivered in the previous year, and that there was a 'great and growing danger to the peaceful trade of the world'; a continuation of the conflict would entail 'the gravest risks, both economic and political'. But when the French government refuted the note no open rupture occured.[20] Lord D'Abernon descibed the effect of the British note as 'magical'; it had helped to restore order in Germany and to inspire the ruling classes with some courage and determination to save themselves.[21] A statement to be made in parliament drafted by the Foreign Office stressed that, in the view of the British government, the occupation of the Ruhr 'was not in accord with the terms of the Treaty of Versailles and could not be justified on juridical grounds'. The government had foreseen that an operation intended to be limited to the despatch of some engineers and technical experts who were to be accompanied by a limited number of troops would soon develop into a large and drastic military operation; meanwhile the French and Belgians 'established a complete and stringent control over every branch of industry in the Ruhr. . . . They have been met with a sullen and formidable hostility by the German government and the German inhabitants, and scenes of disorder and violence have occurred' as an 'inevitable consequence of so sharp an interference by foreign force with the ordinary life of the affected districts.' Every European country, the statement continued, was paying the price for this action, either in a steadily falling rate of exchange, in declining trade, or in growing unemployment:

'The illness of Germany is indeed in danger of growing into an international pestilence; the disease is fast becoming endemic among the stricken nations', and the recovery of the world and the peace were at stake.[22] The British position could hardly be stated more forcefully and more critically of the policy of the French government. No wonder that the wits referred to Anglo-French relations as *la rupture cordiale*.

In Germany, nationalist passion and feelings of hatred against France were aroused to fever pitch by the French action. Mass demonstrations were organized in January in which, according to Lord D'Abernon, half a million people participated in Berlin alone. 'Hatred of everything connected with the French name has reached an intensity which cannot be exaggerated, and which could not be controlled, the hunger and want will add an element of combustion which may well render an explosion inevitable.' If the state of semi-starvation prevalent among the lower middle classes should spread to the working class, revolutionary disturbances 'of which nobody can foretell the outcome' were certain to occur. But he thought it remarkable that the vast crowds uttered not a single cry against the British who had been 'the main cause of Germany's defeat'.[23] The British consul at Cologne also reported on the intensity of patriotic feeling which had spread to the working class. He had discussed this with an Englishman who had long lived in Düsseldorf and employed several hundred workmen there; in his opinion, national sentiments were aroused among many who during the past four years had not thought much of their country. Some months later, in August, he added that the movement of passive resistance to the French was 'entirely spontaneous'; people were convinced that the French aimed at the break-up of Germany, wanted to lay their hands on the Ruhr and intended to enslave the workers for the benefit of the French industrialists and taxpayers; there the French 'have established a regime of sheer militarism the severity of which can surely never have been surpassed'; they had expelled thousands from their homes 'and filled the prisons with countless victims of arbitrary arrests and equally arbitrary sentences'.[24]

Lord D'Abernon also recorded that the mine owners and directors imprisoned by the French for refusing to carry out their orders had become 'national heroes'; the sentences had brought together all parties and all social classes – an effect that could not have been obtained by any other means; they did not deserve to be such heroes, for their policy had been selfish, and they had 'ruined large classes of their countrymen by their inflation policy'. For the moment all working-class hostility to the employers had vanished; and the violence of national feeling among the Socialists equalled that in other social classes.[25] The ambassador further described the attitude of the different political parties to the occupation. As might be expected, the parties of the Right were the most vehement and the least inclined to any compromise; as the French had violated the Treaty of Versailles, it could 'now be denounced as obsolete'. The Social Democrats considered the situation 'a favourable one to regain popularity by vehement endorsement of the nationalist standpoint'; they felt that they had lost much popularity by their failure to formulate a national programme and that the struggle in the Ruhr offered an excellent opportunity to retrieve the position.[26] In March the ambassador met several leaders of the SPD. In contrast with the parties of the Right they did not insist on the evacuation of the Ruhr as a precondition for negotiations; but they realized that negotiations which were not preceded by evacuation would cause 'a violent division of opinion' and thus present 'a grave national danger'. D'Abernon found them disinclined to take any responsibility for such negotiations or even to join a government which might have to negotiate.[27]

From Coblenz, on the other hand, Lord Kilmarnock reported that the working classes were feeling the strain and wished negotiations to start as soon as possible; they suspected that the Ruhr industrialists were reaping large benefits from the government's Ruhr Relief fund; and intensive anti-semitic propaganda against Jewish magnates 'is reported to [be] having some effect'. Thus the German united front was weakening: this was partly due to rumours about nationalist conspiracies, partly to the provocative activity of the Hitler party in Bavaria, partly to an underestimation of the strength of the Communists in the Ruhr by the French.[28] When an official delegation of the Labour Party visited Essen and Bochum in March and interviewed leaders of the miners' union, they were informed that the miners would continue their passive resistance: the German miners had fought for years to win concessions from the mine owners regarding working hours and wages; if they now came under French domination, even only temporarily, they would lose the concessions. The union leaders felt strong enough to 'keep their members with nationalist tendencies sufficiently in check to prevent serious disturbances.'[29] From the outset the Labour Party had strongly protested not only against the French action, but equally against the connivance of the British government in the occupation, and expressed its solidarity with the Ruhr workers; for it considered the French policy, as Arthur Henderson put it, 'a danger to the peace of Europe'.[30]

The measures taken in the Ruhr by the French to enforce their domination were carefully observed. In February the British vice-consul at Essen noted that they 'seem to be systematically making the situation in the Ruhr basin more and more impossible for the inhabitants'; railway services were practically non-existent, and most of the telegraph and telephone lines were out of use; the newspapers were systematically suppressed; all the Ruhr towns, with the exception of only four, had been deprived of their mayors; in Essen, the police had been dismissed so that the inhabitants 'are now a prey to footpads and criminals of all descriptions'; large French units 'seem to roam through the Basin causing disorder and alarm wherever they go.'[31] In March the consul at Cologne wrote that the French might allow the police of Bochum, Recklinghausen and Herne to return to duty, but their discharge seemed to indicate that they intended to remove methodically the whole police force from the Ruhr; 'to the onlooker it seems that no stone is being left unturned to shatter the morale of the inhabitants of the Ruhr and their exhibition of nerve and self-restraint must be a cause for wonder and even admiration to those familiar with the conditions under which they are now living.' The situation was deteriorating 'and there is no ray of light.'[32] Some days later he added that the mayor of Gladbeck had been arrested and carried away, that the police of Dortmund, Gelsenkirchen and Mülheim had been disarmed and removed; in Dortmund and Mülheim the stations had been occupied and the rolling stock seized, 'thus practically completing the paralysis of traffic in the Upper Ruhr'.[33] When a riot occurred at Krupp's in Essen and 14 workers were shot by a French detachment which felt itself threatened, ten directors and managers of Krupp's were tried by a French court-martial and sentenced to between ten and 20 years of imprisonment. When the verdict was announced Curzon commented that 'the sentences were absolutely barbarous'. And even the cautious Permanent Undersecretary Crowe wrote that 'the French authorities can equitably claim the right to put down opposition to their occupying forces'; yet, 'under the cloak of judicial proceedings, they do things which violate all sense of justice and fair dealing. They believe in a system of savage terrorism.' It remained to be seen whether such a regime would succeed in solving the difficulties they met on account of the German resistance.[34] The British consuls on the spot fully agreed with the heads of the Foreign Office in their condemnation of the measures taken by the French to break all opposition.

In June the British chargé d'affaires in Berlin once more commented on 'the intense feeling' of the population. If French or Belgian officers tried to enter a factory, even accompanied by a German liaison officer, they would be met by delegates of the workers who would ask for their papers; as soon as they discovered who they were 'they will kick them out, if necessary very violently'. British officers, on the other hand, could go anywhere, even in uniform.[35] Some weeks later the same diplomat reported on the acts of sabotage which were committed in the Ruhr against the French by so-called 'secret organisations', the existence of which was 'so well known that they hardly deserve the title which they bear'. The German government was well aware of their activities and could if it wanted take vigorous measures against them; its so-called 'helplessness' was simply due to 'the state of public opinion with the consequent fear that adequate measures of repression would provoke disorder'; fear and bad faith together were 'sufficient a cause for doing nothing'.[36]

In July the commercial secretary to the embassy toured the Ruhr and reported on 'the terrific industrial stagnation' he had observed. Canals and inland harbours 'are literally blocked with vessels of all types unable or unwilling to move'; 'postal and telegraph services are seriously impeded and telephone communications cut off. Passenger railway traffic scarcely exists, motor cars have ceased to circulate. . . . The fuel supply and iron ore deliveries to the steel works in the heart of the Basin are for all practical purposes cut off. . . . No figures of coal production are now published but it is certain that the daily output is but a fraction of the previous quantity. Few pits are to be seen working. . . . The production in the Ruhr of pig-iron and steel has sunk to about one-fifth of the pre-occupation output and further diminution of output is in sight.'[37] In the same month the vice-consul at Elberfeld wrote: 'Revenge and a new war with France are openly spoken of on every hand'; in this war, he had been told by many Germans, England would be found on the German side and the munitions would come from Soviet Russia: plenty of them 'are waiting just over the Russian border.'[38] From Bremen the vice-consul reported in November on the constantly heard expressions of surprise that Britain did not intervene 'before it is too late'; there was a 'blind, almost pathetic faith' that she would ultimately do 'something' but in some quarters this was replaced by the conviction 'that she is afraid of France, in the face of whose military might and land and air armaments she is impotent'; France had taken Britain's place 'as the foremost among the nations'.[39] The consul at Cologne saw no reason to doubt the German claim that, while the very best French railway experts could hardly manage the complicated system of the Ruhr, those actually in charge there were of very mediocre quality, otherwise they would hardly have been induced to come and were therefore 'totally inequipped for the task'; in fact, they seemed unable to manage efficiently the very limited number of reparation coal trains.[40]

The British High Commission at Coblenz reported in May on the difficulties meeting British trade with the occupied area. Traders had to go first to Düsseldorf where they found it extremely difficult to get information; the officials, apparently active French officers, did not know the rates of duty according to the tariffs and referred the traders to Essen; but the licensing office there was so badly organized that any doubt was referred back to Düsseldorf so that the unfortunate man had to return there; they then insisted that the British firm had to pay the licence fee and export duty in cash: 'they do not appear to realise that such things as banks exist for the purpose of transmitting funds.' Applicants, it was repeated soon after, were 'continually referred from one office to another or sent back to Coblenz'; the French authorities in Düsseldorf professed ignorance of the requirements of the Essen authorities who had to issue the licences and vice versa.[41] In June Kilmarnock stated 'that it is a fixed idea with a section of the French that they must at all costs prevent export of steel from Ruhr if they are to obtain their ends'; he was nevertheless advising British traders to comply with any fresh French demands 'in order to leave no stone unturned'. A new difficulty arose because the French were putting large German firms on a black list to prevent them from exporting; and British firms were forbidden to receive goods from such black-listed firms.[42] The aim clearly was to impede German trade, even with Britain, by the erection of bureaucratic barriers. In August

Kilmarnock complained to London about the case of a Newcastle firm whose supply of coking coal to the Phoenix works in the Ruhr was suddenly stopped by the French although it was covered by a valid export licence, because the Phoenix works were blacklisted. Three thousand tons had already been delivered without a hitch which indicated that the French had modified their practices without giving notice or informing the High Commission. The black list had always been kept secret so that traders were totally ignorant of the names of the firms listed and of the penalties they incurred.[43]

As active military resistance to the French advance was out of the question, a policy of passive resistance was adopted – a sign of German helplessness rather than an active policy. Before the invasion Chancellor Cuno, in a speech at Hamburg, offered to France and other interested countries a pact of peace: an offer endorsed by almost all the parties, even those of the Right. This offer Lord D'Abernon considered an important development, 'probably contrary to what would have occurred had the offer been made by Dr Wirth or by a Chancellor commanding to a less degree the confidence' of the right-wing parties. In his opinion, it was a hopeful sign that the offer was subscribed 'by those parties in Germany who were considered the most set upon a war of revenge'; for some people still pretended to believe in the possibility of a German attack, 'a pretence made the more easy by some foolish stuff in some English papers'.[44] In March a member of the embassy reported from Berlin that the German government believed the policy of passive resistance would take months to bear fruit and was bound to inflict much loss and suffering upon the country; its only fear was that the extremists of the Left and Right could get out of hand and try to turn passive into active resistance and thus create incidents which might spell disaster; any capitulation on its part would cause a violent division of opinion; if the government were replaced by a left-wing one – 'the only alternative short of civil war' – the Right would refuse to cooperate; the members of the trade unions insisted even more strongly than their leaders on continued resistance to the French. In the writer's opinion, the Germans had regained their unity, their national consciousness and a feeling of self-respect.[45] In May von Rosenberg, the Foreign Minister, told the British ambassador that, even if the government agreed to abandon passive resistance, the people would refuse to do so; 'it would be identical with complete capitulation and humiliation of Germany'.[46]

In July Lord D'Abernon still wrote that there was no sign of any readiness to give up passive resistance; the people in the Ruhr would not obey an order from Berlin to do so unless in exchange definite concessions were obtained by Germany; a leading trade unionist from the Ruhr had even declared: 'We should not give up passive resistance but merely the passivity of our resistance.' The foreign policy of the Cuno government was endorsed by all political parties except a few Independent Socialists; the main criticism of the government was its complete failure to halt the fall of the mark and to stem the rise of all prices.[47] Another member of the embassy believed that the 'intolerable economic conditions' had caused a 'general relaxation of the canons of honesty', and the corruption 'does not tend to increase the prestige of the republican régime'. He had always been of the opinion that the republican form of government was unpopular; wherever he had been, 'I have heard from all classes expressions of opinions ranging from dislike to contemptuous toleration, but never once an opinion which was enthusiastically in favour of the present system'. An observer could visit Saxony, Thuringia, the Ruhr and the poorer quarters of the large cities and come away with the impression that Germany was not only republican, 'but red-hot republican'. If the same person visited Bavaria, Pomerania, East Prussia and many other areas, 'he would equally be persuaded that almost personal rule was on the eve of being introduced.' Two factors which had produced revolution in history were present in Germany: economic distress and political discontent. The abolition of general military service had contributed to the loss of a sense of discipline 'which appears to be necessary to the German character'. All these factors made for disruption, but 'the idea that the world is going to be a gainer by the disruption of this country' was insane, and so was 'the policy which is egging Germany to ruin, or which even allows the ruin to take place in itself'.[48] Kilmarnock at Coblenz, on the other hand, did not believe in 'the prophecies of impending collapse and chaos' which he had heard ever since he had arrived in Germany in 1920; 'at every fresh big slump in the mark we have been told that when that unit of currency reached first 10,000, later 50,000, and later still 100,000 to the £ the end must be in sight', but it had not come. He was reminded of the fable of the boy who was always crying 'wolf' and was tempted to wonder whether the wolf really existed.[49]

Meanwhile secret negotiations were going on between Stresemann, the leader of the People's Party, and the Social Democrats for the formation of a new government. At the end of May the ambassador reported that the 'Socialists were quite ready to come to terms with Stresemann, but Stresemann's followers have deserted him.' Stinnes had exercized strong pressure against Stresemann, and the right-wing *Kreuz–Zeitung* had denounced him as a new Erzberger, virtually inviting the secret associations which had murdered Erzberger and Rathenau 'to devote their attention to Stresemann.'[50] When the Cuno government finally fell after large strikes and severe labour riots Stresemann succeeded in forming a government of the 'Great Coalition' including the Social Democrats. As Lord D'Abernon informed London in August, the view that Stresemann would be too mild to maintain order was not confirmed by his conversation with the new Chancellor; he appeared 'not to recoil from measures of severity' and he well remembered another conversation with him in 1922 about unrest when he declared *'Es muss geschossen werden'* (it is necessary to shoot) and nothing short of this 'would keep things quiet'. Stresemann had also expressed strongly anti-inflationist views and criticized the Cuno government for not exercizing control over the central bank.[51] Soon after Stresemann informed the ambassador that 'he was taking stringent measures to restrict lavish expenditure initiated in the Ruhr by the preceding government'; this would raise a storm of protest from the industrialists and others who profited from it, but it was quite impossible to carry on on the old basis.[52] As to the causes of Cuno's fall, in D'Abernon's opinion it was above all due to the horrendous inflation and the food shortages: 'the people feel that someone must have blundered badly to allow such conditions to come about. Public opinion demanded a scapegoat,' and Cuno and the president of the central bank were sacrificed – deservedly so in the latter case, 'for anything more incompetent that the management of the Reichsbank during the last two years it would be impossible to conceive.'[53] As Stresemann promised to restrict expenditure and to halt the runaway inflation, he had D'Abernon's full sympathy and support.

By mid-September Stresemann was more confident with regard to the maintenance of public order. The ambassador was told confidentially that the Chancellor considered the army and police 'reliable and capable of dealing with any minor outbreak', and cooperation between him and the Social Democrats was 'cordial'; if for some reason they should desert him he would form a bourgeois government and, if he did not succeed in that, dissolve parliament.[54] It was not said what would happen in case of a 'major' outbreak: apparently Stresemann did not think this very likely although there was the ever-present possibility of a 'national revolution' in Bavaria. The most crucial issue facing the new government, however, was the ending of passive resistance because without this there was no hope of bringing inflation under control. As early as June the British chargé d'affaires wrote from Berlin that Germany could not continue indefinitely financing passive resistance in the Ruhr; the effect of the occupation on her finances, i.e. her export bills, was not yet fully felt, as these bills were about three months in arrears; but if and when she could not procure the export bills and the mark fell further as it was bound to do, 'the French will have the German carcass at their mercy by about October.' He feared that Poincaré knew this and that impeded any reasonable solution: 'We don't want Germany to be a carcass. France does not mind very much if she becomes one and if decomposition supervenes.'[55] In early September he wrote privately to London it was 'a well-known fact' that passive resistance could not continue much longer and that the German government could not hold out on this issue; 'the sum required to keep the workers in the Ruhr territory in idleness is between 40 and 50 billion paper marks daily.'[56] At the same time the British 'Kreis' officer at Opladen near Cologne reported that big businessmen such as the directors of large chemical works at Leverkusen admitted that Germany would have to capitulate, that the French measures had 'strangled Germany into submission'; the only thing left was to negotiate with the enemy; the representatives of the Ruhr workers were ready to give up passive resistance if the prisoners were freed and those deported by the French were allowed to return to the area.[57]

In Berlin, Lord D'Abernon learned, Stresemann had discussions with the French ambassador, but he continued to demand the abandonment of passive resistance as a precondition, while Stresemann believed 'that this is an impossibility and that it would lead to chaos and civil war'; if Germany gave up passive resistance the regime of occupation in the Ruhr must be modified and the method of the future settlement must be guaranteed, otherwise they had nothing to gain by accepting the French conditions. Stresemann told D'Abernon 'he would be torn to pieces if he ordered cessation of passive resistance without certainty of counter-concessions'. He therefore asked whether the British government could possibly intervene so as to secure from France terms which he could accept 'without destroying foundations of orderly government and risk of social revolution'. He was hoping that Prime Minister Baldwin would be able to influence Poincaré in this sense and that the British government would participate in the discussions.[58] In London, the German chargé d'affaires called at the Foreign Office and stressed that the present situation could at most last another four weeks; if Germany received no financial assistance, she 'must collapse, or she must "throw herself into the arms of France"', and accept any conditions which the latter might dictate'. The official to whom he explained this minuted that he could not see any alternative: the German government, as the British had been told time and again, could not capitulate and remain in power; its fall would cause anarchy, and the result could be the 'collapse' which was put as the first alternative. He explained to the German diplomat that, if Britain assisted Germany financially, this would mean 'to give up all hope of an allied agreement on the subject of reparations', and the French were bound to misunderstand such an action and to be even less inclined to listen to British representations.[59] On 23 September D'Abernon wired to London that it was essential to find a formula by which Stresemann could 'present the abandonment of passive resistance to the country in such a guise as to render acceptance possible'. Then the immediate crisis could be overcome, but if no such formula were found he expected 'a general catastrophe'.[60]

Three days later the German government officially abandoned the policy of passive resistance and thus admitted defeat. But in Bavaria, as the British consul reported, this was regarded 'as a triumph for the Socialists'; with regard to the future a general feeling of tension existed, and to the National Socialists it simply spelled a 'catastrophe'.[61] Stresemann, on the other hand, was deeply disappointed that this step 'brought about no relaxation from France and obtained very little recognition from England'; he had taken a grave responsibility upon himself, but he was equally determined to take the responsibility for an open break with France if she tried to extract fresh conditions, especially affecting the political future of the occupied area; the differences with Bavaria had become stronger, and there was a marked move to the Right throughout the country. He could not fight this without some support and encouragement; if this government fell the last chance of a constitutional regime would vanish: he was looking to Britain to use her influence 'in saving the cause of constitutional government in Germany'.[62] Only a few days later, at the beginning of October, Addison wired from Berlin he had 'every reason to believe that Chancellor has become convinced that the country cannot any longer be governed constitutionally'; he intended to attempt in the near future to establish a dictatorship with himself as the dictator and 'to dispense with parliamentary forms'. Stresemann, he added soon after, would rather welcome a rejection of the proposed enabling bill by parliament so that he could dissolve it and govern by emergency decrees, while new elections would be postponed indefinitely; he was confident that the Reichswehr would support him. Addison thought that this was probably correct provided that Stresemann 'governs strongly and does not give way to pressure from the Left'. He also reported that Stresemann's own party, the People's Party, had addressed an ultimatum to him that the government must be reformed by admitting the German Nationalist Party and curtailing the influence of the SPD, in particular of the Ministers of Finance and of Justice, Rudolf Hilferding and Gustav Radbruch, an eminent jurist; the eight-hour day should be modified – a proposal totally opposed by the representatives of the SPD who were equally opposed to admitting the Nationalists to the government.[63]

In fact, there was a government crisis. In Addison's opinion, it meant 'a distinct movement towards the Right' which corresponded to the general trend in the country; 'it has become absolutely necessary for the German Government, if they are even to attempt to prevent disintegration and chaos, to conciliate the Conservative elements which, in fact, at the present time, control the national life'; it was essential to conciliate Bavaria as well as the agrarian population in other areas so that they would again supply the industrial centres with food which they were refusing to do (because the currency had become valueless). If the government wishes to remain in power and 'to guide the State to a safe goal' it must try and enlist on its side the 'forces which otherwise would be driven into the camp of disorder'. To Addison Germany appeared 'to be ready to accept a dictatorship resting on the Right'.[64] In fact, however, Stresemann was able to reform the government on the basis of the 'Great Coalition' including the Social Democrats, and only the unpopular Minister of Finance, Hilferding, was dropped and replaced by a conservative without party affiliation.

On 20 October Lord D'Abernon wired to London: 'Disintegration is proceeding at an alarming rate'; Bavaria refused to accept orders from Berlin, and in Saxony 'there is widespread disorder'. He had heard 'from a very confidential source' that a plot existed to establish, within the next few days, a military dictatorship to replace parliamentary government.[65] The telegram hinted clearly at the plans of General von Seeckt to establish a 'directory' – plans which had wide support not only in the army but in right-wing and conservative circles in general. They envisaged sweeping constitutional changes, such as a new Chamber of Estates, the combination of the offices of Chancellor and Prussian Prime Minister, the dissolution of the trade unions and the cancellation of all collective agreements, and in the field of foreign policy the intensification of the economic and military links with Soviet Russia. But these plans were of course not known in detail to the ambassador.[66] In November General Bingham reported from Berlin that, if the Chancellor were to give a definite order to General von Seeckt, 'the military would depose the Republican Government and establish a military dictatorship'.[67] This was probably correct, save that Stresemann was very unlikely to issue such an order, for the relations between the two men were more than strained. It is conceivable that this fact saved the parliamentary constitution – exactly as the strained relations between Seeckt and Ludendorff prevented any co-operation of the two generals against the Republic.

That the Reichswehr in the course of 1923 took measures forbidden to it under the terms of the Treaty of Versailles – such as recruiting volunteers and training retired officers – was known to the British authorities, although the inspection visits of officers of the Control Commission were suspended on account of the Ruhr crisis. In March the social-democratic government of Prussia took action against the illegal paramilitary association led by the former Lieutenant Rossbach and arrested him after a secret meeting with army officers in a suburb of Berlin had been discovered. The British embassy, however, did 'not attach any great importance to the extreme movement' and attributed the 'somewhat sensational action' of the Prussian authorities 'to a desire to placate the Socialists and so facilitate the campaign of passive resistance in the Ruhr'. But it admitted that there was a danger of passive resistance becoming active resistance (which could only be undertaken with the help of the army) and that, if the government were forced to capitulate in the Ruhr, Rossbach's followers would attempt to assassinate the politicians whom they classified as 'defeatist'.[68] In the spring it was discovered in the course of unofficial visits by British officers that German reserve officers were trained at two military camps and that armoured cars looking like tanks were used there.[69] In August the ever active Colonel Morgan reported that in his opinion the German Ministry of Defence intended 'to build up a masked reserve' – an opinion that was supported by many facts. A French secret agent had confirmed this with very detailed information in respect of the East Prussian military district and staff courses were held for the training of senior officers.[70]

In 1924 a British journalist informed MacDonald that, under the Cuno government, the illegal armament was permitted to go on 'with complete immunity' and grew enormously in volume; there was no doubt that the terms of the Peace Treaty had been violated with the connivance of General von Seeckt and Dr Gessler, the Defence Minister; by a strange irony Gessler belonged to the Democratic Party, but 'would be much more at home with the German Nationalists'; when the Prussian Minister of the Interior wanted to suppress the illegal armed organizations of the Right 'he was prevented by Gessler and von Seeckt from doing anything'; the Reichswehr officers 'are as rigorously disciplined as the men of the old German army' and would obey Seeckt's orders 'but the government cannot count on him or them.'[71] It remains true, on the other hand, that Seeckt always hesitated and did not dare 'to jump' as he was urged to do by several right-wing emissaries. When the news of the outbreak of the Hitler Putsch reached Berlin during the night of 8 to 9 November Seeckt was entrusted by President Ebert with exceptional powers under Article 48 of the Constitution, and this move may have put an end to any scheme of his to act outside its limits. It may even have been an astute move of Ebert to prevent Seeckt from acting unconstitutionally. He only retained his powers under Article 48 for a few months and returned them to the President in February 1924 as no longer required.

Among all the dangers besetting the German government – the French invasion, the ambitions of the generals, the activities of the extreme Right and the extreme Left, the conflict with Bavaria and the threatened march on Berlin – probably none contributed more to disintegration and chaos and the alienation of large sections of the people than the runaway inflation, which could only be stopped if the government stopped the vast expenditure on passive resistance in the Ruhr. The Cuno government tried in vain to keep the mark steady – at a rate of about 20,000 marks to the dollar – and in doing so used up large proportions of the German gold reserve. In June a Foreign Office official minuted that 'at least 522 million gold marks have been used for the purpose'. The 'hopeless financial situation' made him wonder 'whether it is now possible to avoid a general social smash in Germany. Perhaps the only bulwark against such a catastrophe at present is the unity of opposition to the French in the Ruhr.'[72] In August Lord D'Abernon wrote that soon a condition would be reached when the mark would be no longer accepted and production would cease; 'fares indicated on the meter of a taxi-cab have today to be multiplied by 150,000; tomorrow the multiplicator will be 200,000; one cannot pay a charwoman without a table of logarithms; a theatre ticket costs over 1,000,000 marks, and a motor car 10,000,000,000.' Unless there was a rapid solution, a grave danger of anarchy existed; the middle as well as the lower classes were complaining bitterly about the exorbitant prices, vast alterations in salaries and wages had to be carried out, and strikes and lockouts were threatening. Certain leaders of industry and finance, he thought, exercized far too much influence and their views were at once selfish and shortsighted.[73]

A few days later the ambassador reported on a meeting of the Council of State at which the president of the central German bank had stated that the daily production of bank notes was twenty billion marks and would be stepped up in the next week to 46 billion; very soon the daily production would reach two-thirds of the present total circulation. 'My comment on above is that such insanity has never been spoken outside a lunatic asylum.' There was no chance of the payment of reparations or the restoration of social order 'if Reichsbank is allowed to follow its own demented inspirations.'[74] Every trade and every class of goods had a different index or multiplier; the most ordinary purchase in a shop demanded a calculation of three to four minutes by an accountant to establish the price to be paid; when that had been done several more minutes were required to count out the necessary notes; the unfortunate housewife had to pay millions of marks instead of single or tens of marks and she had to queue for several hours to buy certain items such as butter.[75] But the inflation was to continue for another three months at an ever accelerating pace. The new currency, the *Rentenmark*, was only issued in mid-November, at the rate of one *Rentenmark* to 1,000,000,000,000 paper marks, or 4.20 to the dollar.[76] The ambassador ascribed this precipitate fall 'to complete absence of any rational control'. He also found that no scheme of stabilization could succeed unless Germany received large scale assistance from abroad, something like 50 or 60 million pounds sterling as cover for a gold reserve – an assistance which would not have been required 12 months before when 'confidence had only been shaken but had not, as now, entirely disappeared'.[77] Meanwhile new paper money and new local 'emergency notes' made their appearance every day, but were often refused acceptance by the population. In the Rhineland, the Separatists issued their own local notes which were only accepted at the order of the Rhineland High Commission, or rather its French section.[78]

After the issue of the *Rentenmark*, however, matters improved rapidly as the government finally adopted a policy of strict deflation. In the Ruhr, 'a wave of optimism' was recorded in early December; 'the shops are filled with new stock and food shops are particularly well supplied.' At Christmas D'Abernon recorded 'the astonishing appeasement and relief brought about by the touch of the magical wand of "Currency Stability".' In the large towns food was once more abundant, potatoes and cereals appeared in large quantities, and even butter was again available at stable, if high prices. The queues in front of the butchers and groceries disappeared. The improvement in the economic situation also brought 'in its train political pacification – dictatorships and putsches are no longer discussed', and even the extremist parties 'have ceased, for the moment, from troubling'. The question which the ambassador naturally asked himself was why 'so beneficial a change' had not been adopted much earlier.[79] Part of the answer was supplied by Lord Kilmarnock from Coblenz who emphasized the enormous benefits which the industrialists had derived from the period of inflation. They had used it 'to turn paper marks into plant . . . often borrowing marks for the purpose and repaying them after further depreciation had taken place'; during the period of passive resistance many workers were employed improving the means of production instead of producing goods, and large scale building operations were carried out, for example at the dye works at Höchst and Leverkusen. At Bochum, Stinnes had built the largest steel tube factory in the world; fixed charges had been paid off at a trifling cost in depreciated marks.[80] As we shall see, the employers also used the social distress caused by inflation and unemployment to get rid of the eight-hour day, one of the achievements of the revolution of 1918.

By the end of November Stresemann was no longer Germany's Chancellor. At the beginning of the month the Social Democrats resigned from the government because of its intervention against the left-wing governments of Saxony and Thuringia, and the government became a rump, with several of the vacancies not filled. On 23 November it lost a vote of confidence in the Reichstag as the Social Democrats and the German Nationalists voted against it. Stresemann, Lord D'Abernon reported, had counted on the willingness of President Ebert to grant him a dissolution in case of defeat, but he learnt that Ebert would not do so because he believed it impossible to hold an election with so large a part of the country occupied by foreign armies. But even those who voted Stresemann down did not know 'of anybody of equal capacity to put in his place'; when a totally unknown deputy of the Bavarian People's Party made a clever speech 'he was at once put forward as a possible candidate' for the chancellorship. D'Abernon believed that General von Seeckt would 'continue to act as the principal controlling authority'.[81] As he possessed semi-dictatorial powers under the state of emergency and as the Bavarian crisis had been settled by the failure of the Hitler Putsch, there was no room for the establishment of a dictatorship, military or otherwise. Within a few days a successor to Stresemann was found in the person of the leader of the Centre Party, Wilhelm Marx, who formed a bourgeois government. Stresemann described Marx to D'Abernon as 'a very worthy man', a strong Catholic and learned judge, but completely ignorant in financial and economic matters and 'rather parades his ignorance of them'. Stresemann apparently had no intention of seeking support either from the Nationalists or the Social Democrats whom he regarded as weak and hesitant; yet no government could have a parliamentary majority without the support of either party.[82]

The vast inflation, the passive resistance and the French counter-measures had produced social distress on a scale hitherto unknown. Already in the summer of 1923 the Food Committee of the Rhineland High Commission recorded deficiencies, chiefly in potatoes (which 'have become a luxury') and fats for which the occupied area depended on other German districts. As the causes of the critical situation it listed: the lack of confidence in the mark and the unsatisfactory distribution of the food available because the inhabitants did not use the trains run by the French Régie; the German representatives feared that the situation would become critical after mid-September.[83] In December the Foreign Office, apparently urged by British public opinion, enquired about the relief of destitution in Germany and received a rather shattering reply from the embassy. About one-fifth to one-sixth of the population of Berlin was suffering distress, and the percentage was likely to increase. The *Berliner Tageblatt* (a well known liberal daily) was collecting subscriptions to relieve hunger, but in one month had only been able to collect about 15,000 of the new *Rentenmark* or about £750; the committee of the stock exchange contributed two tons of dried peas for distribution among needy doctors and their families, and these were the only 'acts of charity by the rich of Berlin towards their unfortunate brethren'. In certain parts of the city the Salvation Army was feeding about a thousand people, but its funds came mainly from British and American sources. 'Neither Stinnes, nor Krupp, nor any of the big industrialists or bankers or business men, appear ever to have contributed more than infinitesimal sums for the relief of distress.' Apart from much misery, 'there is also much vulgar ostentation and luxury and it can easily be understood that a superficial observer should leave the country with the legitimate impression that everybody is a millionaire.'[84]

In January 1924 *The Times* carried an appeal for relief in Germany which was signed by several bishops of the Anglican Church, the Chief Rabbi, and many left-wing or liberal politicians and writers, such as Asquith, Margaret Bondfield, Lady Bonham Carter, Arthur Henderson, Maynard Keynes, Ramsay MacDonald, Lord Parmoor, General Smuts and H.G. Wells.[85] In the autumn of 1923 Lady D'Abernon noted 'the distressing spectacle of gentlefolk timidly stretching out their hands and asking for help', as well as the envious glares of hatred from the poor at people who were warmly clad and well shod.[86] The British embassy's critical assessment of the callousness of the German well-to-do received striking confirmation from a different quarter. Early in

1924 the Pope sent a dignitary of the Holy See to Munich to hand over relief funds, and on his return the British minister to the Vatican asked him for his impressions. He was told 'that the rich are totally disregarding the needs of their poorer brethren'; the Nuncio in Munich 'was dismayed at the utter callousness displayed by opulent Germans towards the suffering of their own countrymen'; they would not 'dig into their own pockets even for the most paltry sums' but would spend money 'with more than pre-war profusion' during the Carnival as well as on holidays in Italy and Switzerland, and rather cynically they preferred aid to be dispensed from papal funds.[87]

During the autumn and winter of 1923 there was widespread looting and plundering from fields and shops all over the country, as noted in a French communiqué as early as August. With the end of passive resistance the large subsidies paid to the Ruhr industrialists came to an end and in October large scale dismissals of workers began. The industrialists declared they could neither sell their goods nor pay their employees.[88] According to a report by Kilmarnock, the local German authorities feared that the workers would be unable to exist on their unemployment relief, could not buy coal or potatoes for the winter and would take the law into their own hands; but he did not expect any serious trouble in the Rhineland itself where people were only too relieved to be spared the restrictions of life existing in the Ruhr.[89] At the end of October the British consul at Cologne wrote of 'wholesale plundering and disorders in many parts of the Ruhr'; shops and depots were looted and the small police forces were unable to prevent it; at Düsseldorf the number of unemployed had risen within 10 days from 25,000 to nearly 100,000 and the streets were crowded with idle men; people armed with stones invaded the fashionable shopping area and smashed the windows of all the great stores.[90] At the beginning of November Lord D'Abernon reported from Berlin widespread looting of food shops in the poorer districts and added rather ominously that the 'movement has assumed a strongly anti-semitic character'; the authorities had prohibited anti-semitic meetings called by the extreme Right.[91]

In November such reports multiplied. At Düsseldorf the food supply was described as precarious because the farmers would not sell against paper marks; flour, meat and butter were lacking, but the potato shortage had been overcome thanks to imports from Holland; the trade unions had formed a committee to control the prices.[92] From Cologne the British consul wrote that practically the entire working class was unemployed; the Tyssen works at Mülheim had dismissed all their employees; unemployment relief amounted to about one billion paper marks per week – an amount insufficient to feed a family even for one day; the dealers were reluctant to keep stocks 'in view of the probability of their being looted by hungry crowds or lawless bands'.[93] In the Ruhr, according to another report, there was complete industrial stagnation. The workers no longer attended at the works because the payments in support of passive resistance which depended on attendance during working hours had come to an end. The 'dole' was 'totally inadequate to provide even bare subsistence'. The local authorities had no funds to pay benefits if the central government could no longer help them, and in December the situation of the population was likely to become desperate.[94] At the end of November it was reported from Cologne that there was increased looting at Düsseldorf, Essen, Gelsenkirchen and other towns of the Ruhr; the unruly crowds were led by Communists many of whom were armed, and frequent fights occurred with the police; the unrest spread to Cologne and the outlying country areas, again with Communist backing; it was difficult to see how the people could be fed as the shopkeepers were reluctant to lay in stocks. In Cologne gangs of unemployed smashed shop windows, overturned loaded vehicles and organized raids on fields of the neighbourhood. In Düsseldorf the looting of shops and vehicles 'was a daily occurrence'.[95]

The Rhineland High Commission was informed that demonstrations of the unemployed took place almost every day and became more and more threatening. In Wald the mayor was only able to retain his authority by conceding the demands of the 'Unemployed Councils', but then the government stopped his supply of money. When additional demands of the 'Councils' were refused the men demonstrated in front of the town hall, forced their way into the building and demanded that the employers must be brought there to negotiate. In Gräfrath the town hall was attacked and damaged by crowds of demonstrators. In Eller the unemployed put up barricades which they defended with light machine guns. In Ohligs a crowd armed with heavy sticks and stones attacked the police who defended the town hall; they were forced to fire, two people were killed and more wounded. In Hilden, although an issue of food was arranged through negotiations, the crowd besieged the police in the town hall while others plundered and wrecked the main shops. Everywhere the police found it very difficult to maintain order and drive back the bands of looters which spread out from Düsseldorf into near-by districts. The police officers were convinced that the riots were inspired and organized by Communists.[96] In December, however, the unrest somewhat subsided although Düsseldorf was still 'in a state of extreme unrest'. Some factories reopened and unemployment began to decline.[97]

The conditions prevailing in Germany favoured the growth of the Communist movement, and in the end a kind of 'revolutionary situation' was created although this seemed to favour the extreme Right rather than the extreme Left. In July an Intelligence report stated that the prospects of a successful Communist uprising were 'very unfavourable', with the only exeption of Saxony, and that this was realized by 'the responsible leaders in Moscow and Berlin'. But, the report continued, the left extremists of the KPD were making vigorous propaganda for immediate action in defiance of their leaders and of the Communist International; in early May the effect of these breaches of discipline was considered so serious by the latter that it summoned representatives of the extremists to Moscow and pressed them to carry out its orders;. but the damage was already done, for in the same month strikes and violent disturbances broke out in the Ruhr, 'initiated by individual Communist malcontents who, together with the Syndicalists, stirred up the unemployed'. But the local Communists were quickly rebuked by the KPD leaders for playing into the hands of the French and the German reactionaries and were ordered to abstain from violence. Karl Radek, however, who had allegedly visited the Ruhr, recommended that a rising should be authorized as the moment was propitious and the French would not intervene. But this was not accepted, and for the time being the Comintern adhered to its waiting policy. The KPD had some success in forming 'Proletarian Hundreds' (which often were more radical than the party leaders), but the internal discussions 'have continued to militate against a successful general rising'.[98] Apart from the doubtful information about Radek, the report was quite accurate: throughout 1923 internal differences were hampering any decisive action by the KPD, and the frequent changes of tactics by the leaders of the Comintern did not contribute to any unity of

action. In July Lord D'Abernon mentioned Communist disturbances in Breslau and Frankfurt which created 'considerable
uneasiness in Berlin'; there and elsewhere the KPD organized
mass meetings on Sunday 29 June, and the authorities took firm
measures to prevent trouble. In Berlin 12 meetings were held in
closed halls which passed without incident, and small meetings
took place in other towns. In Leipzig about 10,000 demonstrated
in the open air and about 5,000 in Dresden; all passed quietly. In
the ambassador's opinion, the danger did not lie in the strength
of the Communists but in the excuse any rioting would offer the
extremists of the Right and the reactionaries to intervene
actively.[99]

Saxony indeed was the Communist stronghold. But a War
Office report of July exaggerated considerably by stating that
'the government . . . is in fact Communist', for it was left-wing
Social Democrat. The report continued even more unlikelily
that the police were allegedly converted to Communist views,
that 'Proletarian Hundreds' were formed under police auspices,
ostensibly to assist the regular force, and that generals of the
former army who tried to attend commemorative parades of
ex-servicemen were threatened with violence. Saxony 'thus
forms a suitable hatching ground for Bolshevik propaganda.'[100]
Nor was the War Office any better informed about south
Germany, for the same report lumped together Baden and
Württemberg with Bavaria as 'dominated by the reactionary
policy of Hitler and Ludendorf' (sic). This was perhaps true of
Bavaria but not of the two other states. From Berlin Addison
wrote in a private letter in September somewhat more accurately
that in Saxony bands of hundreds of men on bicycles roamed the
country districts in search of food; the police were powerless,
and the chief of police was reported to attend Communist meetings and to encourage the workers to revolutionary action.[101] In
August new strikes occurred in the Ruhr and in and around
Dortmund conditions were critical. According to the British
consul in Cologne, at the Union works the workers assembled in
front of the director's office armed with steel bars and demanded
food and higher wages; they were only pacified by the promise
of cheap food. Similar scenes took place at the Hoesch iron and
steel works. At the Phoenix works at Hörde the workmen erected
a gallows and threatened to hang the directors, who had to leave
surreptitiously, but again a promise of cheap food pacified the
crowd.[102] Strikes and labour riots occurred all over Germany in

August, but a general strike called by the Communists failed to such an extent that the slogan was formally withdrawn by them, as Lord D'Abernon wired from Berlin.[103]

In Moscow opinion continued to be divided as to the imminence of the German revolution. At the end of August the head of the British commercial mission reported a curious incident. At a meeting of the Petrograd Soviet a member of the Central Committee of the KPD, Erwin Hörnle, made a speech which stressed the imminence of the German revolution and the support it would receive from the Soviet Union. He was followed by Zinoviev, the president of the Comintern, who declared, according to a newspaper report: 'The German revolution may occur not in a year, but in the course of a few months, or even weeks. The axis of the world's movement has recently been the grandiose events in Germany, and the workers of Petrograd, as well as all workers of the USSR should be prepared with the same readiness to die for the German revolution, protecting it, as in the case of our revolution.' But on the following day the same paper attributed these sentences to an 'unfortunate mistake': according to additional information 'it appears that Comrade Zinoviev did not call upon the workers of Russia to support the German revolution. Comrade Zinoviev made no statement that the German revolution would occur in a few weeks; he only maintained, in his speech, that in the event of obstinacy on the part of the German bourgeoisie the revolution may become inevitable.'[104] Thus the president of the Comintern found himself 'corrected'. Apparently, the German revolution was not just around the corner, and no support from the workers of Petrograd was called for.

When passive resistance was called off in September the Communists of Essen and other Ruhr towns called a general strike in protest against the 'treachery' of the Stresemann government and organized large demonstrations in support of a strike. But this again was a failure and in Cologne it was 'a complete failure'.[105] So was the attempt to win over the trade unions of the Ruhr to a strike against the reduction of wages and of unemployment relief which was made in October, for the unions rejected the proposal and tried instead to negotiate with the employers.[106] But meanwhile the Comintern dramatically changed its policy for Germany and ordered the German party districts to prepare for an uprising; the 'German October' was believed to be at hand, and Soviet military experts were sent to

Germany to assist its birth. Yet the only place where serious unrest occurred – and that apparently through the sending of the wrong communication – was Hamburg where heavy fighting broke out on 23 October. As the British consul reported on the next day, the disturbances were continuing there; especially in the district of Barmbeck there was serious fighting, the pavement was torn up, barricades were built, trees felled and trenches dug. Work at the port was at a standstill. Two days later, however, he wrote that order was more or less restored. About 200 to 300 Communists were taken prisoner by the police who had lost about 20 of their number, while the Communist casualties were much higher (the consul considered the published figures unreliable). Yet the police succeeded in quelling the rising without any help from the army.[107] As the attempt remained completely isolated there was to be no 'German October'. In late November Lady D'Abernon was told by the Undersecretary of State in the *Auswärtige Amt*, Maltzan, that many thousands of Communists had congregated in the centre of Berlin and built barricades; when they threatened to attack the police the latter forced the barricades, opened fire and dispersed the crowd, many of whom were killed; but nothing of all this was allowed to be reported in the censored press.[108] By that time, according to the British military, the political tension in Saxony had abated considerably. The Reichswehr had deposed the left-wing governments of Saxony and Thuringia and removed the Communists from them. The report noted that this had been done very quietly and 'that the Reichswehr have been behaving very reasonably.[109] In truth, by the end of the year there was no longer any Communist danger in Germany as the economic situation began to improve.

When strikes occurred among the municipal employees of Cologne in May and June, the British military authorities simply arrested the strike leaders and applied to the Rhineland High Commission for their deportation from the occupied area as 'dangerous agitators', and this was carried out.[110] In November the workers employed in printing paper money in Cologne struck for higher wages. With the precipitate fall of the mark there was an acute shortage of bank notes, and the British High Commissioner feared that this might 'bring about disorders and endanger the safety of the Army'. The continuation of the strike was therefore prohibited by the High Commission.[111] Early in 1924 there were more strikes in the industrial area, but the employers refused to make any concession to the workers and the strike slowly petered out. As the employers suffered from lack of orders they felt in a strong position.[112] Clearly, the time was not propitious for any militant working-class action. High unemployment and economic crisis drove the unions onto the defensive, and the employers were able to enforce their demands.

These concerned above all the abolition of the eight-hour day which had been legalized by the revolution of 1918, and a return to the ten-hour day. The legal basis for this was provided by a government decree of 21 December which permitted deviations from the principle of the eight-hour day. In early November a confidential British memorandum stated that the industrialists of the Ruhr were determined 'to exploit the present situation to the fullest possible extent to regain' their authority and to impose the ten-hour day as a condition of resuming work: 'it would seem that the industrialists will be able to secure by force majeure the acceptance of their terms', even if this should postpone the resumption of work (after the end of passive resistance).[114] The commercial secretary of the Berlin embassy wrote in October it was safe to assume that the industrialists were 'on almost every point in opposition to the German Government'; they distrusted it because it was 'a Government of the Left; they wish to abolish the existing labour legislation; they have no faith in the capacity of the Government to re-establish any kind of financial and economic order.' They thus preferred to negotiate directly with the French so as to 'make a better bargain for themselves than their Government would ever make for them'. They demanded a day of eight and a half hours for the miners and of ten hours for other workers; the Ruhr magnates desired 'to be invested with sovereign power'.[115] At that time the government was that of Stresemann which was by no means 'a Government of the Left' but in which the SPD was represented by three ministers.

On 8 November, according to a French communiqué, 87 members of the employers' association met in Düsseldorf and decided to establish the ten-hour day and to 'stabilize' wages. One speaker declared that there was a danger of a strike, 'but no resumption of work can take place until the ten-hour day has been accepted'. Yet the unions were determined to oppose the move. In Bochum, the workers of the Bochumer Verein forced their way into the factory and demanded payment of unemployment relief; in

Hattingen, the management proposed the resumption of work – on the basis of the ten-hour day. In Duisburg and Essen, all emergency work was stopped. The miners of the Constantin mine in Bochum threatened to stop work when they were told that their underground shift had been extended to eight and a half hours; in Wanne thousands of unemployed pillaged the offices of the 'Unser Fritz' mine.[116] Early in 1924 the decision of the German government to reintroduce a ten-hour day on the railways caused much indignation among the railwaymen and 60 per cent of them voted in favour of a strike; but the principal railway districts – Erfurt, Halle, Hamburg and Magdeburg – voted against. In the Rhineland not much opposition from the railwaymen was expected once the change had been approved by the Rhineland High Commission.[117] The commercial secretary of the consulate in Cologne noted that the coal owners of the Ruhr were able to make increased deliveries of coal to France on reparation account without suffering financial loss, on the basis of 'increased hours and low wages'. In the spring of 1924 the wages were calculated to have 70 per cent of the purchasing power of pre-war wages, while the coal price was 170 to 190 per cent above the pre-war level. A demand of the miners union for a wage increase of 30 per cent was rejected by the mine owners; their position was secure because they were reimbursed by the government for deliveries on reparation account.[118]

That the employers in 1923 felt in a much stronger position also emerged in East Prussia in August when 'they threw down the glove by locking out all dock labourers and refusing to readmit one at any wage until the whole union gives way and accepts terms', as the British vice-consul reported from Königsberg. Voluntary labour was recruited to load and unload cargoes and the university students took a prominent part in this work. But the crux of the matter was the attitude of the numerous small officials, such as postmen and policemen: 'if these remain unshaken the workingmen in East Prussia will be beaten.'[119] The attitude of the small officials was never in serious doubt, especially in a province so permeated by nationalist sentiment, where it was feared that France was hatching a scheme 'to assist Poland to annex East Prussia' in case of a German collapse, as it was put in the report.

That the university students formed the core of the extreme Right in many towns of Germany was pointed out in a secret military report on a conference of the '*Hochschulring deutscher*

Art' which was held in Göttingen in October. The conference was addressed by an officer of the Ehrhardt Brigade who severely criticized the measures taken by the Prussian government against the *völkisch* movement and urged those present to step up the propaganda for it. He also mentioned his good connections to the military district commands; all students should take advantage of the army's training courses for short-term volunteers and they should buy arms.[120] The Army of the Rhine reported on the activities of the former Lieutenant Rossbach who – in spite of all prohibitions – was able to hold meetings in several towns and was 'collecting all the extreme reactionary elements of the Italian and Bavarian type' in north Germany.[121] In March the British embassy commented on the founding of a new *völkisch* party, the *'Deutsch Völkische Freiheitspartei'* by three men who had seceded from the Nationalist party, Henning, von Gräfe and Wulle: they 'soon gathered to the fold the most rabid ultra-nationalist and anti-semitic hotheads in Prussia, as well as a number of ex-army officers of the Rossbach type.' The party's programme included the 'rejection of the policy of fulfilment and readiness to bear the consequences thereof'; but the report attached no 'great importance to the Extreme movement', especially as the new party was soon suppressed by the Prussian authorities.[122] Reports from the embassy in October, however, pointed to the 'enthusiasm and energy ... to be found in the ranks of those who represent reaction' and to the fact that the Right was armed while the Left was not. It was a 'patent fact that opinion is moving towards a strong government and that it is not impossible that counter revolution will occur before there is any revolution to suppress.'[123] The right-wing trend also showed itself in the support which reactionary circles in Brandenburg and Pomerania were willing to extend to the 'Bavarian action' of November, but it was not said whether this referred to action planned by the Bavarian government or by Hitler.[124]

Violent nationalism manifested itself in noisy demonstrations against France and in violent incidents affecting officers of the Military Control Commission. In Königsberg in January the officers were virtually besieged in their hotel and had to be rescued with difficulty by the police. In Erfurt two French officers were unable to carry out an inspection and were met by hostile demonstrators; 'they finally escaped without injury but after very disagreeable experiences.'[125] In June Addison reported from Berlin: 'that no French or Belgian officer can put his nose into any shop in order to make a purchase, far less into any industrial establishment in order to carry out duties of an inquisitorial nature, without immediate risk to life and limb. This is a situation which the German Government cannot control. The more they warn the people beforehand, the greater the risk of an incident.'[126] In discussing the lack of support for the Republic Addison also mentioned anti-Semitism as well as 'the preponderant power now possessed by the Jews in this country': 'They have penetrated everywhere. They appear to own everything, and, in fact, do own most things, and their vulgar ostentation in these times of general distress and their pushing assumption of power, combined with the corrupting influence which they are supposed to exercise on the needy politicians, who mostly represent advanced opinion, are another cause of discontent with the republican form of government.'[127] Curiously enough, this was not given as an opinion expressed by Addison's German acquaintances but as his own. Some weeks later Lord D'Abernon also noted: 'Jewish influence is great and increasing, so that their hostility is not to be despised. . . . It is remarkable that, amongst Jews, there is little evidence of gratitude for the relatively generous attitude of England towards their race as shown in the absence of anti-Semitism in England, nor is there the smallest recognition of our policy with regard to Zionism. They prefer Paris, where they have been maltreated both before and after the Dreyfus trial, and Germany, where before the war no Jew could become an officer, to England, where they have long had equal rights.'[128] As examples of the alleged anti-British attitude of the Berlin Jews he mentioned Rathenau and Deutsch of the AEG electrical concern and two journalists, but made an honourable exception of Theodor Wolff of the *Berliner Tageblatt*. It seems, however, that the ambassador confused the veneration which many Jews had for French culture and literature with their political attitude, which in the year 1923 was very markedly anti-French as was that of most Germans. In the following year D'Abernon attributed the anti-British bias 'of the average Jewish writer' to the fact that 'we are too austere and anti-intellectual', or alternatively 'to a subversive and nihilistic tendency to [sic] Judaism which is hostile to sober authority and out of sympathy with the success derived from what is usually termed "character".' He remained convinced that 'speaking broadly, the German Jew is Francophile. He regards Paris as the real centre of world civilization. . . . He

155

has more sympathy with French literature and French standards of art than he has with those of the Anglo-Saxon world.'[128] It should be added that, after all, modern Germany had received many of her institutions and inspirations from the hands of Napoleon and that French, not English, was the first modern language taught in most German secondary schools – it was only replaced by English after the Second World War.

Yet among some of the British diplomats a much more strident anti-Semitism existed. In 1920 the British Consul-General in Zürich, E.B. Maxse, sent in a report on the 'International Jewish Clique' which stated: 'There is a club at Berlin which is locally known as the Bolshevic Jewish Millionaire Club. One of the supporters is the publisher [Bruno] Cassirer who is an exceedingly rich man. In past years he made his money by exploiting young literary talent by sweating rates of payment. At present he and the leading men of this club are, I am informed, busily engaged in forming suitable Bolshevic propaganda agents' [sic]. To the consul it appeared 'that the real brain and leaders of the Bolshevist movement in all countries are either Jews or of Jewish descent'; he added that in educated circles the belief was growing 'that the Jewish movement has for final object the destruction of the present civilization based on Christianity and its replacing by a Jewish oligarchy ruling subject races by force and terror.'[129] The consul might not have read *The Protocols of the Elders of Zion*, but his informants certainly had. In the same year the Consul-General at Frankfurt, Cecil Gosling, sent a report which closely reflected German anti-semitic propaganda. He claimed that 'a very considerable number of Jews successfully evaded being sent to the front and obtained safe employment beyond the reach of shot or shell'. From 1917 onwards, he alleged, the Jews 'secretly encouraged' the incipient revolt in the German army and navy; when the revolution broke out and the mob started plundering, 'no Jewish house was intentionally interfered with, though these offered by far the richest prospect of loot' (in truth, the amount of looting in the revolution of 1918 was incredibly small). 'From this time onward', Gosling continued, 'the scum of Jews in Germany devoted itself wholly and entirely to the task of amassing more and more wealth. . . . I have already referred to the *Frankfurter Zeitung*. That daily, at the moment of the armistice, was openly and frankly bolshevist in its sentiments. It had more than one Communist on its staff of leader writers and did all in its power to inflame the masses and to fan the flames of class hatred.' Gosling also observed that the Germans in Frankfurt stayed at home after their work 'in their often cheerless and unheated homes and their place is taken abroad by the vulgar be-jewelled and overdressed Hebrew and his women, who with a lack of prudence unusual in so cautious a race, display their opulence in the choice of the largest and noisiest motor cars and, in the restaurants, in the choice of the costliest dishes and the rarest and most expensive vintages.' Yet, 'when the star of bolshevism appeared to be in the ascendant, they were fully prepared, if necessary, to take a leading part in the adoption of its principles in Germany.'[130] No German anti-Semite could have put it more forcefully.

The report was refuted in a long minute by an official of the Central Department of the Foreign Office, George Saunders. 'This despatch', he wrote, 'seems to me to represent mainly the views of militarists, reactionaries and antisemites.' He thought that the German Jews, like those of other countries, tended to exaggerate 'most of the faults and some of the virtues of the nation of which they form a part'; in the German Empire, 'Jews were often more extravagant in their views of world-policy than Imperialists of pure German or mixed Prussian blood.' There was a larger percentage of clever people among the Jews than among the rest of the population and in this they were like the French Protestants who, small in numbers, exercized a very strong influence in the administration, in commerce and the press, and in public life in general. Among the supporters of the pre-war SPD there were only two wealthy Jews, Professor Arons and Paul Singer, a clothing manufacturer. 'I have not learned that there are or were many, or any, rich Jews among the backers of German Communism. . . . The vast majority of moderately well-off Jews belong to the bourgeois Democratic Party, which was in the cold shade of hopeless opposition' under the Emperor William II. As to the *Frankfurter Zeitung*, it did not deserve Gosling's strictures: as he, Saunders, had read it for 30 years or more, 'I should not say that it takes a specifically Semitic view of affairs. On the contrary, it is at present, perhaps, the best mirror of average educated German opinion among the business classes. It no doubt resents attacks upon the Jewish race, just as many Americans of English origin resent attacks upon the English race and English institutions.

Cet animal est très méchant,
Quand on l'attaque, il se défend.'[131]

157

It was a well informed and intelligent refutation. But no question was asked from what murky sources the consul obtained his information, nor is there any evidence that the Foreign Office replied to his report.

In the occupied Rhineland German nationalism was particularly virulent when directed against those who were Separatists and supported the plan of an autonomous Rhenish Republic. They were considered traitors and became the victims of murderous attacks. In March 1923 an attempt was made on the life of the Separatist leader Smeets in Cologne. He was badly wounded and his brother-in-law was killed. Smeets was rushed to hospital and attended by the best available specialist sent there by the mayor, Dr Adenauer. The Rhineland High Commission immediately ordered the suspension of the Cologne chief of police and announced that it intended to dismiss him 'should he fail to make satisfactory reply to the charge of grave negligence in the exercize of his duties' on account of the ease with which the crime was committed and the escape of the culprit. But the British Deputy Commissioner at Cologne countered that the police had taken all reasonable precautions to guard Smeets; he did not think that any police force could have prevented the entry into Smeets' house of someone who had studied the situation and planned the attempt. He added: 'I have nothing but praise for the action taken by the Police President and his officials after the commission of the crime', and he strongly recommended to let the German authorities proceed with their investigations – an opinion with which the British general in command of the Rhine Army fully concurred.[132] But it took nearly six months before the alleged murderers were arrested in Cologne.[133]

In June 1923 Adenauer had a long discussion with a British official about the possibility of the Rhineland forming a separate federal state within Germany. He began by stating that the whole course of the occupation made the realization of this idea much more difficult: owing to the French actions he and other influential men had completely withdrawn from a project which they had supported in the early days of the occupation. Adenauer continued that, if Germany were in a strong position, he would have nothing to do with the plan, but Germany's position was now desperate and daily getting worse; a grave danger existed that the end would be disintegration and Germany would be divided into two, three or even more independent states – a contingency that would represent a grave threat to the future of these states and to the peace of Europe. Without going deeply into the question, he was therefore at first sight prepared to support the idea if it provided a real solution of the present difficulties; but it could not be put forward as an order or as a suggestion coming from France. An order no German could accept, and a suggestion would be received with such suspicion that it would be turned down at once, without being discussed seriously. If the present German government publicly brought forward such a scheme it would fall; the next government was likely to be a Socialist one, and the Socialists were more strongly opposed to the plan than any other German party. The only way he could suggest was that it should be put forward by the British government, purely on its own merits, without any promise of advantages such as a reduction of reparation payments, otherwise the Rhinelanders would think they were being sold and the opposition would grow. Adenauer promised to think it over. The same official also discussed the matter with other prominent Germans, and 'on the whole the idea has not been unfavourably received.' A Reichstag deputy, a bitter opponent of the Separatists, thought it was an excellent suggestion. The official thought that the majority of the Rhinelanders were in favour of separation from Prussia (not from Germany), but the urban working classes were against it, for the SPD was strong in Prussia but weak in the Catholic Rhineland; thus its power on the Rhine would be reduced as soon as the Rhineland became independent of Prussia. Many Germans, however, feared that, as soon as the Rhineland separated from Prussia, Hanover would follow suit, and possibly other provinces too; what was left of Prussia might then become Bolshevist; such assertions could be heard frequently.[134]

In November 1923 the same British official reported that the anti-Prussian feelings in the Rhineland, always latent, began to assert themselves when it became clear that passive resistance had failed; it was felt that the Berlin government 'neither knew nor took steps to know the difficulties which faced the population, and did not give the help which might have been given.' The Rhinelanders were first German, secondly Rhinelanders, and only thirdly Prussian; 'but what is perhaps more important is that they are anti-French and terrified at the prospect of being annexed by France or of falling under the control of the French.' They knew that the Separatist movement was supported by

France and refused all collaboration with it.[135] At Coblenz Tirard, the President of the Rhineland High Commission, was negotiating with Adenauer and other leading Germans from the Rhineland about the formation of a new German federal state. According to the British Commissioner at Cologne, Adenauer's opinion was that it was useless for the French to demand a federal state, separated from Germany by a customs barrier and with its own currency and budget, for such a state could not possibly support the burden of the armies of occupation; even a constitutionally created federal state would only be viable if the Allies made concessions which substantially reduced the cost of occupation, and the issue could not be considered separately from the reparations question as a whole. Thus there seemed little prospect of progress in the discussions at Coblenz.[136]

In late October 1923 the Separatists acted; a Rhenish Republic was proclaimed at Coblenz and elsewhere 'by comparatively small bodies of men, majority of which [sic] belong to the lowest classes of the population', as the Acting British High Commissioner wired to London; in Coblenz the action was undertaken 'by at most 400 Separatists'. This was made possible by the apathy of the people, caused 'by feeling of despair present in all minds in regard to hopeless outlook for the future, dissatisfaction with Berlin . . . and misery into which the country has fallen'; people were convinced that the French were behind the movement and that it was hopeless to fight against it. But there was little enthusiasm for the Separatist cause, 'except possibly in country districts: to say Separatist movement is at present spontaneous would be wide of the mark.'[137] From Cologne the British consul reported that the Separatists would be speedily suppressed by the opposition of the population but they were clearly supported by the forces of the Belgians and the French; they were arming the Separatists and conveying them from town to town by lorries or trains; they were 'drawn from lowest depths of population', and the general public 'will never willingly endure them'. Their advent to power 'under allied bayonets' could only aggravate the desperate economic situation. If the French and Belgians could be persuaded to adopt an attitude of neutrality, the 'movement would obviously collapse'.[138] Another British official wrote from Cologne he could not find words to describe the gravity of the situation; in nearly all the towns of the French zone Separatist bands had occupied the public buildings and were protected there by French troops and tanks; among the mass of the people there existed 'a bitterness so intense that they would literally rather die than live under a Government of such description'. In the industrial areas there were hundreds of thousands of practically starving unemployed and hunger riots were to be expected. To this should be added 'the administrative chaos which must result from the setting aside of all regular administration, and the hatred and bitterness which the events of the past two days have called forth'. The dire warning given by Dr Adenauer and the secretaries of the Rhenish trade unions must be taken seriously; every effort must be made to persuade the French government 'to replace with as little delay as possible the band of adventurers now ensconced in the public buildings of the Rhineland by the responsible and accepted leaders of the Rhineland population.'[139] The French High Commissioner at Coblenz, Tirard, however, declared that, until further notice, he regarded the partisans of the Rhineland party as the *de facto* authority in those places where they had seized the public services and as responsible for the maintenance of law and order.[140]

At the beginning of November the Central Department of the Foreign Office summed up the situation. The Rhenish Republic had been proclaimed 'by a group of political adventurers under French influence', but without any 'real support whatever from the local inhabitants'; the French and Belgian authorities refused permission to the German police 'to resist the usurpers and in many cases actually permitted the latter to carry arms and to issue orders in complete violation of the provisions of the Rhineland agreement'. The British representatives in Paris, Brussels and Rome were instructed to make it clear to the government to which they were accredited that the British government 'would view any attempt to set up separate states independent of the Reich' with 'extreme dissatisfaction'.[141] In its opinion, as Curzon emphasized at the Imperial Conference at the end of October, a dismemberment of the Reich 'would materially affect the status of Germany as a contracting party to the treaty' of Versailles, so that in certain important aspects it would automatically cease to operate and would require complete revision. No such independent states should be recognized and no attempt to constitute them should be supported.[142] Lord Kilmarnock at Coblenz was instructed to press for the rearming of the German police and for the disarming by it of all unauthorized persons; it was contrary to the Rhineland Agreement that the 'provisional separatist administration' at Coblenz continued to issue decrees and enjoy armed support.[143] Lord D'Abernon informed the German government of the contents of the British note; even the autonomy of the Rhineland within Germany could only be recognized if it were established at the express wish of Germany. He added that Britain had taken this exceptional step because she had full confidence in the person of Stresemann and in his government and was convinced that the committee of experts would reach a satisfactory solution on the reparation issue and thus bring about a détente and more stable conditions in Europe.[144]

In early November Kilmarnock informed London that, thanks to French support, the Separatist movement had established itself; the Separatists were holding all the large towns and many smaller ones and country districts; the movement had received no support from any social group in the larger towns, but in some country areas 'the population appears to have accepted the change and joined the movement more or less spontaneously'.[145] The British consul at Cologne reported that the situation had become 'infinitely more dangerous' and that the events 'have fanned the feeling of the public to a white heat'. He had received a deputation from the town of Düren: its factories were closed, and no food came into the town; the armed Separatists, numbering about 2,000, were protected by Moroccan troops and were forcing the tradesmen to accept the worthless paper money they were printing; but the banks did not accept it and the shopkeepers could not use it or exchange it for a stable currency with which they could buy new stocks, so that people went hungry. In Kreuznach in the Palatinate too, the Separatists printed their own money 'in enormous quantities' and forced the local authorities to accept it; the branch of the German central bank had closed down and its staff left. In the Siebengebirge close to the Rhine villagers armed with axes fell upon the Separatists and killed some 30 whereupon the rest fled in panic.[146]

In mid-November Kilmarnock reported that the Separatists sent small bands of armed men into a town who then evicted the local authorities and replaced them by their own followers; the main body then returned to the base and repeated the same operation elsewhere; but it seemed that, even where they held power for some weeks, they exercized little influence on the administration which remained in the hands of the old officials, and did little more than to requisition food and money for their own use; with the possible exception of Trier, they had not managed to form an effective administration. In Trier there was more enthusiasm for Separatism and the Separatists were better organized and advised. In the Palatinate, too, the movement had taken a firmer hold and a section of the population was in favour of Separatism, including workers; this was due to the reactionary policy of Bavaria and its conflict with Berlin as well as the fear aroused by the Hitler Putsch: there 'the movement must be taken seriously'.[147] Four weeks later Kilmarnock wrote that he possessed considerable evidence that in the Rhine province the Separatist movement was coming to an end; in Bonn the Separatists had withdrawn from the public buildings and taken over a small house; they had evacuated several towns of the Palatinate such as Ludwigshafen, Frankenthal and Zweibrücken; they no longer made requisitions, and no recent complaints had been made about the issue of their money; the whole movement seemed to be nearing its end owing to quarrels between its leaders and lack of funds.[148] As it turned out, however, his view was only correct for the Rhine province which was part of Prussia, but not for the Palatinate which belonged to Bavaria.

Early in 1924 an 'Autonomous Government of the Palatinate' was proclaimed which requested the Rhineland High Commission to register its decrees. The French High Commissioner then proposed that this should be done but was opposed by the British High Commissioner because this would mean the recognition of the so-called 'government'. The Belgian High Commissioner was in favour of registering the decrees which would not imply a recognition of the 'government', and the proposal to do so was adopted by a majority vote.[149] Two days later Kilmarnock reported that, according to the French High Commissioner, 607 out of 650 communes of the Palatinate adhered to the movement and that police services were satisfactorily maintained either by the Separatist police or by the regular police acting under Separatist orders. He did not doubt that the movement was considerably more successful than it had been in the Rhineland, but equally that French support had to a large extent contributed to its success.[150] On 4 January the Foreign Office telegraphed to Lord Crewe, the British ambassador in Paris, that according to its information the movement in the Palatinate 'is an artifical product, which, but for outside coercive pressure, would have no continued existence'; in the opinion of the British government the declarations recognizing the government which were allegedly signed by numerous mayors were not made voluntarily, but were the 'deplorable result of the removal of normal police protection against violence and blackmail, and the systematic expulsion, or threatened expulsion, of the constituted authorities', carried out with the connivance of the French authorities. The ambassador was instructed to make 'personal representations of the strongest nature' to the French government.[151] In a further telegram to Paris it was pointed out 'that the alleged spontaneous movement in the Rhine Province proper in favour of separation had been purely fictitious'; there was no evidence to the contrary that the situation in the Palatinate was any different; it there was a genuine desire for local autonomy, why did it 'not follow the course made available by the terms of the German constitution'?[152]

The British government then proposed that its Consul-General in Munich, R.H. Clive, should visit the Palatinate officially and report on his findings. But the French government classified this course as 'incorrect' – an attitude which left the British 'frankly astonished' as they had 'long submitted without any protest to the visits and presence of numerous French officials in the zone of British occupation'. In an interview with Sir Eyre Crowe the French ambassador said that his government, 'out of regard for their prestige', could not allow the consul to make enquiries in the Palatinate in his official capacity but only as a private person, and that he would have to be accompanied by a French official. Crowe replied that this 'was no less unfriendly, and, in fact, insulting, and that it would be regarded by His Majesty's Government as clear evidence that the French authorities were afraid to let the truth be revealed', so as to 'prevent the consul-general from seeing and hearing things which the French authorities were determined to hide.' He threatened it might be found necessary to apply the same rule to the French officers in Cologne.[153] In Coblenz the British High Commissioner protested formally against the registration of the decrees of the so-called 'Autonomous Government' as being *ultra vires*.[154]

In spite of all French opposition, Clive's visit took place in January 1924; but before he went to the Palatinate he took the precaution of calling to Frankfurt about 30 people from the Palatinate – trade union officials, mayors, lawyers, industrialists, journalists and the heads of the Catholic and Protestant churches. He found that all were 'united in a common detestation of separatist movement' and he received 'abundant evidence of French support of movement'.[155] He spent five days in the Palatinate and interviewed 'people from every class and from every part'. On 18 January his conclusions were wired to London: that the 'overwhelming mass of population are opposed to autonomous government', that this 'could never have come into existence without French support', that both churches, the majority in the large towns and the official classes rejected the idea of separation from Bavaria, that a considerable section was indifferent to Bavaria but opposed to separation from Germany. Only among the peasantry and the socialist workers did he find a feeling 'in favour of Rhineland state including Palatinate, politically independent but economically bound to the Reich' because they feared the 'militarist policy of Berlin and Munich'; among these two social groups many just wanted 'peace at any price'.[156] After his return to Munich Clive received many letters complaining about persecution by the Separatists of people who had given evidence to him, in spite of a French guarantee that no action would be taken against them. Many were threatened with arrest, others had their property confiscated 'as a result of their plain speaking'.[157]

A few weeks after Clive's visit the Separatist movement in the Palatinate was terminated by a violent outbreak of German nationalism inspired and led from unoccupied Germany. In early February Clive reported that a 'state of anarchy' existed in Pirmasens, that the regular police had disappeared or been expelled, so that it was impossible to get the unemployment funds there, that the unemployed had formed an 'additional government siezing and requisitioning goods'. Some days later, after attempts to re-establish order had failed, fighting and serious disorders broke out and an attempt was made to storm the District Office in which the Separatists had established themselves. In Kaiserslautern too disorders occurred. Apparently the French were withdrawing their support and the nationalists were seeking revenge on the Separatists. The police summoned them to surrender and when they refused to do so opened fire; this was returned by the Separatists. When French troops appeared on the scene the crowd dispersed and began to plunder the houses and shops of known Separatists. In Pirmasens a large armed crowd finally succeeded in setting fire to the office occupied by the Separatists and 28 of them were burnt alive or otherwise killed.[158] A few days later Kilmarnock reported a decision taken by the Rhineland High Commission that the Separatists were to be disarmed and the German police to be rearmed so that they could maintain public order; the Separatists were to be dispersed. Their disarmament was carried out quickly, and the active Separatists were evacuated from the occupied area. It was assumed that many would enlist in the Foreign Legion or otherwise enter French service.[159] In March 1924 a special committee appointed by the High Commission found that peace reigned in the Palatinate. Order had been restored in Kaiserslautern and Pirmasens. Many of the former Separatists had returned to work and lived on good terms with their fellow-workers. But the pacification was endangered by the nationalist agitation in Baden and Bavaria, the attitude of the German press, the arrests carried out in unoccupied Germany, and the institution of a special 'Palatine Week' by the Bavarian government with its 'slogans of hate and excitement'.[160] That was the end of the Separatist movement: it too had aroused violent German nationalism and once more shown up the vital differences between French and British policy in Germany.

That Germany survived the year 1923 as one state was due partly to the revival of a strong nationalist sentiment – an integrating factor in spite of all local feeling in Bavaria – partly to Stresemann's skill in finding a way out of an apparently hopeless situation, partly to the (very belated) stabilization of the currency, and last but not least to the policy of the British government. Although it officially declined to be a mediator between France and Germany, it did in fact play a mediating part and time and again countered French actions which could have brought about a general catastrophe. Although the democratic Constitution was temporarily suspended on the basis of Article 48 and General von Seeckt established a kind of military dictatorship, the Constitution survived the year 1923. But it did not survive the next, even more severe, political and economic crisis.

V

GUSTAV STRESEMANN

In 1923 Stresemann was Germany's Chancellor for less than four months, but during that period of stress and deep crisis a close personal relationship developed between him and the British ambassador, to whom he often turned in times of trouble for help and advice, and could unburden himself and reveal his fears and apprehensions. In his turn Lord D'Abernon considered Stresemann 'the cleverest politician' among the German Chancellors he had got to know; 'if he has a defect, it is that he believes everything can be arranged by a certain amount of lobbying and a rousing speech.' What the ambassador found especially praiseworthy was Stresemann's determination to put the German finances in order and to stabilize the currency – a determination strengthened by British wishes. But he found it difficult to explain the violent attacks of the Right on Stresemann which accused him of being 'a mere catspaw of the Socialists' and of having been 'brought into office by the street'. One possible explanation of this bitter hostility D'Abernon found in the 'marked aversion' of the Right to taxation; 'they will attack any Government which effectively taxes them' – an attitude in which they were supported by certain big industrialists 'whose patriotism does not extend to voting their own taxation'.[1]

The bitter hostility of the Right persisted throughout the following years of gradual stabilization during which Stresemann, until his death in October 1929, remained the Foreign Minister, under three different chancellors and in ever-changing cabinets. In June 1924 the ambassador noted that the antipathy of the German Nationalist Party to Stresemann was 'bitter and persistent'; it was above all due to the belief that, without his influence over his own People's Party, the latter would have combined with the Nationalists; another reason was that Stresemann's wife was suspected of being Jewish (the Nationalists were strongly anti-semitic). Lord D'Abernon thought that they would even be willing to swallow the report of the experts on German reparations 'provided that Stresemann is sacrificed to them'.[2] A few days earlier he reported that the question most acutely dividing opinion was whether Stresemann should be dismissed as Foreign Minister; Stresemann himself was confident that he would be a member of any new government and the line of foreign policy would remain the same, but he was being attacked, or only very weakly defended, by his own party. The Nationalist Party meanwhile was putting forward the candidature of the former Grand-Admiral von Tirpitz for the post of Chancellor, without realising 'the deplorable impression this appointment would make abroad'; curiously enough, they had no confidence in Tirpitz, 'whom they have always considered a political trimmer, but they can discover in their own ranks no other name which carried weight.'[3] In May D'Abernon found Stresemann depressed 'by the ingratitude of various political parties, particularly his own', the People's Party. Stresemann was unpopular; 'he is regarded as arbitrary and not a sound party man, so most of the political leaders woud like to turn him out of office'. Yet in the ambassador's opinion Stresemann had rendered great services to Germany and her position had vastly improved within the past six months: 'the currency has been stabilized, the Experts have produced a workable scheme for Reparation, Poincaré has fallen, the Ruhr is about to be restored economically to Germany.' D'Abernon found Stresemann easy to deal with; he did not 'think that any change would be for the better' — an opinion that was shared by the French and American ambassadors in Berlin.[4]

Stresemann had a very uneasy relationship with the more conservative members of his own party, while the German Nationalists deeply distrusted his whole policy of détente and reconciliation with France. In the autumn of 1924 the People's Party promised the German Nationalists that they were to join the government — a bourgeois government under Chancellor Marx. Then Stresemann, according to a report from the British embassy, started a minor government crisis by insisting that the promise of his party must be honoured by the Cabinet, possibly with the intention of getting rid of Marx. The writer suspected that Stresemann saw himself 'as the great Chancellor of the Moderates leading Germany towards the ideals of strong government' and rather unfairly added: 'he only thinks of himself and all his actions are directed "ad majorem Stresemanni gloriam".'[5] Lord D'Abernon probably would have taken a more charitable view of Stresemann's motives. As Stresemann had started his political career on the Right and had been a strong advocate of annexations during the war, he felt always troubled by right-wing opposition and tried to 'tame' the Nationalists by bringing them into the government and making them share in political responsibility – without any conspicuous success. Marx only survived another three months and was then replaced as Chancellor by Dr Hans Luther, the former Minister of Finance; and four Nationalists joined the new government.

A few weeks later President Ebert died, and in April 1925 Field-Marshal Paul von Hindenburg was elected president with a very slight majority of only 900,000 votes over his rival Marx: a victory of the right-wing parties over the moderates, demonstrating the strength of nationalism and conservatism and the weakness of the republican forces. Soon after Lord D'Abernon found Stresemann 'rather troubled about political outlook'. Not that he feared any difficulties from the new president; he believed that he was not interested in political questions and would refuse to become the tool of the extreme Nationalists. When the latter tried 'to foist upon him a pronounced anti-democrat as president's secretary he turned them neck and crop out of his house saying that he intended to appoint Meissner who must be a most faithful servant of the State since he had contrived to work during five years with Ebert'. According to Hindenburg's friends, he did not want to listen to long speeches or lengthy explanations; he preferred a 'friendly cup' to long arguments and above all he did not want to be troubled and liked to go to bed early. But what Stresemann feared was that the German Nationalist Party, who had remained hostile to him and suspected him of opposition to Hindenburg's candidature, would take advantage of Hindenburg's success to challenge the whole policy of conciliation; they would accuse him of making concessions dangerous to Germany without any quid pro quo: 'What is the use of renouncing all title to Alsace Lorraine if in turn nothing is received?' Their principal ground of attack would be the security pact which the German government wished to conclude as part of its policy of reconciliation.[6]

The security pact, which became the Treaty of Locarno, was indeed a major aim of German foreign policy for which Stresemann and D'Abernon worked in unison. In March 1925 the latter wired to London: 'the public in Germany is at present unaware of far-reaching character of German communication. Strict secrecy has been observed. When text of this communication becomes public there will be a general surprise at boldness of policy indicated – a surprise which in many circles will be accompanied by resentment. The government will be in for heavy weather. The only line on which they can fight the question is broad basis of a regeneration of Europe through obliteration of war animosities and allaying of war alarms.' An official of the Central Department of the Foreign Office minuted that all of them would welcome a comprehensive pact which included Germany; but they had grave doubts whether this would be possible 'before the first stage of an Anglo-Franco-Belgian arrangement has been gone through'; there were signs, however, that Herriot, the French Prime Minister, 'is trying to educate his public opinion. It would be a disaster if Herriot were to fall just at this moment.'[7] In May 1924 the reactionary government of Poincaré had fallen and been replaced by that of Edouard Herriot which aimed at a general pacification. Thus the German initiative met with a favourable response in France. In Germany, too, the discussions were proceeding favourably. As D'Abernon informed London in March 1925, the discussions in the State Council (*Reichsrat*) had 'passed off smoothly' and the representatives of the federal states were for the pact. In the Foreign Affairs Committee of the Reichstag lively discussions took place and strong opposition came from the German Nationalists as well as the Communists; Russia would make 'a desperate endeavour to prevent Germany taking part in any western European combine'.[8] Sauerwein, the editor of *Le Matin*, who had strong anti-German views, went to Berlin in the spring to observe the presidential election. On his return he recorded 'a distinct feeling in Germany in the direction of a "rapprochement" towards France'; there should be an immediate reply to the German offer of a pact, for Stresemann could not wait much longer for a French answer.[9] In the Foreign Office it was noted that the value of the proposed pact was that it would 'prevent Germany from running amok in Europe again without once more rousing against her the whole moral opinion of the world'.[10]

But a dissentient voice came from the British minister in

Warsaw, Max Muller, who in a private letter doubted the value of the German renunciation of the use of force and her guarantee of the eastern frontiers of France and Belgium: 'do you really maintain that, after our experience in 1914, we are justified in considering that future generations in Germany would hold themselves bound by any such declaration? Surely the very fact that the Germans themselves draw a distinction between the Western and Eastern frontiers indicates a sneaking doubt in their minds as to the binding force of their promise with regard to the latter.' In his opinion, the real question was whether the German word could be trusted or not; he could not forget 'former instances of German perfidy, and the Poles have even more reason for remembering them.' He believed 'that the real object of the proposals is to pave the way for a revision of the Eastern frontiers', thus no doubt reflecting the apprehensions of his Polish hosts. A few months earlier the German minister in Warsaw had told him that the Germans would never accept the Polish Corridor: 'I must confess that I find it difficult not to regard this attitude of the Germans as natural and indeed inevitable.'[11] The regaining of the Polish Corridor certainly remained one of the principal aims of Stresemann's foreign policy: he was willing to accept as final Germany's frontiers in the west as drawn by the Treaty of Versailles, but not those in the east which should be revised – an attitude that was supported by nearly all political parties.

The Foreign Office, on the other hand, tried to impress upon the German government that it should not make the acceptance of the pact or the admission to the League of Nations dependent on conditions, such as the evacuation of the northern zone of the occupied Rhineland or the reduction of the armies of occupation. In September 1925 the Foreign Secretary, Austen Chamberlain, wired to Lord D'Abernon: 'Surely the German government should not at this stage indulge in such destructive tactics. They must realise that any controversial reply to the invitation [to attend a conference] might wreck prospect of verbal discussions for which they always protested their desire.' The ambassador replied he had already impressed upon Stresemann that the only sensible attitude was an acceptance without conditions; any points the Germans wished to raise should be reserved for verbal discussions; Stresemann fully realized this and intended to obtain authority from the cabinet to accept without any conditions; but he intended to state verbally that, in entering the

League, Germany was maintaining her position that she was not responsible for the outbreak of war in 1914. Such a declaration was considered 'most ill-timed' by the Foreign Office and 'likely to have most unfortunate effect'. Once more D'Abernon acted and then replied that the German government realized the 'soundness of policy indicated', but it was meeting 'obstinate resistance from nationalist organisations' which aimed at adding conditions to the German acceptance of the invitation and to limit severely the powers of the German delegates at the conference. On the next day, however, he was able to report that the Germans accepted without conditions and that Stresemann would only make a verbal declaration about the views of his government.[12] A few weeks later the conference of Locarno led to the conclusion of the well known treaty by which the contracting powers renounced the use of force, and guaranteed the maintenance of the *status quo* along Germany's western frontiers, as well as the demilitarization of the Rhineland.

On 17 October Chamberlain wired to D'Abernon from Locarno: 'To the German Government will belong the honour of having taken the initiative in the course of action which has led to the Treaty of Locarno. I am convinced that the agreements which have been initialled here will mark a turning point in the history of Europe and I trust that the friendly personal relations established between the British and German delegations are the sure tokens of the new relationship between our nations.'[13] But Stresemann's difficulties were by no means over. In late October D'Abernon wired to London that the discussions between the ministers and the party leaders and in the Foreign Affairs Committee had 'been at times very violent'; Luther and Stresemann had both lost their tempers, and the German Nationalist leader Count Westarp 'was acrimonious and critical'. His party adopted a resolution that it could not accept the treaty and the Nationalist ministers resigned from the government. Stresemann nevertheless reckoned with a large majority in favour of acceptance; the Social Democrats would vote for it, but 'they will not tolerate again a government with a large German National admixture.' From a secret source the ambassador heard that an 'influential section of Prussian nobility' was collecting signatures to a declaration approving the government's policy, endorsing the treaty and protesting against the action of the German Nationalists 'as injurious to German interests'. In the final debate in parliament D'Abernon noticed the moderation of the Nationalist leaders and their refusal to support an amendment put forward by the *völkisch* deputies asking the President to postpone his signature and hold a referendum on the issue. The veteran Communist leader Clara Zetkin delivered a violent speech and a tirade against Britain which she claimed had emerged victorious in the struggle for hegemony in Europe; as she had come straight from Moscow, this was apparently due to 'Moscow inspiration'. Even the German Nationalist papers accepted the result 'with moderation and almost good grace', and only a *völkisch* newspaper declared that it could not regard the treaty as binding.[14]

At the end of November Luther and Stresemann were able to travel to London to sign the treaty which marked a turning point in German foreign policy. It was ratified by the Reichstag with the large majority of 300 to 174, as Stresemann had anticipated. And Lord D'Abernon commented: 'they have to contend with unrestrained and unlimited party intrigue and party ambition.' In his opinion, the German Nationalists as well as the Social Democrats were subordinating solid gains for Germany 'to their thirst for political advantage', but the SPD had voted in favour. The Foreign Office too sharply criticized not Stresemann, but the German political parties and the German ministers. 'The attitude of the Nationalists', it wired to Berlin and Paris, 'makes more difficult the grant of the concessions for which we are prepared nor are we in any other way helped by the attitude of the other parties'; the Nationalists had repudiated the treaty; the Social Democrats were showing no courage or resolution in its support, and the German ministers 'open their mouths wider and wider, demanding the impossible'; they and their supporters 'use language incompatible with the spirit of Locarno, create the appearance of *marchandage* and give the impression of a condition or even an ultimatum.' This course was full of danger; the Germans could obtain rehabilitation in general opinion and the almost immediate evacuation of the northern zone of occupation, but their present course was endangering these prospects; they were also making 'things exceedingly difficult for Briand', the French Foreign Minister.[15] To Lord D'Abernon on the other hand, the principal gain of Locarno was that it 'puts an end to the war against Germany. It brings Germany into the European consortium of Western Powers, and finishes "the wicked disturber of the peace", "the aggressive militarist", and "the mad-dog" conception of the diplomatic position.' It also diminished 'the danger of her [Germany] being attracted into the Russian communistic orbit': France and Britain had accepted her as an equal.[16]

A few weeks after the signing of the Treaty of Locarno the debate was resumed over Germany's admission to the League of Nations. At the beginning of February 1926 Lord D'Abernon wired to London that Stresemann was 'elated at his success' in getting the Foreign Affairs Committee of the Reichstag to accept entry with a majority of 18 to eight; the majority was larger than he had expected because two smaller parties – the Bavarian People's Party and the Economic Party – voted in favour; the strenuous moves of the opposition to achieve a postponement were vigorously countered by Stresemann; if necessary, he declared, the committee would have to sit all night, but a clear decision must be reached. Another difficulty arose because Poland demanded to be treated on a par with Germany and to be made a permanent member of the Council of the League, a demand which was supported by France. But the British Cabinet decided that this would prevent or delay Germany's entry, that only great powers should be permanent members of the Council and that any further change of its composition should be discussed after the admission of Germany so that she could fully participate in it. A British compromise proposal to create an additional non-permanent seat which might then be given to Poland with the consent of the Locarno powers was considered by the German delegation. But in the end Chancellor Luther informed Chamberlain that it was unacceptable because 'the new proposal was simply another way of giving a seat to Poland'. In the Foreign Office it was assumed that the proposal was referred to Berlin and that President Hindenburg had declined to make any such concession.[17] In September 1926 Germany was solemnly admitted to the League. Chancellor Marx and Stresemann left Berlin by train for Geneva. They were seen off at the station by British and French diplomats, from the former royal waiting room where a large crowd of officials and journalists had assembled. With only a few minutes to spare Stresemann appeared, 'out of breath, hat in one hand, stick in the other, and beads of perspiration coming from his bald pate. One felt he had just come from a prolonged struggle with a recalcitrant suitcase.' But the legal adviser to the *Auswärtige Amt*, Dr Gaus, was still missing and only just managed to jump on the slowly moving train. 'Germany was en route for Geneva.

Thus began a momentous journey', the British embassy recorded.[18]

From Geneva Stresemann returned 'delighted with the reception which he met at Geneva and still more by the reception accorded him on his return'. His house was full of flowers so that he could hardly enter, and there were presents of wine, chocolates and many other things. The presents did not come from political organizations but from members of the middle and lower middle classes: 'this demonstration was an excellent augury for the maintenance of the Locarno and Geneva policy.' Stresemann, in a long conversation with D'Abernon, stressed that his aim was 'the complete liberation of the Rhineland from foreign occupation'.[19] A few months later, in March 1927, he returned to the question and complained to the new British ambassador, Sir Ronald Lindsay, 'with impatience and some bitterness of the stoppage of all progress and said it was poisoning the whole political system'. Some people did not mind the presence of foreign troops on the Rhine because they were good for trade, but they were 'distorting the whole political outlook'; without them, the German Nationalists would lose half their parliamentary seats and the conduct of foreign policy would become much easier. He earnestly hoped that the evacuation would be completed in the course of the year. 'His case, he maintained, was an unanswerable one and he had never heard a decent argument formulated against it.' In the Foreign Office it was minuted that Stresemann would be well advised to leave the question of total evacuation alone and to concentrate on the less ambitious issue of obtaining a reduction of the occupation armies – which, in Stresemann's eyes, would only be the first step towards total evacuation; in these circumstances, 'the French very naturally feel that if they now make a generous concession to the Germans as regards numbers, Dr Stresemann far from accepting it as such will only use it as a pretext to "ask for more"'.[20] Stresemann then told the ambassador that 'a sensible reduction would be a great thing, and he was convinced that it would so be regarded by the public at large'; only the right-wing Hugenberg papers were maintaining that a reduction would mean little or nothing. Lindsay added that in his opinion the whole occupation had only a 'nuisance value', it provided no serious guarantee for the payment of reparations, 'and if the French Government have millions of money to bury in fortresses along their eastern frontier, they can bury them equally well whether they have an army of occupation in the Rhineland or not.'[21]

In June 1926 the War Office reckoned that the armies of occupation in the Rhineland still numbered about 77,500 – after the evacuation of the northern zone by the British army which then had a strength of 8,000. This was a considerable reduction, for in March 1924 the French and Belgian forces alone numbered more than 128,000, 15,000 of whom were still in the Ruhr; the French army on the Rhine included 1,227 'colonial natives' and 17,927 'North Africans'.[22] Yet Chamberlain, the Foreign Secretary, found the figure of 77,500 difficult to reconcile with 'what was said at Locarno' and informed Paris 'that Stresemann fully realises what a weapon this breach of faith has given him; and he will certainly use it to the full every time he has an opportunity. It is a bad business, and I do sincerely wish that Briand, pressed though he be by other cares, would take a strong line and have done with it. The present position is indefensible.' In March 1927 Chamberlain told Stresemann at Geneva that he had a very bad conscience in this respect, and that the German complaint was fully justified; he was willing to help so that the French too would recognize this. He had put the question whether the British army of occupation could be withdrawn to the Cabinet and had met with opposition; the Chancellor of the Exchequer, Churchill, pointed out that these 8,000 men were paid for from the reparation account and thus were cheaper than they would be elsewhere, whereupon Stresemann interjected: 'Poor old England'. More important, however, was the political consideration: as long as Britain had an army on the Rhine she could use her influence in Paris in favour of evacuation by both countries; when no British soldier was left there the British interest in the issue would quickly diminish; now a question in parliament could always be arranged and he could then stress the necessity of evacuation.[23] In August Lindsay confidentially informed the German Undersecretary of State that Chamberlain had undertaken a very energetic *démarche* in Paris and Brussels to achieve a really tangible reduction of the troops in the Rhineland – his information being an example of a 'new secret diplomacy' for which he had received no instruction. According to Stresemann, Chamberlain was for a reduction by 15,000 men, but the French would only agree to 10,000. Once more opposition had also come from Churchill who calculated that any thousand British soldiers withdrawn would burden the budget with £100,000. By the end of 1927 the Allied forces on the Rhine were reduced to 67,000, 6,500 of which were British.[24]

At the end of 1928 Stresemann returned from a conference at Lugano 'especially pleased with two things': he was convinced that Briand was determined to evacuate the Rhineland, and Chamberlain had stated that 'evacuation would follow as a matter of course' as soon as the technical problems permitted if the Experts' Committee produced a satisfactory solution of the reparations question. In his conversation with the British ambassador Stresemann continued: there existed a common belief that after the evacuation of the Rhineland Germany would pursue other issues, such as the *Anschluss* or the Polish Corridor, but 'this was a complete misapprehension'; he had recently discussed the *Anschluss* with the new Chancellor, Herman Müller, and told him that it 'could only come about through a unanimous vote by the Council of the League'; it was not a question of practical politics; 'racial and linguistic ties existed between Germany and Austria and one could never get over that fact'. But the North Germans looked down upon the Austrians as too easy-going, and the Austrians believed that the North Germans were only living for work and did not know how to live properly: the real issue for Germany was only the Rhineland.[25] Stresemann finally succeeded and the Rhineland was evacuated in June 1930 – eight months after his death; but further German demands were raised soon after. As to the Corridor, at the end of 1927 Stresemann himself told Chamberlain that 'Germany could never admit that East Prussia should permanently remain "a colony".' Quite recently the Soviet Deputy Foreign Minister, Litvinov, had suggested to him that the moment war broke out between Poland and Lithuania Germany should occupy the Corridor, and no one would prevent her from doing it. He, Stresemann, had replied that he knew what the consequences would be for Germany: 'it might be all very well for Monsieur Litvinov who sat at Moscow, but Germany would not take the risk'.[26]

Less realistic was Stresemann's attitude towards the colonial question. When the new British ambassador observed to him in 1928 that the desire for colonies, in Italy as well as in Germany, seemed to him a strange phenomenon, Stresemann replied that the reasons were mainly psychological: 'the more developed any civilization became, the stronger would be the desire in considerable classes to escape from it'; if by chance Germany obtained a colony tomorrow, 'the day after tomorrow it would be overpopulated with Germans'; in his public speeches he only seldom mentioned colonies but, if he did so, there always was enthusiastic applause, especially from the young. Yet it was an illusion to believe that they would emigrate en masse to any German colony. As the ambassador remarked, 'it is no use saying that the old German colonies were only a source of expense and weakness, or that no German ever went to them, or that they served no really useful purpose'; their loss was resented 'and in the course of time the resentment is likely to become bitter'; the yearning for colonies in Germany and Italy 'defies all mere reasoning'. Like Stresemann he sought the explanation in psychological factors which he felt unable to analyse, but they would have to be reckoned with.[27]

Always plagued by bitter attacks on his foreign policy and by criticism even from the ranks of his own party, Stresemann found much to admire in the British political system. When in June 1929 the Conservative government was replaced by a Labour government under Ramsay MacDonald and this aroused strong expectations in Germany, Stresemann regarded it as quite mistaken to extend 'a special greeting' to the new government; that would imply that a complete change in British foreign policy was expected. But he had been delighted to see that the new American ambassador to London was welcomed by the outgoing Foreign Secretary, Chamberlain, as well as by his successor, Arthur Henderson. 'Thus did the Government party and the great opposition party together meet a foreign representative because both were of one mind in their conception of England.' In this way, it was reported to London, Stresemann voiced his 'respectful and almost jealous admiration' for the attitude of the British parties and apparently he was not the only German to do so.[28] In 1928 Stresemann treated the ambassador to a 'dissertation' on political education in the two countries. His son had gone to Cambridge and returned greatly impressed 'by the way in which young men were educated to play a part in politics by attending meetings of the Union'; this did not exist in Germany; the German idea of a political speech was that it 'must be crammed full of facts and based on a perusal of countless reports and papers'; but an Englishman who delivered a speech of the German variety would merely bore his listeners; his talk would be witty, while humour was out of place in a German political discourse.[29]

In his turn Austen Chamberlain greatly admired Stresemann, but his admiration did not extend to the Germans in general. In 1926 he wrote to Lord D'Abernon: 'If I am ever inclined to despair of our policy of conciliation, it is because the German authorities seem incapable of realising what is necessary for the execution of Stresemann's great idea. The moment that pressure upon them is relaxed they become intolerant and even insolent; they seem to understand nothing but a clenched fist; a concession provokes not gratitude but some new demand which, but for the concession, they would not have ventured to put forward – give them an inch and they take an ell.'[30] In December 1926 Chamberlain remarked to a German diplomat at Geneva that he greatly admired Stresemann's courage; after Locarno he had won the fight against public opinion in Germany, but he had won and was now strong enough to impose much more upon public opinion than he was willing to admit; Briand was in a much weaker position, and the Germans should not go too far, otherwise they might have to welcome Poincaré as Foreign Minister instead of Briand and Poincaré would never deign to make any concessions; in this respect all Germans were like Poincaré: always eager to receive but never to make any concessions. It was astonishing, the diplomat noted, how openly Chamberlain conversed with him in a leisurely fashion.[31] Two months later Chamberlain requested the British ambassador to tell Stresemann how much he recognized his statesmanship and the difficulties with which he had to contend; he had put forward proposals on the remaining military issues – war material and eastern fortifications – which made it unnecessary to remit them to the League of Nations. 'He has thereby helped to demonstrate in a tangible manner the benefits of a policy of cooperation and reciprocal concessions which we both have at heart.'[32]

In 1926 another incident occurred which caused friction between Britain and Germany and forced Stresemann to intervene to smooth troubled waters. In May Lord Kilmarnock reported from Coblenz that the Rhineland High Commission had received a complaint from the Commander-in-Chief of the occupation armies about a German intention to illuminate, on the occasion of a visit by an agricultural council, the Niederwalddenkmal on the hills above Bingen – erected to celebrate the German victories of the Franco-Prussian war – an intention which he considered 'a direct provocation on the part of the Germans'. The general asked the High Commission to prohibit the illumination, but the British High Commissioner persuaded his colleagues to let him try to arrange a peaceful solution. He accordingly saw the German Commissar for the occupied territories who averred that he knew nothing of the matter and thought the report incorrect. The general in command of the British troops sent his chief of staff to see the German official responsible for the district and urged him to intervene, and in addition sent two British officers to the mayor of Bingen with the request that the illumination should be cancelled. The mayor asked the officers whether they intended to prohibit it and, when they replied in the negative, declined to do so himself. The illumination took place. 'The German authorities', Kilmarnock commented, 'showed no sense of any real spirit of reciprocity' in a case 'in which it would have been extremely easy to do so'. Chamberlain saw the German ambassador and expressed his strong doubts whether the German government intended to abide loyally by the policy of Locarno.[33]

Stresemann immediately asked Lord D'Abernon to tell Chamberlain he 'should not take these difficulties, however irritating, as indicating in the slightest any desire on the part of the Central Government not to carry out to the fullest extent the policy of Locarno'. He declared: 'I stand and fall by Locarno'; the German government did not 'have the slightest intention of deviating by one hair's breadth from that policy'. A few days later the councillor of the British embassy wrote that it seemed incredible to him how any human being should not see that the illumination 'was so tactless and offensive as obviously to constitute an intended affront'; Stresemann had pointed out to him that unfortunately a total incomprehension of other people's mentality was a principal trait of the German character and that the local authorities in the Rhineland were unreasonable and pettifogging. As an example Stresemann mentioned that the area already evacuated was by no means satisfied and was continually putting forward new demands; probably the chief instigator of obstruction was Dr Adenauer, who had led Cologne into a terrible financial mess with his lavish building schemes; 'his only chance now lay in continuing to pose as the champion of the oppressed', and so he concerned himself with matters which were none of his business. Only a few days later Chamberlain informed D'Abernon that the illumination was to be repeated; if this were not prevented he would have to regard it 'as directly and wilfully provocative'. The ambassador replied that Stresemann had 'shown himself ready and indeed anxious to prevent any incident'; he had spoken strongly to the local authorities and he knew 'how injurious to the whole policy of Locarno these episodes may be'. The illumination was not repeated and thus the incident was closed. It had shown how fragile the policy of reconciliation was and how easy it was for obstreperous local officials to create difficulties which only considerable tact on both sides was able to overcome.[34]

The relationship between Stresemann and Lord D'Abernon was so close that they often referred to the Treaty of Locarno as their 'child'. Rather surprisingly Stresemann also used the ambassador to ventilate topics which were close to his heart and which he could not easily discuss with his German colleagues. One of Stresemann's favourite topics in these private conversations was the German army, its structure as prescribed by the Treaty of Versailles and its commander-in-chief, the ambitious General von Seeckt. In February 1924 a worried Stresemann explained to D'Abernon that the German President and the Chancellor had far less authority than General von Seeckt; no one outside Germany realized how great the difficulties of the civil government were in relation to the Reichswehr and its generals; the government had to be extremely careful how they dealt with Seeckt.[35] Two days later, however, Seeckt returned the exceptional powers granted to him by President Ebert in November 1923, for he believed that the authority of the state was sufficiently strong to make a continuation of the state of emergency unnecessary. In early March Stresemann returned to the subject. He had always held, he said, that the 12 years' service stipulated by the Peace Treaty 'was a fatal error. It made the army a caste apart – a kind of Pretorian guard divorced from and in opposition to the mass of the people'. In his opinion the army officers were 'more trustworthy from the point of view of the Republic than the men, and von Seeckt he considered quite trustworthy'.[36] Two months later, however, Stresemann's opinion of Seeckt had changed once more: he 'was a very astute man . . . but it was by no means certain how he would decide which was right and which was wrong'; before the Hitler Putsch in Munich it was not at all certain whether Seeckt would side with Ludendorff and Hitler; only when he heard that the post at the head of the army was entrusted to Ludendorff did he decide not to join the Putschists. Gessler, the Minister of Defence, had little influence, and the officer corps was too independent of him; it was 'too much imbued with the aristocratic traditions of the past' and 'no more democratic than it had been under the Emperor'. The officers respected Seeckt 'beyond measure', but they felt no affection for him.[37]

At the beginning of June 1924 Stresemann 'reverted to his usual theme that a long service army was a grave political danger to Germany'. On this occasion he even called the army a 'Wallenstein soldateska', referring to the most famous mercenary leader of the Thirty Years War: all might be well if Wallenstein was loyal to the civil authority but very often he was not; it was vital to reach an agreement with the Entente 'under which a democratic stream might pass through the arteries and veins of the army'. As D'Abernon noticed, Stresemann always waxed very eloquent on this theme which he had deeply at heart.[38] In the same month Stresemann also discussed the subject with a British officer attached to the embassy. According to the officer's notes Stresemann classified the Reichswehr as 'a state within the state', aloof from the people and out of sympathy with the majority of the nation. Officers as well as men were strongly nationalist; the rank and file, lacking the education of their superiors, were generally *völkisch* in politics; if they had been able to vote in the last election (a few weeks ago) the National Socialists would have received an additional 100,000 votes, and on this army Germany's internal security depended. The officer interjected that the preservation of the traditions of the Imperial army doubtless played a part in fostering such sentiments. Stresemann agreed that the young soldiers were easily blinded to realities by the pomp and circumstance of 'the good old times', revealed to them by regimental celebrations and the unveiling of war memorials; when they attended these they 'compared the old uniforms, military march tunes and the Hindenburgs, Mackensens and Ludendorffs with their modern counterparts, to the inevitable disadvantage of the latter', and all this increased their contempt for the republican Constitution. Stresemann also criticized the fact that officers and men when off duty had to wear plain clothes, a practice 'totally foreign to the German nature'; when in uniform the soldier was a servant of the state but out of uniform he would forget his responsibilities and was easily induced to discuss and absorb political ideas. The right-wing extremists then took good care to impress him with his importance as the future 'saviour' of Germany. If Germany were allowed a national short-service militia, it would be an agent of internal unity, it would be 'of' and not 'apart' from the people; but the Reichswehr was 'a perpetual menace to interior peace'.[39] What is remarkable about these views is not their content – which is confirmed by many documents – but that they came from a politician who was as strongly conservative as Stresemann, and not from the political Left. In a way, all the latter's criticisms of the army and its politics were confirmed by Stresemann.

For two years the British documents do not add much to this subject, but after Seeckt's dismissal in 1926 Stresemann told Chamberlain at Geneva how glad he was that Seeckt had gone. 'Von Seeckt never spoke and the Minister of Defence . . . never saw him and knew nothing of what was going on.' Seeckt was always considered a very able man, but Stresemann never knew whether his silence 'concealed real ability or merely an empty mind'. In any case, General Heye, the successor, was entirely different; he had informed Stresemann that he regarded himself as an organ of the government, that there could not be two governments or two policies in Germany; he would make his proposals to the government, take his instructions from them and carry out their policy. Chamberlain added that clearly Stresemann 'is much happier with the new commander-in-chief' and that he anticipated far fewer difficulties from him; he would loyally observe his obligations to the government.[40]

In a conversation with the new British ambassador soon after Stresemann even stoutly defended the Reichswehr. He could not understand, he said, how the French with their vast army, their guns, poison gas and air force, could have any apprehensions with regard to Germany. Lindsay replied that this was understandable if one remembered the past and thought of the future; the Germans had exerted themselves to evade disarmament and military control and there were many 'signs of the old, soldierlike spirit'; a favourite topic of discussion among army officers was the next war, which would bring Germany new victories within a few years. Stresemann, however, denied the existence of a considerable military spirit in the country; the army 'was not a popular institution' and its officer corps was not 'in the least bellicose', for the last war was still too close.[41] In April 1927 Stresemann further told the ambassador that the resentment against himself amongst senior army officers had diminished to such an extent that many of them had recently met him socially 'and had received him with encouraging cordiality'; but he admitted at the same time that 'things were still bad'.[42] What is really surprising in all this is to what extent Stresemann's views had changed after Seeckt's dismissal. It is understandable that he considered Heye's remarks a hopeful sign, and we know from other sources that under Heye an attempt was made to effect a rapprochement with the Republic.[43] But we also know that the attempt was short-lived and that there was strong opposition in the officer corps to the 'new course'. On this occasion Stresemann's optimism seems to have got the better of him, and a friendly 'social gathering' of senior officers seems to have exercised an unwarranted influence on him.

Stresemann's health was undermined by years of strenuous work and bitter personal attacks, but by 1928 his position was secure, as the ambassador reported. 'Although Dr Stresemann would not have sufficient physical strength today to conduct the violent campaigns of previous years, yet, so far as he is concerned, the battle has been won, and he can now continue his programme and his policy with the slighter effort required from one whose prestige and whose authority is universally recognised.' Stresemann, the report continued, was anxious to secure the permanence of the present coalition government and would use the whole weight of his authority to strengthen the government of Hermann Müller in which the Social Democrats were strongly represented.[44] Ten months later, indeed, Stresemann courted death in trying to save the coalition government. In October 1929 he found on returning from Madrid a government crisis 'in full swing', caused by the desire of the People's Party to withdraw from the coalition. Stresemann devoted all his time and energy to a solution of the crisis. He was suffering from a severe cold but left his house to attend a meeting of his own party and to see the Chancellor, and for the moment he succeeded in saving the government. When he returned home towards the evening he suffered a stroke and never recovered consciousness. As Sir Horace Rumbold, the ambassador, put it: 'if ever a man sacrificed his health and life in the service of his country it was Stresemann.' A week later Rumbold added:. 'The German public awoke on 5 October frankly astonished to find the whole world regarding Germany with undisguised respect as a great country which had made a remarkable recovery, and which had shown herself capable, in time of need, of producing a really great statesman. . . . There can be no more talk of outcasts. Germany has now really taken her place again as one of the leading nations of the world.'

Stresemann's aim of 'winning back for Germany the respect of the outside world' was achieved at the moment of his death. 'Never again, says the man in the street, can an important question in international affairs be decided without Germany's voice being heard.' But the ambassador realized that there was no one with Stresemann's authority who could give the People's Party a clear line and that the Centre Party showed much resentment at the appointment of Dr Curtius, also from the People's Party, to succeed Stresemann as Foreign Minister.[45]

The financial adviser to the British embassy also commented on Stresemann's death. He pointed to the internal troubles in Germany, such as severe unemployment and a sharp financial crisis in the spring: to this had to be added the disappearance of a man 'regarded by all as one of the few stable factors on which reliance could be placed'; Stresemann's foreign policy called for a kind of truce between employers and employees, and his death might be the signal for a renewal of the struggle between them. Stresemann had always been in advance of the other deputies of the People's Party and at times he and his party seemed to have little in common. But by the sheer force of his personality he 'kept them in some sort of relation with the Moderate Left', and his foreign policy provided the industrialists with a period of quiet – to the benefit of industry; but the People's Party had to pay a price and acquiesce in a financial policy under 'socialist' auspices – a price which the party became more and more unwilling to pay. The report pointed clearly to the growing conflict between the People's Party and the SPD, especially in matters of finance, which was to break out in full strength a few months later and to cause the overthrow of the Müller government. Yet a minute by the historian E.H. Carr only said: 'This is all rather vague and speculative.'[46] In his annual report for 1929 the ambassador came back to an assessment of Stresemann's role: 'Germany lost her greatest statesman since the days of Bismarck. History will decide which was the greater statesman of the two. Bismarck built up the pre-war German Empire on the basis of three successful wars, but Stresemann's work was, on a basis of defeat, to restore that empire as far as possible to its former position among the nations of the world. His task was infinitely the more difficult of the two, and he disappeared from the scene before it was completed. But he had set the ship of State on a right course, though many of his countrymen only recognised that fact after his death.' Three facts, he added, endeared Stresemann to the people of Berlin: he was a Berliner, he was the first real peace minister since the war, and he sacrificed his life for Germany.[47]

Another British diplomat in Berlin, Harold Nicolson, emphasized the gap which Stresemann's death had created. The Germans, he wrote to a friend in London, do not understand what is meant by a compromise; they think that in each case there must be a winner and a loser; 'Stresemann was far above the ordinary German mentality and you could thus negotiate with him on an equal basis'; now that Stresemann had gone the old difficulties were reappearing. There was a further difficulty, 'the anarchy of the German parliamentary system'; the Germans had no idea of the proper relations between the executive and the legislature; if the new Foreign Minister gave way on a controversial issue, 'every one of his colleagues in the Cabinet would have to attend a meeting of their own separate parties in order to convince these parties that it was not necessary for them to resign their portfolios as a protest.'[48] After Stresemann's death Lord D'Abernon wrote: 'As one who knew him well through difficult years, who saw his triumph over grave opposition from without and from within, I hold that Germany has never had a wiser or a more courageous adviser.'[49] When a Stresemann memorial was inaugurated in Mainz in July 1931 a book was published in his honour with contributions not only from D'Abernon but also from two British Prime Ministers, Lloyd George and MacDonald, apart from American, French and German contributions, and MacDonald sent a fulsome message of praise to the Memorial Committee.[50]

There is no doubt that in the inter-war period no other German statesman or politician enjoyed in Britain the fame and prestige of Stresemann. This was above all due to his policy of reconciliation which corresponded to a widespread sentiment that the catastrophe of 1914 must not be repeated, that Germany must be readmitted as an equal partner to the family of nations, that the Treaty of Versailles had been a mistake. But it was also due to Stresemann's skill as a negotiator, to his transparent honesty and good will, to the difficulties with which he had to contend in his own country, and to the circumstances of his death. In March 1933 *The Times* in a leader still praised Stresemann's 'real patriotism' and his policy of making Germany a 'good neighbour' and contrasted this with the policy of the new German Chancellor, Adolf Hitler, who had just won a resounding electoral victory.[51] Unfortunately, even before that event Stresemann's cautious foreign policy was discontinued by his successors. Whether Stresemann's policy could have survived the onset of the new economic crisis if he had lived, is a question which the historian cannot answer. We can only say that after 1929 Stresemann's diplomatic skill was sadly missing and that the close personal contacts he had built up with his British and French counterparts came to an end with his sudden death. Germany has not been blessed with many great statesmen, but he was certainly one of them.

VI

STABILIZATION –
AND NEW PROBLEMS

The most urgent issue to be settled at the beginning of 1924 was that of German reparations – a precondition of the evacuation of the Ruhr and of better relations between France and Germany; a committee of experts under the chairmanship of the American General Charles C. Dawes was appointed to assess Germany's capacity to pay. As early as January the Berlin embassy reported that what the French desired was 'a real scheme of settlement' and 'broad negotiations' between Paris and Berlin; the German government was strongly pressed by the industrialists of western Germany to negotiate because their financial position was getting critical owing to the payments and free deliveries they had to make to France; thus the government 'could not refuse to negotiate, but they would not negotiate too rapidly' and would keep the British government fully informed. Lord D'Abernon added that the industrialists were feeling the pinch and were 'in great financial straits'; this was confirmed by the fact that several big firms were trying to sell off subsidiary enterprises against cash; allegedly they were also trying to sell blocks of shares to foreign buyers.[1] In Britain a new Labour government under Ramsay MacDonald successfully attempted to mediate and to bring about a general settlement. A change of government in France from Poincaré to Herriot in the spring of 1924 greatly facilitated these efforts.

In April the committee of experts submitted its report which suggested German reparation payments beginning with 1,000 million gold marks and rising to 2,500 millions within five years, to include all the obligations arising from the war. From Berlin D'Abernon wired that the first impression was unfavourable; 'people spoke of exaggerated annuities, of unjustified infringement of sovereign rights, of Turkification'. But more recently opinion had changed because German economic unity was to be re-established and the Ruhr to be economically evacuated; Stresemann was making great efforts to secure a favourable reception in the press and spoke of 'idiots who think of rejecting experts' proposals'. At the end of April the ambassador wrote that even the German Nationalists were coming round to acceptance; they realized now that their only hope of joining the government rested on approval of the experts' report. According to Stresemann, the Nationalist speakers in the election meetings were very uncertain as to what attitude to adopt towards the report, and the favourable attitude of the industrialists 'has left them in a quandary'.[2] In the same month MacDonald, speaking at York, declared that the greatest danger emanating from Germany was 'not the danger of arms; it is the danger of industrial deterioration. . . . That is caused by the policy of foreign Governments imposing tributes upon Germany which Germany can only pay out of the degraded life-blood of the German working-man. (Cheers.)'[3] The Prime Minister set himself to gain French and German consent to the Dawes proposals. When D'Abernon reported in May that the popularity of the scheme in governmental and financial circles had considerably diminished, MacDonald replied that he appreciated the difficulties and the 'delicate position' of the German government, but it would be 'singularly unfortunate' if the whole scheme were endangered by their reluctance or a policy of making acceptance dependent upon certain conditions; 'it is both useless and unwise for German Government to look for anything of the sort at this moment.' D'Abernon was empowered to convey to them his personal assurance 'that as soon as the French Government have been constituted and are in the saddle, His Majesty's Government are determined to spare no effort to secure prompt execution of the experts' scheme in its entirety.' And he appealed to the ambassador 'to speak with all the authority at your command in endeavouring to instil into German Government some element of common sense.'[4]

In July D'Abernon was able to inform London that in the debate in the Council of State all the German federal states, with the sole exception of the small Mecklenburg-Schwerin, had approved the government's policy with regard to the experts' report: an unexpectedly favourable result because even Bavaria gave its consent; but in the debate all speakers had insisted on the necessity of obtaining a firm date or dates for the military evacuation of the Ruhr. He was told by the German authorities that they had tried to keep this issue separate from the discussion on reparations, but had found it impossible to obtain approval without a clear assurance about evacuation which need not be given directly to them. In the Foreign Office it was minuted that any such suggestion 'would merely make confusion worse confounded': the request should be turned down. Stresemann told D'Abernon that the refusal of the French to give any promise of evacuation made the position of the government 'absolutely impossible'; if he went to parliament and was unable to make a definite statement 'he would be voted down by his own party'.[5] Already on the same day, however, the ambassador wired to London that the position of the government had improved and that it was confident of obtaining a majority; the German Nationalists had no real alternative to offer and were 'afraid to come out too violently against a policy of acceptance on account of anxiety of financial circles to reach a solution'. If no majority could be obtained President Ebert was willing to grant a dissolution, and in an election the two extremist parties, the *Völkische* and the Communists, would lose seats and probably a fair majority could be gained.[6]

At the end of July D'Abernon's impression was that all the parties, with the exception of the two extemist ones, were anxious to reach a settlement; the German Nationalist attitude had become more moderate, and they only stipulated that acceptance of the Dawes Plan should be accompanied by evacuation of the Ruhr, that the Rhineland should be evacuated as stipulated in the Treaty of Versailles, and that there should be no more sanctions. In the debate in parliament the eminent historian Professor Otto Hoetzsch spoke for the German Nationalists and exclaimed: the 'Government should not go to London except on a footing of complete equality', whereupon Stresemann interjected: 'that is entirely my view'. Hoetzsch continued that his party was not averse to making sacrifices, for throughout history the defeated had to make contributions.[7] Reason seemed to prevail even among the German Nationalists who indeed a few months later entered the German government. In early August the ambassador reported that the terms of invitation to the London conference on reparations were welcomed in Berlin and had strengthened the government; the German desire to arrive at a settlement was genuine, but apprehension still existed regarding the military evacuation of the Ruhr and a fixed date for this was indispensable; if it were agreed to within a reasonable time and there were no 'dangerous loopholes', he was convinced that the Reichstag would ratify the Dawes Plan.[8]

At the end of July MacDonald wrote to the French and Belgian Prime Ministers that their governments had occupied the Ruhr solely to obtain economic results; therefore, as soon as the economic position was cleared up by the Dawes Report, it was illogical to continue the occupation; now the two Prime Ministers were trying to bargain on the subject and raising the question of inter-Allied debts; this issue had to be kept outside the London conference, and the British government had never recognized the occupation of the Ruhr.[9] The French government then made a tentative offer to evacuate the Ruhr in 1926, but MacDonald made it clear that he regarded the occupation as illegal and could not possibly agree to an occupation for another two years which would be resisted by the Germans.[10] Meanwhile the London conference had opened and was attended by Chancellor Marx, Stresemann and Finance Minister Luther. The German Undersecretary of State, von Schubert, at lunch with Miles Lampson from the Foreign Office stressed that the German government had no hope of obtaining in parliament the required two-thirds majority for the Dawes Plan (necessary for any change of the Constitution) unless the question of evacuation was settled. Marx as well as Stresemann was committed to find a solution, failing which the government would fall. When Lampson reminded Schubert that the French Prime Minister too had to take account of his public opinion, Schubert replied that a solution was imperative, and equally that of another controversial issue, that of putting Allied railwaymen on the Rhenish railways. Lampson's impression was that on these points Marx and Stresemann were 'definitely committed to the various political parties in Germany' and 'that the chance of their giving way is very small indeed'.[11] When *The Times* and *The Daily News* published reports that MacDonald had at the conference supported the French thesis – reports which he ascribed to leakages from the German delegation – he made strong representations to Marx who insisted that no one could have been so foolish as to leak such a report. When similar accounts appeared in the London evening papers MacDonald sent the cabinet secretary, Sir Maurice Hankey, to the Germans to repeat his protest:

all that MacDonald had done was to tell the Germans that the maximum concession Herriot was able to make on account of his parliamentary position was a withdrawal from the Ruhr within a maximum of 12 months (not six as the Germans demanded). Schubert assured him that the German delegation had very strict rules about communications to the press and that only the delegates themselves were permitted to speak to it.[12] It could not be established who was responsible for the leak. In the end MacDonald's compromise formula was accepted by the conference, and Herriot obtained a large majority for it in the Chamber.

In Germany the press was at first critical of the decision and doubtful whether the Reichstag would pass the Dawes Plan with the required two-thirds majority. But a French promise to evacuate Dortmund and other towns brought about a change and only the right-wing papers maintained their hostility.[13] The Reichstag then passed the railway bill (putting the German railways under Allied control as a security for reparation payments) but only by a simple majority, not the necessary two-thirds, which amounted to a government defeat. Stresemann entered into long negotiations with the German Nationalists who 'finally stated that they would detach forty to fifty members of their group to vote for the Bill provided they could save their face by showing some concession in regard to question of evacuation of the Ruhr', as the ambassador wired to London. Two days later the embassy was able to inform London that the Dawes legislation had been passed by the Reichstag with a sufficient majority. As Addison wrote to Lampson: 'I was always of the opinion that the German Nationals would funk it at the last moment and would, to use Stresemann's expression, "detach" a sufficient number of members from the party to vote for the Railway Bill.'[14] The Dawes Plan came into force on 1 September 1924 and remained valid for five years, a monument to Stresemann's negotiating skill, and equally to 'MacDonald's skilful mediation between France and Germany'.[15]

The Ruhr was evacuated by the French in July 1925. According to the Treaty of Versailles the northern zone of the occupied Rhineland, the area around Cologne, was to be evacuated by the Allied armies five years after the conclusion of peace 'if the conditions of the present Treaty are faithfully carried out by Germany'. But the Allies found that Germany had not carried out the provisions with regard to disarmament and Cologne was not evacuated in 1924. In February 1925 Chancellor Luther visited

Cologne. In his welcoming speech Dr Adenauer, according to the British Deputy High Commissioner, 'referred to the continuation of the Occupation as intolerable, stated that the population were labouring under the strain of lack of freedom . . . and resented the treatment meted out to them': as the report said, it was 'a remarkable statement in view of the Carnival festivities now in progress'. Luther replied that his government was willing to negotiate and to remove any abuses connected with disarmament: the Rhineland should trust the government and do nothing likely to provoke discord.[16] The Allied decision aroused strong anti-British feeling in Germany. General von Seeckt was reported to be 'very angry', believing 'that the English Government are being dragged at the heels of the French'. An official of the *Auswärtige Amt* told a British general that this failure made it impossible for any German to have any confidence in British actions.[17] In the Foreign Office much of the blame for the unsatisfactory state of Anglo-German relations was laid on the German Nationalists and their representatives in the government. From Paris Lord Crewe wrote in October that he failed to understand the 'subservience of the Nationalist ministers to demands which they know to be unreasonable and contrary to true interests of their country', for they seemed to care less about the evacuation of Cologne than about their party prospects. And the Permanent Undersecretary of State wired to D'Abernon: 'Are there not enough good men in the Nationalist camp to save the Rhineland and free Cologne? That is the question of the moment.' The Nationalist leader Count Westarp and his friends were doing all they could to prove 'that the Germany that counts does not want peace and desires to bring to nought our efforts to promote it.'[18]

By November 1925 when the evacuation of Cologne had been agreed on Lord D'Abernon urged that it 'should be carried out with the utmost rapidity'; Britain should do something striking, 'even at cost of inconvenience and money'; if it could be done in advance of German expectations, it 'would constitute a great diplomatic and political gain here'. Lampson, however, minuted his doubts whether they could press the War Office any further; and another official agreed: 'if we push the soldiers too much at present I fear "passive resistance".'[19] By the end of January 1926 the British evacuation of Cologne was completed, bringing to an end the first phase of the occupation. Adenauer, who had been only too pleased to welcome the British to

Cologne as protection against 'anarchy', then spoke of 'the hard fist of the victor for seven long years'. But the *Rheinzeitung* stated that the British troops had 'done much in the service of international peace'.[20] When the evacuation was celebrated in March 1926 in the presence of President von Hindenburg, Adenauer's speech was in British opinion 'calculated to revive bitter memories'. He complained about the 'unbearable burdens of countless families', the 'many hundred years imprisonment awarded by British courts', and exclaimed: 'unbearable was the triumphant blare of their regimental music'. The Prussian Minister of the Interior, Severing, on the other hand, 'confined himself chiefly to historical enthusiasm for the Rhine'; and a Foreign Office official minuted: 'Germans will be Germans.'[21]

In general too, the British officials in the Rhineland complained about the non-co-operative attitude of the German officials. After the conclusion of the Treaty of Locarno the Deputy High Commissioner wrote to London: 'If conciliation is to be effectual it must be mutual'; the German attitude of 'non-cooperation, not to say antagonism' showed itself in the press, in exaggerated demands on the Allies, in the behaviour of local officials, and in the orders they received from Berlin; it was an unfortunate German characteristic 'invariably to ask for an ell as soon as he has received an inch' and the concessions made by the French had been received with bad grace. Soon after similar sentiments were voiced by D'Abernon in Berlin: the very substantial alleviations of the occupation regime on the Rhine had not been received with satisfaction or contentment; the political Right would not admit that any gain made by the government was good, and the Centre and the Left on the whole did not recognize the great benefits or ignored them for political reasons; 'The art of expressing gratitude, with a view to obtain an increase of future favours and benefits, is one which the Germans do not practice.'[22] In 1927 the British consul at Mainz wrote at length about the feelings aroused by the occupation which in reality did not constitute a severe burden and did not seriously interfere with economic and social life. In his opinion, it was 'a very great moral burden', for it implied a limitation of German sovereignty and symbolized defeat; 'it recalls the bitterness, the hatred and the mistakes of the Great War and the final catastrophe' of 1918. 'For many Germans the occupation is the insolent crow of the vainglorious Gallic cock'; once the Germans stood in Metz, but now the French tricolour waved over the citadel of Mainz. 'The

French parades have not the same standard of cleanliness and efficiency as the Germans once knew, and in Mainz the pathetic crocodiles of ill dressed recruits from the country districts of France headed by detachments of resounding *clairons*, instead of impressing the Germans with a sense of the military might of France, seem to provoke at best a patronising good humour not unmixed with pity.' In his opinion the French really had nothing to gain by staying on in the Rhineland; they had won neither liking nor respect, while Britain had achieved much more of both without seeking them.[23]

Apart from national sentiment and the memories of defeat, there also existed very definite issues, such as the 'troublesome question of the Rhineland railway system' which was discussed in the Foreign Office in 1928. According to the terms of the Treaty of Versailles, the 'upkeep of all permanent works of mobilization' was forbidden in the occupied area, and the French military believed that certain railways constituted such works and must be destroyed before the final evacuation. The British military did not disagree with the French although they thought that the coming of mechanized warfare had greatly reduced the importance of railways. The question became more complicated when the Germans in 1927 asked for permission to carry out new railway construction — a request to which no reply was given by the Allies until the whole question of what constituted a permanent work of mobilization had been decided. As such the Rhineland High Commission could forbid any railway construction which might endanger the safety of the armies of occupation, but in the British view the construction envisaged did not fall into this category, nor were the Allied governments since the Treaty of Locarno entitled to decide unilaterally what was a permanent work of mobilization. If the British acquiesced in the French policy they would have to refuse to allow any new German construction works, 'on the entirely unjustifiable ground that we may, at some future date, consider them to be permanent works of mobilization'. In that case, the Germans would be fully justified in appealing to the Council of the League against such arbitrary action. In the opinion of Lindsay, then the Permanent Undersecretary of State, two reasons existed for taking immediate action: in the first instance the merits of the case 'which I consider very strong', and secondly, apprehension that the French government might use it for bargaining with the Germans in the forthcoming negotiations about the final evacuation. Another official minuted: 'It is inconceivable at the present date that H.M. Government could join in any attempt to blow up German railways or to hamper German railway development on the ground that the Germans contemplate using their railways for military mobilization. The thought of a British delegate to the League Council defending such a thesis is sufficient to show its absurdity.' Another official added that the issue must be settled once and for all because the Germans were beginning to point to the obstruction of the development of the Rhenish railways 'as a further proof of the failure of the Locarno spirit': the British 'must make it clear that we have no responsibility for this policy.'[24]

During these years the British willingness to meet legitimate German demands and to soften the provisions of the Peace Treaty increased. But side by side with that there was considerable apprehension about the growth of German nationalism and of the military spirit and critical assessments were made of German national characteristics, some of which have already been quoted. Before the German elections of May 1924 which resulted in considerable gains to the right-wing parties and a decline of the democratic ones, Prime Minister MacDonald wrote privately to D'Abernon that he felt much concern about the election: 'If they go Right and the mind of the Right is pure military reaction, this country will be dragged into a policy of continued coercion against every wish which it now entertains. . . . As you know, I came in hoping to begin a new policy. . . . If a Germany Right victory defeats me, I must submit to make the best of very much worsened conditions. . . . As the left parties have failed to gain confidence on party grounds, is there any chance of their coming together in the interests of their country and agree upon an Opposition policy? Or is German politics in complete chaos? Is there daylight anywhere?' The ambassador replied that he shared MacDonald's concern, but the danger should not be exaggerated; most probably a few German Nationalists would join the government (they did so some months later); there was no real risk of violent action against the Peace Treaty 'nor of any real departure from a reasonable policy of fulfilment'; the dominant influence would most likely remain with the Centre Party which would oppose any adventure and constitute an effective brake. But even if the German Nationalists should win enough seats to dominate the next government, British moderating influence would prevent any violent departure from the present policy. While the German Nationalists held erroneous opinions on almost all subjects, they had rather sound opinions on the necessity of keeping on good terms with Britain. They would listen to British advice provided they were convinced 'we were taking a line of our own and not acting in obedience to Paris suggestion or dictation.' Another possibility was a coalition of the People's Party with the Social Democrats in which case MacDonald's policy 'would have a clear run.' British influence was 'the most effective force conducive to a sensible and conciliatory policy in this part of Europe', and by any false step Britain might lose 'what others have lost already and what they would not weep to see us lose'.[25]

In June 1924 D'Abernon wrote that the growth of the German Nationalist vote was above all due to the French policy in the Ruhr and to the failure to make adequate concessions when Germany abandoned the policy of passive resistance; but if the German government could show that a policy of fulfilment brought 'rapid acts of conciliation', such as a liberal release of prisoners or the restoration of autonomy in the occupied area, the government and the moderate parties would gain strength; 'on a broad and reasonable basis success is within reach.' In November D'Abernon reported that most thinking men in Germany wanted to establish firm relations with England and with the USA; unless Britain made grave mistakes 'this orientation will remain dominant in German foreign policy for the coming years.' As to German-Soviet relations – an ever present fear since the Treaty of Rapallo of 1922 – nothing much had come of it, commercial relations had not developed, and the military connection 'was and is a mere bogey'. The reason for this last very surprising claim the ambassador found in 'the antipathy between the German military caste and the Jewish communist of the Soviet' and the Social Democrats' hatred of Communism: 'Germany turns to Russia when there is no one else to turn to.'[26] There was much truth in the last sentence. But in spite of all antipathy of the military caste German-Soviet military relations flourished under General von Seeckt because both armies benefited from them: the Reichswehr from the secret installations put at its disposal in Soviet Russia, and the Red Army from German military know-how. On the side of the Reichswehr the determination to circumvent the restrictions of Versailles overcame all ideological or other considerations.

At the beginning of 1925 the nomination of the president of the commission administering the Saar territory was the occasion of a minute by Crowe: 'I am afraid it is true that he and his officials systematically abuse their power and strain their rights under the treaty to the utmost in a sense hostile to the population.' Unfortunately, the Council of the League with its always overcrowded agenda could not control the proceedings of the Saar Commission; any attempt at interfering with its activities was frustrated 'by the up-in-arms attitude of the French member' and the complaisant attitude of its other members, and the situation was 'not made easier by the cantankerous attitude of the Germans'. Austen Chamberlain added: 'This is unfortunately true. It would be less difficult to do something for the Germans if they showed greater discretion and moderation in their demands.'[27] In August of the same year D'Abernon could inform London of the final acceptance of an Anglo-German commercial treaty by the Reichstag, against only the votes of the Communists and the *Völkische*. He did not think that there had ever been a serious danger of its rejection but 'the colonial party here is strong and one never quite knew what the Government would do or not do'; but 'with the help of a good deal of pressure they have done their part quite well and are delighted to have the conclusion of so important a commercial treaty to their credit.'[28]

In the presidential elections of 1925 the right-wing parties thought of putting forward the candidature of the Minister of Defence, Gessler. As the ambassador reported, this plan was abandoned thanks to the efforts of Stresemann who forcefully argued that 'his selection at the present time would create the worst possible impression in Western Europe'. D'Abernon even thought of an 'inexorable fate which so often impels German opinion to select the most tactless of all the courses available, and the one most offensive to public opinion abroad', but on this occasion the natural impulse had happily been checked.[29] In the end, however, Field-Marshal von Hindenburg was elected, a hardly more suitable choice from the point of view of western opinion. D'Abernon thought that his election would not make any great immediate difference, as the constitutional rights of the president were limited. A memorandum drawn up in the Foreign Office even found the election 'a perfectly natural event': if the positions were reversed 'the great majority of Englishmen would no doubt vote for a Hindenburg'. On the other hand, his election would give a fillip to the German

Nationalists: 'The danger is not with Hindenburg himself but with those behind him, and it is idle to suppose that their influence will not be felt and responded to by the government.' But it would be a mistake to assume that the policy of conciliation had failed; 'the fundamental impossibility of keeping Germany down' remained the same, and there was no reason to change the British policy 'to bring Germany back into the Comity of Nations'. Germany 'must be put on probation for a period', and the Allies must receive more tangible proof of German good faith before they could conclude any further binding agreements, for example on disarmament or Germany's admission to the League of Nations.[30]

In the following year, 1926, it was the conclusion of the Treaty of Berlin between Germany and Soviet Russia which perturbed the British government although Lord D'Abernon assured the Foreign Office that the Germans were acting in good faith and had reaffirmed their loyalty to the Treaty of Locarno and the Covenant of the League. In the Foreign Office, however, it was found that Germany's preoccupation was 'to run with the hare and hunt with the hounds'. Chamberlain wrote to D'Abernon that the language of the text was 'singularly ill-chosen' to inspire confidence in the minds of the western governments; he should tell Stresemann that the British government felt very uneasy, and that a first perusal of the texts seemed to increase the fears and suspicions of German intentions. In a personal telegram he added that he had used all his influence 'to secure fair and even friendly consideration of the German action in other capitals'; he relied on the ambassador to persuade Stresemann 'to make this time a speech directed to foreign audiences and calculated to reassure them. The trouble with the Germans is that they never think of any public opinion except their own. You can help greatly by showing Stresemann what are the points which he ought to make.'[31] According to his own notes Stresemann replied to the ambassador he should inform Chamberlain that there was no reason whatever to doubt in any way the continuation of the policy of Locarno; he should make any use he considered appropriate of this declaration, and an interview with *The Times* was envisaged to reinforce this impression.[32] When Chamberlain and Stresemann met in the autumn at Geneva Stresemann begged Chamberlain to consider the difficulties facing the German government in the Rhineland: it 'was the playground of Germany'; masses of German tourists went there, honeymoons were celebrated there, and the Germans 'could not help singing' perhaps under the influence of the wine; 'even the Brandenburger took to song in the Rhineland though it was contrary to his nature and produced a disagreeable noise'.[33]

In the autumn of 1927 the German ambassador in London noticed a renewed interest by the London papers in German internal and external affairs. In spite of the great confidence Stresemann enjoyed in England, there always reappeared a strong distrust of the German Nationalists in the government as well as fear of a monarchical restoration which would lead to a less pacific foreign policy; on the other hand there was a general understanding of the German wish to see the end of the Rhineland occupation, and only a minority was in favour of continuing it.[34] In 1928 the German embassy reported from London, on the occasion of a speech of Prime Minister Baldwin to the League of Nations Union which stressed cordial relations with France as well as with Germany, that the speech was quite honest and corresponded entirely to the views of Churchill; the latter advocated cooperation between the four West European powers and his opinions probably counted for most within the Cabinet; but during the past months the policy of the Foreign Office, in the negotiations on disarmament and the Rhineland evacuation, diverged from this line and emphasized unilateral friendship with France while ignoring the United States and Germany; the Entente with France, based on common political and military interests, had prevented a really reciprocal, triangular relationship between Britain, France and Germany, and there were no indications of a change of policy by the Foreign Office.[35] But the favourable result of the German elections of May 1928 gave an opportunity to Chamberlain to express his satisfaction. The steady improvement in Germany's foreign relations, he wrote to Paris, 'has cut the ground from under the feet of the Nationalists. We have the reward of our moderation, and the result should encourage us to go further on the same lines. We have made it possible for the Republic to live and for the German people to give a striking proof of their desire for peace.' The 'ex-Allied Governments' [sic] should not delay the settlement of certain outstanding issues, such as the withdrawal of the military experts from Berlin and the early evacuation of the Rhineland, for in German eyes they perpetuated the 'abnormal relations between the German and ex-Allied Governments which it was the object of the Treaty of Locarno to terminate.'[36]

Stabilization – and new problems

The general election of 1928 resulted in a remarkable defeat for
the German Nationalists and the National Socialists and a
victory for the Social Democrats whose leader became the new
Chancellor, and Chamberlain responded immediately. His
alleged anti-German bias was in reality a bias against the
German Nationalists who in 1927–28 had once more joined the
government, and this bias was fully justified.

Later in 1928 a memorandum written by the British consul in
Mainz gave occasion to ventilate British official opinions on the
German issue. He admitted that German colonial and naval
ambitions had 'receded very much into the background', but
there remained 'an essential will to *Weltgeltung*, and the confidence in Germany's power and right to achieve this *Weltgeltung*
which is as great in 1928 as it was in 1914.' Only the method of
giving effect to this will had changed out of necessity; having
been completely disarmed, the Germans were 'probably the
most convinced pacifists on the continent'; they saw that the
victors of the Great War were no better off than the vanquished
and in some respects worse off; German power politicians now
thought more and more in terms of industrial trusts and international agreements instead of military might. An official of the
Rhineland High Commission, William Seeds (a former consul in
Munich) disagreed. 'German commercial and economic efforts',
he wrote, might well develop into renewed 'colonial and marine
aspirations', and issues such as the eastern frontier, the
Anschluss and a possible revival of militarism might in time
touch British interests very closely; 'the renascence of Germany
is, in view of the German character, not to be contemplated
without a certain anxiety.' The evacuation of the Rhineland
alone, he feared, would produce a remarkable effect, but not
'quite the effect which we all desire and hope for.' And venturing
into the field of past history he concluded: 'The great and the bad
qualities of the Teuton [sic] make Germany a potential danger to
an extent which France, properly handled, can never attain. Past
history is not encouraging to constructive cooperation with the
forces of aggression. . . . It may be argued that Germany will
busy herself with economic development to the exclusion of
territorial or military questions. . . . But I see no guarantee whatever of this. Rather I do see her, once Rhineland evacuation and
similar problems have been nicely settled, combining her economic advance with a dogged pursuit of a highly rectified Eastern
frontier.'[37] These were prophetic words. In the Foreign Office a

201

memorandum was drawn up which supported the view that Germany aimed at establishing 'an economic hegemony over Europe'; but this policy was not new:. 'it was followed with great persistency and determination before the war' and there was every reason to believe that all Germany's energies would be devoted to that policy. In spite of all the alleviation of the German difficulties since Locarno the Germans 'have continued to parade their grievances' and suggested that the former Allies were failing in the undertakings they had given; the allegation that the British government had ceased to mediate between Germany and France was unfounded if the word was interpreted in the widest sense, for the government continued to exercise pressure on the French in a number of very controversial issues.[38]

Manifestations of German nationalism and the military spirit were registered on many an occasion. In 1924 the British vice-consul at Königsberg in East Prussia reported that, on the occasion of a Kant festival, the university and public buildings were all bedecked with the black-white-red flag of the former Empire; the rector, 'whose branch of teaching is the instruction of the theological students in practical pastoral work', addressed the assembled students and exclaimed amongst cheers that he had no use for internationalism, only for a Germany united and independent, and 'every student must be ready to give the last drop of his blood to bring Germany to power again'.[39] The British consul at Munich quoted from the *Fränkischer Kurier*, the leading paper of Nuremberg, the following: 'The day may well arrive when instead of Separatists, Frenchmen are thrown into the fires. Perhaps not today, nor tomorrow, but surely the day after. And cracking French skulls make [sic] the same noise as smashed Separatist ones.' He would have assumed, the consul commented, there must be a limit to journalistic criticism, if only for the sake of prudence and decency, but the article showed no such limit. He also pointed to the growing intensity of the national movement, 'fostered largely by non-Bavarians'.[40] At the beginning of 1925 when the decision was announced to postpone the evacuation of Cologne, the Bavarian 'patriotic societies' published an appeal to boycott all nationals of the countries responsible for the decision and the Bavarian papers were 'unanimous in expressing disapproval'; while the hostility to France showed signs of diminishing, that against England 'has been resuscitated'.[41]

In the occupied Rhineland a tremendous national fête was

organized, the so-called 'millenary celebration', in honour of the defeat of Duke Giselbert of Lorraine by King Henry I in AD 925 as a result of which Lorraine became part of the Frankish Empire: an occasion barely mentioned even in the German history books. Special trains were to bring large numbers from unoccupied Germany to take part in the fête. In the village of Burg an open-air performance was prepared with an expected audience of 150,000. 'It is evident', Lord Kilmarnock wrote from Coblenz, 'that these patriotic demonstrations will be attended by Nationalists, rather than the members of parties of the Left, and that the presence of large numbers of reactionaries from unoccupied Germany ... presents grave dangers of the outbreak of disorders.' What irritated the Foreign Office most, however, was the intended presence of President von Hindenburg. An irate telegram was sent to Lord D'Abernon asking him 'to draw Dr Luther's attention confidentially but in unmistakable terms to the extreme inconvenience and indeed real perils of such a project'; it would be 'the depth of folly' to remind the Allies that Hindenburg's name figured on their lists of war criminals: 'we are ready to forget it.' The visit did not take place. Looking back on 'the tremendous preparations' for the fête and its enormous cost, Kilmarnock was 'more than ever convinced that the Millenary celebrations were primarily organised by Berlin as a political move'; the claim that they were a spontaneous expression of patriotism and loyalty by the local population was disproved 'by the apathetic attitude and utter lack of enthusiasm displayed towards these celebrations by the majority of the inhabitants of the Rhineland.'[42] When Cologne was finally evacuated in 1926 there was another big celebration. At the university Stresemann addressed the students on the spirit of Locarno, but not a single republican flag was to be seen, and the students, 'resplendent in their high boots, white breeches and gorgeous tunics, replied with well-known war songs directed against the French.' In the city itself, however, the activities of the Nationalists were well checked by strong forces of the *Reichsbanner*, the republican para-military association.[43] When the French army evacuated Düsseldorf and Duisburg this was celebrated by 'a three-day drinking bout', with many cafés and pubs remaining open all night; 'not a republican flag was to be seen in the town', military marches were played, the hardships of passive resistance were recalled in patriotic speeches, and a movement was organized to erect a memorial in honour of Schlageter, the nationalist 'martyr', who had been executed by the French for acts of sabotage.[44]

In 1927 the Foreign Office explained to Lord Kilmarnock that in Germany there existed a bellicose minority and a pacifist minority; between these two extremes there was 'an amorphous mass of opinion' which at times tended to the one and at times to the other; it was to be hoped that in the course of time this mass would 'throw its weight definitely on the side of peace'; yet the minority which harboured ideas of revenge 'consists of the best trained and most determined part of the nation – a nation which is accustomed to being led, and which readily bows its head to an order', so that the fact that the aggressive section was only a minority afforded a limited assurance, especially to the French.[45] Two years later, in 1929, an official of the *Auswärtige Amt* expressed similar apprehensions to the British ambassador, this time on account of the activity of the Nationalist leader Alfred Hugenberg, who 'was causing the German Government considerable preoccupation'; while Hugenberg had lost influence with sensible people, his 'influence with the masses, and especially with German Fascists, was as great as ever', and the situation was 'not without danger'. The ambassador thought that it required careful watching and that 'the political atmosphere was not healthy'.[46]

Particularly unhealthy were the activities of the nationalist secret societies and para-military associations which were commented on very frequently. In 1924 the Central Department of the Foreign Office commented on a report by the Intelligence Section of the British Rhine Army according to which there existed hundreds of such secret societies; they were largely military in character and some of them carried out rifle practices and military exercises. This was contrary to Article 177 of the Treaty of Versailles which forbade all German associations to occupy themselves with military matters, and many had been dissolved by the authorities but they always reappeared. In west Germany they were working in a more underground manner, but in the east quite openly, as shown by the recent demonstration of the *Stahlhelm* in Königsberg where its members paraded in uniform. These societies were illegal and the German government should be asked to dissolve them, but such suppressions were not likely to be very effective: 'they will be less so than ever at present, in view of the spirit which is evidently abroad in Germany.'[47] Soon after a British diplomat wrote from Berlin that Article 177 was 'chiefly honoured in the breach'. A large section of the population was working with enthusiasm at their military training, 'varying in proportion to their age and to their experience or ignorance of the realities of war'; the British must reconcile themselves 'to the fact that the German military spirit is so hardy and so carefully cultivated a growth that no amount of Treaty provisions or controls will extirpate it. It would, indeed, be folly to expect in a virile race with a tradition of 150 years expansion by conquest.' He went on to mention 'the political murder organizations': it could not be the policy of any government to tolerate them, as little as any British government would tolerate the Fenians, but they continued to exist; as the Bavarian 'patriotic associations' had been tolerated by the Allies, the German could hardly be expected to be 'plus royalist que le roi'. He believed 'that the cult of war is so ingrained in his nature – even after the experience of the last decade – that he will not give up until he has had at least another try.' The one force in Germany making for pacifism was the socialist movement which was likely to grow 'owing to the shameless exploitation of labour which reigns throughout Germany today'. When the Communists succeeded in blowing up a statue of Moltke in Halle in 1924 a new one was unveiled there in May. The ceremony, it was reported, was attended by numerous uniformed members of the para-military associations such as the *Stahlhelm* and the *Wehrwolf*, as well as a tradition company and a band of the Reichswehr, and the band played the old Imperial hymn.[48]

A British Intelligence officer, who had served in Germany since 1920, even took the line that the efforts to suppress the para-military associations had 'tended to convert them from useful elements to dangerous encumbrances'. He also drew attention to the fact that their members were in many places trained in intensive short courses by the Reichswehr. He thought that their development resembled in many aspects that of the Italian Fascists: only that in Germany there was no Mussolini and that it seemed 'extremely improbable' that a man could be found 'with sufficient skill, character and powers of leadership, to unite the various nationalist societies under one banner for the successful execution of a coup'. Owing to their lack of coordination and of central leadership, the societies were 'not at present a danger to peace'.[49] At the end of 1924 the Military Control Commission reported that it had not yet succeeded in securing the disbandment of the well known militant associations of the *Stahlhelm, Oberland* and *Wehrwolf* on account of obstruction by the German authorities, which 'pretend to regard these societies as childish'. The British General Staff commented that it was desirable to suppress their activities, but that this appeared impossible because they 'quickly reappeared in another guise'.[50] The British vice-consul at Königsberg who watched a *Stahlhelm* parade there, noted the large numbers marching in uniform (many of them carrying guns), the youthful age of the majority, and the participation of working men; 'the movement has a strong hold on the coming generation and is not confined to one section of the population'; it possessed a central organization for the whole province, with 'district', 'company' and 'group' commanders.[51]

In November 1924 26 leading members of the 'Organisation Consul' (which was responsible for a whole series of political murders) were tried at Leipzig for membership of a secret society, but its leader, Captain Ehrhardt, had succeeded in escaping from custody. At the end of the proceedings the public prosecutor demanded sentences varying from two months' imprisonment to small fines for nine of the accused, and the remainder should be discharged as innocent. According to a report forwarded by D'Abernon, 'the speech for the prosecution resembled the speech for the defence so closely that it is difficult for the reader to distinguish which is which'. The public prosecutor stated *inter alia*: 'Anybody who was at the front during the war can understand the bond between Ehrhardt and the accused. Anybody who was at the front must have pledged and received loyalty. . . . Loyalty is the loftiest feeling known to the soldier.' 'We have men before us whose world collapsed with the Revolution, whose calling was annihilated, who were thrown naked out into life. The German Army and its Officers were insulted by the Revolution and met with no protection. That has to be admitted.' The verdicts, however, were in excess of those demanded by the prosecutor. Four men were sentenced to eight months' imprisonment and 12 received sentences varying from three to five months, while ten were acquitted. Miles Lampson minuted: 'The leopard has not really changed his spots but he is less vocal than he used to be.' Crowe added: 'German justice has for generations been a cruel farce.'[52]

During the following years more attention was paid to the *Stahlhelm* than to any other para-military association, for it became by far the most important militant organization of the Right. In 1927 the British consul at Bremen noted that it 'has gradually increased its strength through the virtual or complete absorption . . . of the Wiking, Wehrwolf, Olympia and Konsul' organizations, the financial support given by Hugenberg, and the weakening of rival associations such as the *Jungdeutscher Orden*. The Berlin embassy reported the speech of the Brandenburg *Stahlhelm* leader, Elhard von Morosowicz, at a rally in Hamburg: 'France is still our enemy', and the League of Nations nothing but 'an authority for the suppression of Germany'; the German race was not defunct; even in Austria it had, thanks to the *Heimwehren*, succeeded in throttling revolution; 'the spirit of Potsdam and of Frederick the Great would be grafted' on to the youth of the *Stahlhelm* which must be prepared to redeem Germany's honour. 'The speech was received with tumultuous applause.'[53] In 1928 the Director of M.I.3.b reported that of all the nationalist societies, the *Stahlhelm* was the most important; its members were trained by the army as *Zeitfreiwillige* (short-term volunteers) and possessed quantities of arms; it was considered the 'special reserve of the Reichswehr and is treated accordingly'.[54] The same point was made in 1929 by the British military attaché in Berlin. 'In his opinion there is not the slightest doubt that the Reichswehr are continually helping the *Stahlhelm* in all sorts of illegal little ways, such as lending them material for training and assisting them in night marching'; the relations between the *Stahlhelm* and the army 'are undoubtedly good and are probably getting better.'[55]

In November 1928, on the other hand, the British embassy emphasized that the *Stahlhelm* was not the strongest organization in Germany: 'the *Reichsbanner* [the pro-Republican para-militay association] is more numerous and represents a far wider and more influential body of opinion.' The Fascist victory in Italy and the anti-parliamentarian coup of Primo de Rivera in Spain were made possible by social and political disintegration and the absence of an organized opposition: neither of these conditions existed in Germany and any 'march on Berlin' would require 'some serious and improbable accident in the political machine'; the *Stahlhelm* might be foolish enough to attempt a Putsch, 'but so long as Germany remains economically, socially and politically as sound as she is to-day, there is no chance of any such Putsch being successful.' This was quite true, but how long would Germany remain 'economically, socially and politically sound'? That was impossible to foresee in 1928, at the height of economic prosperity. A minute added in the Foreign Office pointed out that the *Stahlhelm* was drawing its principal strength from the agrarian districts and thus might become 'a controlling force in the predominantly agricultural districts' to the east of the Oder and in Silesia; in the event of difficulties, for example with Poland, a base might be formed there from which resistance to the pacifist policy of the parliamentary majority might be organized.[56] Early in 1929 another Intelligence report stated that General Groener, the new Minister of Defence, had terminated the system of training *Zeitfreiwillige* in the army; this threw the responsibility for the military training of the members on to the shoulders of the *Stahlhelm* leaders. It was carried out by former officers or members trained by the army, and probably machine guns and other weapons were still 'privately' borrowed from army units. But the Defence Ministry no longer paid subsidies to the *Stahlhelm*. The new system adopted by the army consisted in enlisting men for three years, instead of 12 as prescribed by the Peace Treaty.[57]

By comparison with the *Stahlhelm* no other militant right-wing organization received similar attention in the reports from Germany. Little notice was taken of the para-military associations of the Left, for obvious reasons. In May 1926 Addison reported on the Whitsun rally of the Communist *Rotfrontkämpferbund* which he had observed from close quarters. According to the estimates, about 30,000 men marched through the streets of working-class Berlin to a public park 'where they arrived travel stained and exhausted' and were addressed by the KPD leader Ernst Thälmann. In general Addison found that 'the programme was mild to the point of boredom', but 'the men were of unusually fine physique, and compared well with police or Reichswehr troops in discipline and military training.'[48] A curious statement in view of the generally rather unsatisfactory training and armaments of the *Rotfrontkämpferbund*, but a compliment to its discipline and marching order.

Even more curious was a report on the republican *Reichsbanner* by the Intelligence department of the British Rhine Army of 1924 which claimed that its actions and aims showed 'that the movement is comparable to that of the "Fascisti".' The new organization was 'combating the activities of Communist and Monarchist societies'; it 'constitutes another more or less trained military organization' and might 'become a serious factor in promoting the military training of the youth of Germany'. If a *Reichsbanner* branch were formed in Cologne, it would cause 'a weakening of the power of the Allied and German authorities to deal with the subversive "Left" and "Right" movements', and conflicts between the *Reichsbanner* and rival associations were certain to occur.[59] Yet the *Reichsbanner* was formed to defend the Republic and its whole tendency was pacifist and anti-militarist. What is true, however, is that it added yet one more para-military organization to the German spectrum. As Lord D'Abernon reported in 1926, if one drove on a Sunday through any German province one always saw the same sight: 'men of every age and every corpulence, similarly dressed, marching rigidly in rank, accompanied by bands and banners, amid the applause of the attendant womankind and young'; companies of country squires with their retainers and proletarian units were 'performing the same evolutions and carrying with the same invincible solemnity the emblems of Imperial Germany and revolutionary Russia': it was not surprising that so many Germans could 'think of foreign policy only in terms of war' and could 'not conceive future frontiers otherwise than on the time honoured scale of batteries and battalions.'[60] It was a sad picture that emerged, even in the eyes of so benevolent an observer.

As the Communist danger subsided after 1923, the German Communist Party received little attention in the British reports – only when its parliamentary deputies voted against the Dawes Plan, the Treaty of Locarno and Germany's entry to the League of Nations. Much more important from the British point of view was the German Nationalist Party, whether in or out of office, because its vote was often crucial on issues of foreign policy. D'Abernon's comments on the party were frequently scathing. In 1924 he wrote privately to MacDonald that they were 'divided between their desire for office and their unwillingness to go back on all their election pledges' and that 'the idea of putting [the former Admiral] Tirpitz at the head of a German Government could only have occurred to a German National': if the Germans intended to bring about a combination hostile to them 'I do not think they could take a step more appropriate than putting Tirpitz in as Chancellor.'[61] Yet the embassy's annual report for 1925 took a more positive view and considered it probable that the German Nationalist Party, in spite of its preference for monarchy and class prerogatives, 'is the best qualified to give to Germany an efficient and dignified internal administration'; it admitted, however, 'that its ideals and methods are still those of the barrack square, and would, in the long run, prove a source of intolerable misgiving to Germany's neighbours'.[62] Whoever wrote these lines must have had in mind the Prussian administration of the pre-1914 period which was dominated by the Conservative Party, the predecessor of the German Nationalists: but was it really so 'efficient and digni-fied'? and so much better than the Prussian administration of the 1920s? It most certainly was an administration in the interests of a narrow social class.

It was readily admitted that the chances of a monarchical restoration were very slim, at least outside Bavaria. But the appearances of the former Crown Prince were carefully regis-tered. In 1924 he attended a performance at the Munich opera house; the whole house rose when he entered and all eyes were fixed upon him, the British consul wrote. His annual report mentioned that the Bavarian Prime Minister, Dr Held, was a monarchist and would very much welcome a return to the Bismarckian federal system, but only by constitutional means. Prince Rupprecht of Bavaria was 'far too wise and prudent a man to allow himself to be rushed into any hasty action'; his popu-larity among the people continued to grow, but the idea of establishing a Bavarian monarchy within the German Republic which was propounded by some Bavarian monarchists was ludicrous; and a 'King under Ebert' was an impossibility.[63] In 1926 Sir Ronald Lindsay, the ambassador, believed that the majority of the German states would welcome a return to the monarchy, for most of the local princes had been popular, the local courts 'lent a grace and dignity to the capital . . . and gave a stimulus to local trade, the loss of which is a source of dis-content.' But unfortunately for these princes their cause was associated with that of the Hohenzollerns: outside Prussia the ex-Emperor and his family were disliked, and in Prussia 'they are largely despised' – with the only exception of the former Crown Princess. William II was considered impossible 'because he ran away instead of facing his troubles like a man', and for a variety of reasons his sons 'are equally impossible'.[64] There obviously was no hope for a restoration.

The rise of Alfred Hugenberg within the German Nationalist Party was followed with interest. In October 1928 the ambassa-dor reported from Berlin that he had been elected party leader in place of Count Westarp who had 'fallen between the stools of the

extreme reactionaries and the more moderate elements';
Hugenberg would certainly make strenuous efforts to purge the
party of what he believed to be its weaker elements; some of
these moderates hoped that his election would ultimately lead
to the breakaway of the extremists, 'leaving the party free to
reconstruct itself on a sounder and healthier basis'.[65] In
November 1929 it was expected that the annual party conference
would bring the internal differences out into the open,
especially on account of the recent unexpected successes of the
National Socialists in local elections. But, as Harold Nicolson
reported from Berlin, there was no 'washing of political linen';
the oppositionists within the Nationalist Party left the conference en masse before the public discussions started and left the
field to Hugenberg; even the leaders of the Agrarian League who
openly opposed his course did not attempt to disturb the peace
of the proceedings.[66] Hugenberg's extremist course remained
unchallenged, and the oppositionists ultimately had no choice
but to leave the party and to form unimportant splinter groups of
their own.

As to the largest German party, the SPD, it was believed in the
British embassy that they were 'all the more anxious to beat the
patriotic drum' because of their many denunciations of reactionary tendencies in the army and the para-military associations,
which caused their opponents to claim that they were siding
against Germany. Thus Social Democrats talked about the
Anschluss, and in Prussia they found in their criticisms of the
occupation regime in the Rhineland a theme which permitted
them to claim that they were good Germans and to reinforce
their cooperation with the Centre Party in the Diet. This also
enabled them 'to be as disagreeable as possible to Stresemann,
and thus to show him, according to true German methods, that
he is not the great man that he thinks he is.'[67] The endless
bickering among the party leaders and their constant manoeuv-
ring for position never ceased to irritate the British diplomats. It
certainly led to frequent government crises and to political in-
stability which were a feature of this period of relative stability.

Hardly any notice was taken of the moderate parties, the
Centre or the Democrats, which formed part of the governing
coalition. But – after the events of 1923 – the extreme Right
attracted much attention, although during the years of prosperity its following remained small. In September 1924 the
British consul reported from Munich that the Hitler party was

divided into no less than four groups and was disintegrating; 'though no one would make bold to say that Hitler with his demagogic oratory and persuasive personality could not if he returned [from detention] restore the broken ranks and reunite the party'. But his greatest enemy was the stabilization of the mark, the beneficial effect of which could not possibly be overestimated, and the acceptance of the Dawes Plan had 'damped the war spirit of the man in the street'. In December the acting consul added that Ludendorff with his personal quarrels 'has nearly ruined the prospects of the party which Hitler has so laboriously built up'; its funds 'seem to have reached a very low point' and its propaganda had to be curtailed; only one insignificant paper was still supporting the party.[68] The Berlin embassy, on the other hand, noticed the surprising success of the *Völkische* in the elections of May 1924; they polled 1,900,000 votes and gained 32 seats in the Reichstag – a success which alarmed the German Nationalists.[69] Perhaps it was for that reason that the latter refused to make common cause with the *Völkische* in requesting President Hindenburg not to sign the Treaty of Locarno and to hold a referendum on the issue.[70]

For three years thereafter the National Socialists were not mentioned although this was the time when Hitler reunited the party and brought it under his sole control, with a strictly hierarchical structure embracing the whole of Germany. After the election of May 1928 which strengthened the moderate parties the British ambassador commented on the NSDAP, which had polled a mere 800,000 votes: 'These crazy people are actuated by a combination of anti-Semitism and acrid nationalism carried to its extremest logical conclusions.' Stresemann called them 'Communists who sing the "Wacht am Rhein" instead of the International', and their militant nationalism created a gulf between them and the Communists. 'The only pleasant thing about them is that they have lost three out of 15 seats in the Reichstag.'[71] In September 1929 the Foreign Office received a reliable report that von Morosowicz, the leader of the Brandenburg *Stahlhelm*, had said that the Young Plan (reparations settlement) proved a blessing in disguise, for hitherto it had been a hopeless task to bring together the Agrarian League and the National Socialists, that their inclusion in the common front against the Young Plan introduced a radical element necessary to prevent stagnation in the nationalist movement, that men like himself and Duesterberg (the second in command of the *Stahlhelm*) welcomed the inclusion of Hitler in this common front – in contrast with the more cautious policy pursued by the *Stahlhelm* leader Franz Seldte. The informant, however, thought that Hitler could not give up 'his radical socialism' without losing many followers to the Communists.[72] It was this united front against the Young Plan which elevated Hitler to a figure on the national stage and made him 'respectable' in middle-class eyes. It also brought large funds to him. In November local elections were held in Prussia in which the National Socialists succeeded in more than doubling their vote compared with 1928. Harold Nicolson, the First Secretary, wrote to London that the mass defection of the Nationalist voters to the NSDAP had greatly alarmed the Nationalist leaders. They had provided funds for Hitler's campaign, and Count Westarp and his advisers now deplored 'the fact that they ever assisted these young people at all'. In Nicolson's opinion 'the refreshing vigour' of the National Socialists was certain to appeal 'to German youth who are always impressed by extreme idealism'.[73] He was clearly impressed by the vitality of the party.

A few weeks later Sir Horace Rumbold, the ambassador, commented on the 'unexpected successes' of Hitler's party. Until a few weeks ago, he wrote, the Germans outside Bavaria and the south 'paid not the smallest attention to Herr Adolf Hitler and his doings'; it was vaguely known that he was an Austrian, was implicated in the Putsch of 1923 and was the leader of a dwindling Bavarian party, 'mainly composed of hot-headed young men who sang anti-republican songs and willingly took part in riots'. Why did 'such an illogical and confused programme appeal to Bavaria, Thuringia and even Pomerania with like cogency?' The party was aiming at something new, 'it aims at something less than reconciling opposite political poles. The catchwords of the extreme right and the extreme left are jumbled together in a manner which defies analysis.' It seemed to him that the National Socialists owed their success 'to the vigour, the sincerity, and above all, the youthfulness of their following'; their appeal was addressed 'to German youth, eager, progressive, curious, conscious of its vigour but deprived of opportunity'. The National Socialists rejected pacifism and toleration and extolled bigotry; they denounced internationalism and extolled xenophobia; 'in a country where landlords and tenants alike are groaning under an intolerable burden of debt, they preach war against capitalism, against interest, against the tyranny of the mortgage banks and, above all, against usury, profiteering, and the Jews. . . . Among the more sober party orchestras they have the magnetic attraction of a jazz band.'[74] It was a shrewd analysis which brought out many of the causes of the National Socialist success. Written at the end of 1929 it in many ways anticipated later events. Like Nicolson, Rumbold was impressed by 'the vigour, the sincerity' of their propaganda, the youthfulness of their followers, compared with the dull and staid propaganda efforts of the established parties which only at election time bothered about the inhabitants of the small towns and villages of Germany. Although 'sincerity ' may be a big word, there can be no doubt that the youthful adherents of the party took the propaganda slogans seriously and honestly believed in them, especially at this early time, before many fellow travellers found it opportune to jump on the band-waggon.[75]

Side by side with a virulent nationalism, directed against the 'fetters' of Versailles and all German 'traitors', anti-Semitism was a principal part of National Socialist propaganda. That anti-Semitism was on the increase was noticed by General Wauchope, the head of the British section of the Military Control Commission, as early as 1925. 'Jews and anti-Jews all tell me', he wrote, 'that the anti-Jew feeling in Germany grows stronger every month. Nothing like it existed before the war; it is more violent now than a year ago, and it is by no means confined to the Nationalist and Clerical parties. Anti-Jew feeling is rather like the poverty and distress in Berlin.' But the general was not unbiased although he considered himself a 'shrewd and patient observer' of the Berlin scene. He wrote these notes after a lunch with 'two fat German Jews'; one of them was a senior civil servant 'whose unpleasant exterior . . . conceals a most powerful brain' but whose name the general misspelled. What he disliked in his lunch partners was that 'being Jews and having principles about as straight as their own noses, they naturally had a lot to say about the honour of the Fatherland.'[76] These notes were written a few months after the eruption of the Barmat scandal, a corruption affair in high circles which aroused strong anti-semitic feelings, and this may have influenced the general's remarks. His second lunch partner was a director of one of the leading German banks. As the British embassy reported, the Barmat scandal involved many leading Social Democrats and Centre Party politicians; large sums were involved – well over two million pounds – which had been furnished to the Barmat firm by way of credits, partly through the Prussian State bank and partly through the official postal system. The German Nationalists immediately claimed that corruption was rampant in the whole administrative system, but some of the officials involved had served since before the war and held nationalist views. According to the report energetic attempts were made to hush the matter up, and 'the unpleasant truth is mostly to be found in the Communist papers, such as the *Rote Fahne*.' The Minister of Posts, a Centre deputy, and another deputy of the same party were forced to resign in consequence of the scandal.[77] This and similar affairs of later years certainly were grist to the mill of anti-republican and anti-semitic propaganda, and they weakened the government.

Of the three chancellors of these years – Marx, Luther and Müller – the ambassador was clearly most impressed by Luther, 'a simple strong man of an antique type', as D'Abernon described him. He praised him together with Dr Schacht for saving the German mark: 'The fact that he is Chancellor of the Reich is a guarantee for moderation, for stable conditions, and for a maintenance of rigorous financial administration.' The man behind Luther's throne was supposedly Stresemann 'whose judgment of political probabilities has been proved, on several occasions, singularly correct'.[78] In November 1925 Chamberlain wired to D'Abernon that he would greatly regret any change in the chancellorship; did the German parties not see 'that for us Luther and Stresemann stand for the Locarno reconciliation, that they have won our confidence as we have I trust won theirs and that it is a bad moment to swop horses. . . . I have worked with Luther and I have confidence in him.' And on another occasion: 'We must strengthen Luther and Stresemann who are behaving with complete loyalty and marked courage.'[79] When the German Nationalist ministers resigned from the government over the Treaty of Locarno Luther found it very difficult to form a new cabinet from the moderate parties. As D'Abernon informed London at the beginning of 1926, it required the personal intervention of President von Hindenburg, who insisted that the Democratic Party must join the cabinet in spite of its quarrel with the Bavarian People's Party over the question of filling the Ministry of the Interior. It was stated that Hindenburg had absolute confidence in Luther and was strongly opposed to the alternative candidate, Marx, who had been Hindenburg's principal rival in the presidential election of the previous year.[80]

This was one of the first occasions – but not the last – when the new president intervened in the formation of the government.

A few months later, however, the Luther government fell and Marx became the next Chancellor. As the British embassy reported, Stresemann was widely suspected of being 'not altogether guiltless' and Luther fell into a skilfully prepared trap. He had so often said 'no' that 'he had antagonised practically everybody including his own colleagues'; he had driven his officials to despair by constant demands for full information on every possible subject; 'he would suddenly ask for memoranda on the estimated number of cows at the armistice in the territory ceded to (a) Denmark, (b) Poland, (c) France, with a full account how the cows came to be there'; he felt entitled to interfere in departmental details and thus antagonized his colleagues, especially Stresemann, and he equally irritated the parliamentarians. It also was evident that no one could remain at the head of the German government for any length of time unless he was a prominent member of one of the leading parties, and Luther did not belong to any: 'he stood alone'.[81]

In 1925–26 the old president was mentioned several more times in the British reports. He was said to receive daily numerous abusive letters, 'largely from old comrades in arms', vilifying him for his approval of the Treaty of Locarno and his acceptance of Germany joining the League of Nations, thus 'ratifying for a second time the scandal of Versailles'. But Hindenburg was behaving with sense; he had never pretended to favour entering the League, 'but he has the constitutional sense to follow the advice of his ministers.' In August 1926, shortly before Germany was officially admitted, the British ambassador wired to London that the President might make difficulties about Geneva and might even refuse to sign the necessary decree. In preliminary conversations with members of the government he indicated that three conditions would have to be fulfilled before he would sign: a considerable reduction of the armies of occupation, an agreement about its duration, and the termination of the work of the Military Control Commission. Stresemann was seriously worried and would try to concentrate on the issue of troop reduction and to shelve the other two questions; he would point out to the President 'how inopportune their immediate discussion would be'; in his view there was no real connection between them and Germany joining the League.[82] D'Abernon also suspected that Germany hesitated to

216

enter the League out of fear of alienating Soviet Russia. The Germans would 'only risk forfeiting Russian support when they are sure of getting something equivalent on the Western frontier'; they would not enter a bargain as long as 'the positive gains are remote and nebulous'.[83] These obstacles were overcome and in the autumn of 1926 Germany joined the League.

Yet in spite of prosperity and considerable successes in the field of foreign policy the position of the government remained weak. In January 1928 the ambassador reported that 'decay proceeds apace; the Government is weak, a reed shaken by the wind, subservient to every vote-catching cry and everyone is dissatisfied.' Stresemann had long ago insisted that only a new government would be able to face the new French government and Chamber that would come into being in May. Now it was generally agreed that the budget had to be passed, and after the despatch of the essential financial business there ought to be a general election; it was expected that this would bring a considerable shift from the Right to the Left.[84] The election of May 1928 did bring this shift: Chancellor Marx resigned and was replaced by the Social Democrat Hermann Müller. In December the new Chancellor made a speech at a banquet given by the Press Association, which the British ambassador considered 'truculent' and 'indiscreet', in particular with regard to the *Anschluss*. He feared that the remarks were a deliberate statement of the new government's foreign policy and a rejoinder to recent statements in Britain and France. Müller stated *inter alia*: 'There is no Austrian people. There are only German races in Austria. Just as the Bretons are French, so are the Austrians German. We are one nation.' In the Foreign Office his speech was considered 'very tactless', but the official who commented on it was not certain whether the Chancellor was 'altogether to blame'; for the French press had been 'exceedingly rabid about this lately and M. Briand introduced a long and apparently quite unnecessary diatribe about it into his recent speech in the Chamber', while Millerand declared that a realization of the *Anschluss* would mean war: with all this it could be argued that the German Chancellor 'was forced to make some rejoinder.'[85] The Foreign Office thus once more adopted a mediating attitude to issues which remained highly controversial between France and Germany and tried to avoid siding with one or the other in what was still a verbal contest about the fate of Austria.

In 1929 the settlement of German reparations by yet another

committee of experts headed by the American Owen D. Young figured very prominently in the reports. At the beginning of the year Stresemann expressed his irritation to the ambassador about the long drawn-out formalities; he hoped that the experts would not take as long over their report as the powers needed to appoint them; business men would have done this in a few days.[86] When the conference held in Paris threatened to break down the French ambassador in Berlin blamed the intransigence and arrogance of Dr Schacht, the president of the German Central Bank. In the opinion of the commercial secretary of the British embassy Schacht was 'an ambitious man who would bring about his own extinction in so unnecessary a manner', and Germany's foreign credit 'would be severely injured' by a failure of the conference.[87] In the end even Schacht bowed to what he believed was 'inevitable' and the experts' report was accepted by the German representatives and the German government. But immediately the Hugenberg press launched violent attacks on the Young Plan and claimed that the German delegation admitted that the compromise reached was 'purely political and . . . not based on economic realities'. Even some moderate newspapers were critical of certain details of the plan, but – apart from the nationalist papers – the German press 'seems to have made up its mind to swallow the pill'. In the Foreign Office E.H. Carr minuted: 'The Germans seem to have, on the whole, good reason to be satisfied. They have gained something (not, of course, all they hoped), and given up nothing; and they can live in hopes of further reductions later on.'[88] He did not mention that, according to the Young Plan, German reparation payments were to continue until the year 1988, as they were to cover the inter-Allied war debts the settlement of which would take equally long. It was this 'slavery' for 60 years which aroused the fury of the nationalists.

The debate in the Reichstag on the Young Plan had to be postponed because of Stresemann's illness. When it took place the German Nationalist leader Westarp launched a violent attack on Stresemann and repeated the party's determination to fight the plan. Stresemann, 'who looked pale but was in fighting spirit', devoted most of his reply to a shrewd and aggressive criticism of the Nationalists; he reminded them that they helped towards the acceptance of the Dawes Plan, had then demanded its revision and were now objecting to the revision; he declared that Germany was not alone guilty of causing the outbreak of war in 1914; but the war debts did not result from the Treaty of Versailles but from a lost war; according to a British observer his speech 'was undoubtedly effective and discomforted them [the Nationalists] not a little.' It was warmly applauded.[89] A few months later Schacht launched his public attack on the Young Plan, thus openly playing into the hands of the Nationalists and National Socialists who were organizing a referendum against its acceptance. Harold Nicolson discussed Schacht's 'outburst' with von Schubert, the German Undersecretary of State, and found him 'puzzled and indignant'. Schacht's publication of his rejection, without the knowledge of the Finance Minister, was 'unforgivable' and would cause the government 'the most acute embarrassment': what made it worse, Schacht had also attacked other countries such as Britain and the Chancellor of the Exchequer 'with whom the Reich Government was desperately anxious to be on easy terms', and the whole affair placed Germany 'in an intolerable position'. Nicolson added that the actions of Hugenberg and Schacht 'cannot but strengthen the hands of those who are continually contending that democratic institutions are not suited to Germany, and that Government by Parliamentary coalitions means only weakness and confusion'.[90]

At the time of the Reichstag debate on the Young Plan the ambassador wrote to London that the advanced age of the President (he was almost 82 years old) and the precarious state of Stresemann's health formed serious elements of weakness in the German situation and that the Chancellor too was an ill man. By the time Nicolson made his comment Stresemann was dead. Rumbold also considered it essential that the next President 'should command the confidence of the country as a whole', and could think of no one to fulfil this condition except General von Seeckt[91] – a man deeply distrusted by the entire Left, who at best would have enjoyed the confidence of the conservatives, a rather small section of the voters. In 1928 Nicolson attempted a more general analysis of the German character. In his opinion the Germans had not yet regained self-confidence and 'this temperamental uncertainty was much increased by the events of the war'. During the agonizing years of the post-war period they also lost their pride: they clung to Chamberlain and D'Abernon 'as the two prophets who, armed with wisdom, would (and did) lead them from the waste'. They had now recovered their pride but not yet their self-confidence; 'their excess of caution tempts them to reject any proposal which they are not obliged, either by

219

treaty or by obvious self-interest, to accept'; if they appeared to be obstructive this could 'be explained by their fear of criticism, by their dread, if they once leave the narrow path prescribed by the Treaties, of making some mistake. . . .'[92] This unwillingness to compromise was also noticed by another British observer and concerned the bitter controversy over the German flag, which in his opinion was 'full of unrealities'. 'No German soldier', he wrote, 'ever fought under the Red, White and Black', for they fought under the colours of their separate states to which they took their military oath; the new flag of black-red-gold was violently supported by the Republicans, 'yet it is useles to pretend that the Republic is now dear to the hearts of the nation'; black-red-gold was attacked with even greater violence by the Right, 'but those people have nothing to put forward to replace the Republic' and a return to the monarchy was 'unthinkable'.

To him it seemed a pity that the Weimar Republic ever produced a new flag, for it had become a cause of quarrel, but the whole issue was unreal.[93] It certainly made the Republic unpopular with the conservatives. There was another issue which in the 1920s led to violent political controversies, that was the question of compensation for the former ruling houses and the property rights claimed by them. At the end of 1925 Addison reported from Berlin that the courts were recognizing these rights to such an extent that Prussia would lose very considerably while 'the smaller Federal States are liable to be crippled financially by the magnitude of the settlement with their ex-reigning houses'; the proposed settlement had led to violent outbursts in the left-wing press, while that of the Centre was torn between respect for the letter of the law and annoyance at the practical results; private claims in paper marks against the state (for example from those who had bought war loans) were only honoured to the extent of five per cent of their face value, and this was one of the principal arguments against a settlement with the former princes on purely legal grounds. In 1926 the left-wing parties, for once united, launched a plebiscite demanding the expropriation of the former ruling houses without compensation, but this was opposed by the government as well as the President. In spite of this, 36 per cent of the electorate supported the plebiscite. 'It is clear', D'Abernon commented, 'that several million voters who do not belong to the Socialist or Communist parties, have voted in favour of expropriation.' A provisional analysis showed 'that Prussia has yielded the greatest amount of localities where the percentage in favour of the referendum was over 50 per cent of the total number of persons entitled to vote. The highest percentage was in Berlin, namely 63. . . . On the whole the figures show that the feeling was strongest in Prussia, where many of the Democrats and Centre must have voted in favour of expropriation' out of dislike of the House of Hohenzollern.[94] As the referendum had failed the princes received ample compensation through treaties between them and the different states. There was no further comment on the disparity between the treatment of the princes and that of ordinary citizens. But in the same year D'Abernon commented on the verdicts of the German courts in cases of treason. In these cases 'judges, who are ordinarily men of broad views and enlightened humanity, administering a code which in many aspects is remarkably humane, inflict sentences of a savagery that leaves an English observer aghast.'[95] He could have added that these sentences, in their vast majority, concerned partisans of the Left, usually the extreme Left, and that the sentences revealed the political bias of the judiciary.

The German army was as conservative in it higher ranks as was the judiciary. The loyalty of both was to the *ancien régime* rather than to the unloved Republic. But the election of President von Hindenburg provided the army with a commander-in-chief who enjoyed their loyalty. As a junior British officer wrote in 1926, 'the Reichswehr, as such, is united in its allegiance to the Commander-in-Chief, the President, who, as Germany's military hero, has, in the eyes of the soldier, now filled a gap which, until his election to the presidency, was very noticeable in the Republican Constitution, and which could only be adequately filled by the "Chef der Heeresleitung", General von Seeckt.' He thought that henceforth the army would refuse to cooperate with the para-military associations in the erection of a right-wing dictatorship.[96] But the connections between the army and these associations, in particular the *Stahlhelm*, continued to exist because the army needed their members for illegal defence formations on the eastern frontier and for providing suitable recruits and temporary volunteers. When details about the army's recruiting methods leaked out in 1926 Chamberlain instructed the British ambassador to hint to Stresemann what anxiety this caused in foreign countries: 'Dr Stresemann may contend that this is an internal question merely affecting Germany herself, and I am ready to admit that the first aim of

221

these societies is probably to overthrow the republican regime. But the question has an international side as well, and Dr Stresemann must surely perceive that the nations who were fighting for their lives against the German army less than ten years ago cannot remain indifferent when they see the old Nationalist forces attempting, with apparent success, to recapture the Reichswehr and to make it once more a willing instrument of their nefarious designs.'[97]

The Inter-Allied Military Control Commission was well aware of the training of *Zeitfreiwillige* by the army, usually in one of the military camps or training grounds, of young men 'definitely recommended by some nationalist organisation', as was reported frequently in 1924.[98] According to the British Intelligence Summary, it was believed that possibly up to 100,000 men were trained in the course of a single year: 'it constitutes a flagrant breach of the Treaty of Versailles' and should be stopped 'before the matter gets more serious'.[99] In the autumn of 1924 it was confirmed by the War Office that members of the *Jungdeutscher Orden* as well as university students were trained at the Sennelager and that a new course was planned to start there early in 1925. Large numbers of temporary volunteers had been recruited in Bavaria, especially in 1923; but when officers of the Control Commission visited the military headquarters in Munich and a local Reichswehr regiment early in 1924, the German officers questioned strenuously denied that any reserves had been called up or that any *Zeitfreiwillige* were attached to their units and claimed that only men engaged for the legal 12-year term were present, that no volunteers had been enlisted since the rising in the Ruhr of 1920. Confusion on that score had probably arisen, they alleged, because during the Hitler Putsch units from outside Munich had been brought in; the 'replies were made frankly and without hesitation', and the officers' attitude was 'perfectly correct and polite'.[100] It clearly would not do for one gentleman to accuse another of lying.

At about the same time a British pacifist attended a meeting of the International Peace Bureau in Brussels and met Dr Ludwig Quidde, a leading German pacifist. On her return she reported to the Foreign Office that Quidde and his German friends were very disturbed about the training of German youths all over the country in military courses lasting eight or more weeks. The German pacifists had addressed a memorandum on the subject to their government but had been warned by General von Seeckt that procedures would be taken against them if they published it; thus Dr Quidde preferred to make his communication by word of mouth rather than in writing.[101] A few weeks later, however, he was arrested on a charge of treason on account of an article about German infractions of the Peace Treaty published in the *Welt am Montag*. A Foreign Office official suggested to put it to the German government 'that they should at once have the proceedings annulled'; he admitted that this was an intervention in German internal affairs but felt Britain 'ought to act' so as to prevent 'infinite future complications'. MacDonald and Crowe thought that Lord D'Abernon should speak informally to Stresemann to stress the grave complications the case might cause; and a telegram was sent to Berlin instructing the ambassador to warn Stresemann 'that in the interests of his country, he would be well advised to take immediate and drastic action to stop the proceedings', unless Quidde's arrest was not connected with his claims of violations of the Peace Treaty. Soon after Quidde was released but the proceedings against him were not stopped.[102]

Possibly because of these revelations and the strong German desire to terminate the activities of the Military Control Commission, the number of temporary volunteers enlisted by the army declined during the following years. When the allegation was repeated in 1927 the new Chief of the Army Command, General Heye, denied it 'on his word of honour'; and the British ambassador commented: 'If men had passed through the Reichswehr in excessive number the fact would hardly have escaped the knowledge of trade unions and would almost certainly have been utilized by the Social Democratic opposition in an attack on the hated Government, and still more hated Minister of the Reichswehr.' Lindsay was well 'aware of the unpleasant propensities of the German authorities in such questions', but he believed that a mare's nest had been discovered. And a British colonel added that it would be 'of little importance' if a few thousand extra men were trained every year.[103] Early in 1929, however, an Intelligence report stated that in late 1927 and early 1928 members of the *Stahlhelm* were trained by the army 'for short periods', but that the system had been abandoned some time after the appointment of General Groener to the Defence Ministry. Some reports also indicated that another system existed, that of enlisting men not for 12, but for only three years; and one report mentioned that the head of the *Truppenamt*, General von Blomberg, was responsible for 'making all the necessary arrangements'.[104] If the army leaders became convinced that courses of six to eight weeks were insufficient for training a soldier, as well they might, enlistment for three years would be preferable. In December 1929 the British military attaché stated there was little doubt that *Zeitfreiwillige* were still being trained; from the evidence at his disposal he estimated their number as some 7,000, and 'the large number of extremely youthful faces in the ranks of the Reichswehr' convinced him that the practice continued; locally the army was still cooperating with the *Stahlhelm* in numerous ways.[105] The unpublished autobiography of General von Blomberg confirms that at least in East Prussia numerous *Zeitfreiwillige* were still trained by the army in short courses and during manoeuvres.

It seems that the existence of another illegal force, the *Grenzschutz* along the east German frontiers, was at first a little better guarded. By 1928, however, the Allies were surprisingly well informed about it. In June the military expert attached to the British embassy in Berlin, Colonel Gosset, confidentially told an official of the *Auswärtige Amt* that a French officer had been entrusted with the task of investigation. From his remarks the German drew the conclusion that the Allies had procured secret German material through the good services of Polish Intelligence. Gosset used expressions such as *Bezirksleiter* and *Kreisleiter* which had never occurred in the diplomatic documents, and the Allies were also informed of the existence of organized military units in East Prussia and Silesia.[106] That there were other sources of information was confirmed in a letter of Harold Nicolson to the Foreign Office. He mentioned the evidence from recent German treason trials; and the Italian military attaché had told his British colleague that the eastern *Grenzschutz* was able to put 50,000 armed men into the field at three days' notice; its units included members of the *Reichsbanner* as well as the *Stahlhelm* (which was true of East Prussia but not of the other provinces). Nicolson added that 'for the moment' the army was still 'incapable of sudden or dramatic expansion'; he believed that 'it is better to shut one eye to such subterfuges in view of the fact that far more trouble or, in other words, far more danger to peace will be created by an endeavour to stem such leakage than is constituted by the actual dribble itself', for 'there will always be subterfuges, some of which will be discovered, and some of which will never be disclosed.'[107] Letters such as this explain a lot of the British attitude of 'shutting one eye' – not to mention the very much improved relations between Britain and Germany at the time of Stresemann which seemed to remove the danger of war. A senior official of the Foreign Office wrote that all its information confirmed a French report on the *Grenzschutz*, but any protest 'would appear to be a sheer waste of breath unless they are prepared to take it up as a matter of primary importance and to carry it to the League'; even if they did so, 'the result could not possibly compensate for the bad blood which would be aroused', especially as the *Grenzschutz* included members of all parties to the Social Democrats on the Left.[108] And there the matter rested.

At the beginning of 1933 the British military attaché in Berlin thought that the *Grenzschutz* was only part of a wider policy of the Ministry of Defence for the eastern frontier districts. When the German military reviewed the situation after the conclusion of peace 'they found a very alarming state of affairs' there and decided 'to begin at once the formation of fresh German wedges to isolate the Polish blocks in Pomerania and Silesia'; ex-soldiers were settled who would thus be available on the spot in case of war; in the centre, where the population was sparser, frontier defence units were organized under energetic officers who had recently left the army; and the same policy of colonization was adopted in East Prussia, in particular the area of the Masurian lakes; there the problem was aggravated by depopulation which for economic reasons had set in at the beginning of the twentieth century.[109] That illegal measures for defence were not only taken along the eastern frontiers but even in central Germany became known to the Allies in 1929 when an employee of the Defence Ministry sold to the French a complete collection of secret material relating to the Prussian province of Saxony, allegedly for the sum of 100,000 French francs. To camouflage it the material was dated 1924, but the army did not doubt that the Allied military experts would immediately recognize it as up to date; it would provide them with a complete purview of the defence organization and its tasks.[110] From a perusal of the internal telephone directory of the Defence Ministry the British also knew that, contrary to the provisions of the Peace Treaty, the General Staff – with four sections and a chief of staff – had been resuscitated in 1929 (or earlier), although the published Army List said nothing on this. Furthermore, several retired officers were 'really employed on General Staff work'.[111]

In some other matters Allied pressure was a little more successful. In 1927 a British colonel visited the island of Borkum and discovered that of the 119 guns Germany was permitted to retain for coastal defence four had been removed and placed on a cruiser. The Army Council insisted that the four guns must be put back on their old sites and an undertaking given that such infractions would not be repeated. But a Foreign Office official minuted that the Admiralty 'do not attach much importance to the question'.[112] On this occasion General Wauchope had insisted that the assurance of the German military that all the guns had been placed according to an agreed formula must be accepted and that no visit of inspection was required to verify this. But after a lively discussion in the Control Commission the majority decided against him, and it was then found that the four guns had been moved. In the same year the German government intended to give a formal assurance that the pill-boxes built along the eastern frontier contrary to the terms of the Peace Treaty would be blown up: as the Reichswehr opposed any verification by the Allies, this assurance 'must suffice'. Thereupon the British ambassador told von Schubert the story of the four guns and General Wauchope. Schubert listened carefully, asked some questions about the when and where and remarked that 'the German military authorities too were resolved to behave with scrupulous regard'. He even claimed that the government might fall if it permitted visits of inspection, and the ambassador expected some very violent criticism of the government. Chamberlain and Stresemann then arranged at Geneva a compromise by which Allied experts would witness the destruction. Some weeks later certain of the fortifications were blown up in the presence of Allied officers. In certain cases 'portions of the shelters have been thrown a distance of four to five hundred yards', a British officer reported. The German officers present 'treated the Allied experts in a most friendly manner, as did all the officers they met, and also the local inhabitants', and relations were 'most cordial throughout the visits'.[113] The government did not fall – and the few blown up pill-boxes could be quickly rebuilt.

As to the equipment permitted to the German army by the Peace Treaty, officers of the Military Control Commission in 1924 discovered considerable quantities of arms and equipment above the permitted levels. The German News Agency then denied that differences of opinion existed on this issue between the Defence Ministry and the *Auswärtige Amt* as alleged by the British papers. As Addison wrote to London, every child knew that constant friction existed between them, but 'some of the leading spirits in the German Army are so absolutely thick-headed that they cannot realize that it is to their obvious interest . . . to get rid of the Commission as soon as possible by means of an apparently full and frank attitude'.[114] In 1925 an inspection of a factory at Wittenau revealed 113,000 rifle barrel forgings and 17,000 machine gun barrel forgings plus other war material but no complete weapons. Obstruction was encountered and later some of the incriminating material was removed. It seemed that the arms were produced for export to South America and not for use in Germany. The attitude of the Foreign Office officials was to play down the incident. The British should try, one of them minuted, 'to prevent the French from making too much of it'.[115] In 1928 two Communist deputies placed a large gas shell on the table of the Reichstag and another deputy declared that it was a specimen of many thousands produced at the Schichau ship-yard near Danzig. Colonel Gosset, however, considered that 'it would not be possible or desirable to raise the matter with the German authorities' on account of a Communist demonstration, and the ambassador simply reported the incident to London.[116]

In the same year a large explosion occurred in Hamburg when a quantity of phosgen gas stored by the firm of Stolzenberg blew up although the Control Commission had ordered the stock to be destroyed. It was not clear whether this was a stock dating from the war or of recent manufacture, and the Allied governments addressed an enquiry to the Germans how the possession of the gas could be reconciled with Germany's treaty obligations and the war material law. The German reply was found 'evasive and argumentative', and no conclusive evidence existed that there was an infraction of the Peace Treaty; it was therefore believed that it was useless to pursue the matter further and it was dropped. Colonel Gosset reported several times that there was 'reason to suppose that secret stores of poison gas exist in this country and that certain factories are still employed in the manufacture of gas shells'. The ambassador, however, consider-ed it pointless to pursue the matter: the Allied governments would not 'obtain satisfaction or even information in respect of incidental violations' unless they could produce 'incontrovert-ible and independent proof'.[117] Thus even the production of poison gas could take place in Germany because the Allies felt unable to prevent it, or did not feel strong enough to act. German obstruction and evasion carried the day.

In 1923 the visits of inspection by Allied officers to German military establishments were abandoned after a number of violent incidents (see page 154). They were to be resumed in 1924 with the beginning of rapprochement between France and Germany; but, as D'Abernon heard 'very confidentially', this was violently opposed by General von Seeckt in a Cabinet meeting of 8 January because Germany had completely disarmed and military control had to be terminated according to the provisions of the Peace Treaty. Seeckt was opposed by Stresemann who urged that the control must be carried out for political reasons, and his view was supported by the Cabinet. Orders were sent to the military districts 'which should facilitate peaceful execution'. The inspection visits were resumed and there were no violent incidents. A new conflict with Seeckt developed in June after the Ambassadors' Conference had demanded a 'general inspection' to ascertain the state of German disarmament. The German government was willing to accept this — so as to speed up the termination of the Control Commission's work — but Seeckt declared any visits to barracks 'incompatible with the honour of the German Army' and the Treaty of Versailles: he would resign rather than allow it. As the British embassy heard 'from a most reliable source', the Cabinet was of the opinion that 'the honour of the German Army lay in obeying the orders of its superiors and that it ceased to be an Army if individual officers, be they Generals or Lieutenants, could oppose' such orders. The government was prepared to let Seeckt go and began to consider names of a possible successor. Then President Ebert had a long conference with Seeckt and the Defence Minister during which he pointed out that Seeckt would have to resign if he declined to obey the government. Seeckt asked for 24 hours to consider his position and consult some other generals and then informed the government that he would accept their ruling: 'In short, when he found that his bluff was called, he threw in his card.'[118]

It was suspected at the time that Seeckt's real reason for refusing the inquiry was that it would reveal the extent of illegal rearmament and result in a continuation of military control either by the Control Commission or by the League of Nations. A British journalist working in Germany mentioned to an official of the *Auswärtige Amt* that the reason for Seeckt's opposition must be that he had something to hide and received the reply:

'Of course he has.'[119] In spite of all this, the British attitude to Seeckt remained surprisingly positive. In June 1924 D'Abernon wrote: 'Although Herr Stresemann has hinted to me on more than one occasion that General von Seeckt and a long-service Reichswehr are a thorn in the side of a moderate Republican Government, I am inclined for my part to believe . . . that he stands for the maintenance of internal order against the extremists of either wing.'[120] Early in 1925 the Director of Military Intelligence, in a letter to General Wauchope, was even more positive: 'I agree we must avoid anything which the Germans could interpret as a direct attack on von Seeckt. Doubtless he has plans for the future and his statue may one day adorn the Siegesallee, as the man who has delivered Germany from the consequences of the Versailles Treaty, but at the present time he supports the Republic and is a force on the side of existing law and order.'[121] For the British authorities the maintenance of law and order was a primary consideration, but any other German general would have been equally capable of doing this, and on this issue Stresemann knew better: Seeckt was a highly political general with very ambitious plans for the future; and it was above all due to him that the Reichswehr became 'a state within the state'.

In November 1924 D'Abernon reported that military control, 'which it was generally considered impossible to re-establish', had proceeded for two months with only minor incidents. The inspections had discovered 'a large number of minor infractions, but no evidence whatever of military preparations of such a nature as to involve a danger of war'. But the French officers of the Control Commission were still deeply suspicious and would not subscribe to any favourable interpretation of German intentions. The Control Commission had drawn up a 'list of German delinquencies' which were mainly minor ones, but listed considerable quantities of surplus equipment. It also stated that the control of the army was 'ineffective' because the Allied officers were not allowed into any room marked 'private', they had to accept the German figures of the strength of the units, and any information for the period when control was suspended was refused. In general, however, the Army Council agreed with the opinion of General Wauchope, the head of the British section of the Control Commission, that 'Germany cannot be regarded as having carried out the military clauses of the Treaty of Versailles, either in the spirit or in the letter', but that she was sufficiently disarmed 'to prevent her being able to go to war with a civilized Power armed on a modern scale'. General Wauchope also thought that, after the destruction of the surplus war material, the work of the Control Commission could safely be terminated, but certain factories should be converted to peaceful production and the militarized police forces should be reorganized.[122] At Stuttgart the Allied officers visiting the headquarters of the 5th Division were assailed by a hostile crowd, two officers were struck on the head and a car was damaged. Strong police reinforcements succeeded in dispersing the rioters who sang the 'Watch on the Rhine' and other patriotic songs. A youth who had distributed stones was arrested.[123]

After conferring with General Wauchope Lord D'Abernon believed that the principal difficulty concerned the quartering of German police units in barracks. Both were of the opinion that the German government needed an 'efficient and fully armed police force living in barracks as a protection against communism and internal disorder'; it would be unwise 'to press for a modification which might endanger public tranquillity'; recent Communist demonstrations in Berlin had proved 'a genuine necessity for rapidly available means of repression'. The Director of Military Intelligence at the War Office, however, felt that the ambassador overestimated the Communist danger: 'this is not so great now as it was four or five years ago,' and the only serious Communist trouble of recent times was put down by the army (in 1923) not the police; the French, on the other hand, were exaggerating the danger emanating from the police.[124] He might have added that the Prussian police was controlled by the Social Democratic government of Prussia, which did not see eye to eye with the generals and often clashed with them on defence and other issues. The police presented a threat to the Communists but not to Allied security.

At the end of 1924 the British General Staff assessed the military situation in Germany and stated 'that their mistrust and apprehension of Germany remain undiminished'; they did not fear France but they feared for France; there were dangers to civilization beyond Germany (meaning Soviet Russia), 'and the sooner Germany can be brought to range herself on the side of western civilization, the better chance will that civilization have of maintaining itself against these dangers', but the conversion of Germany required discipline. Germany was temporarily cowed by defeat but would reassert herself, and 'pressure must be maintained on Germany till she is led or forced into higher standards', and this pressure could only be exerted by France and Britain acting together. The tone became more strident when the General Staff discussed the German nation, 'a primitive people scientifically equipped – vigorous, prolific and unscrupulous, combining the height of modern efficiency with the mentality and brutality of the middle ages'. A few months later the General Staff came back to the issue when it commented on the final report of the Military Control Commission after its general inspection; it declared that the infractions were 'against the spirit rather than the letter of the treaty'; they were made possible 'by the military spirit which animates a large section of the German people'; this constituted a 'grave danger', but the peace treaty 'makes no provision for dealing with it.'[125] There was no second flight into the realm of medieval history, and the possibility of exercising pressure on the German government to dissolve the numerous para-military associations was not even discussed.

In February 1925 Lord D'Abernon reported that Chancellor Luther was determined to rectify any failure in matters of disarmament which the Allies could point out; no positive advantage could accrue from more visits of inspection. In his opinion and that of General Wauchope the outlook for a general solution was 'distinctly favourable' and anything imperilling it should be avoided; on the difficult issue of the militarized police a compromise would be best. Some months later General Wauchope reported that he had seen General von Seeckt only once in recent weeks; Seeckt had made it clear 'that though delighted to talk about the weather' he would not discuss the disarmament question. Wauchope had been told that Seeckt was very angry because of the Allied note demanding rectification which he attributed to French pressure on Britain.[126] It was obvious, however, that unless there was sufficient rectification the Military Control Commission would not be wound up all that quickly. In November 1925 D'Abernon wrote that at last the Control Commission appeared to be nearing its end and that Lord Crewe in Paris had negotiated 'with skill and vigour'; the final delay concerned 'points of no real importance', and all the measures of disarmament carried out since 1924 had 'a military value of 0.0001'. It would have been preferable to declare that disarmament was completed. Twelve months later Stresemann, in a conversation on the same subject with the British ambassador, feared that, if military control were not terminated, the German Nationalists would dominate German public opinion in matters of foreign policy and that would mean a throw-back to out-of-date methods. Lindsay replied that he too considered the situation rather strange: there was agreement on 99 per cent and conflict about the last one per cent; Chamberlain had written to Paris and Rome and suggested to meet the German wishes; but France was making difficulties, and Chamberlain advized the Germans to make a concession on the issue of the para-military associations. But Stresemann refused to admit that these could constitute a nightmare for France.[127]

Meanwhile a new difficulty had arisen, following the retirement of General von Seeckt in October 1926. He had permitted the eldest son of the former Crown Prince to take part as an officer in the autumn manoeuvres without previously informing either the Defence Minister or the President. Stresemann told D'Abernon that the incident itself was not all that important but it was 'quite intolerable' for Seeckt to authorize this on his own responsibility. Dr Gessler declared publicly that he was not prepared to defend Seeckt in parliament and was supported in this by the Cabinet; in due course Hindenburg too insisted that Seeckt must retire.[128] Seeckt's successor was Lieutenant-General Heye who was promoted full general in the same month. General Wauchope noted immediately that this was 'most unfortunate' and showed a lack of political sense on the German side. Previously, the French had agreed to regard the question of the High Command structure as settled, but now they might reopen it because Heye's promotion showed that the 'Chief of the Army Command' exercised the functions of an Inspector-General and Commander-in-Chief: in January 1926 the Germans had accepted the Allied demand that the commanding generals of the army must be directly subordinate to the Minister of Defence, and not to the 'Chief of the Army Command'. Some days later General Wauchope had lunch with Stresemann who enquired whether the issue of the Higher Command structure could be regarded as settled. Wauchope replied that a week ago he would have said yes, but the promotion of Heye had complicated matters a little. Stresemann then explained that Seeckt's natural successor would have been either General von Lossberg or General Reinhardt, the most senior generals of the army. But the first was a monarchist which made his appointment impossible, and the second a Württemberger, 'and Prussia and the other States would not have accepted the appointment'; therefore Heye was appointed, but Lossberg and Reinhardt declared they could not serve under an officer junior to them in rank and threatened to resign. Stresemann feared that public opinion would not have countenanced this on top of Seeckt's retirement, and thus the 'only thing to do was to promote General Heye'.[129] Unfortunately, General Wauchope did not know that Reinhardt had been Seeckt's predecessor as 'Chief of the Army Command' and before that the last Prussian Minister of War, so that any objection from Prussia to his appointment was extremely unlikely. It may, of course, have been that Stresemann invented this curious 'explanation' on the spur of the moment: it certainly sounded quite convincing.

Before the end of 1926 it was announced that the Military Control Commission would be withdrawn. General Wauchope noted that 'outside official circles and the Army, comparatively few people knew or cared whether the Commission existed, but the Press campaign, cleverly organized ... has made the withdrawal of the Commission a much needed and valuable diplomatic triumph for Dr Stresemann.'[130] At the same time the general received information from the American military attachés in Berlin, who were in close touch with Reichswehr officers, on the true spirit animating the officer corps. Both stated 'most emphatically that after constant meetings, discussions and attendances at manoeuvres and in camps of exercise, they are convinced that the great bulk of German officers believe that in very few years they could wage a successful war against France'; initially, the Germans would have to retreat to the east of the Ruhr and perhaps further, but 'final success would come to Germany, thanks to the National spirit of the people, capacity for endurance', purchase of arms from neutral countries and the inability of the French to fight a long war. Wauchope himself did not share this view but thought that the date when Germany would be capable of waging war would be near as soon as she possessed factories equipped to produce war material at very short notice: therefore the control of the special tools needed for the production of arms was 'most important, practicable and legitimate'.[131]

Another contentious point concerned the training of army officers as aviation pilots, which was desired by the Reichswehr as a question of prestige, as Stresemann told the British chargé d'affaires in January 1926. No one, he added, dreamt of training

7,000 officers as military pilots, but the officers felt declassed if this remained forbidden to them; as little as they could be forbidden to become drivers, as little could they be prohibited to take part in sports flying, and any such prohibition would be deeply resented. A few days later Addison once more visited Stresemann to explain the British point of view that no flying training should be allowed to the Reichswehr. In March Stresemann told D'Abernon one should not forget that hitherto Germany had been permitted flying training as a sport and that now she was being asked to make a concession beyond the prohibitions of Versailles; no intention existed to create a German air force, nor of training 200 officers simultaneously: the Allies had misunderstood the German request and their note was a very retrogressive step. D'Abernon replied that the best solution might be to fix a definite number of men to be trained per year; the figure could be relatively small and would not cause the disquiet aroused by the number of 200, and he admitted that even that figure would not constitute a danger.[132] At that time Stresemann knew of the German aerodrome at Lipetsk in Russia where dozens of German officers were trained as pilots and observers but the British did not yet possess this knowledge.[133] Apparently a compromise was eventually reached; in 1929 the British air attaché, Group Captain Christie, stated that officers and other ranks of the army were trained as pilots and observers at the German flying schools at Munich and Staaken and that of the Albatross works near Berlin, with funds supplied by the Ministry of Defence. In addition, the German navy had seaplane stations at Kiel and on the island of Norderney in the North Sea, which were maintained by the 'Luftdienst G.m.b.H.', a concern employing 135 people and possessing 30 aeroplanes. In the same report Christie for the first time mentioned the secret agreement with Soviet Russia and the German flying school there, only he placed it at Vitebsk in White Russia instead of Lipetsk (to the north of Voronesh), with German 'fighting and bombing squadrons all concentrated on this one large aerodrome'.[134]

In December 1928 the British military attaché in Berlin also discussed German-Soviet military relations and noted that General von Blomberg, the head of the *Truppenamt*, with members of his staff had attended the Red Army manoeuvres in the Ukraine, while Red Army officers in uniform observed the training of certain Reichswehr units; as Blomberg's mission infringed Article 179 of the Peace Treaty (which forbade

Germany to send military missions to foreign countries) the
Germans had kept very quiet about it. In the same report the
attaché called General Heye 'affable and rather pompous . . . an
insignificant figure compared with his very able predecessor
von Seeckt'; by someone who knew Heye well he was described
as 'little in stature and little in mind'. Twelve months later the
military attaché reported that the new head of the *Truppenamt*,
General von Hammerstein-Equord, accompanied by two other
officers had also attended the Russian manoeuvres and then
made an extensive tour of Russia, the Ukraine, the Urals, the
Caucasus and the Crimea; the German military authorities were
'bent on keeping close touch with their most effective potential
ally in a future conflict with Poland'. In spite of all this, the
attaché claimed to notice 'a distinct cooling-off in Russo-German
relations', compared with 1928 when it looked as if the 'Eastern-
ers' had gained the upper hand in German military policy. But
he did not say on what evidence this surprising judgment was
based. He was considerably more correct in his claim that the
Reichswehr leaders were 'building up the foundations of a large
expansion some years hence'.[135] The financial adviser to the
British embassy noticed that the Reichswehr budget for 1925–26
amounted to 624 million marks, well over a third of the budget
for 1913–14 when the army had been eight times as strong. A
minute of the Foreign Office stressed this discrepancy as well as
another: that the German navy had been 'reduced from a strength
comparable with that of our own to an almost negligible quantity'; if the expenditure on the police were added to that on the
Reichswehr, it came to nearly one half of the pre-war figure.[136]
The implication clearly was that some of these very large funds
were being diverted to illegitimate purposes and, as we now
know, this was quite correct.

In 1929 the British ambassador summed up what he knew of
German military plans: 'minor illegalities are taking place, and
will continue to take place, on an extensive scale', but it was
impossible to obtain convincing evidence as to the actual extent
of the illegalities; as long as democracy existed in Germany it
was likely to be pacifist, and with the passage of time Germany's
disarmament would be fused into general disarmament, subject
to general methods of supervision. If Britain made representations regarding German infractions of the Peace Treaty, this
'would be negatived by the impossibility of proving our complaints or enforcing our demands'; not even 'the most optimistic

framer of the Treaty of Versailles' could have thought 'that every single enactment of that instrument would remain in force for over a quarter of a century.'[137] Yet this was only ten years after the signing of the treaty, and in practice its military provisions had already broken down, for the Reichswehr generals were determined to pursue a course of expansion.

So were the German admirals. In August 1928 the Müller government authorized the construction of the first armoured cruiser or 'pocket battleship', thus abandoning the attitude of the Social Democratic Party when it was in opposition. Harold Nicolson reported from Berlin that this change of policy was due to pressure by the President on the Chancellor (another instance of the extra-constitutional use of the presidential powers); the right-wing papers were exploiting 'this instance of Democratic and Social Democratic insincerity' and insisting that the decision involved the building of three more ships of the same class. Outside Berlin and especially in Saxony there was violent criticism of the decision; this became so serious that the SPD leaders summoned a joint meeting of the parliamentary party and the executive committee. There Paul Loebe, the president of the Reichstag, proposed that the party should continue the fight against the building of the cruiser with all the means at its disposal, which would have meant the resignation of the government; but the motion was defeated by a small majority. Another resolution, expressing opposition to the construction but not asking for the withdrawal of the SPD ministers from the government, was then passed with a large majority. But several provincial party papers continued to express resentment and to insist that the second instalment for the cruiser should be withheld.[138] The first pocket battleship was launched by Hindenburg in May 1931 in the midst of the economic crisis; and, as predicted by the right-wing papers, this was only the first of a series which Germany continued to build in spite of the severity of the crisis. In June 1931 the SPD leader Otto Wels visited Arthur Henderson in the Foreign Office and explained that his party could not possibly break with General Groener, the Defence Minister, 'the main bulwark of the Republican regime', nor with President Hindenburg, 'whose personal position in German politics is virtually supreme': when he and Groener were united 'as they usually are on questions of armaments', no government could stand up to them. Wels could only suggest rather feebly that the British ministers should hint in private conversations that the building of the next pocket battleship should be post-poned.[139] So they did, but the suggestion fell on deaf ears (see page 249).

The years of relative stabilization, with the election of President von Hindenburg and the growing weight of the army, brought new strength to the conservative forces in state and country. In the industrial field the British reports noticed a marked tendency to concentration and amalgamation, especially in the heavy and chemical industries. In 1925 the financial adviser to the embassy composed a memorandum on the subject which discussed the proposal to amalgamate some of the leading concerns in mining and steel production, such as Thyssen, Rhein-Elbe Union, Phoenix and Rheinstahl, with Krupp adopting a position of benevolent neutrality; 'the production apparatus has become too big; it cannot be used advantageously and it involved too costly overhead charges.' In the chemical industry too an attempt was made 'to transform the present federal system of independent companies into one great economic unity, whereby it will become possible to reduce the amount of duplicated labour as well as to increase the productivity of each concern.' A complete fusion of their interests under the name of 'I.G. Farbenindustrie' had been announced, and a similar tendency was noticeable in the artificial silk, petroleum and electricity industries.[140] In 1926 the commercial secretary reported on the formation of the 'Vereinigte Stahlwerke', a Ruhr steel trust, with a total output capacity of nearly six million tons of steel, after nine months of difficult negotiations. The four firms mentioned above had decided to join hands; with reduced costs they hoped to find larger markets abroad, and the finishing industry could be supplied with cheaper material and thus with 'greater competitive ability in the world market'. Schacht, the president of the central German bank, told D'Abernon over dinner in 1926 that since Locarno the position of the bank had become stronger every week, while until Locarno it had always lost gold; the tide had now turned, confidence increased and he was very optimistic about the future; unemployment was the black spot, but against that might be set the amalgamation of the large concerns, especially of the chemical and steel industries. Schacht insisted that German colonial interests should be developed as a means of maintaining the stability of the mark, and for good measure also that the frontier system in the east with the Polish Corridor and the partition of Upper Silesia was 'unworkable'.[141] Stresemann, on the other hand, assured the ambassador that the political influence of German heavy industry 'had greatly diminished'; this was due to the death of Stinnes who had the whole of heavy industry behind him and wielded 'a well-nigh irresistible weight of authority'. But since 1925 the president of the employers' association was Dr Carl Duisberg of the great chemical trust, and its new secretary was Dr Kastl who held liberal views; Duisberg and other leading industrialists supported the People's-Party and the Democratic Party, and not the German Nationalists.[142] Thus the growing power of the German chemical industry, especially of the new I.G. Farben trust, was duly noticed. It was founded at exactly the same time as Imperial Chemical Industries, and for the same reasons.

The German industrialists used their growing power against the working class, especially in the Ruhr where a superficial national unity had existed in 1923. Early in 1924 the British vice-consul at Essen reported that in the cement industry the unions other than the 'free' unions had agreed to a ten-hour day and that agreement had been reached on the wages of the metal workers, but that the employers refused to negotiate with the metal workers union, the DMV, as long as it would not give in to the ten-hour day; the number of strikers in the metal industry had declined, partly because the workers who refused to work ten hours were not entitled to any unemployment relief.[143] In April the British section of the Rhineland High Commission noticed that the unions had to call off the strike over the issue of the ten-hour day; it 'ended with a complete victory for the employers', and now a 54-hour week was being worked. A similar strike of the brown coal miners lasted seven weeks, with the Communists playing a very active part; at the end of February the 'Christian' union advocated a return to work but were overruled by the other unions and the proposal was voted down. But the number of those returning to work grew daily; the employers reported an increased willingness to work, in spite of the longer hours. They used the opportunity to reduce the work force by 23 per cent owing to the introduction of two shifts of ten hours each and to dismiss the strike leaders: they had gained a complete victory over the 'free' unions which had lost much of their support. As a result of the improving economic situation and the resumption of work the number of unemployed had declined.[144] At the same time the 'free' unions were attacked by the Catholic Church. The hierarchy of Cologne, Münster and Munich published an edict denying the sacrament to any of their members, so as to induce them to join the 'Christian' unions.[145]

In the Ruhr the situation of the working class continued to be extremely bad. In March 1924 the American organizer of a fund to aid the workers found that real wages were about 25 per cent lower than in the pre-war period and that the cost of living had risen substantially; those fortunate enough to have work 'are living on an unbelievably scanty margin which must mean real hunger and slow starvation for the masses'; more food was now available but people could not afford to buy it, and the situation of the unemployed 'is really desperate'.[146] In the autumn a Foreign Office official who visited Mainz and Cologne commented on the high cost of living; wages approximated to the pre-war level but the hours were longer. In Cologne he did not observe any actual signs of poverty but from Crefeld there were reports of distress. During the inflation many fortunes had been made and lost; many of the imposing modern buildings he had seen 'were built on the paper mark'; most of them were banks some of which were 'magnificently housed'.[147]

In Ludwigshafen the workers of a chemical factory in 1924 refused to comply with the extension of their working day from eight to ten hours and left the factory after eight hours' work. Thereupon the management declared a lockout and the workers tried to occupy the factory. The police were then called in, used their arms and several workers were wounded, while the mayor appealed to the Rhineland High Commission for the assistance of troops.[148] A much bigger lockout was declared by the employers of the steel industry of the north-west in the autumn of 1928, affecting more than 200,000 workers. The Ministry of Labour had declared an arbitration award legally binding, but the employers contested this on the ground that the award had been made by the arbitrator alone and not by a majority of the committee. 'The action of the employers is difficult to understand', the commercial secretary of the British embassy commented, 'unless they have determined to use this occasion to contest once and for all the authority of the State to interfere by means of an arbitration system in matters which they regard as purely economic'; the employers had repeatedly demanded the revision of the law governing arbitration and the abolition of the government's power to intervene in labour disputes, except where a well defined public interest was concerned. The situation deteriorated when the central office for unemployment decided that the locked-out workers were not entitled to unemployment relief; many of them were not union members, and the funds of the unions proved insufficient. The socialist papers published articles threatening the capitalists with dire consequences if they persisted in challenging the authority of the democratic state, but this was a rather empty threat.[149] There can be little doubt that by the end of the stabilization period the whole position of the employers was considerably stronger than it had been in the early years of the Republic.

In general the British attitude towards Germany had become much more friendly and conciliatory, for example in overlooking German infractions of the military clauses of the Peace Treaty or in speeding up the final withdrawal of the Military Control Commission. This may have been partly due to the great prestige of Stresemann, partly to a reassertion of the old principle of the balance of power on the Continent (although this was no longer mentioned in the official records), partly to a desire to strengthen the west as against the east. Even in the vexed question of German-Polish relations which so often occupied the attention of the League of Nations, the British attitude was by no means anti-German. When the Poles in 1927 expelled several Germans – railwaymen, managers and directors of firms – a Foreign Office official minuted: 'So far as discrimination against Germans as such is concerned, I think the Poles are in the wrong'; but it should be remembered that Germany was 'in a position to overwhelm the native element in Polish commerce, professions, etc.'; if the Poles, as they should do, applied most-favoured-nation treatment they would give Germany 'a very considerable advantage over the other nations with which Poland chiefly trades'. This seemed inevitable, however, and 'the Poles will have to realise in the long run that their economic life cannot develop save in close connection with that of Germany'. In the same year this official visited the town of Beuthen in Upper Silesia which had been allocated to Germany after the plebiscite and found there 'every appearance of prosperity': the shops well stocked, the cafés crammed full, the women and children of the working class well fed and clothed, the town engaged in an ambitious housing scheme, 'not designed with a strict eye to economy'. He had gone to Beuthen to take part in a meeting to promote German-Polish understanding and found it well attended, especially by women.[150] Clearly, not everything was black in German-Polish relations.

Occasionally, however, irritation with German demands or the behaviour of the German authorities would show itself at the Foreign Office, as in the case of the illumination of the Niederwald monument mentioned in the previous chapter (see pages 179–81). A similar incident occurred in 1927 when the German government asked for permission for army officers to attend a scientific meeting on aeronautics at Wiesbaden in the British zone of occupation, to which no Allied representatives had been invited. Apparently for this reason the Rhineland High Commission refused permission and Chamberlain declined to intervene. An official of the Foreign Office considered that this episode illustrated 'the gross want of tact and psychological intuition inherent in the German mentality', and particularly prevalent among former officers and the German Nationalists. The episode 'also served to show the weakness of the permanent officials in the Ministry of Foreign Affairs' who – in the absence of Stresemann – had to cope with the Ministry of Defence ' in which questions of internal politics so frequently override the dictates of diplomacy'.[151] Yet the principal aim of British policy was the integration of Germany with the Allied countries through the League of Nations and good commercial and political relations. In retrospect it seems that this policy might have been successful if the world economic crisis had not intervened and if democratic institutions had survived in Germany: it was a big 'if'. But in the years before 1930 few people seriously doubted that the Republic and democratic institutions had come to stay in Germany.

VII

THE FINAL CRISIS

During the years 1930 to 1932 British policy towards Germany did not change in any important aspect. There was the same worry about a revival of German nationalism and militarism and the possibility of another European war, side by side with a willingness to meet German wishes and to assist Germany, especially the government of Heinrich Brüning, to stem the growing flood from the Right. Fears about the rising tide of German nationalism were voiced by Arthur Henderson, the Foreign Secretary, when he saw von Schubert, now the German ambassador to Rome, early in 1931. Henderson enquired what the prospects of the 'Hitlerites' were; if they came to power it was feared – less in England than elsewhere – that they would tear up the treaties and drive to war; some people were asking themselves whether there was any point in pursuing disarmament if certain circles in Germany wanted war. He, Henderson, had always stood for a revision of the Peace Treaty, when the ink of the signatures was hardly yet dry; he had advocated this within the Second International, to the French Socialists as well as at Geneva in 1924; but a policy of obtaining a revision of the treaties by force would lead to disaster. Schubert could only reply that hitherto no German government had shown such an intention (which was quite true but did not answer Henderson's fears).[1] Three months earlier similar fears were expressed by Churchill, then an opposition MP. To a German diplomatic visitor he expressed his satisfaction about the parliamentary success of the Brüning government and his sharp rejection of National Socialism which had brought about a considerable deterioration of Germany's position abroad. He reminded his

visitor of a meal they had in 1925 when he had said that France
was still afraid of Germany – and this was still the case. Hitler
denied any intention of waging war, but he, Churchill, was
convinced that Hitler or his followers would use the first opportunity to resort once more to arms. Churchill showed himself
very well informed about German developments and had clearly
studied the press reports in detail.[2] Although neither politician
was quite representative of public opinion in Britain at that time,
the reports indicate a growing awareness of the National
Socialist menace among leading politicians. Both Henderson
and Churchill had been members of the War Cabinets of Asquith
and Lloyd George and were clearly afraid of a repetition of the
great catastrophe of 1914.

Henderson and the Labour government were above all
interested in disarmament and the discussions on this subject at
Geneva. In June 1931 he warned another German visitor of the
impression prevailing in England that Germany was not really
interested in disarmament and unwilling to cooperate honestly
to achieve it, but was determined to rearm ultimately; in the
circumstances Britain was inevitably pushed towards France,
for in one respect the two countries were united – to prevent
German rearmament. The German embassy in London considered this attitude symptomatic of the growing distrust of
German policy 'in wide circles of English friends of peace who
as such are friendly towards Germany'.[3] When the British
ambassador saw the German Foreign Minister Curtius in Berlin
he expressed similar worries: Henderson and the British government were counting on success at the disarmament conference
and therefore regretted the pessimism noticeable in Germany;
the British government was not satisfied with a stabilization of
the existing state of armaments, and was demanding their reduction, but it had the impression that a large section of German
public opinion intended to use the conference to achieve the
renunciation of the disarmament clauses of the Treaty of
Versailles; this section was rendering a bad service to the
German government and to international cooperation. Curtius,
however, considered this criticism of German policy unjustified
and repudiated it rather sharply: Henderson ought to be able to
tell him at their next meeting that the criticism no longer stood.[4]

When Sir Horace Rumbold reported this conversation to
London two officials of the Central Department of the Foreign
Office minuted that in their opinion, 'the German Government

and probably the majority of Germans do not at present want to adopt the policy of rearmament if they can help it', because it would raise such serious political issues 'that no German Government would willingly embark on it'. Yet Germany seemed determined to use the disarmament conference to raise the question of the Polish Corridor. If this were settled to her satisfaction she would be reasonable with regard to disarmament; if not, she would adopt the thesis that claims and quarrels likely to lead to war had not been eliminated and that 'she must reserve all the forces available to her in order to secure her national rights'. Any solution acceptable to Germany would entail sacrifices by Poland, and the French were the people best suited to persuade the Poles to accept such sacrifices.[5] It was rather optimistic to expect the French to bring pressure for the revision of the treaty to bear upon Poland and even more optimistic to think of a Polish willingness to make such sacrifices to a hostile Germany. Sir Robert Vansittart, the Permanent Undersecretary, expressed scepticism. His mind, he wrote, 'has long been moving toward treaty revision (of which the Polish Corridor is the salient feature) as an essential European necessity for safety'; but revision was not yet possible: 'The Poles simply would not look at it, and have already said so. Treaty revision is a thing to have in our minds, and to work *towards* – not immediately *for* – gradually. I believe there are wise people in France who also see this.' He proposed to go to Paris for a few days to sound his opposite number at the Quai d'Orsay but he was sceptical in advance as to his answer.[6] The German attitude to Poland was descibed at that time by Rumbold in 'its crudest form': let Poland come down to the German level of armament or let Germany arm to reach the Polish level; one day France would realize that Poland was more of a liability than an asset and would stand aside; Soviet Russia, 'though utterly untrustworthy', would contain a large Polish force on Poland's eastern frontier; then Poland 'must give way and then at last we will have peace in Europe.'[7] Shades of 1939 – only that the concerted German-Soviet action against Poland did not bring peace but a general war.

In July 1931 a memorandum on German-Polish relations was drawn up in the Foreign Office for the use of the Prime Minister. It stressed that Germany's eastern frontier 'constitutes one of the most dangerous infection spots in Europe'. This view was reinforced by the great *Stahlhelm* rally in Breslau in June in honour of the twelfth anniversary of its first demonstration; the rally was 'particularly provocative and aggressive', and the speeches frankly anti-Polish; all French comments were 'acid'. The official German attitude was 'that they are unable to control an unofficial organisation such as the *Stahlhelm*; but this is bunkum, and if necessary the Germans should be told so.' The demonstration was playing directly into the hands of the Polish Nationalist Party and would only strengthen Polish suspicions and distrust. What was not mentioned was that the demonstration was adorned by the presence of General Heye, just retired as Chief of the Army Command, who strongly emphasized his sympathies for the *Stahlhelm* and his enmity to Poland – on the basis of his study of the problem while he was the commanding general in East Prussia.[8]

Twelve months later, after the fall of Brüning, a Foreign Office minute once more stressed that the Poles were 'doubtless right' to fear that the Germans would use any increase of power 'to force the pace later over the Corridor' and that this issue was next on their list; for the moment they seemed anxious 'to let matters rest in the east till they have settled up accounts in the west', but this was 'only the lull before the storm'. Soon after, another Foreign Office official wrote it was no use to think that, if the German demands on rearmament were granted, 'any measure of finality' could be gained; on the contrary, the grant of equality of status to Germany would only 'hasten, in fact precipitate, the opening of the Corridor question and with it the whole territorial system of 1919' – an opening that was 'inevitable'. This was what the French feared and 'we cannot blame them for foreseeing it.'[9] Thus the problem was clearly seen but there was no British action to try and cope with it. Perhaps the development was seen as 'inevitable' because meanwhile a German government much further to the Right than Brüning had come into power: as the earlier of these minutes said, 'it was Papen and Schleicher & not Hitler who called the tune in Germany.' For the German claims to territorial revision it would have seemed that this made little difference, for Hitler would press the same claims, only more vociferously.

At the end of 1932 the issue of granting Germany 'equality of rights' in armaments was once more discussed in the Foreign Office. It was recognized that, if this were done, other German claims to 'equality' were bound to be raised. The demilitarization of the Rhineland, 'unaccompanied by the corresponding demilitarization of the adjacent territory of France, is unequal treatment for Germany'; possibly concessions could be made there, such as the recruiting of Rhinelanders for the envisaged national militia or a system of purely defensive fortifications; the prohibition of the *Anschluss* 'is in a sense incompatible with equality of treatment' as no such restriction was imposed on any other country; if Austria remained determined to join Germany, 'it would surely be not only unjust but useless for the Council of the League to veto such a step'; as to 'the deletion of the war guilt clause', this 'would surely be a great advantage to get rid of at the proper moment' and would be 'a gesture which really costs us nothing'. If Britain and France abandoned it they would not give up the view that 'Austria-Hungary and Germany were in a peculiar sense directly responsible for the crime' of 1914, but they would be 'freeing the Germans from the, to them, odious duty of publicly confessing against their will that they agree with us on this at least disputable proposition.' To this memorandum envisaging far-reaching concessions to be made to Germany Alexander Cadogan added: 'The Germans are never backward in raising their claims, and will doubtless bring up all these points seriatim.' He suggested a policy to stall and to say that Britain could not consider these claims while working out equality of rights in armaments.[10] A few weeks later the appointment of Hitler as Chancellor put an end to the discussions for the time being. They indicate how far certain people in the Foreign Office were willing to go to meet German claims whether they considered them justified or not, and in spite of all their suspicions about a revival of German militarism.

The efforts of the Brüning government to cope with the economic crisis were anxiously followed in London. In December 1930 the ambassador informed Arthur Henderson that the difficulties of the government would increase during the winter: 'It is difficult to think of anybody in the Germany of to-day more capable of directing the affairs of the Reich than the present Chancellor, and it would be a misfortune for the country if he had to go.'[11] Early in 1931 Henderson wrote to Rumbold that, if there were a real danger of the Brüning government not being able to weather the storm, the British government ought to give it support and encouragement to strengthen its position. Rumbold replied that Brüning enjoyed great prestige in Germany; he was backed by President Hindenburg and by Otto Braun, the Prussian Prime Minister, 'one of the most powerful men in Germany'; the government had to face two immediate difficulties, to get the Reichstag to accept the agrarian proposals and to pass the military budget (including a vote for the second 'pocket battleship'); when these difficulties had been surmounted the Reichstag would be adjourned and not meet again until the autumn, giving Brüning 'a clear run of some six months'. The important thing, however, was a fall of the unemployment figures, 'for if the figures of unemployment do not appreciably fall, the next winter will be very serious indeed and anything might happen.' He then suggested a friendly gesture by the British towards the Brüning government, such as an invitation to London to exchange views, which would give Brüning 'an international prestige which would be helpful to him in Germany itself', or a public statement by the Prime Minister 'testifying to the statesmanlike and energetic manner with which Brüning is grappling with difficulties which are common to practically all the great countries of the world at the present moment.'[12] The suggestion was taken up, Brüning and Curtius were invited and came to Chequers in June to discuss reparations, the Young Plan and economic questions. But sadly MacDonald had to tell them that 'nothing could be done by the British Government alone'.[13]

Shortly before the visit of the German ministers Rumbold wrote from Berlin that the Germans had 'been seeking some avenue of escape from their miseries and every avenue seems closed in turn, whether it be the Customs Union [with Austria], Reparation or a general revival of world prosperity. It is the lack of any hope which makes the situation seem to them so depressing and makes it difficult for Brüning to keep them in hand.' No hope on the reparation question could be held out to them and it was necessary above all 'to avoid any risk of an imputation of bad faith in this matter'. After the visit to London the ambassador reported that confidence in Brüning 'is still unimpaired'; it was thought that he was determined to grapple with the problems and that he knew what he was doing, that he was 'not likely to make political concessions in a moment of panic'. There was considerable criticism of the German financial and industrial leaders, of their extravagance and their excessive salaries, and a very general feeling that the present crisis must be the last of its kind and that Germany must not accept international commitments which she could not fulfil. For the moment Hugenberg and Hitler were content to point out that they had been right all the time, that the Young Plan could not be fulfilled 'and that everything they have foretold, including internal bankruptcy, has come to pass.'[14] But by October 1931 Rumbold was told by a source he considered absolutely reliable that Brüning had lost 80 per cent of his prestige and that his best friends were deserting him; he was taking no one into his confidence and only his prestige abroad was keeping him in office; Hugenberg would not take the Chancellorship unless he received full powers to dispense with the Reichstag, but the President 'refuses to be a party to anything in the nature of a coup d'état'; the situation was 'both obscure and disquieting'.[15] Fifteen months later Hindenburg was to refuse these powers to General von Schleicher: he felt bound by his oath to the Constitution and rejected methods of unconstitutional government, exactly as President Ebert had done in the year 1923.

In June, just before the visit to Chequers, the Brüning government issued its second emergency decree 'for the protection of the German economy' which imposed heavy sacrifices on large sections of the population. Brüning declared that the limit of the privations which could be imposed upon the people had been reached. In the Foreign Office Vansittart minuted that this was *not* the case, but the point was 'that the German people and Govt. have convinced themselves that this is the case, and that the Brüning Govt. – the only decent Govt. that we can see – can therefore do no more without falling': therefore the French view, though partly justified, was 'beside the fundamental point'. Henderson's Parliamentary Private Secretary, Philip Noel Baker, expressed his agreement, 'since further sacrifices by the poorer classes can only drive them further towards Communism'. Orme Sargent found two weak points in the Brüning decree: the failure to attempt a reform of the defective system of financial administration, to eliminate the waste and overlapping which prevented the government from enjoying the full yield of the revenues – a task that had always been shirked; secondly, the failure to reduce the military budget which was 'suspiciously high in comparison for instance with our own'; until this was substantially reduced the Americans and the French would argue that the German government had not reached 'the limit of possible sacrifice'. Noel Baker agreed that, if possible, the Germans should be induced to postpone the next 'pocket battleship', 'of which the psychological effect would be enormous'.[16]

Henderson accordingly wired to Berlin 'that, as Germany

during the "Hoover year" will be living on charity of other nations, it would be only decent that during that period she should not be spending money on the construction of the new battleship' (President Hoover had just proposed a postponement of all reparation and reconstruction debts by one year). Henderson refused to take into account the threat of Hindenburg's resignation if the battleship were delayed; surely, the President would not allow 'the satisfaction of his personal wishes to complicate negotiations which have for their object the economic salvation of Germany.' In a conversation with the German ambassador Henderson stressed that such a gesture 'would have convinced Europe of the sincerity of the desire of Germany to make her contribution to the general work of pacification'.[17] The only concession, however, which Brüning was willing to make was not to proceed with the building of the third 'pocket battleship'; as he told the British ambassador, nine out of ten million marks voted for the second one had already been spent; if work on it were stopped 'he ran the risk of antagonizing the younger element in Reichswehr. . . . He had to be very careful, for he depended on Reichswehr for maintenance of order in the country.'[18] This was the reality of political life in Germany at the end of the Weimar Republic; the influence of the officer corps was paramount. In October 1931 the ambassador reported that what was criticized most in Brüning's social policy was the failure to bring down the cost of living; this had been immovable for two years or longer; the masses felt that a government which so rigorously cut wages and unemployment relief should find the means to reduce food prices which were kept high by subsidies and protection. The industrialists were worried by the economic and financial situation and wavering in their allegiance to Brüning. His position had become 'very much more difficult'; he had been forced to give up the position of intermediary between Right and Left 'and it seems as if he could only retain power by himself following the movement towards the Right.'[19]

In March 1932 it was minuted in the Foreign Office that, since the beginning of the year, the prices of most staple foods and of the public services in Germany had been reduced on average by ten per cent, while wages had been brought down to the level of 1927 (i.e. considerably more): this was a remarkable achievement, comparable to that of Mussolini who had also succeeded in forcing down prices, 'backed up, however, by the whole

Fascist machinery of terrorism and punishment'. The writer had strong doubts whether similar measures could be equally successful in 'more independent-minded countries' such as France or Britain, for it must be remembered that 'both Italy and Germany are today living under dictatorships'.[20] Yet the Brüning government was certainly not a fully fledged dictatorship. An official British visitor who spent a week in Berlin during the same month found that the situation was not improving. 'Drastic exchange control, standstills, general bureaucratic government, extension of State control over banking, shipping, etc., interference with private contracts by, e.g. reduction of interest rates, freedom of all tenants to cancel leases' were bringing things to a stop and reducing production. Brüning disliked the constant extension of state control but saw no way of avoiding it. Schacht condemned the existing state of affairs: nothing good would happen 'unless a government of the Right came into power'. The greatest danger was 'arising from the growing paralysis of private enterprise'; unless some freedom were reintroduced this would lead to an extension of government control over much of industrial life; it was obvious 'that no Reparation payments at all are possible for a long time', and the German government would have to face 'the possibility, even the probability, of a moratorium on foreign debts'.[21] A high official of the Treasury, who also visited Berlin in March, had an impression 'of almost unrelieved gloom' and 'a grave feeling of nervousness as to the future', caused by the decline of German exports, the mounting difficulties of the central bank in providing cover for the mark, and the growth of the Hitler movement; and this feeling was shared by the British and French representatives on the spot.[22]

In April 1932 the commercial councillor of the British embassy drew up a memorandum on the economic situation. In mid-April the total number of unemployed stood at 5,934,000 compared with 4,628,000 12 months before; during the summer of 1931 the figure had dropped by about one million, but a similar drop in the current year was unlikely as no real revival in building activity could be hoped for; Germany did not have the means to help herself but depended on an improvement elsewhere. The small towns and districts found it impossible to carry their share of the burden of unemployment relief and had to be hurriedly helped by a nearby large town or a federal state; as these could not meet the additional charge it was passed on to the central government which had to meet more and more of the expenditure. The German nation possessed a 'remarkable power of resistance', and if one thought what the Germans had had to put up with since 1916–17, 'one is reluctant to assert positively that such a people could ever give way to social and economic disorder', but they too must 'have their breaking-point'. He believed that Germany would be able to hold out until the end of June 'through a continual tightening of the control of foreign exchange and by the Government taking an increasing share in the financing of industry'.[23] But before the end of June Brüning had ceased to be Germany's Chancellor. In the last week of May a British officer who had been invited to Berlin by Brüning reported that his position 'had become intensely difficult'; Schleicher, supported by Hindenburg's secretary, Meissner, and Hindenburg's son, was urging the President to get rid of Brüning and was aiming at establishing a military dictatorship. Brüning had challenged Schleicher to act, but Schleicher seemed to hesitate. Brüning intended to visit Hindenburg and to demand a public announcement of support and his signature to another financial decree which would be highly unpopular with parliament and the people, including a further curtailment of unemployment relief. He had suggested to Hindenburg that Schleicher ought to be dismissed, 'but the President was not prepared to go so far'.[24]

After the fall of Brüning the ambassador supplemented this information. Ever since his appointment as Commissioner for Eastern Settlement Hans Schlange-Schöningen (who was himself a conservative landowner) had maintained that the uneconomic large estates of East Prussia should be reduced in size; he worked out a scheme of colonization which provided for compensation for the landowners who were to be expropriated, although they were bankrupt and estates were unsaleable in East Prussia. About ten days before his dismissal Brüning was summoned to visit the President on his East Prussian estate, but he refused to go and made it clear that he would not yield on this issue. He let it be known privately that he intended to establish where he stood and to obtain unmistakable proof of his continued confidence from the President. At the final interview Hindenburg 'was adamant in his insistence that there should be no agrarian Bolshevism, no confiscation of land for settlement purposes'. He also demanded the resignation of several ministers, including those of finance and of labour. In dismissing the

Brüning government 'Hindenburg undoubtedly subordinated foreign affairs to internal considerations to an extent without precedent in recent German history . . . and this is the first occasion on which internal and indeed local affairs have been given pride of place.' On the eve of the reparations conference Hindenburg dispensed 'with the services of a man who had acquired the position of one of the leading statesmen of Europe, who enjoyed the confidence of foreign statesmen and to whose unsparing efforts on his behalf the President mainly owed his re-election' only a few weeks earlier.[25]

As to the appointment of Franz von Papen as Brüning's successor, it was hoped that a section of the Centre Party would support his government or that the whole party would tolerate it until after the elections. 'They did not foresee the extreme hostility of the Centre electorate in the country, nor did they realise that Bavaria would adopt so unfriendly an attitude'; the leaders of the Centre were 'beside themselves with annoyance at what they regard as unpardonable duplicity.' The Papen government reckoned with a split in the Centre and toleration by Hitler and his party: 'two bold assumptions' which could not 'be affirmed with any certainty'. The hostility of the Centre was also aroused by the plan to appoint a Reich Commissioner for Prussia: 'there appears indeed to be no legal justification for interference by the Government of the Reich, especially in view of the fact that many of the larger Federal States have been or are being governed by defeated Ministries which cannot be replaced for political reasons.'[25] Thus Papen's removal of the Prussian Social Democratic government which took place on 20 July was considered illegal by the British embassy; but there was no comment on Hindenburg's unceremonial dismissal of Brüning which was carried out on the same doubtful legal basis: a more than elastic interpretation of Article 48 of the Constitution. As early as November 1931 an official of the *Auswärtige Amt* had told the British chargé d'affaires that Papen 'was doing his best to bring about an Alliance between the Centre party and the National Socialists', a course favoured by the party's right wing but resisted by Prelate Kaas, the Centre chairman.[26] At that time no one expected that Papen, a comparatively unknown deputy in the Prussian Diet, would be the next Chancellor.

At the beginning of August Rumbold reported he had heard 'on very good authority' that those who had brought about Papen's appointment were now turning against him. It was suggested to get rid of him by making him German ambassador in Paris; if Papen resigned the next Chancellor could 'only be General von Schleicher'. But Papen himself showed no sign of giving up; in a press interview he stated that he had no intention of bothering about forming a coalition or trying to find a majority in parliament, but he expected 'to rope Hitler and other Nazi leaders into his Cabinet and shoulder them with responsibility'; neither the Centre nor the National Socialists would prove difficult when the new Reichstag met; a provision for an Upper House should be inserted in the German Constitution, and the electors should vote for personalities rather than for party lists.[27] That changes of the Constitution would require a two-thirds majority in parliament did not seem to worry Papen and his optimism regarding the attitude of the Centre and the National Socialists proved totally unfounded. In October, after the second dissolution of the Reichstag by Papen, the embassy's financial adviser believed that the really pressing question was whether Papen 'can hope to obtain from such a Reichstag the majority necessary for his far-reaching plans of voting and constitutional reform'; he might seek no more than the required two-thirds majority for a reform of the voting system so as to obtain a parliament elected by a restricted franchise, which might 'allow him in due course to proceed with his schemes for constitutional reform'. But the government rested 'on the favour of President Hindenburg and the control of the armed forces', and the only party supporting it were the German Nationalists.[28] How then could Papen hope to gain a two-thirds majority for his far-reaching plans? In September the ambassador reported 'that the old field-marshal is the only fixed point in the present state of flux'; he was 'indispensable' and this 'perhaps constitutes the most serious feature of the political situation'.[29]

The Papen government was unable to solve the economic crisis and the unemployment figures remained as high as ever. In November Rumbold considered that in this 'all important question' little had been achieved; the elaborate and expensive scheme to create jobs 'has, for all practical purposes, proved a failure'; after six months of 'authoritarian' government the situation was still dominated by the figure of more than five million unemployed. The President had given Papen 'a very free hand in this as in other fields', but the problem could not be solved by methods strongly opposed by the parties of the Left and some cooperation with them seemed essential.[30] Two weeks later

Papen had gone and, as predicted in August, General von Schleicher was the new Chancellor. On the day of his appointment, 2 December, the embassy wired to London that it 'is regarded as a victory for Constitutional principles and a defeat for reaction'. Schleicher was 'a suave, moderate and very intelligent man'; business circles were 'jubilant'; at the stock exchange, prices had fallen in the morning on rumours of Papen's reappointment but 'showed great buoyancy this afternoon'. A few days later the information was supplemented by more favourable comment: 'Schleicher is no machiavellian intriguer as his enemies allege. His political instincts are keen, and his experience teaches him to be on good terms with all the political leaders'. It would be wrong to think that he aimed at power, and 'more correct to say that his intelligence forced him to intervene or to give honest counsel at different moments'. During his years at the Ministry of Defence he had kept the army on good terms with successive democratic governments, defended and explained military policy and expenditure and 'imbibed the "sweet poison of politics."'[31]

On 21 December Schleicher received the British ambassador and expressed his hope for friendly cooperation between the two countries. He explained that he had some hope to win the support of the National Socialists; 'a section of the party was quite ready to follow this course but Herr Hitler himself was an incalculable personality and nobody could forecast his line of action.' Schleicher disclaimed any hostility to the Hitler movement and said he would regret its collapse; he wanted to harness it 'in the service of the State'; as to the Social Democrats, he believed it possible 'to parley with them', and in any case 'it was healthy for the Government to have to face an opposition'. At this stage Schleicher was still optimistic but all his calculations about differences within the National Socialist and Social Democratic parties were to be proved wrong very soon, and Hitler quickly succeeded in reasserting his authority over the waverers. MacDonald replied to Schleicher's message of good will with the assurance 'that I am looking forward to nothing with more hope than warm co-operation between our two countries in all that makes for European friendship, neighbourliness and co-operation'.[32] Unfortunately, there was little time to prove these sentiments in practice because five weeks later Hitler was appointed Chancellor. The ambassador's telegram of 2 December already hinted at sources of opposition to

Schleicher: circles of the army, he wrote, disliked the 'establishment of such a direct connexion between the Army and political
affairs.' More opposition soon came not only from all the major
political parties, but also from the Agrarian League and the
circles around the old President. Schleicher was virtually on his
own and could not even rely on the army.

That Schleicher had vast political ambitions was noticed by
the British military attaché as early as the summer of 1930. At a
dinner his wife was told by Schleicher 'apparently in earnest'
that one day he would be the President of Germany. Schleicher
according to the report belonged to 'a gang of pushing officers
who monopolise all the leading posts' in the army, and it
included the brothers von Hammerstein, at that time the heads
of the *Truppenamt* and the *Personalamt*; 'it is not improbable
that this gang is working for the setting up of a military dictatorship, possibly under Schleicher's leadership', after the death of
Hindenburg. Some weeks later the attaché added: 'Schleicher
poses as the *fidus Achates* of General Groener, the Reichswehr
Minister, but in reality he practically runs the Ministry. . . .
Schleicher is a born intriguer with boundless ambition, who is
undoubtedly playing for high stakes'. He favoured a forward
German policy in cooperation with Soviet Russia against
Poland, 'and the senior and saner officers of the Reichsheer who
distrust Russia as an ally have now been eliminated.'[33] At
another dinner, held about the same time, Schleicher told
Rumbold that Brüning, 'a great friend of his', would be in office
for some time, that 'his sincerity and honesty are so transparent
as to have impressed the Reichstag and German public
opinion.'[34] Eighteen months later Schleicher's intrigues were
one of the causes of Brüning's fall.

The Minister of Defence under Brüning was Schleicher's old
chief, General Groener, who was willing to serve the Republic
and to prevent right-wing extremism from spreading in the
army. In April 1930 a British Intelligence report stated that
Groener had issued a secret order to the Reichswehr which
stressed that it was the servant of a democratic republic and had
to carry out its demands; the word 'national' only applied to the
state and not to political parties hostile to the present form of
government; and the officers were to explain political issues to
the men from a point of view favourable to the government.
According to the report this order was badly received by the
officer corps and protest meetings were held at which it was

claimed that the army served the state, and not a particular government which was subject to political influences. This proved, the report concluded, 'that the idea of democracy is not intelligible to many German officers and that the Reichsheer is a distinctly political factor'.[35] After the discovery of secret National Socialist activities in the army Groener had indeed issued a special order which emphasised the officers' duty to combat tendencies hostile to the existing state, but the word 'democratic republic' did not occur in it, and nothing is known about 'protest meetings' against this order. In October the British military attaché reported that the 'discontent with the prevailing lack of political leadership' had brought about 'a spirit of revolt among the younger officers' against their seniors. They were accused of 'having stifled their patriotic consciences to eat the bread and butter of a republican government'. Groener in particular was charged with 'kow-towing at every turn to the Social Democrats . . . and is becoming more unpopular with the Army every day.' Yet, surprisingly, the attaché regarded Groener 'as the greatest and perhaps only political genius in Germany today'.[36] There can be no doubt that there was growing opposition to Groener within the officer corps, and not only from junior officers, on personal and political grounds.

The strength of this opposition also emerges from an interesting report of a member of the Berlin embassy who had spent the Whitsun weekend of 1932 at a house party given by a Count Dohna, a leading East Prussian landowner. There he met Colonel Walther von Reichenau, the chief of staff of the East Prussian division (later one of Hitler's field-marshals), who spoke to him very freely on the subject of Groener's resignation. According to Reichenau, Groener 'was the son of a "little paymaster Sergeant-Major"' and had never learnt how to treat an officer as a gentleman'; his position had become impossible through 'his unfortunate marriage last year with an elderly housekeeper of a small hotel, with whom he had been having a liaison'. 'It was intolerable to the officers corps to have this woman, who looked what she was, as their social leader. She was ugly, excessively stupid, had developed ambitions and had urged Groener to keep in the political limelight.' He had constantly interfered in the internal affairs of the army 'as if he were still an active general.' 'The last straw', however, was the decree dissolving the SA (in April 1932): 'Schleicher had advised against it, but Groener, egged on by his wife, without saying anything had gone, as it were, behind Schleicher's back to Hindenburg and obtained his signature to the decree under threat of resignation.' This attack on the SA movement 'which they regarded as essentially patriotic and healthy' had caused indignation in the officer corps and this had induced Schleicher and Hammerstein to take action. In this they were backed by the officer corps which had always thought Groener 'slippery and unreliable'.[37] The report sheds new light on the enforced resignation of Groener, which finally led to a cabinet crisis and the fall of Brüning, and on the role of Schleicher who had acted against his own minister. The report brings out very clearly the snobbish attitude of the aristocratic officers who looked down upon Groener on account of his parentage and his belated marriage to a woman who was 'ugly and excessively stupid', and obviously socially very inferior. Under strong pressure from the governments of the federal states Groener had dissolved the SA, but the officers regarded the movement as 'patriotic and healthy': the whole dichotomy between the army and the democratic republic is highlighted by this one report.

In conversations with senior as well as junior officers the British military attaché also found 'marked disapproval' of Groener's action in suppressing the SA and their 'military activities'. Groener had become unpopular, and the officers 'are inclined to look upon him as a "traitor" to their cause'; the suppression would drive the SA underground as had happened with the IRA in Ireland. In general, the officers felt 'that the Nazi movement is the best available means of disciplining the youth of the country . . . and that it keeps them out of the Communist ranks'; it gave them an opportunity 'of expressing their devotion to the country'. The Reichswehr officers were clearly impressed by this 'patriotic' movement, and inclined to disregard its countless deeds of violence. In 1931 the attaché regarded Colonel von Reichenau 'as one of the coming men', but he was much more impressed by Reichenau's chief, General von Blomberg, the commanding officer of the East Prussian division. Blomberg 'towers, physically as well as mentally, above the mediocrities who at present hold most of the leading commands in the Reichsheer. . . . I consider him to be vastly broader and more objectively minded than any other German soldier I have met, except perhaps von Hammerstein, but Blomberg I would consider a much better soldier than Hammerstein, with far more energy, quickness and decision.' In politics Blomberg was somewhat critical of Groener and Social Democracy but 'eminently level-headed and sensible, without any ultra-national or monarchical delusions'. The *Stahlhelm*, Blomberg thought, did good work by promoting patriotic ideals among the young but had ruined the effect by being 'used for party political purposes'; he even condemned General Heye for joining the *Stahlhelm* on the day after he left the army.[38]

At the end of 1931 the attaché recorded his general appreciation of the German army after four years of observing it at close quarters: 'The officers are undoubtedly well trained in theory and the men are fine human material. Practical training is, however, carried out on rigid lines, the troops get no collective experience with modern weapons, and the higher commanders, who are frequently changed, have little opportunity of handling large formations. The whole system labours under a sense of artificial restriction.' For these reasons the German army could not be considered a danger to any neighbouring power. But the attaché added a warning that a tendency had recently developed to disregard the restrictions of the Treaty of Versailles; there were 'frequent violations of the military clauses with scarcely an attempt at concealment', even in the official military documents, 'and the movement for liberation, once launched, will be difficult to arrest.'[39] These words, written in December 1931, were to be proved true very soon.

Evidence of the violation of the disarmament clauses was found in the first instance in the published figures of the German military budget. In 1930 it contained the sum of 2,250,000 marks 'for improvement of the land fortresses', and E.H. Carr minuted: 'The element of fake in the German military budget is, I am sure, very large, and most of this money is probably not going in fortresses at all' [sic].[40] The British embassy's annual report for the same year found that nearly 3½ million marks *above* the previous year's vote (which was considerably in excess of what was required for the British army) were demanded for arms and ammunition, while the army estimates in general had risen by ten million marks. The report thought that these funds were in reality used to subsidize the armament industry.[41] In 1931 a memorandum compared the expenditure of the British and German armies on arms, ammunition and war material and found that the German army expended nearly three times the amount, and on some items – small arms and artillery ammunition – more than three times the sums required by the British army. The British military attaché and the embassy's financial adviser calculated that in all the British army spent on these items £940,000 and the German army £2,731,000.[42]

In 1930 a secret British memorandum listed German violations of the military clauses such as the 'illegal training of improperly enlisted or discharged recruits', 'technical experiments ... with forbidden weapons', 'important subsidies to industrial firms, particularly for experimental purposes', and the use of foreign firms for the manufacture of war material. A study of German manpower, industry and military expenditure, conducted by Military Intelligence, concluded that Germany was unable to mobilize 'a highly mobile striking force of 21 divisions with the armament and equipment such a force will need'; this the Germans realized, hence their campaign to be permitted a larger army, with shorter service and modern weapons.[43] Thus the fact that the Germans were planning an expansion from seven to 21 infantry divisions was known to British Intelligence. Early in 1932 the British and Belgian military attachés in Berlin compiled a list of four Dutch, two Swedish and two Swiss firms, most of them subsidiaries of German firms, which were manufacturing war material according to German patents or designs. But they considered the notion that Germany was rearming by means of these subsidiaries 'absurd': 'If the French General Staff continue to cry "Wolf!" too often, they will merely forfeit all credibility.'[44] In March an appreciation of the German breaches of the Peace Treaty written in the War Office stated that 'so far Germany has refrained from flagrant violations, such as a resort to conscription, an increase in the total strength of the army, or the formation of large additional units'. But her ultimate object was the demolition of the military clauses, and she has already achieved 'a considerable measure of success in evading them'. The German army was developing into 'a highly organized and efficient modern army', it possessed 'excellent technical equipment' and improved arms, but was still deficient in the prohibited weapons such as tanks, heavy artillery and aircraft, and she possessed 'at least the nucleus of an efficient military air force'. In spite of this, the General Staff believed that the German military preparations 'are mainly defensive in character'. Germany, the memorandum continued, could not contemplate waging an aggressive war against France until the treaty restrictions had been removed and could not 'defend herself successfully against France and

259

Belgium, even if Poland and Czechoslovakia did not intervene'.[45]

Evidence that German junior officers were seconded for about two years or were retired temporarily and then reappeared on active duty was obtained from the published army lists. By the spring of 1931 the British military attaché had compiled a list of 66 officers who had thus 'returned to the fold' – a list that was not 'by any means exhaustive'. In August 1930 a German captain was killed while flying in Russia. 'There are strong grounds for suspecting', Rumbold wrote, 'that he, in common with many other Reichswehr officers, was illegally seconded for flying service in Russia with the connivance of the German military authorities.'[46] In December 1931, however, the military attaché reported that the practice of seconding German officers for flying duties in Russia, which had been 'prevalent from 1927 to 1930', seemed to have ceased, that the relations between the German and Russian armies 'have been less cordial of late' and that fewer exchange visits of senior staff officers had taken place. To him, the relations between the two armies 'remain somewhat of a mystery'. The ambassador even informed London in 1930 that Hammerstein as well as Schleicher had been described as 'partisans of an understanding with the Russian military authorities, but there is nothing to prove that there is such an understanding.'[47]

The Air Ministry, however, possessed very concrete evidence about the German flying school at Lipetsk in Russia. In 1929 it received the first reports that a German school existed and that Reichswehr officers were trained there during the summer months. In 1930 another report stated that every year 50 German officers were sent to Lipetsk and stayed there for two or three years. In a report of 1931 the number was given as 48, half of them being replaced every year, and the aircraft in use as Junkers K.47 and Albatross 78 two-seater fighters. A report of 1932 stated 'that only the best men who have completed their flying training in Germany are sent there' and gave the number of aeroplanes belonging to the army as 86 and to the navy as 11. In April 1932 the so-called 'Gentlemen's Agreement' about the use of Lipetsk expired and was later renewed for one year, at a cost it was said of three million marks p.a. The Air Ministry estimated that in 1931–32 45 bomber pilots and 120 fighter pilots were trained at Lipetsk.[48] There is no indication where these reports came from, but the information was surprisingly accurate and was apparently provided by someone familiar with Lipetsk, either German or Russian. In London it was recognized that these activities were a breach of Article 175 of the Peace Treaty which stipulated that German officers had to serve for a minimum of 25 years, but no action was taken. The Air Ministry specifically warned against 'any reference to the suspected training in aviation of these officers while struck off the list', for, if pressed for evidence, it would be necessary to quote 'confidential sources', which it 'would be most unwilling to do'. When the British military attaché early in 1932 provided 'an exhaustive account . . . of the recent systematic flouting of the Treaty' which made 'fairly formidable reading' and the French government again pressed for action, the reaction of the Foreign Office was once more negative: 'the view that the Foreign Office have consistently maintained is that a policy of pin-pricks against Germany on account of these minor [sic] infractions of the military clauses just before the Disarmament Conference would serve no useful purpose, and they certainly adhere to these views a fortnight before the Conference is due to open.' If the conference should fail, 'the military clauses of the Treaty will become a dead letter.'[49] And there the matter rested. Thus Germany was able to create the nucleus of a modern air force (which she was forbidden to possess): a factor of enormous value to Hitler and Göring in the creation of the *Luftwaffe*.

After attending the rally of the *Stahlhelm* at Breslau in May 1931 the military attaché reported on its military qualities: 'The physique of the men varied very greatly, and the considerable number of the war veteran, n.c.o. type, with corpulent figure and red, bulging neck, tended to catch the eye and make the whole thing rather laughable.' But every *Gau* also contained 80 to 90 'stalwart young men, fit, trained and earnest-looking' whose discipline resembled that of army recruits. In his opinion the *Stahlhelm* contained a nucleus of men, 'partially trained in essentials, such as marching, shooting and scouting, and, at any rate, imbued with the right spirit.' Of the *Stahlhelm* leaders, Seldte 'is a jaunty, rollicking type, with side-whiskers, who might be mistaken for a Spanish bull-fighter or the mate of a tramp-steamer', but he 'has great personality and can carry a crowd with him.' The second in command, Lieutenant-Colonel Duesterberg, 'is evidently a capable and ruthless organiser', 'shrewd, cold and calculating', in correct military turn-out and with a row of decorations, in striking contrast with the casual attitude of Seldte. In an earlier report the attaché pointed to the spirit of revolt, 'sanctified under the name of *Frontkriegergeist*' (front fighters' spirit), which animated the *Stahlhelm* as well as the Hitler movement. One day the 'waves of the older and newer patriotism' were bound to coalesce, and in his opinion this would happen quite soon.[50] Clearly, the spirit of the trenches animated not only the older generation but also large numbers of the young, and these forces did coalesce in 1933, to the benefit of the National Socialists.

The Nationalist allies of the *Stahlhelm* were mentioned from time to time in the diplomatic reports, not as frequently as at the time of Stresemann and Locarno or the Dawes and Young Plans. During their campaign against the Young Plan Hugenberg and his friends sent a former general to see President Hindenburg and to inform him that, if he signed the Plan he would be a traitor to his country and he would never shake his hand again. As Rumbold reported, the old President was much shaken by the interview and even indicated 'that he might wish to resign'.[51] After the election of July 1932 in which the National Socialists gained more than 37 per cent of the vote and the German Nationalists less than six, the ambassador commented that Hugenberg's dream of a right-wing coalition in which he would play the dominant part had not been fulfilled because the two parties failed to gain a majority; 'indeed, one of the features of the elections is the fact that in any possible combination in the new Reichstag the Hugenberg party need not be taken into account.' A few months later, before the general election of November, the embassy considered the prospects of the Nationalist Party 'excellent'; the smaller bourgeois parties were now 'homeless'; 'with a little more tact and adaptability' Hugenberg could gather 'all the debris of small parties between his own and the Centre', but the party was handicapped 'by his cast iron adherence to every comma of his programme', and no other leader was available. Hugenberg had not forgiven Papen for forming his government without consulting the German Nationalists or giving any posts to them.[52] The conservative People's Party, the ambassador wrote in 1930, had after Stresemann's death 'proved an unreliable factor in German party politics'; some of its members inclined towards the Nationalists, others towards the SPD; 'they are neither fish, flesh nor fowl.' As a Prussian minister told him recently, the People's Party was the worthy successor of the National Liberals, whom their opponents called the 'National Miserables'.[53] In the two elections of 1932 the party polled a mere 1.2 and 1.9 per cent of the total vote.

The German Communist Party interested the British diplomats mainly from the point of view of Russo-German relations and Russian interference in German politics. In 1930 Otto Braun, the Prussian Prime Minister, told Rumbold that he knew for a fact that members of the Soviet trade delegation were stirring up trouble among the Communists and provoking them into action, with Russian money provided for the purpose. The *Auswärtige Amt*, Braun claimed, always tried to shield or exculpate the Russians, but if these activities continued the Prussian government would act against the Russians whatever effect this might have on Russo-German relations; it was intolerable that the members of the Russian trade delegation should enjoy diplomatic immunity. Braun spoke 'with great vehemence' and the ambassador was convinced that his threat was not an empty one.[54] Yet the *Auswärtige Amt* too was moved into action by the continuous interference of the Communist International in internal German affairs. In March of the same year Curtius, the Foreign Minister, as well as his Undersecretary of State spoke 'very strongly' on the subject to the Soviet ambassador, Krestinsky: the 'interference was intolerable and could not be allowed to continue', and a violent discussion ensued. Curtius told Krestinsky that, if Stalin really wished to stop this interference, he had the power to do so; von Schubert added that, even if the Soviet government gave a written undertaking that the Comintern would no longer incite the German Communists to revolutionary action, the promise would not be worth the paper it was written on; 'with Russians it was only deeds and not promises which counted.' Rumbold added that Schubert had begged him to treat his remarks as very confidential.[55] We know from the German diplomatic documents that there were more German protests on this account but they proved equally fruitless. In spite of this, the close relations between Germany and Russia continued to exist in the military as well as the commercial field, above all German assistance in the creation of Russian heavy industry and the fulfilment of the first Five Year Plan.

The British embassy in Berlin does not seem to have been seriously worried by the prospects of Communist revolution in Germany, but the threat emanating from the National Socialists was taken more seriously. In October 1932 the financial advizer pointed to the threat of a rapprochement between the three principal 'anti-capitalist forces' – the Communists, the trade unions and the left wing of the National Socialists – and to the alliance between Communists and National Socialists in recent strikes. He added that Papen was ready enough to suppress these movements when he was talking privately: but that was all.[56] The rise of the National Socialists was followed with growing interest and anxiety. When the Rhineland was finally evacuated by the Allied armies in July 1930, the National Socialists used the opportunity to take vengeance on Germans who had associated with the Separatists, to smash their windows, break into their houses and destroy the furniture, and the efforts of the police to stop the pillage had little success. Vansittart saw the German ambassador and described the incidents as 'most deplorable': it was a great pity that an era of improved relations should be started in this way. Sthamer replied that the outbreaks had come as a surprise and his government had done all it could to suppress them by sending in reinforcements. But Vansittart thought that the Germans had provided 'very inadequate police protection to France's former friends'. The French made strong representations in Berlin but these were not joined by the British government.[57]

During the following months interest concentrated on the September elections which were to bring the National Socialists their first great victory. A week before the election Rumbold commented on the 'youthfulness and vigour' of the movement which appealed 'to all those in Germany who are feeling dissatisfied'. The party was confident of winning over three million votes and some 50 to 60 seats in the Reichstag; many people thought that they would win that number but to him it seemed 'somewhat high'; the propaganda methods of the National Socialists were 'original and often ingenious'.[58] On 14 September they polled 6,410,000 votes and won 107 seats. In December the ambassador discussed the causes of Hitler's surprising success. He promised 'all things to all men, assuring the farmers that he would abolish interest and the small shop-keepers that they would obtain five per cent on their savings'. But undoubtedly the principal reasons were the inflation of 1923 'which either wiped out people's savings or passed them into the pockets of the Jews', and the severe economic crisis.[59] Apart from the anti-semitic remark the analysis was quite correct. What Rumbold did not seem to know was that the German Jews, who were to a large extent members of the middle and lower middle classes, were – like the Germans from the same classes – the victims and not the profiteers of the inflation. His views were probably derived from the upper-class Germans whom he met and to whose opinions he listed.

In September 1931 there followed a report about the first large anti-semitic riot in Berlin. On the evening of the Jewish New Year's Day more than 1,000 National Socialists invaded the Kurfürstendamm and fell upon passers-by who looked Jewish. 'The whole street was soon in uproar and at about 9 o'clock a party of about 80 "Hitler boys" stormed the café Reimann which is frequented chiefly by cinema stars and members of the theatrical profession, many of whom are Jews.' But after the first half hour the police gained the upper hand and about 60 rioters were arrested; 27 of them were sentenced to imprisonment.[60] In December 1931 the ambassador reported on many rumours of a moderate and an extremist section of the National Socialist Party, but he did not attach much importance to them: 'for the moment the Nazi movement holds its followers in a grip resembling that of a religious revival. The hypnotic effect of an order from the Brown House is admitted by Hitler's enemies to be even more alarming than heretofore.' Hitler only had 'to issue a command to ensure instant obedience'; even if he contradicted his lieutenants or reduced them to ridicule this did not undermine party loyalty. In talking to the Undersecretary of the *Auswärtige Amt* Rumbold expressed the opinion that one of the main dangers of the rise of the party was its lack of leadership, that it 'contained nothing but fifth rate men'. His partner replied that Hitler was well aware of this and would welcome an election so that he could get 'rid of the riff raff who posed as leaders' and replace them.[61] The report clearly reflected the illusions prevalent in the German establishment as to the true character of the National Socialist movement and the intentions of its leader.

But some of these dangerous illusions were shared by the British embassy. Its annual report for 1931 stated boldly that the 'movement was markedly affected by the influx of better-class people sincerely afraid of communism', as well as by masses of people in town and country 'who are determined to wrest all control of public affairs from the Social Democrats, and if possible to check the corruption which, during a period in which that party has played a major part, has crept into nearly every walk of German life'. These people believed that they would be able to control Hitler and make use of him, 'and Hitler seems to be prepared to fall in with their plans'. In teaching youth to strive for freedom the party used the lessons of German history, such as the War of Liberation against Napoleon or 'the discipline, frugality and self-denial of the time of Frederick the Great': 'the good effect of this teaching is already visible in German youth, which had become very undisciplined since the last war, the revolution and the abolition of conscription. The Nazi instruction halls which now exist in nearly every village throughout the land are models of cleanliness and would gladden the heart of any British scoutmaster.'[62] Clearly, Nazi propaganda had to some extent seeped into the British embassy, quite apart from the inane reference to the Scout movement. The alleged ill-discipline among German youth and the ill-effects of the abolition of conscription seem to point to a military source of this startling piece of information: exactly the same ideas were current in the higher circles of the Reichswehr.

After the general election of July 1932 in which the National Socialists became the strongest party Rumbold thought that they were 'in a difficult position. It would appear that they have shot their bolt and have exhausted the reservoir from which they drew many of their adherents, and yet have failed to obtain an absolute majority in the Reichstag.' The men of the SA would soon begin to ask what was the purpose of all their marchings and their state of mobilization: 'in other words, the time is fast approaching when Hitler will be expected to deliver the goods. He cannot indefinitely play the role of a revivalist preacher.' Hitler had swallowed up the small bourgeois parties of the centre and the Right but made no breach in the three large parties, the Centre, the Social Democrats and the Communists. He even lost ground in Berlin's more prosperous districts as well as in the Catholic areas of Lower Bavaria, Westphalia and Silesia.[63] All this was correct, especially the reference to the growing impatience among the SA which to a large extent consisted of unemployed youngsters who wanted to see the 'fruits' of their efforts and were not prepared to wait much longer. Before the next general election, that of November, the embassy's financial adviser predicted correctly that 'the National Socialists will suffer a reverse, and popular opinion puts their probable losses at 30 to 40 seats.'[64] But he did not attempt to analyse the causes of this decline – at a time when economic recovery was still far away. At the same time the British chargé d'affaires reported the wedding of Prince Gustavus Adolphus of Sweden to Princess Sybil of Coburg-Gotha (a relative of the royal family) whose father had given strong financial support to the early Hitler movement. When the marriage was first announced the National Socialists declared that Hitler would attend it in person and that the wedding would be the occasion of an imposing National Socialist demonstration. But Hitler did not appear although he had spoken in Coburg shortly before. Uniformed detachments of the SA as well as the *Stahlhelm* were in attendance 'despite the outbreak of open political warfare' between them (on account of their differing attitude to the Papen government), as was a unit of the Reichswehr: as the authorities claimed, because members of foreign royal families were present who were entitled to military honours.[65] It must have been a strange gathering, but in a way typical of the dying months of the Weimar Republic. The report even mentioned rumours that 'nationalist circles' were hatching 'plans for the restoration of the monarchy'. But as the ambassador pointed out in November, 'a serious stumbling block' was the lack of a suitable candidate: no one was in sight who would be able to count on wide support.[66]

As to the general mood of Germany during the years of crisis and severe unemployment, in May 1931 Rumbold mentioned 'one important new symptom, namely the wave of depression, even hopelessness, which has swept over the German people'. Two months later he described the scene in Berlin as 'a mixture of almost oriental lethargy and fatalism'; the people were consumed with anxiety but seemed content to fold their hands and to wait for something that would save them. He stressed the 'docility' with which the country had accepted the government measures and the decrees 'which have brought business practically to a standstill', practically destroyed the freedom of the press and set up a kind of 'inquisition into people's private affairs'. The main cause of this docility he saw in the fear of another inflation, after the experience of 1923.[67] This was true of the middle classes, but it affected the working classes and the peasantry to a much smaller extent; and these classes provided the National Socialists and to a lesser extent the Communists with masses of enthusiastic followers. The picture of the mood of Germany in 1931 drawn by the ambassador was an imperfect one. Many of the features of the rising National Socialist movement, on the other hand, were decribed quite correctly, although at times through rather rose-coloured spectacles. Its totally destructive and nihilist character was not perceived, and exactly the same applied to the vast majority of the Germans. That within a few months Hitler would be an all-powerful dictator was not considered a realistic possibility. After all, too many forces were ranged against him and in November 1932 the National Socialists suffered a serious electoral defeat, which might have marked the beginning of the end; and the economic crisis was showing the first signs of abating.

VIII

THE NATIONAL SOCIALIST TAKEOVER

The National Socialist 'seizure of power' in the early months of 1933 was preceded by elaborate intrigues against the Chancellor, General von Schleicher, whose plans to gain mass support had failed. The intrigues partly emanated from the National Socialists, eager to obtain power at last, partly from the German Nationalists and von Papen who felt betrayed by Schleicher, partly from the Agrarian League which totally rejected his plans of settling peasants on bankrupt or derelict estates of East Germany – plans which had already caused the downfall of Brüning (see page 251). On 11 January 1933 Rumbold reported: 'There are a great many intriguers at work and there are signs of incipient hostility to von Schleicher in the Nationalist camp, but the Chancellor is well able to cope with his opponents as long, of course, as the President supports him.' But how long would the old President support Schleicher, and especially his plans of settling peasants on noble estates? The occasion of the ambassador's report was the secret meeting of Hitler and Papen in Cologne on 4 January in the house of the banker Kurt von Schroeder at which Papen suggested a coalition of the Nationalists and National Socialists and told Hitler he would ruin his movement if he persisted in his policy of negation. Rumbold was informed that Hitler's initiative was due to 'two things, a desire to stave off an early election at which he knows he would lose seriously, and an almost equally strong desire to stave off bankruptcy. The debts of his party are becoming more and more pressing.' Hitler needed the help of 'the Nationalist section of the Ruhr industrialists who lent him money some years ago'. On 8 January the Berlin correspondent of The Times reported that

269

the motive behind the meeting in Cologne was not a wish to support Schleicher; 'covert hostility' to him was developing in Nationalist circles, 'ironic references to the self-named "social General" betraying the suspicion with which any attempt at a conciliation with the masses is regarded.' This impression was deepened by the memory of 'the tenacious struggle' of Papen and the German Nationalists to retain the leadership of the government from which Schleicher had removed them some weeks previously. These circles wished to preserve the strength of the National Socialists and to enlist them 'as a constructive force in the work of government'.[1] Exactly the same had been Papen's plan in the summer of 1932, but Hitler was playing for higher stakes and rejected it.

Meanwhile the National Socialists threw themselves 'heart and soul' into the election campaign in the tiny state of Lippe. The ambassador thought that, by concentrating all their strength there, they 'may register a success which they could not repeat at a general election' in which they were likely to lose. The Times correspondent reported the results 'which hardly justify belief in a Nazi success in a general election', and assumed that they would induce Hitler to stiffen his terms for any sort of cooperation. In Lippe the National Socialists gained nearly 40 per cent of a total vote of about 90,000: a result which in their eyes figured as a great victory.[2] A few days later the same correspondent watched a large SA demonstration in the heart of working-class Berlin, in the square where the headquarters of the German Communist Party stood. The police had taken the most elaborate precautions; 'streets were cordoned off, and foot police with loaded rifles suspiciously watched the windows of tenement houses. Mounted police patrolled the neighbourhood and an armoured car thundered by with two machine-guns, admonishing the populace to order, so that one furtive inhabitant muttered to your correspondent: "I wonder they don't bring the pocket battleship out too."' The SA units were led by more lorry loads of police, paraded round the square with defiant looks and marched away to the adjacent cemetery, where Hitler unveiled a monument to the National Socialist hero Horst Wessel who had been murdered by a Communist.[3]

On 24 January Rumbold saw Papen who made no secret of his plan 'to get rid of the Reichstag and rule in what he described as an "authoritative" manner'. In discussing the National Socialists Papen maintained: 'it would be a disaster if the Hitler movement collapsed or were crushed for, after all, the Nazis were the last remaining bulwark against Communism in Germany.' When the ambassador interjected that he did not believe the German people 'were receptive to Communist ideas', Papen replied that 'Communism was receiving recruits from the ranks of young men who had passed difficult examinations but could find no posts'; the ambassador would be surprised if he knew how many intellectuals cherished Communist ideas. According to Rumbold, Papen had 'revealed himself in his true colours', as a monarchist and a partisan of government 'by force and without parliament'.[4] On 27 January Rumbold dined with Otto Meissner, Hindenburg's state secretary, who informed him that Schleicher demanded that the Reichstag should be dissolved and new elections be postponed by six months; the President would not agree to such a 'violation of the constitution' (which provided for elections within 60 days after a dissolution). Meissner further told the ambassador that Hitler might become Chancellor, with Papen as Vice-Chancellor and Hugenberg as Minister of Economics; the National Socialists would have one or two other ministerial posts; 'Hitler has shown signs of late of being more moderate and has realized that his policy of negation was leading nowhere.' According to the report, Schleicher's position 'was seriously shaken' and the German Nationalists were leading the offensive against him; by his negotiations with the trade unions he had also antagonized the industrialists. When Rumbold asked Meissner whether Schleicher, after his resignation as Chancellor, would remain Minister of Defence, the reply was that this depended on the composition of the new government, from which Rumbold concluded 'that Schleicher is finished'. Thus Meissner knew the precise details of the formation of the new government three days in advance. On 28 January the ambassador heard privately that the 'campaign against Schleicher has been given a strong impetus by the President's friends in East Prussia'; during the past week gross irregularities had come to light concerning the fund to support the agrarians of East Prussia and the eastern frontier districts (the *Osthilfe*); many landowners and friends of Hindenburg were openly accused of obtaining large sums for their private purposes: 'to avoid a debate in the Reichstag and a Commission of Enquiry, these circles are anxious that Herr von Papen should return to office and adjourn the Reichstag indefinitely.'[5]

Already on 26 January the *Manchester Guardian* wrote of a 'Hitler-Hugenberg Conspiracy' which intended to persuade Hindenburg to dismiss Schleicher and 'to appoint a Nazi-Hugenberg dictatorship'; but the paper considered it doubtful whether the President would agree to such a scheme, 'even if he preferred Hitler to Schleicher, which is at least equally doubtful'. On the 28 January *The Times* also reported on the intrigues against Schleicher. It was believed likely that he would go to the President and ask for a reaffirmation of his confidence; but it was expected that the latter would refuse him the plenary powers he was asking for and that he would have to resign. Then Papen and Hugenberg would suggest that Hitler should become Chancellor; the government would include Hugenberg, and it was hoped that it would be tolerated by the Centre Party and thus obtain a parliamentary majority. The National Socialists were negotiating with the German Nationalists for the restoration of a 'united front'. They and the Junkers were convinced that this was the last chance 'for obtaining a dictatorship and the indefinite shelving of Parliament' and were more determined than ever to achieve this because of the debates in the budget committee of the Reichstag about the maladministration of the *Osthilfe* funds.[6]

On 30 January *The Times* announced the fall of the Schleicher government, by methods which the paper compared 'to those of a sixteenth-century Italian Court': 'advisers with social or family connexions have had constant access to the aged President; Herr von Papen has never been away, and the strongest influence of all has been attributed to Colonel von Hindenburg, the President's son and ADC. The Chancellor, on the other hand, has had to await the grant of definite appointments.' The *Manchester Guardian* added that it was generally known that Papen worked hard behind the scenes for the overthrow of Schleicher; he was considered too 'democratically inclined'; but that was a 'compliment which Schleicher only deserved in a very limited sense. But then, everything is relative.'[7] Rumbold even found 'a poetic justice' in the fall of Schleicher, who had now become the victim of intrigues which he himself had spun in earlier years; Hindenburg had listened 'to unsound advisers who have kept as far as possible in the background and have acted through his son.' Rumbold found it difficult to imagine that the leaders of the new government, Hitler and Hugenberg, would 'be able to work together in harmony for any length of time',[8] which was a perfectly correct forecast.

The composition of the Hitler government led to extensive comment in the British press. A first leader of *The Times* stressed that, apart from the Minister of the Interior (Frick) and the Prussian Minister of the Interior (Göring, in charge of the Prussian police), 'the new Cabinet is Nationalist'; foreign affairs and finance remained 'in the hands of experienced Ministers'; 'it is clear that the Hitler Government is to be regarded as an attempt to balance the greater experience of the Conservative Nationalists with the numbers, the enthusiasm, and the popular appeal of their allies.' Hindenburg had taken a risk, but a return to a Papen government, rejected by the vast majority, might have caused a first-class crisis. It had always been desirable to give Hitler a chance 'of showing that he is something more than an orator and an agitator'; the experiment would be followed with some anxiety abroad, notably in France and Poland. 'In this country, moreover, as in France, the effect of the change of Government on the German attitude towards armaments will be watched with some misgivings. But in fairness to the Nazis it must be admitted that they have in fact said little more on the subject of German disabilities under the Treaty of Versailles than the most constitutional German parties, although they have said it much louder.' The *Manchester Guardian* commented: 'That the Nazis are determined to maintain their power is to be seen in the allocation of the command of the police and military and Civil Service to Nazis or Nazi sympathisers.' It might almost seem a bargain by which Hitler had given the Nationalists control of economic matters 'in return for control of the organized force of the nation'. At the same time the paper believed rather optimistically that, if the National Socialists chose the way of suppression, 'they run the danger of uniting all elements of the Left in a single Marxist front'.[9]

The *Daily Mail*, on the other hand, warned: 'All the forces of Germany which are determined to tear up the Peace Treaty and make Germany a Power capable of imposing her will on Europe are now united. . . . Past animosity and past antagonism are forgotten in the common aim: the restoration of Germany's might and the regaining of her lost territories.' But the paper also expected 'keen and active opposition' from the Left which feared the loss of trade union rights and a lowering of wages. 'If provoked too far, they will use their sharpest weapon, the general strike. . . . Germany is now divided into two camps whose hostility is deeper and more bitter than it ever was before.' What the papers did not reckon with was the deep-seated animosity between Social Democrats and Communists, which made any common action virtually impossible, and the equally deep-seated tradition of complete passivity on the side of the SPD and the trade union leaders, who might have acted against a *coup d'état* of the army, but not against a government which had obtained power 'legally'.[10] The British papers clearly did not believe that the National Socialists would succeed in establishing their power without a severe struggle.

The British ambassador, however, pointed out at the beginning of February that 'the Hitlerites are united while the Nationalists represent conflicting interests, big landowners, farmers, peasants, industrialists and ex-service men. The internal divergencies in the Nazi party will come to light in due course but not until the torch-light election is over, whereas there are already rifts in the Nationalist lute.' Rumbold also thought (wrongly) that Papen had 'persuaded Hitler to drop his claim to exclusive power, to admit that his party is not an intangible movement but a political party like any other, and to cease aping Mussolini.' But, the report went on, if Papen thought that he had 'harnessed the National Socialist movement to the chariot of the Right', he was probably mistaken, for it was much more likely that the former would benefit at the cost of the Nationalists in the coming election. Hitler was now the Chancellor, many of his followers had been given office, in the Prussian civil service officials were ousted and replaced by his men, and all this would increase the number of place hunters and add to his poll at the election. In late February Rumbold wrote: 'Hitler may not be a statesman but he is an uncommonly clever and audacious demagogue and fully alive to every popular instinct. By the simple process of iteration and re-iteration he has convinced the youth of this country that the present unemployment is the work of successive Governments of the Left. Germany, he says, is a heap of ruins. The elementary truth is that Germany was a heap of ruins in 1918 and that the German parties of the Left, meeting with a certain amount of sympathy even at Versailles, salved the structure of the Reich, maintained its unity and ultimately rebuilt it.' But the youngsters who composed the mass of the National Socialist audiences 'appear to be ignorant of the most elementary historical facts, and when Hitler declares that the revolution of 1918 led to Germany's defeat his audience seems to believe him.' The credulity of the listeners was even more astonishing than the audacity of the speaker. The parties of the Left had committed grievous errors in internal policy, especially in education: if they had insisted on teaching the true facts of the history of the war, Hitler could not so easily mislead the young; the Left had failed to show 'that authority and even ruthlessness which Germans seem to expect from their rulers'.[11] Much of this analysis was shrewd and correct; but perhaps it attached too little importance to the enthusiasm and expectation of a great national revival which then permeated so many young Germans (and not only the young ones).

About the same time the *Times* correspondent commented on Hitler's speech in one of Berlin's largest halls: Hitler was the knight to slay 'the dragon which had caused all Germany's ills', Marxism, 'and with this simple allegory, told in accents of almost religious fervour, the rapt thousands were not only content but enthusiastically happy'. Only some days later, on 15 February, the same correspondent reported that the National Socialists had taken 'the first unmistakable step' towards a Fascist regime by arming sections of the SA and the *Stahlhelm* and employing them as an auxiliary police; Communist and 'disguised Marxist' meetings and demonstrations had been forbidden. These instructions, issued by Göring, clearly had the purpose 'to place the whole machinery of the State at the disposal of the parties of the Right and render the holding of normal elections impossible.' The *Manchester Guardian*, too, considered the turning of SA units into an 'auxiliary police force' as the first step towards the formation of an armed militia on the Italian pattern: 'If the Nazis have their own way Germany will be Fascist within a few months, perhaps within a few weeks.'[12] The *Times* of 16 February stated 'on the best authority' that the National Socialists were 'avowedly working to establish the "Nationalistic State" . . . irrespective of opposition, and expect to realize their ambition in the immediate future.' They believed they could 'find "legal" means to their end; but the conception of legality has already suffered so much damage that the word is losing respect.' The National Socialists were looking forward with enthusiasm to the final struggle with Communism and were resolved to root out the idea for which six million Germans had voted; 'they are prepared to be "brutal" and at all costs to have their way.' In their calculations the result of the elections of 5 March and the prospect of a parliamentary opposition had disappeared.[13]

In mid-February the commercial councillor of the British

embassy reported that the determination of the new rulers to pursue an extreme nationalist policy was confirmed by the sweeping changes of personnel from the permanent heads of the ministries downwards, by their control of Prussia and by their attempts to establish their authority in the other federal states; there was an 'atmosphere of dangerous emotionalism and political irresponsibility'. Yet he believed that two men stood out who possessed sound judgement and were capable of visualizing the consequences of hasty decisions: von Neurath, the Foreign Minister, and von Schwerin-Krosigk, the Finance Minister; 'as long as these men remain at their posts there is a guarantee that the worst follies will not be committed or, if committed, will be remedied.'[14] Both had served in the same capacity under Papen as well as under Schleicher; they were the representatives of an older social order, and were to continue to serve Hitler most loyally into the years of the Second World War. Neither seems to have objected to any of the 'worst follies' of the new regime. If the commercial councillor found that the National Socialists were 'not wanting in energetic ruthlessness', this is precisely the quality which their allies were lacking.

Later in February Rumbold reported that, as a result of three weeks of Hitler government, Germany was divided 'into two hostile camps and political tension has increased to such a degree as to be a matter for serious concern'; the two camps were divided by a narrow neutral zone which was occupied by the army and the Prussian police. But his assessment was wildly optimistic when he counted on the Federation of German Industries, the great shipping and export firms, the Protestant and Catholic Churches 'and what I might call moderate and reasonable people in all ranks' to oppose 'a minority composed very largely of millions of immature young men and women'.[15] At that time large numbers of the 'moderate and reasonable people' were busy making their peace with the new regime and jumping on the bandwaggon. At the end of the month a leader in the *Manchester Guardian* stated the position much more correctly: the elections of 5 March would be held 'not before but after the event. Herr Hitler has made it clear that the Government has the power and, in its own view, a divine right to it. If the electorate judges otherwise, so much the worse for the electorate.' The elections were taking place, as the leader of the Centre Party, Prelate Kaas, had said, under conditions appropriate to the Balkans but not to Germany. 'The Nazis, indeed, enter this election with a programme which is simply, in effect, "All power to the Storm Troops".' The Berlin correspondent of *The Times* gave details of the persecution of the Left and commented that a large class of people existed who could be expected to be moderates but who viewed 'current developments in Germany with complacency and even satisfaction'; no serious misgivings were aroused by 'the condonation of political murder, discrimination in the administration of justice, the muzzling of the Press, the unbridled calumniation of political enemies'. People believed that these measures were necessary, 'that there is now a clash of naked force in Germany', that National Socialism would win and, if it failed, only Communism could follow.[16] The National Socialist propaganda that the choice was only between the swastika and the Soviet star had fallen on very fruitful soil.

The propaganda effort was given a new impetus by the Reichstag fire of 27 February which caused an immediate stepping up of measures of persecution against the Communists – and not only against the Communists. The fire naturally made banner headlines in the British papers. *The News Chronicle* immediately queried whether prominent Communists were involved, and its Berlin correspondent thought the claim that the German Communists had any official connection with it 'just nonsense'. But he also disbelieved 'the stories that it was done by Nazis', which 'would be Machiavellism carried to the extreme'. Conditions in Germany resembled those of martial law; 'the liberties which the country has enjoyed almost since the era of Frederick the Great have vanished overnight, and they may not be re-established for years.' Communists, Socialists and pacifists were arrested without ceremony and thrown into prison. 'The Crusade against the "Red Terror" serves as a pretext for relentless war upon all democratic institutions.' The correspondent added that he still had to meet an intelligent German – not blinded by party passion – who believed that the Communist Party was responsible for the Reichstag fire or had been 'hatching a revolutionary plot, of which hair-raising particulars are being printed hourly in the Nazi and Nationalist newspapers – the only ones in Germany now enjoying freedom of expression.'[17] The *Manchester Guardian* reported that Germany was under 'virtual martial law', that actual martial law would have involved the army and was rejected in order to keep it out of politics. The facts of the fire were puzzling and many people were beginning to ask questions which were difficult to answer; how could one man (van der Lubbe) 'have started fires in scores of places and bring enough petrol into the Reichstag and work for hours undisturbed without the attendants on duty noticing him'. It was equally strange that, as was alleged, he should have poured petrol on his shirt to start the fire when the building contained so many curtains and other inflammable material. Until these puzzles had been solved many would prefer to have their own views about the origin of the fire, 'especially as it has provided a welcome excuse for the Government to adopt more vigorous measures of repression than ever towards the Communists.'

A leader of *The Times* commented on the silencing of the opposition and the severe curtailment of public liberties. 'Clubs have been trumps, and most of the trumps are in the hands of one of the best known Nazi leaders, Captain Göring.' Shootings and beatings were continuing; songs like 'The Night of the Long Knives' might have been 'dismissed two months ago as crude bravado' but could not be treated so lightly any longer; 'and in the present state of Europe the continuance of this high tension in Berlin must remain a danger to international peace.'[18] Rumbold considered the Reichstag fire 'as mysterious as it is suspicious'; although the leaders of the Communist Party were of poor quality, they 'are not entirely devoid of intelligence, and it is difficult to see what advantage they could gain by attempting to burn down the Reichstag a few days before the election.' The tension was great and 'the hysterical measures adopted by the Government' had only increased it. 'One cannot help thinking that a spectacular effort is being made to stampede the electorate into the Nazi-Nationalist camp on Sunday next.'[19]

On the eve of the election *The Times* stated in its first leader: 'There cannot, of course, be the slightest doubt that the present Government intend to remain in office whatever the result of the election; and to that extent the consultation of the people is a farce.' The police 'may arrest without giving a reason and detain without preferring a charge. They are encouraged to discriminate arbitrarily in the performance of their duties. They have been officially instructed, in fact, to allow wide licence to members of the parties of the Right, but to use their weapons ruthlessly against anybody suspected of Marxist sympathies.' The paper's Berlin correspondent reported that almost the only sign of opposition activity was an occasional Centre Party poster 'against civil war'; fear possessed the minds of the adherents of the Left; the reasons could be found in brief announcements, such as that of a workman murdered in his house, or of a Communist deputy from Oldenburg taken from his home and shot, or in the flight and going into hiding of prominent Socialists and Communists. The correspondent of the *Manchester Guardian* noticed that in the dreary working-class quarters of Berlin 'no flags at all are to be seen – except a Nazi flag here and there'. The inhabitants 'are grimly silent', for one had to be a brave and reckless man to hang out a red flag in Berlin now. With the open persecution of the opposition 'and with monstrous charges brought against it which it was not even allowed to answer', it would have been indeed a surprise if the election had not brought a success to the government; the election 'marks the triumph of a propaganda campaign which was brutal and unscrupulous, but in its own demagogic way enormously skilfil'.[20] In spite of all this, the National Socialists did not succeed in gaining an absolute majority but only 43.9 per cent of the vote and their Nationalist allies another eight per cent: insufficient for a change to the Weimar Constitution.

During the weeks of March the British embassy as well as the correspondents of the British papers reported on the terror unleashed in Germany. As the Communists had gone to ground, Rumbold wrote, 'reprisals were visited in most cases on Social Democrats, Democrats, Jews and members of the Centre Party'; even Dr Brüning had changed his residence when a man resembling him was attacked in the street. Rumbold thought it possible 'that the rumours of abductions, floggings and other personal visitations which have been in circulation here are exaggerated, but that a great deal of injustice has been done is undeniable,' and for this the government must be held responsible. Now a reaction had set in on the Right: 'The flying squads of irresponsible young men who arrested private individuals, assaulted Jews, destroyed printing presses and inflicted horse-whipping on lawyers and journalists, are now disappearing from the streets and a little more confidence is felt by the law-abiding section of the community.' The British consuls too reported summary arrests from all parts of Germany; 'in a great many cases it is evident that the fate of the persons who have disappeared will remain a mystery.' The Communist leaders, the report continued, were held in the fortress of Spandau 'and rumour has it that they are none too well treated.' Prominent Social Democrats had gone into hiding and charges of corruption were raked up against former ministers. The ambassador believed that 'the regime of violence and outrage which has so shocked foreign countries during recent weeks' was modelled on methods practised by soldiers of the Black Reichswehr in 1923–24; those suspected of treachery were punished by a self-appointed court in so-called 'Feme trials'; 'the more notorious of these gangsters were gladly enrolled in the first SA formations, and they brought with them the tradition.'[21] There was, of course, another model – that of the Italian Fascists.

In April Rumbold wrote that the campaign of violence was showing no signs of ending; a prominent Jewish lawyer had been murdered in Chemnitz and the son of President Ebert had been maltreated; 'one of the most inhuman features of the present campaign is the incarceration without trial of thousands of individuals whose political antecedents have rendered them obnoxious in the eyes of the new regime. The establishment of concentration camps for politicians and pacifists on a wholesale scale is a new departure in civilised countries.' This, like the assaults and murders, seemed often 'to be the work of irresponsible members of the Nazi party.'[22] Much of the initial violence indeed came from 'irresponsible' members of the SA and SS who were seeking vengeance on their enemies, but a large amount of organized violence was carried out with the connivance and at the command of the National Socialists, especially of Göring and his underlings. A leader in the *Manchester Guardian* on 'The Secret Terror' mentioned some of the 'sinister buildings' in Berlin which recalled the prisons of the Russian Cheka and of the Italian Fascists: 'How can a great and civilised nation like the Germans tolerate these horrors?' In the last week of March the paper continued to publish 'Facts about the Nazi Terror', 'the beating and robbing of Jews', 'German workers under the Nazi Terror', 'Examples of beatings and murder'. One case of a political murder in public its horrified correspondent witnessed in a Berlin street. Other British papers too carried detailed stories of the terror, from Berlin as well as many provincial towns.[23] As Rumbold put it at the same time, the National Socialists 'have succeeded in bringing to the surface the worst traits in the German character, i.e. a mean spirit of revenge, a tendency to brutality, and a noisy and irresponsible jingoism.'[24]

The 'Day of Potsdam' of 21 March, when Hindenburg, Hitler, the members of the government, the leaders and former leaders of the armed forces and many other German dignitaries assembled in the famous garrison church of Potsdam for a religious ceremony, was interpreted by the majority of British papers as a triumph of the Prussian spirit. 'The scenes within the church and in the streets', the *News Chronicle* wrote, 'were at once a repudiation of Germany's recent past and a challenging avowal of pride in the spirit and tradition of Potsdam.' The *Daily Mail* saw in the placing of a wreath by Hindenburg near the coffin of Frederick the Great 'the final triumph of Prussia and Prussianism over the whole of Germany'. A first leader in *The Times* declared: 'The new spirit of Potsdam will be innocuous to the rest of the world if it implies only a resurrection of German self-respect. That President Hindenburg interprets Prussian traditions in that sense is clear from the words which he used at the Potsdam ceremony. . . . There is ample and legitimate space in Europe for the kind of Germany which is the old Field-Marshal's ideal.'[25] Several papers stressed that Hindenburg had saluted the former Crown Prince when he entered the church: did this indicate the possibility of a monarchical restoration? And would the Prussian traditions prove stronger than the spirit which inspired the National Socialists? Prussianism had been the enemy of Britain in the First World War; but – in the atmosphere of 1933 – a revival of the Prussian traditions seemed preferable to unlimited National Socialist power.

The reports of the British papers on the meeting of the Reichstag on 22 March and on the acceptance of the enabling bill by all parties except the SPD (the Communist mandates were declared null and void) were on the whole limited to large extracts from Hitler's speech and the result of the decisive vote – 441 votes for the bill against 94 votes of the SPD. But the *Daily Mail* warned: 'If the Reichstag accepts this Bill it extinguishes itself, and the Government will possess greater powers than any other Government in Europe.' And the *News Chronicle* stated: the Reichstag would be called upon 'to sign its own death warrant' and to give legal sanction to the dictatorship.[26] *The Times* briefly mentioned that Otto Wels, 'a rather pathetic figure', opposed the bill 'in an atmosphere laden with hostility' and that Carl Severing, the former Prussian Minister of the Interior, was arrested on his way to the Reichstag session, but was allowed to cast his vote against the bill – and then rearrested. Only the *Manchester Guardian* reported in detail that Wels had 'reminded the Government that nothing in the world was eternal' and that a change from the present system would come one day. 'You can take our liberty and our lives but not our honour', he declared, and 'he charged the Government with cowardice for eliminating the people's representatives at a time when popular control was most necessary.'[27] None of the papers said that Wels's speech constituted an act of great courage in the atmosphere of terror which surrounded the session in the Kroll Opera house; nor was any importance attached to the 'yes' vote of the Centre and the small bourgeois parties which enabled Hitler to claim that he had assumed power quite legally. There was no comment either on the end of the Weimar Republic and its Constitution which was abrogated by the enabling law.

There was a great deal of comment, however, on the measures by which the Hitler government extended its control over the whole of Germany and all branches of public life. Even before the fateful meeting of the Reichstag the papers reported in detail how the National Socialists seized power in the Free Cities and other towns, forced their mayors – such as Adenauer in Cologne – to resign and eliminated the elected councils and aldermen. Everywhere the swastika flag was hoisted on the public buildings and mayors, officials and university rectors who protested were removed by force. In many places the police and SA units occupied the buildings of the trade unions and socialist newspapers and hoisted the 'patriotic flags'. There were, finally, detailed reports of the violent intervention in the south German states, the enforced resignation of the Bavarian and Württemberg governments and the arrest and maltreatment of their ministers.[28] On 11 March *The Times* correspondent wrote from Berlin: 'Within four days of the election the Federal States have been transformed into Nazi citadels; the oft-proclaimed resistance of the great Catholic or Liberal States south of the Main, undermined in advance by the strength of the local Nazi organisations, crumpled into nothing before the order from Berlin. The Nazi nominees are called "Police Commissioners", but actually their powers are almost unlimited.' Four days later a leader of the same paper stated: 'The "seizure of power" by Herr Hitler's Government is almost complete. . . . So complete has been their victory that the rest of the world hardly yet realizes that what has happened through the length and breadth of Germany is no mere change of Government, no sudden swing of the political pendulum from Left to Right, but a real Revolution. No other term indeed can fairly be applied to the change from a more or less constitutional democracy to what is to all intents and purposes a two-party Dictatorship in which one party has almost a monopoly of dictation.'[29]

On the same day Rumbold wrote to London 'that the counter-revolution which began when the President appointed Herr Hitler to the Chancellorship on 30th January has now come to an end with the capture of the entire administration of this country. The term revolution is perhaps inapplicable in the strict sense, because the means employed were partly legal and partly illegal, and the illegal measures were at all events tolerated by the head of the State. . . .' While the National Socialists seized the federal states largely by force, they used the ballot box to gain control of local and municipal government in Prussia. 'The National Socialist revolution is now complete and the parties of the Left have suffered an eclipse from which they will take some time to recover. The resolution with which the new Government have seized power and overcome difficulties has undoubtedly made a favourable impression on a people who instinctively prefer definite action . . . to inaction and hesitation. A policy of ruthlessness will always appear in Germany to be a strong policy and therefore a wise one.' He added that the Nationalist allies of Hitler were 'completely bewildered by the violence of the landslide which has swept the ground from under their feet'. He still had some doubt whether the ruthlessness of the new regime would be able to 'overcome the resistance of all the forces which have hitherto constituted the political life' of Germany.[30] But by that time resistance, or even opposition, was no longer a practical possibility. The other question he discussed, whether Hitler's takeover was a revolution or a counter-revolution, is still being discussed by the historians: it clearly had elements of both. Hitler himself always stressed that he had come to power by 'legal' means; but this meant stretching the term legality to its limits, and the limits were not those of the Weimar Constitution which had ceased to exist.

Germany had always been a federal state. The establishment of a completely unitary centralized state was achieved by a law of 7 April. In his comment on the law the ambassador wrote that this step 'may perhaps be the logical development of Bismarck's work but which that statesman never hoped to achieve'. Henceforth it was the Chancellor 'who, through his nominees, will directly control the affairs of all the Federal States. In every sphere of public life the Reich Government will henceforth be able to count on a political unity hitherto unknown, and as a result of this unity, will be able to exercise an authority hitherto undreamt of.' The Prussian Diet would no longer be able to elect a government, nor would it be able to overthrow it; like all the other Diets it would become a purely advisory body. The old federal system had come to an end.[31] In the ambassador's opinion there was only one force which so far had not identified itself with National Socialism – the Reichswehr. 'Of course there are Nazi cells in the army', he wrote, 'and some of the officers sympathise with it.' He knew that the new Undersecretary of State in the Defence Ministry, Colonel von Reichenau, had strong sympathies with the National Socialist movement. But the report wrongly assumed that the minister himself, General von Blomberg, 'is quite aloof', for Blomberg shared these sympathies. Rumbold also thought 'that Hindenburg would not hesitate to impose martial law . . . for the theatrical Nazis with their incessant agitation are foreign to his simple straightforward military nature.'[32] Yet the President was much too old and quite incapable of taking any such drastic action; nothing could be expected from him or from the *Stahlhelm* whose 'great bitterness against the Nazis' was mentioned by the ambassador.

According to another of his reports two principal arguments were advanced by those who supported Hitler. The first was that he had saved Germany and Europe from Bolshevism, but this was 'a considerable assumption'. No doubt 'a hard kernel of Communism of the Russian variety' existed in Germany, but it was 'doubtful whether Communism really presented the dangers with which the Hitler party invested it'. The second argument was 'that the Hitler experiment must be made a success, failing which Germany will be plunged into chaos', an opinion held 'even by men of sensible views such as Baron Neurath'. Rumbold, however, thought that this argument left two factors out of account: the army and the 'two large bourgeois parties, namely the Centre and the Social Democrats'.[33] On both points he was certainly right. The German Communist Party was feeble, had done nothing when Hitler became Chancellor, and its voting strength of six million concealed the fact that it was unable to take any action because its following consisted almost entirely of the unemployed and semi-starving. In the early months of 1933 there were still considerable forces, such as the (not quite 'bourgeois') Social Democrats and the trade unions, willing to support an alternative government if Hitler had been replaced: but who was to achieve this feat? During the spring these alternative forces were destroyed one after the other by the

National Socialists – with the only exception of the army whose support Hitler needed and which he only brought under his complete control five years later. What is perhaps even more important, all this Hitler was able to do with the support of the majority of the German nation, and the opposition was driven into small isolated pockets. In June Vansittart could write: 'Hitler's magic has already transformed the German outlook: self-confidence and hope now fill the German heart. He has blown with his trumpet, and the Jericho of moral depression has fallen. Other Jerichoes are as confidently expected to fall. . . . What else, in the field of foreign affairs, may it not be expected to achieve? Frontier revision? "Mitteleuropa" under German control? Return of the Colonies?'[34] It sounded very pessimistic, and not without reason. But was it really Hitler's 'magic' which had achieved this? In reality, his path had been smoothed by the severity of the economic crisis and the inability of earlier governments to cope with it, and above all by the many bitter enemies of the Weimar Republic and the complete passivity of its defenders.

There was one other aspect of the new regime which occupied the attention of the British press and the embassy, that is, the measures of persecution taken against the Jews. In early March *The Times* correspondent reported that the Jewish department stores in Berlin were picketed by uniformed SA men who exhorted customers not to enter them and argued with them while the police looked on. In the Ruhr, according to an official statement, the action was not ordered by the National Socialist Party but was a spontaneous act of 'the patriotic population' which demanded the closure of the stores. The *Manchester Guardian* carried a similar report and added that many Jews had been attacked in the streets and some seriously injured. A 'wave of violence' was unleashed. A few days later all Jewish judges were banned from the courts.[35] At the end of March the papers reported on the general boycott of all Jewish enterprises which was 'to begin in every town and village of Germany' on 1 April. 'In some cases', the *Daily Mail* wrote, 'the racial ardour of true Germans is such that they have already begun the boycott', giving relevant details from ten German towns. So did the *News Chronicle* which further reported that windows of Jewish shops had been smashed and Jewish judges, lawyers, doctors, dentists and business men put under 'protective custody'. The paper stated that 'millions of Germans are entirely out of sympathy with this anti-Jewish outburst, and they hold in particular that it is unfortunate that it should be launched at a moment when the German Government's protests against "atrocity" stories are beginning to carry weight with foreign public opinion.' The *Manchester Guardian* commented: 'The Dictatorship is completely ruthless – a fact which is not sufficiently realized as yet. It is undoubtedly perturbed by the world-wide protest against atrocities for which it alone is responsible, and as it cannot terrorise the population of London, Paris, or New York, and cannot suspend British, French or American newspapers, it resorts to blackmail as far as it can.' It would be a great triumph for Hitler and his dictatorship if protest demonstrations outside Germany were confined to the Communists and the Jews stopped their protests.[36] Looking back on the boycott of 1 April the British ambassador believed that it had not been popular throughout Germany; 'on the other hand there has been no noteworthy revulsion of feeling in favour of the Jews', but only 'apathy' and a 'lack of sympathy' on the part of the public, while the persecution and maltreatment were continuing.[37]

In late March Rumbold reported that the Jewish community was faced by 'a much more serious danger than mere bodily maltreatment or petty persecution'; Jewish doctors, lawyers, judges, professors and persons with any sort of official appointment 'are being ruthlessly dismissed for no other reason than the accident of race'. Any observer could notice that the average German was superior to a Jew in many respects, but 'distinctly inferior in an artistic sense and even in a purely intellectual sense . . . and in every domain of intellectual efforts the achievements of the Jews are entirely out of proportion to their numbers.' He considered it 'only natural that the academic youth of this country should bitterly resent the success of the Jews, especially at a moment when the learned professions in Germany are hopelessly overcrowded.' This explained why the National Socialist Party 'comprises in its ranks most of the academic youth of this country'. Rumbold also believed that 'in the domain of finance' a Jewish supremacy was established at the time of the collapse of the German currency in 1923 and of the stabilization of the mark: 'Jewish financiers were quick to seize the opportunity to lay firm hands on the financial machinery of the country', and 'the best elements of the Jewish community will now have to suffer and are suffering for the sins of the worst, and more especially for the sins of the Russian and the Galician Jews who came into this country during the revolution of 1918.' The report clearly reflected the general German and German-Jewish prejudices against the 'Eastern Jews' which had been fanned by some notorious financial scandals; it was also coloured by the anti-semitic sentiments prevalent in German academic circles which the ambassador found 'only natural'. Yet some days later he added that his Polish colleague had shown him 'a lengthy list of cases of physical maltreatment of Polish Jews . . . frequently illustrated and confirmed by photographs'. All his diplomatic colleagues were as shocked as he was himself, and these actions were severely condemned in all non-Nazi circles with which he and members of his staff were in contact. Indeed, some of his German acquaintances 'made no secret of their shame that their country should have resorted to such medieval methods'. Among those mentioned by name as feeling 'the stigma of their country very deeply' were General von Seeckt, the former leader of the army, and Dr Wilhelm Solf, a leading diplomat. The German Foreign Minister told him that Hindenburg had tried for one hour to persuade Hitler to cancel the boycott of 1 April, but that all his efforts and those of several ministers had been in vain; there had been 'a serious struggle amounting almost to a presidential crisis'.[38]

In June 1933 Vansittart tried to sum up the situation in Germany in a top secret memorandum and in particular to assess to what extent Germany's economic recovery might be assisted and her economic and financial difficulties might be eased by British help. From past experience, he wrote, Britain had every reason 'to fear the re-emergence of Teutonic hubris'. Under successive post-war governments the German army and navy 'have managed to get their hands pretty deep into the pocket of the Reich'. The Reichswehr Ministry was as independent as ever and 'now almost the only organ of executive authority outside the Nazi sphere of influence': a too rapid recovery would undoubtedly ease German rearmament. These grave political considerations should not be omitted in a discussion of Germany's economic difficulties: 'Otherwise we may live to learn that the immediate material benefit of a prosperous Germany under Hitler may be more than outdone by the great damage to international confidence and security which will result from the dangerous uses to which the Nazi Government will be tempted to put any such material prosperity.'[39] The dangers emanating from Hitler's Germany were clearly recognized, but there was no suggestion of what might be done to contain them. Britain wanted a stable and prosperous Germany, but a stable and prosperous Germany could also become dangerous and the experience of 1914 had not been forgotten. The real fear was that history might repeat itself.

What surprised all British observers in Germany was the speed with which the National Socialists established their power and eliminated all opposition as well as the lack of any resistance to the dictatorship. They did not reckon with the utter ruthlessness of Hitler and his henchmen, nor with the scruples and bitter rivalries among their opponents. As one of the British diplomats in Germany remarked as early as 1923, the Weimar Republic had very few ardent supporters (see page 135): in the hour of its need even fewer were prepared to defend it at the risk of their lives. Above all, the Republic completely failed to arouse the enthusiasm of the young, and in this, as the British ambassador so clearly recognized, the National Socialists were past-masters. In the early 1920s as well as in the early 1930s millions of Germans had known nothing but economic misery and semi-starvation, in 1923 many hundreds of thousands had lost their property and their security. They blamed the republican governments for all the ills that had befallen them and believed that the 'system' was responsible. The prophets of the new system promised them a 'Third Reich' of plenty, of stability and of glory, and they followed these prophets, to their own doom.

CONCLUSION

The foregoing chapters have shown the wealth of information in the British documents on developments in Germany between 1918 and 1933, much of it new or at least shedding new light on what is known from German sources. Several British officers witnessed the revolution of 1918 in Berlin and other German towns. They saw 'no signs whatever of rioting'; outwardly things were 'more or less normal', where they might have expected revolutionary upheavals. The German army was well and truly beaten, and even a division of the Prussian Guards returning to Berlin presented 'a very pitiful display', clearly unfit to cope with serious disturbances of law and order. To soften the terms of the armistice, the German representatives as early as November played the card of the 'Bolshevik peril' which would 'certainly spread to other countries'. That was the message passed on to the Allies by none other than two members of the soldiers' council attached to the German High Command — one more proof how moderate these councils were in politics and how easy it was to manipulate them. That a leading industrialist like Stinnes was blowing into the same trumpet is of course less surprising, but it is rather startling that he should invite the Allies to occupy more German lands if 'the present state of chaos' continued to exist in Germany. The numerous reports by British officers on the conditions in many German towns do not confirm Stinnes's assessment. Considering the conditions of defeat, semi-starvation and collapse of the old order, law and order were on the whole preserved amazingly well. The often-quoted German sense of discipline quickly asserted itself. Only in Munich a prominent German pacifist who returned there

289

from his Swiss exile noticed signs of disorder and 'Bolshevik domination' – but that was after the murder of Prime Minister Eisner in February, which inaugurated a more radical wave in the Bavarian capital. Some British officers visited Munich and Nuremberg during the days of the so-called 'Soviet Republic' in April 1919, and their accounts provide a vivid picture of revolutionary events in the German south. So does the report given by another leading pacifist, Professor Foerster, of the anti-Prussian wave in Bavaria after the suppression of the 'Soviet Republic', leading to a movement which aimed at the foundation of an 'Alpine republic, agricultural, pastoral and Catholic'.

There is much new information on the events of the Kapp Putsch and its sequel, the rising in the Ruhr. As early as July 1919 Colonel Bauer, Ludendorff's adjutant, announced the Putsch plan to a British officer in Berlin, but the latter thought that the result would only be an assumption of power by the extreme Left. When the Putsch took place the Allied representatives from the outset adopted a negative attitude and in the end informed Kapp and Lüttwitz that they had to resign. The Allies supported the legitimate government under Ebert which in their opinion ought to be strengthened against the forces of the extreme Right and Left. The left-wing rising in the Ruhr against the free corps and the Reichswehr is extremely well documented by British officers who visited the industrial area from which the German army had been driven. They found that the claims of the workers were 'well founded', that the military leaders were responsible for the events, that the workers were able to maintain law and order, that their movement was directed against military reaction, and that there was no need for the reconquest and the punitive measures taken against the insurgents. Coming from professional officers whose instinctive tendency was to sympathize with their German counterparts, this testimony is all the more valuable. Equally interesting are the reports on the survival and transformation of the 'dissolved' free corps, either by their transfer to the navy or by settlement on east German estates, where they could wait for the day when they would come again into their own. In general, the British experts were not convinced that Germany had fulfilled the military clauses of the Treaty of Versailles; many infractions were discovered by Allied control officers and there was much obstruction from the German side. With regard to other equally controversial clauses of the treaty – those on the trial of alleged war criminals – the

Conclusion

British law officers attending the trials found that they 'were conducted very impartially with every desire to get at the truth', with the president condemning the conduct of the accused German soldiers. What aroused the ire of the British was the lenient treatment of the condemned men after the trials and the ease with which they made their escape – with help from inside and outside the prison.

Until 1923 Bavaria was the centre of reaction in Germany, with the *Einwohnerwehren* and their successors dominating the scene. Their disbandment was demanded by the Allies but stoutly resisted by the Bavarian government. On this and many other aspects of the Bavarian scene – from Prince Rupprecht to Adolf Hitler – the detailed reports of the British consuls in Munich provide fascinating reading. The incredible atmosphere of Bavaria comes to life in the description of the visit of President Ebert to Munich in 1922 or of the Hitler Putsch of 1923 when the local populace sided with Hitler and against Kahr who to them was a coward and a traitor. Equally vivid are the many accounts of the German inflation and the terrible misery caused by it. The strong revival of German nationalism, of hatred of the French and of a thirst for revenge are stressed time and again. So is the egotism and shortsightedness of the industrialists of Rhine and Ruhr who used the crisis of 1923 and the vagaries of the German currency for their own selfish purposes. The highly critical British views of the Rhenish separatists tend to confirm the German picture of the movement, and in addition there are detailed reports on the attitude of Dr Adenauer and the Centre politicians who originally favoured a Rhine province separate from Prussia (but not from Germany) but were alienated by the French policy of supporting the Separatists. British policy and the report of the British consul in Munich, who was sent to investigate events in the Palatinate, certainly contributed to the liquidation of the Separatist movement early in 1924.

The reports on the years of stabilization and rapprochement between Germany and her former enemies shed new light on the policy of Stresemann, who enjoyed an enormous prestige in Britain, greater than any other German statesman. Entirely new are his highly critical comments on the Reichswehr – called by him a 'Pretorian Guard', a 'Wallenstein Soldateska' – and its political attitude, with the other ranks even further to the Right than the officers. The general trend to the Right was symbolized by the election of Field-Marshal von Hindenburg as President

291

and contributed to Stresemann's worries. That even in these years the new President was by no means a passive onlooker but intervened directly in politics was shown in 1926 when he did not want Marx to become Chancellor and made difficulties about Germany joining the League of Nations, or in 1928 when he pressed for the construction of the first German 'pocket battle-ship'. When Otto Wels, the SPD leader, visited the Foreign Office he even described any opposition to Hindenburg and Groener (the Defence Minister) as impossible. The British possessed detailed and correct information on the many German violations of the Treaty of Versailles, whether it was the recruiting of 'temporary volunteers', the formation of frontier defence units and the building of fortifications on the eastern frontier, the production of poison gas or the establishment of the nucleus of an air force. But all these were considered 'minor' infractions in London; at a time of amicable relations with Berlin the Foreign Office was opposed to a policy of 'pinpricks' against Germany.

Amicable relations could also lead to cooperation of a very different kind – against dangerous 'agitators' – and the Foreign Office willingly fell in with a German suggestion that was welcome to it. In 1924 an official of the *Auswärtige Amt* in passing mentioned some Indian refugees who had helped the German cause during the war and, unable to return to India, lived in Berlin. From the German point of view they were 'most inconvenient guests' because they had become Communists, 'were supplied with Bolshevist funds, and generally assisted the cause of Bolshevist propaganda in Germany'. The Germans would welcome an opportunity to expel them and would supply information about their activities when available. The British government replied that it had no objection to the removal of the Indian agitators from Germany, provided that they were deported to India on a German ship and not merely expelled. The German Undersecretary of State, Maltzan, promised that this would be done and that information on their journey would be given so that their escape en route, for example in Egypt, could be prevented. Later the German government also handed over the information it possessed on Indian agitators who were or had been living in Germany.[1] Any method of cooperation against the common 'enemy' was permitted.

As far as the Reichswehr was concerned, the ultra-conservative spirit animating the officer corps emerged most clearly in the incredible comments made by Colonel von Reichenau, the chief of staff of the First Division, to a complete stranger at a house party in East Prussia in 1932. This was immediately after the enforced resignation of General Groener, the Minister of Defence, against whom his own subordinates had formed a united front on political and social grounds. The aristocratic officers looked down upon Groener as the son of a 'little pay-master Sergeant-Major', who had concluded an 'unfortunate marriage' with an elderly housekeeper. Allegedly egged on by her, Groener had committed the cardinal sin of dissolving the SA – a movement which the officers 'regarded as essentially patriotic and healthy', and which they needed for their illegal frontier defence units. Nine months after these 'revelations' Colonel von Reichenau was the new Undersecretary of State in the Defence Ministry under General von Blomberg, the Minister of War. The facts of German rearmament were well known in London (and in Paris) and the information on German violations of the disarmament clauses was very accurate, but the will to counter them was lacking. In defence of the British attitude it might be said that as yet there was no danger and, as long as Germany remained a parliamentary democracy, the forces opposed to any adventure in foreign policy would remain strong. But how long would Germany remain a democracy? The weight and the influence of the army were constantly growing and any later action might be very difficult, if not impossible. Action was not even taken against the many para-military associations which were flourishing in the country, such as the *Stahlhelm*, and which were assiduously fostered by the army. It is a story of missed opportunities: that they existed can hardly be doubted, and the French were strongly pressing for action.

As early as 1919 the War Office and British officers in Germany were urging a lifting of the Allied blockade and a strengthening of the German government which was under Social Democratic influence – to prevent a spread of Bolshevism to Germany. Several times Winston Churchill circulated papers advocating such a policy to the Cabinet. At the time of the Kapp Putsch the Foreign Office advocated a policy of maintaining the Ebert-Bauer government in power, as it was 'genuinely demo-cratic', and of giving assistance to it. This line remained a constant element in British policy. Germany should be allowed to recover, to the benefit of British trade and of the stability of Central Europe. This policy was strongly supported by the British diplomats in Germany and led to serious conflicts with

France. In 1923 a British member of the Rhineland High Commission believed that 'the real issue' between Britain and France was 'whether Germany is to be allowed to recover', and another wrote: 'We don't want Germany to be a carcass. France does not mind very much if she becomes one and if decomposition supervenes.' On the controversial issue of Upper Silesia the Foreign Office adopted an attitude highly critical of French policy and by and large it supported the German claims to the area. A similar attitude was taken to the sanctions imposed by the French because German troops had marched into the Ruhr to suppress the left-wing rising of 1920 and, of course, in 1923 when the French army occupied the Ruhr. The British government always claimed that it had no wish to mediate between France and Germany, that it was neither anti-French nor pro-German; but in practice it often supported the German attitude and at times it certainly and effectively mediated between the two countries.

In the immediate post-war years the Foreign Office also intervened on behalf of individual Germans whose entry into Britain was considered undesirable by the Home Office. When Eduard Bernstein, one of the best known German Socialists, intended to visit London in November 1919 to attend a meeting of the 'Fight the Famine' Council and the Home Secretary opposed his visit, Curzon wrote to the Home Office and pointed out that Bernstein, owing to his long residence in London, 'understands the English point of view as few Germans do' and had opposed the pro-war policy of his own party 'as soon as he had found out the truth regarding the origins of the war'. But the Home Secretary did 'not think it advisable to admit any former enemy aliens' unless the visit was 'of importance to the British Government or to some specific British interest': if Curzon intended to invite Bernstein for such a purpose he promised to reconsider the matter.[2] In June 1920 a repetition occurred when the liberal *Berliner Tageblatt* wanted to send the well known journalist Paul Scheffer to London as its correspondent and the Home Office refused permission, this time on the basis of secret Intelligence reports about Scheffer's war-time activity as a German propagandist in Holland. In the Foreign Office it was minuted that Intelligence reports were often unreliable and Scheffer's exclusion was to be deplored, even if it could be shown that his war-time activities amounted to more than what journalists of a belligerent country had done normally during the war. Crowe added that the ideas

Conclusion

of the Home Office 'of dealing with aliens are more Prussian than anything done in Prussia, and the odium for acting on their advice has to be borne by the FO'; the Home Office should be told that the Foreign Secretary could not make himself responsible for excluding Scheffer unless there was precise evidence that he was guilty of acts prejudicial to British safety. But again the Home Office accepted the responsibility for refusing his admission – a view with which the General Staff concurred.[3]

A third case occurred early in 1921 when the well known German writer and art collector Harry Count Kessler intended to apply for a British visa and Lord D'Abernon enquired whether this would be granted. Simultaneously General Malcolm sent the same enquiry to MI5 and received a negative reply, based on Count Kessler's alleged 'Bolshevist and communist opinions' (a perversion of the truth). Crowe minuted that Malcolm should never have put the question to the War Office which had taken 'a decision for which they have no authority whatever'. And a telegram was sent to Berlin by Curzon that General Malcolm should not have intervened: 'I must beg that questions of granting or refusing visas be submitted to me by the Embassy in the proper way.'[4] In general, there was much inter-departmental friction. On a different occasion Crowe minuted, full of irritation: 'Our generals, like the officers in the War Office who lay down the law about foreign policy, are a terror', and 'there is no real discipline in the upper ranks of the army'.[5] Foreign policy and everything connected with it must remain a prerogative of the Foreign Office.

After 1923 the attitude of the Foreign Office towards Germany became more friendly and more willing to meet German wishes. This was due above all to Stresemann's successful foreign policy which struck a responsive chord in Britain at a time of general pacification and stabilization. Many old suspicions, however, remained, in particular those of the German Nationalist Party and its opposition to a policy of reconciliation, of the growth of German nationalism and militarism, of the German tendency to ask for more as soon as any concession had been gained. It was recognized in London that these tendencies were not those of official German policy and it was hoped that they would be overcome in due course. To promote the policy of rapprochement the Foreign Office was willing to contemplate far-reaching revision of the Treaty of Versailles, to support German claims to 'equality' of rights, and there can be little doubt that this policy would have prevailed if the Weimar Republic had continued to exist. If its premises were too optimistic, it is somewhat difficult to criticize them from hindsight.

Faced by the rise of the National Socialist movement some of the Foreign Office officials took too rosy a view of its 'youthfulness', its 'vigour' and its 'sincerity', and praised its determination to restore 'discipline' in German youth and 'the good effect of its teaching'. Yet these illusions did not last, and the diplomatic reports on the 'seizure of power' were completely realistic and made no effort to conceal or condone the terror unleashed in Germany. It is also true that some of the diplomatic reports from Berlin – and much more so those of certain British consuls and officers – showed a marked anti-semitic tendency and considerably overestimated the extent of Jewish influence in Germany and the Jewish gains from the German inflation, reflecting the views of the conservative circles from which they derived their information. On at least one occasion, the crude anti-semitic bias of a consular report was immediately corrected in the Foreign Office, and an interesting comparison was made between the influence of the Jewish minority in Germany and that of the Protestant minority in France.

Apart from these examples, the Foreign Office reports and those made by British officers and officials in Germany were remarkably free from bias, well informed and incredibly detailed. They are of primary value for our understanding of the history and of the causes of the failure of the Weimar Republic. If the efforts of Lord D'Abernon and many others like him to promote Anglo-German understanding failed, that is no reason to condemn them or to accuse them of shortsightedness. In general, the British diplomats, officials and officers concerned with Germany during this period showed understanding and knowledge; they cannot be accused of anti-German bias or of insular arrogance. They showed compassion for the ills that befell Germany after 1918 and much sympathy with the German efforts to recover and to regain an important position in Europe. Allowing for certain lapses, British policy towards Germany after the Great War emerges with considerable credit.

NOTES

CHAPTER I

1. For details see F.L. Carsten, *Revolution in Central Europe 1918–1919*, London, 1972, pp. 21–24, 50–53.
2. Memorandum of 1 November 1918: PRO, Cab. 24, vol. 68, fo. 355.
3. Report by Lieutenant G.H. Beyfus, s.d.: PRO, WO 144, file 6, fo. 135.
4. Report by Brig.-General H.C. Rees, s.d.: ibid., fo. 134.
5. See Carsten, *Revolution in Central Europe*, p. 62; Ulrich Kluge, *Soldatenräte und Revolution*, Göttingen, 1975, pp. 234f.
6. Haking's despatch, 16 November 1918: PRO, WO 144, file 3, fo. 7.
7. Despatch of 20 November 1918: ibid., fo. 64. These despatches are General Haking's own copy, now in the War Office files at the PRO.
8. Information given by a German General Staff officer, 19 November 1918: ibid., fo. 56f.
9. Unsigned memorandum, 17 November 1918: ibid., fo. 33f.
10. Notes volunteered by Lieut.-Commander Kiep, 25 November 1918: ibid., fo. 172.
11. Haking's despatch, 22 November 1918: ibid., fo. 103.
12. Report by Lieutenant G.H. Beyfus, s.d.: PRO, FO 371, file 3776, fo. 110.
13. For details see Carsten, *Revolution in Central Europe*, pp. 68–71; Kluge, *Soldatenräte und Revolution*, pp. 117, 196f., 199–204. For the earlier history of the Spartacus Group, see F.L. Carsten, *War against War*, London, 1982, pp. 85ff., 152ff., 158f., 190ff.
14. Memorandum by Winthrop Bell (who had left Germany on 22 November), 11 December 1918: PRO, Cab. 24, vol. 71, fos. 252–58. Italics in the original.
15. Information by von Haniel, 20 November 1918: PRO, WO 144, file 3, fo. 66.
16. Notes on General Nudant's meeting, 26 November 1918: ibid., fo. 180.
17. For Stinnes' activities, see Erich Eyck, *A History of the Weimar Republic*, Cambridge, Mass., 1962, pp. 166f., 224f.

18. Memorandum by Winthrop Bell, 11 December 1918: PRO, Cab. 24, vol 71, fo. 259.
19. Report by Lieutenant G.H. Beyfus, s.d.: PRO, WO 144, file 6, fo. 135f.
20. Meeting of Armistice Commission, 7 December 1918: ibid., file 4, fo. 159. The coup of 6 December actually was a right-wing soldiers' attempt to proclaim Ebert President of the German Republic and to arrest the Executive Council of the Berlin workers' and soldiers' councils: see Kluge, *Soldatenräte und Revolution*, pp. 225–33.
21. Report by S.8, Stockholm, 23 December 1918: PRO, FO 371, file 3776, fo. 51f.
22. Intelligence Department to Sir William Tyrrell, 28 December 1918: ibid., fo. 50.
23. Haking to War Office, 6 January 1919: PRO, WO 144, file 7, fo. 27.
24. Haking to War Office, 10 January 1919: ibid., fo. 102.
25. Haking to War Office, 9 January 1919: ibid., fo. 83. For the Spartacus Putsch, see Carsten, *Revolution in Central Europe*, pp. 214–18; Kluge, *Soldatenräte und Revolution*, pp. 268f.; Arthur Rosenberg, *Geschichte der deutschen Republik*, Karlsbad, 1935, pp. 67ff.
26. M.A. Abrahamson to Lord Kilmarnock, 9 January 1919: PRO, FO 371, file 3776, fos. 148ff.
27. Copy of note from Maj.-General Sir R.H. Ewart, Spa, 12 January 1919: PRO, WO 144, file 7, fo. 167f.
28. P.I.D. Memorandum, 15 January 1919: PRO, Cab. 24, vol. 73, fo. 251.
29. M.I.6.B report, 2 February 1919: PRO, WO 144, file 9, fo. 148.
30. Ibid.
31. Report of 16 January 1919: ibid., file 8, fos. 41ff.
32. Report by Captain E. Christie Miller and Captain E.B. Trafford, 15 February 1919: PRO, Cab. 24, vol. 75, fo. 271.
33. Report by Captain A.D. Seldon, Captain H.M. Henwood and Lieutenant H.A. Rose, 10 February 1919: PRO, WO 144, file 10, fo. 144f.
34. Report by Captain G.B. Sommerville, Captain J.E. Broad and Lieutenant D. Pease, 14 February 1919: ibid., fo. 217.
35. Report on visit to Frankfurt-on-Oder, 10 March 1919: ibid., file 11, fo. 189.
36. Major Knyvett to War Office, 20 March 1919: PRO, FO 371, file 3776, fo. 413. Italics in original.
37. Maj.-General Ewart to General Haking, 7 March 1919: PRO, WO 144, file 11, fos. 325ff. For the events of March 1919, see Rosenberg, *Geschichte der deutschen Republik*, p. 75.
38. Report by Captain R. Hodson, 2 February 1919: PRO, FO 371, file 3776, fo. 255.
39. General Haking to War Office, 21 March 1919: PRO, WO 144, file 12, fo. 249.
40. Maj.-General Neill Malcolm to Director of Military Intelligence, 31 July 1919: PRO, FO 371, file 3777, fo. 326f.
41. For Muehlon before 1918, see Wolfgang Benz, 'Der "Fall

Muehlon" – Bürgerliche Opposition im Obrigkeitsstaat während des Ersten Weltkrieges', *Vierteljahrshefte für Zeitgeschichte*, xviii, 1970, pp. 343–65. For Bavaria in general, see Carsten, *Revolution in Central Europe*, pp. 201ff., 218ff.

42. Rumbold's telegrams to the Foreign Office, Bern, 24 and 28 February 1919: PRO, FO 371, file 3788, fos. 130, 140–43.
43. Report by Captain Thornley Gibson, 5 April 1919: PRO, WO 144, file 14, fo. 192.
44. Report by Lieutenant G.H. Beyfus, 9 April 1919: ibid., file 15, fo. 77.
45. Report by Lieutenant Wareing, 19 April 1919: ibid., file 22, fo. 188.
46. P.I.D. Memorandum of May 1919: PRO, Cab. 24, vol. 80, fo. 84f.
47. Minute signed G.S. (George Saunders), 8 May 1919: PRO, FO 371, file 3777, fo. 5.
48. Report by Captain T.J. Breen, 13 August 1919: PRO, WO 144, file 25, fo. 211.
49. General Haking to War Office, 5 April 1919: ibid., file 13, fo. 294.
50. General Haking to War Office, 8 April 1919: ibid., fo. 371. Apparently Haking was impressed by the German arguments and the 'despair' among the German officers.
51. General Haking to War Office, 1 May 1919: ibid., file 15, fo. 166.
52. Minute signed G.S. (George Saunders), 2 May 1919: PRO, FO 371, file 3776, fo. 542.
53. Report by V.77, Bern, 28 February 1919: PRO, Cab. 24, vol. 76, fos. 383, 389f.
54. Note circulated to the Cabinet by Churchill, 10 April 1919: PRO, Cab. 24, vol. 77, fo. 457.
55. Note by General Staff circulated to Cabinet, 23 April 1919: ibid., vol. 78, fo. 200.
56. Martin Gilbert, *Winston Churchill*, iv, London, 1975, p. 277.
57. Report by Maj.-General Neill Malcolm, 1 August 1919: PRO, WO 144, file 24, fo. 130.
58. Report by Lieut.-Colonel W.L.D. Twiss, circulated to Cabinet, 20 December 1919: PRO, Cab. 24, vol. 95, fo. 309.
59. For details see Eyck, *History of the Weimar Republic*, p. 89.
60. Report by Maj.-General Malcolm, 27 June 1919: PRO, FO 371, file 3777, fo. 226.
61. Report by the same, 18 July 1919: PRO, WO 144, file 23, fo. 91.
62. Report by the same, 25 July 1919: ibid., fo. 256.
63. Report by the same, 1 August 1919: ibid., file 24, fo. 128.
64. Report by Colonel C.E. Pollock, 7 July 1919: ibid., file 23, fos. 75, 81f.
65. Thomas Gooding to Foreign Office, 13 November 1919, and minute by George Saunders, 18 November: PRO, FO 371, file 3778, fos. 314, 319.
66. Minute by the same, 2 December 1919: ibid., fo. 390.
67. Report by Maj.-General Malcolm, 20 November 1919: PRO, WO 144, file 33, fo. 35.
68. Malcolm to War Office, 4 May 1919: PRO, FO 371, file 3789, fo. 458f.

69. Report by Lieut.-Colonel W.L.D. Twiss, 20 December 1919: ibid., file 3779, fo. 100f.
70. General Haking to War Office, 14 June 1919: PRO, WO 144, file 19, fo. 222; Lord Kilmarnock to Curzon, 23 January 1920: DBFP, series i, vol. x, London 1960, no. 1, p. 2.
71. War Office to Foreign Office, 20 November 1919, and Foreign Office to Director of Military Intelligence, 2 December 1919: PRO, FO 371, file 3795, fos. 41 and 50.
72. P.I.D. Memorandum, 4 February 1919: PRO, Cab. 24, vol. 74, fo. 302.
73. Viscountess D'Abernon, *Red Cross and Berlin Embassy 1915– 1926*, London, 1946, p. 80.
74. General Staff, War Office, 5 February 1920: PRO, WO 155, file 2, no. 180.
75. Rumbold to Curzon, 13 March 1919, report on conversation with Haase: PRO, FO 371, file 3787, fo. 535.
76. Lieut.-Colonel F. Thelwall to General Malcolm, 25 May 1919: PRO, WO 144, file 18, fo. 87.
77. Report by General Malcolm, 10 May 1919: PRO, FO 371, file 3777, fo. 72f.
78. Minute by George Saunders, 27 March 1919: ibid., file 3787, fo. 534.
79. Michael L. Dockrill and J. Douglas Goold, *Peace without Promise – Britain and the Peace Conference 1919–1923*, London, 1981, pp. 31f., 35, quoting a minute by James Headlam Morley of 16 February 1919; Harold Nicolson, *Peacemaking 1919*, London, 1945, pp. 287, 293f.
80. 'The Dictated "Peace"' ', leader of *The Labour Leader*, 10 June 1919, p. 6. In general see G.D.H. Cole, *A History of the Labour Party from 1914*, London, 1948, p. 92.
81. MacDonald, 'Labour and the Peace Treaty', *The Labour Leader*, 22 May 1919, p. 5; and 'The Municipal Elections and Foreign Affairs', *Forward*, Glasgow, 15 November 1919.
82. Report by Lieutenant G.H. Beyfus, December 1918: PRO, WO 144, file 6, fo. 136.
83. Report by an unnamed officer, 16 January 1919: ibid., file 8, fo. 43.
84. von Lersner to British Armistice Commission, Spa, 28 December, and General Haking to War Office, 31 December 1918: ibid., file 6, fos. 80A, 102.
85. General von Winterfeldt to President Armistice Commission, Spa, 10 December 1918: ibid., file 5, fo. 14.
86. P.I.D. Memorandum, 30 October 1919: PRO, Cab. 24, vol. 92, fos. 290ff., 307ff.
87. Report by General Malcolm, 29 August 1919: PRO, WO 144, file 27, fo. 98.
88. Report by the same, 19 September 1919: ibid., file 29, fo. 97. For D'Annunzio and Fiume, see Denis Mack Smith, *Italy*, Ann Arbor, 1959, pp. 333ff.; F.L. Carsten *The Rise of Fascism*, London, 1980, pp. 51f.

89. Reports by General Malcolm, 3 and 24 October 1919: PRO, WO 144, file 30, fo. 85; file 31, fo. 103.
90. Report by General Malcolm 30 October 1919: ibid., file 31, fo. 197.
91. Weekly Intelligence Report, British Army of the Rhine, no. 25, 8 October 1919: PRO, FO 371, file 3778, fo. 135.
92. Report on the Marloh trial by Colonel C.E. Pauvels, 9 December 1919: PRO, WO 144, file 34, fos. 110ff.; E.J. Gumbel, *Vier Jahre Politischer Mord*, Berlin, 1922, pp. 20ff.
93. Report by General Malcolm, 18 December 1919: ibid., fo. 192.
94. Report by General Malcolm, 27 November 1919; ibid., file 33, fo. 162f.
95. General Malcolm to War Office, 4 May 1919: PRO, FO 371, file 3789, fo. 464.

CHAPTER II

1. General Malcolm's report, 25 March 1920: PRO, FO 371, file 3783, fos. 528ff.
2. Lord Kilmarnock to Foreign Office, 13 March 1920: ibid., file 3780, fo. 226.
3. See F.L. Carsten, *The Reichswehr and Politics*, Oxford, 1966, pp. 78ff.; Johannes Erger, *Der Kapp-Lüttwitz Putsch*, Düsseldorf, 1967, pp. 116ff, 139ff., 146ff.
4. Kilmarnock to Foreign Office, 13–14 March 1920: PRO, FO 371, file 3780, fos. 232, 234, 261.
5. 'Annual Report on Germany for 1920', 7 May 1921: ibid., file 6060, fo. 143f.
6. Kilmarnock to Foreign Office, 14 March, Foreign Office to Sir Harold Stuart, 15 March 1920: ibid., file 3780, fos. 264, 306.
7. Robertson to Foreign Office, 17 March 1920: ibid., fo. 409.
8. Kilmarnock to Foreign Office, 16–17 March 1920: ibid., fos. 341, 356.
9. The same to Foreign Office, 18 March 1920: ibid., fo. 444.
10. The same to Foreign Office, 20 March 1920: ibid., file 3781, fo. 128. The name 'of the most moderate of Independent leaders' is not given.
11. Minutes by Curzon, 24 March, and by S.P. Waterlow, 26 March 1920: ibid., fo. 208.
12. Robertson to Foreign Office, 18 March 1920: ibid. fo. 7.
13. Minute by S.P. Waterlow, 29 March 1920: ibid., fos. 377, 388.
14. Kilmarnock to Curzon, 13 April 1920: DBFP, 1st series, ix, 1960, no. 396, p. 411.
15. Memorandum by Lieut.-Colonel R.S. Ryan, Cologne, 14 April 1920: ibid., no. 409, pp. 420–25.
16. Report by Robertson, Coblenz, 27 March: ibid., no. 227, pp. 256f.; FO 371, file 3781, fos. 517–21, with minute of 30 March, ibid., fo. 512.
17. Robertson to Foreign Office, 27 March and 2 April 1920: DBFP, 1st series, ix, nos. 227, 263, pp. 259, 299.

18. Political report, signed J.J. Hertbertson, 20 April 1920: PRO, FO 371, file 3784, fo. 343f. For the Bielefeld agreement and the Ruhr rising in general, see George Eliasberg, *Der Ruhrkrieg von 1920*, Bonn, 1974, pp. 173ff.
19. Report by Captain R. Garrett, 14 April 1920: FO 371, file 3784, fos. 218ff.
20. Robertson to Foreign Office, 8 April 1920: ibid., file 3782, fo. 473f.
21. General Headquarters Rhine Army to War Office, 10 April 1920: ibid., file 3783, fo. 472.
22. Robertson to Foreign Office, 7 April 1920: ibid., file 3782, fo. 407; FO 894, file 2, fo. 406.
23. French Embassy in London, 9 April, Curzon to Cambon, 14 April 1920: ibid., FO 371, file 3783, fos. 198ff.
24. Robertson to Foreign Office, 8 April 1920: ibid. file 3782, fo. 473.
25. Lord Derby to Foreign Office, 16 March 1920: DBFP, 1st Series, ix, no. 130, pp. 159f.
26. Crowe's minute of 19 March: PRO, FO 371, file 3781, fo. 14.
27. DBFP, 1st series, vii, no. 68, p. 585.
28. ibid., p. 590; Curzon at Allied Conference in London on 24 March 1920: ibid., no. 70, pp. 606—9.
29. Curzon to Derby, 1 April 1920: ibid., ix, no. 245, pp. 276ff.
30. Crowe's minute of 5 April 1920: PRO, FO 371, file 3782, fo. 138f.
31. Foreign Office to Derby, 6 April 1920: ibid., fo. 352f.
32. Sir G. Grahame to Foreign Office, 5 April 1920: ibid., fo. 160f.
33. Conclusions of Cabinet Meeting, 8 April 1920: ibid., file 3784, fo. 46; Earl of Balfour to Hardinge, 24 May 1922: PRO, Cab. 24, vol. 136, fo. 571.
34. General Malcolm's report, 22 January, and P.I.D. Memorandum on the Berlin Disorders, 19 January 1920: PRO, FO 371, file 3779, fo. 466; Cab. 24, vol. 96, fo. 335.
35. War Office to Foreign Office, 20 April 1920: PRO, WO 155, file 2, no. 24A.
36. Kilmarnock to Foreign Office, 25 June 1920: FO 371, file 3803, fo. 253.
37. Viscount D'Abernon, *An Ambassador of Peace*, i, London, 1929, p. 57.
38. Harold Stuart to Curzon, Coblenz, 12 March 1920: DBFP, 1st series, ix, no. 90, p. 132.
39. Kilmarnock to Curzon, 4 June 1920: ibid., no. 509, pp. 519f.
40. Morgan's report, 12 May 1920: ibid., no. 72, pp. 88, 103. In civil life Brigadier Morgan was a professor of law at University College, London.
41. Morgan's report, 12 March 1920: PRO, WO 155, file 5, no. 55A, p. 19. Cp. his *Assize of Arms – Being the Story of the Disarmament of Germany and her Rearmament*, London, 1945.
42. Report by Captain Colin Moad, 12 July 1920: PRO, FO 371, file 4792, fo. 173f.
43. Military Notes, British Army of the Rhine, 31 January 1921: ibid., file 5957, fo. 87f., with the exact distribution of the force.

44. Morgan's report, 25 June 1920: DBFP, 1st series, x, 1960, no. 107, p. 147f.
45. Report by Lieut.-Colonel A.L. Longhurst, 18 March 1921: PRO, FO 371, file 5982, fo. 278, 'The Trial of Hauptmann Pfeffer'.
46. Morgan's report, 20 June 1921: DBFP, 1st series, xvi, no. 806, pp. 906, 908f., 914.
47. Kilmarnock to Curzon, 1 January 1921: ibid., xvi, no. 557, p. 596.
48. Kilmarnock to Curzon, 1 February 1921: PRO, FO 371, file 6013, fo. 169.
49. D'Abernon to Curzon, 31 October 1922: ibid., file 7547, fo. 237f.
50. Military Notes, British Army of the Rhine, 23 August 1920: ibid., file 4784, fo. 107.
51. Kilmarnock to Curzon, 8 July 1920: ibid., file 4762, fo. 93.
52. Report by Lieut.-Colonel A.L. Longhurst, 4 February 1921: ibid., file 5981, fo. 9f.
53. Minute by S.P. Waterlow, 29 December 1920: ibid., file 5853, fo. 46.
54. Robert T. Smallbones to Foreign Office, Munich, 31 August 1920: PRO, WO 155, file 3, no. 63A.
55. Military Notes, British Army of the Rhine, 6 September 1920: PRO, FO 371, file 4784, fo. 157.
56. Report by Captain P.G.E. Warburton, 10 November 1920: DBFP, 1st series, x, no. 318, p. 438.
57. D'Abernon to Curzon, 23 November 1920: ibid., x, no. 325, p. 449.
58. D'Abernon, *An Ambassador of Peace*, i p. 87 (3 November 1920).
59. B.B. Cubitt to Foreign Office, 20 April 1920: PRO, WO 155, file 2, no. 24A.
60. B.B. Cubitt to Foreign Office, 24 December 1920: PRO, Cab. 24, vol. 117, fo. 355.
61. Memorandum by General Staff, War Office, 15 January 1921: ibid., vol. 118, fo. 369f.
62. Monthly Review of Intelligence Directorate, Home Office, March 1921: ibid., vol. 122, fo. 233.
63. Morgan's report, 20 June 1921: DBFP, 1st series, xvi, no. 806, p. 909. Cp. for the whole issue James M. Diehl, *Paramilitary Politics in Weimar Germany*, Bloomington, 1977, pp. 32–8, 55–67, 79–93.
64. Foreign Office Memorandum, 19 April 1921: PRO, FO 371, file 6010, fo. 122f.
65. Kilmarnock to Curzon, 21 June 1921: ibid., file 5857, fo. 113.
66. D'Abernon to Curzon, 1 August 1921: ibid., file 5878, fo. 79.
67. General Staff Memorandum, 31 March 1922: DBFP, 1st series, xx, 1976, no. 202, p. 428.
68. Ibid., no. 202, p. 426f.
69. D'Abernon to Curzon, 30 January 1922: PRO, FO 371, file 7554, fo. 596f.
70. Minutes by R.F. Wigram, M.W. Lampson and E.A. Crowe, 30 June 1922: ibid., file 7451, fos. 28–31.
71. Jürgen Heideking, *Areopag der Diplomaten – Die Pariser Botschafterkonferenz der alliierten Hauptmächte und die*

Probleme der europäischen Politik, Husum, 1979, p. 230.
72. D'Abernon to Curzon, 20 March 1922: PRO, FO 371, file 7449, fo. 122f.
73. Notes by R.F. Wigram, Genoa, 16 May 1922: ibid., file 7572, fo. 266f.
74. Such cases are in FO 371, files 7530–31; the case quoted in file 7531, fos. 89ff.
75. Report by Captain H.P. Atkinson, Munich, 25 October 1922: ibid., file 7453, fo. 40f.
76. Foreign Office to Treasury, 1 December 1922: ibid., file 7454, fos. 28, 197.
77. William Seeds to Curzon, Munich, 3 December 1922: ibid., file 7455, fo. 22f. von Knilling's speech was quoted in a French note of 26 December: ibid., file 8700, fo. 16f.
78. Seeds to Curzon, Munich, 1 February 1923, and British Embassy Paris to Foreign Office, 13 January 1923: ibid., file 8700, fos. 16f., 19f., 30. Cp. Heideking, *Aeropag der Diplomaten*, pp. 241ff.
79. Report by Major-General F.R. Bingham, 6 February 1920: PRO, Cab. 24, vol. 98, fo. 42.
80. Report by Colonel W. Stewart Roddie, 30 January 1920: ibid. vol. 97, fo. 651. Italics in original.
81. General Staff Memorandum, 5 February 1920: FO 371, file 3780, fo. 78f.; WO 155, file 2, no. 18c.
82. Göppert to Millerand, Paris, 6 and 14 July 1920: FO 371, file 4796, fos. 76, 94.
83. Minutes by Curzon and Crowe, 17 December 1920 and 5 March 1921: ibid., file 4733, fo. 1, file 5860, fo. 199f.
84. Reports by R.W. Woods and Ernest M. Pollock (the Solicitor General), 24, 26 and 30 May 1921: ibid., file 5862, fos. 20f., 38, 52.
85. Viscountess D'Abernon, *Red Cross and Berlin Embassy*, p. 94 (4 June 1921).
86. Intelligence Notes, Lieut.-Colonel A.L. Longhurst, 22 July 1921; PRO, FO 371, file 5984, fo. 208f.
87. Minute by R.F. Wigram, 9 July 1921: ibid., file 5863, fo. 187.
88. Crowe's record of conversation with German ambassador, 3 February 1922: DBFP, 1st series, xx, no. 170, p. 375f.
89. D'Abernon to Rathenau, 10 February 1922: PRO, FO 371, file 7528, fo. 291f.
90. R.M. Kohan to Curzon, Leipzig, 11 July 1923: ibid., file 8809, fos. 188ff. For the account of the escape of the two U-Boat officers with the help of former members of the Ehrhardt Brigade inside and outside the prison, see Ernst von Salomon, *Die Geächteten*, Berlin, 1930, pp. 318–29.
91. Kilmarnock to Curzon, 26 May 1920: PRO, FO 371, file 3802, fo. 376.
92. D'Abernon to Curzon, 28 August 1921: ibid., file 5974, fo. 116f.
93. Seeds to Curzon, 31 August 1921: ibid., file 5975, fo. 25.
94. Addison to Balfour, 26 June 1922: ibid., file 7536, fo. 66.
95. Seeds to Balfour, 27 June 1922: ibid., file 7536, fo. 128.; Gosling to

Balfour, 5 July 1922: ibid., file 7537, fo. 22.

96. Minute by J.W. Headlam Morley, 3 May, on report of 16 April 1920: ibid., file 3784, fo. 477.

97. Army of the Rhine report, 9 June 1920: ibid., file 3787, fo. 16.

98. Report by Director of Military Intelligence, 10 September 1920: ibid., file 4841, fo. 59f.

99. J.J.W. Herbertson to President Rhineland High Commission, 4 July 1921: PRO, FO 894, file 9, fo. 105.

100. Colonel M. Ryan to Kilmarnock, 29 March 1922: FO 371, file 7520, fo. 191f.

101. J.I. Piggott to the same, Cologne, 29 July 1922: FO 894, file 12, fo. 300.

102. H.D. Beaumont to Curzon, 25 March 1920: DBFP, 1st series, x, no 542, p. 736.

103. Gosling to Curzon, Frankfurt, 12 June 1920: ibid., ix, no. 523, p. 548.

104. Kilmarnock to Curzon, 27 August 1920: ibid., x, no. 204, p 299f.

105. Report by Major R.T.G. Tangye, 29 October 1920: PRO, FO 371, file 4785, fo. 67.

106. Kilmarnock to Curzon, 25 January 1921: DBFP, 1st series, xvi, no 581, p. 624f.

107. Robertson to Curzon, Coblenz, 7 July 1921: PRO, FO 371, file 5883, fo. 71f.

108. Lieut.-Colonel C.W.W. McLean, MP, to Cecil Harmsworth, MP, 25 January and 1 February 1922, Foreign Office reply of 2 February and minute by H.W. Brooks, 11 February: ibid., file 7549, fos. 281, 285, 286f.

109. Minutes by G. Goschen and S.P. Waterlow, 29 September 1920: ibid., file 4798, fo. 199. E.D. Morel's *The Horror of the Rhine* (August 1920), is in file 4799, as is the German pamphlet literature on the subject.

110. Military Notes, British Army of the Rhine, 10 February, and Gosling to Curzon, 2 February 1921: ibid., file 5957, fo. 97, file 5962, fo. 111.

111. Seeds to Curzon, 3 February 1921: ibid., file 5962, fo. 132.

112. Kilmarnock to Curzon, 1 February 1921: ibid., file 5962, fo. 69.

113. Gosling to Curzon, 24 February 1922: ibid., file 7559, fo. 120.

114. D'Abernon to Curzon, 21 April 1921: ibid., file 6003, fo. 22f. Potsdam was, of course, the shrine of the Prussian monarchy, and it might have been difficult to stage such a demonstration elsewhere.

115. Intelligence Notes by Lieut.-Colonel A.L. Longhurst, 15 April 1921: ibid., file 5982, fo. 300.

116. Report by Mrs Kathleen Jones, s.d. (May 1922): ibid., file 7514, fos. 139, 141f.

117. Statement by Sir Somerville Head, 26 February 1921: ibid., file 5964, fo. 93.

118. D'Abernon to Curzon, 21 April 1921: ibid., file 6025, fo. 200.

119. The same to Curzon, 2 April 1921: ibid., file 6056, fos. 2 and 5.

120. Intelligence Notes by Lieut.-Colonel Longhurst, 9 September

1921: ibid., file 5985, fo. 52f.

121. Report by Mrs Kathleen Jones, s.d.: ibid., file 7514, fo. 134f.
122. Directorate of Intelligence, Home Office, report for March 1921: PRO, Cab. 24, vol. 122, fo. 234.
123. Colonel F.H.P. Percival to Curzon, 5 September 1920: FO 371, file 4816, fos. 93ff.
124. Colonel F.H.P. Percival to Curzon, 14 September 1920: ibid., file 4817, fos. 48, 53ff.
125. Rumbold to Curzon, Warsaw, 4 September 1920: ibid., file 4816, fo. 144.
127. Hardinge to Curzon, 24 December, and Crowe's minute, 25 December 1920: ibid., file 4823, fos. 51, 53.
128. Colonel F.W. Tidbury to Wigram, Oppeln, 12 January 1921: ibid., file 5887, fo. 146.
129. Curzon to Percival, 22 March 1921: DBFP, 1st series, xvi, no. 1 p. 1. The result of the plebiscite, ibid., no. 22, p. 45.
130. Minutes by Wigram and Crowe, 24 March 1921: PRO, FO 371, file 5891, fos. 152ff.
131. Percival to Foreign Office, 8 and 15 May 1921: ibid., file 5898, fo. 35, file 5900, fo. 165.
132. W.G. Max Muller to Foreign Office, 8 May 1921: ibid., file 5898, fo. 113.
133. Aide-Mémoire handed to Briand, 13 May 1921: ibid., file 5905, fo. 59.
134. Percival to Curzon, 20 May 1921: ibid., file 5904, fos. 4ff.
135. D'Abernon to Curzon, 22 May 1921: ibid., file 5905, fo. 141.
136. The same to same, 31 May, and minute by L.E. Ottley, 1 June 1921: ibid., file 5908, fos. 35, 56.
137. Foreign Office to Hardinge, 14 June 1921: ibid., file 5911, fo. 15f.
138. J.I. Craig to Major Ottley, 25 May 1921: ibid., file 5909, fos. 15–18.
139. Stuart to Curzon, 1 July 1921, with draft Proclamation of Inter-Allied Commission, s.d.: ibid., file 5915, fos. 8, 10f.
140. Stuart to Curzon, 16 July 1921: ibid., file 5916, fo. 99.
141. Crowe's minute, 18 July 1921: ibid., fo. 184.
142. Stuart to Curzon, 20 July 1921: ibid., file 5917, fo. 136.
143. W. Heneker to Foreign Office, 7 August 1921: ibid., file 5921, fo. 74.
144. D'Abernon to Foreign Office, 7 October 1921: file 5926, fo. 331f., quoting Loebe's plea.
145. Rosen to Curzon, private, 6 October 1921: ibid., file 5927, fos. 106ff.
146. Draft Cabinet Conclusions, 12 October 1921: ibid., file 5928, fo. 81.
147. D'Abernon to Curzon, 10 October 1921: DBFP, 1st series, xvi, no. 325, p. 344.
148. Petition of December 1921, with minutes by S.P. Waterlow and Crowe, 14–15 December: PRO, FO 371, file 5933, fos. 89, 91.
149. General Heneker to War Office and Balfour, 2 and 22 July 1922: ibid., file 7467, fo. 229; file 7468, fo. 79.
150. Report by Major Keatinge, 5 March 1922: ibid., file 7471, fo. 59f.

151. D'Abernon to Curzon, 10 February and 11 April 1922: ibid., file 7463, fo. 72, file 7496, fo. 81f.
152. Stuart to Curzon, Oppeln, 6 June 1922: ibid., file 7466, fo. 186; Heideking, *Areopag de Diplomaten*, pp. 98–100.
153. General Malcolm's report, 22 January 1920: DBFP, 1st series, ix, no. 14, p. 14.
154. General Staff, War Office, 5 February 1920: PRO, WO 155, file 2, no. 18c.
155. D'Abernon to Curzon, 2 July 1920: PRO, FO 371, file 4781, fo. 6.
156. Report by Director of Military Intelligence, 20 June 1920: ibid., file 4791, fo. 158.
157. D'Abernon, *Ambassador of Peace*, i, pp. 180, 182 (5–6 June 1921).
158. Weekly Report, British Army of the Rhine, 28 July 1921: FO 371, file 5959, fo. 13.
159. D'Abernon to Curzon, 6 June 1921: ibid., file 5971, fo. 132.
160. J.I. Piggott to British High Commissioner, Cologne, 12 May 1921: ibid., file 5970, fo. 186f.
161. Crowe's minute, 24 March, and Foreign Office to Kilmarnock, 31 March 1920: ibid., file 3781, fos. 304, 431.
162. D'Abernon to Curzon, 23 March 1922: ibid., file 7476, fo. 7.
163. Kilmarnock to Curzon, 21 February 1922: ibid., file 7520, fo. 124.
164. Addison to Balfour, 27 May 1922: ibid., file 7535, fo 178.
165. D'Abernon, *Ambassador of Peace*, i, pp. 310, 314 (10 and 15 May 1922).
166. Ibid., ii, pp. 48f., 60 (29 June and 14 July 1922).
167. Kilmarnock to Curzon, 3 January 1921: PRO, FO 371, file 5980, fo. 48.
168. D'Abernon to Curzon, 13 October 1921: ibid., file 5929, fo. 12.
169. The same to same, 15 and 22 November 1922: ibid., file 7539, fos. 71, 86f., 107f.
170. The same to same, 13 October 1922: ibid., file 7538, fo. 215.
171. The same to same, 27 November 1922: British Library, Additional MS.48925A, fo. 67.
172. Addison to Curzon, 5 December 1922: PRO, FO 371, file 7489, fos. 11–14.
173. The same to S.P. Waterow, private, 13 and 19 December 1920: ibid., file 4730, fos. 105, 180.
174. D'Abernon to Curzon, 19 November 1922: ibid., file 7487, fo. 186f.
175. D'Abernon to Curzon, 11 April 1922: ibid., file 7516, fo. 134f.
176. Kilmarnock to Curzon, 24 June, minutes by R.F. Wigram and H.W. Malkin, 1 July and 5 August, and War Office to Foreign Office, 30 July 1921: ibid., file 6063, fos. 1f., 7–10.
177. D'Abernon to Curzon, 2 February 1922: ibid., file 7556, fo. 137.
178. Kilmarnock to Curzon, 31 January and 10 February 1920: DBFP, 1st series, ix, nos. 23 and 38, pp. 28, 57f.
179. General Haking to Chief of Imperial General Staff, 21 March and minutes of 3–4 April 1920: PRO, FO 371, file 3782, fos. 37, 40.
180. Martin Gilbert, *Winston Churchill*, iv, London, 1975, p. 384 (24 March 1920). Italics in the original.

181. General Staff Memorandum, 16 August 1920: PRO, FO 371, file 4741, fo. 71.
182. Minute by S.P. Waterlow, 20 January 1921: ibid., file 5854, fo. 206.
183. J.I. Piggott to M.W. Lampson, Cologne, 8 November 1922: ibid., file 7522, fo. 173.
184. Minute by S.P. Waterlow, 9 May 1922: ibid., file 7567, fo. 136.
185. General Malcolm to Director of Military Intelligence, 28 January 1920: DBFP, 1st series, ix, no. 19, p. 22f.
186. H.D. Beaumont to Curzon, 23 February 1920: ibid., no. 56, p. 91.
187. D'Abernon to Curzon, 8 November 1920: ibid., x, no. 233, p. 329f.
188. Report by F. Thelwall, 21 October 1920: PRO, FO 371, file 4743, fo. 94.
189. Report by the same, 25 October 1920: ibid., file 4787, fo. 122f.
190. Viscountess D'Abernon, *Red Cross and Berlin Embassy*, p. 73 (6 November 1920).
191. D'Abernon to Curzon, 29 November 1922: PRO, FO 371, file 7519, fo. 155.
192. Report by Mrs Kathleen Jones, s.d. (May 1922): ibid., file 7514, fo. 137.
193. D'Abernon to Curzon, 8 September 1922: ibid., file 7505, fo. 167.
194. Addison to Curzon, 14 September 1921: ibid., file 5987, fo. 22.
195. Kilmarnock to Curzon, 18 January 1921: ibid., file 5968, fo. 197f.
196. Thelwall to Department of Trade, 21 February 1921: ibid., file 6044, fo. 8f.
197. Addison to Curzon, 4 December 1922: ibid., file 7488, fo. 182f.
198. Kilmarnock to Curzon, 31 January 1920: ibid., file 3779, fo. 483.
199. Reports by Sir Harold Stuart, 7 April, and Alfred Scattergood quoted by General Malcolm on 1 April 1920: ibid., file 3798, fo. 73.
200. General Morland to War Office, 11 May, Foreign Office to War Office, 22 May, War Office to Foreign Office, 16 June, and minute of 18 June 1920: ibid., file 3802, fos. 295, 296A, 305f.
201. Report by Lieut.-Colonel Stewart Roddie, 4 June 1920: ibid., file 3786, fo. 591.
202. General Staff report circulated by Churchill, 28 June 1920: PRO, Cab. 24, vol. 108, fo. 198.
203. Report by Lieut.-Colonel Longhurst, 22 December 1920: PRO, FO 371, file 5939, fo. 205.
204. Stuart to S.P. Waterlow, 26 April 1920: ibid., file 3784, fo. 526.
205. E.W.P. Thurston to Curzon, 18 August 1920: ibid., file 4771, fo. 130.
206. British Forces of the Rhine, report for week ending 22 October 1920: ibid., file 4785, fo. 22.
207. Report by Captain W.C.M.M. Georgi, 6 January 1921: ibid., file 5952, fo. 11f.
208. Report by E.C. Campbell, 30 November 1921: ibid., file 5997, fo. 97.
209. Annex to Minute 162 of the Rhineland High Commission, 14 February 1920: PRO, FO 894, file 1, fo. 297.
210. Kilmarnock to Foreign Office, 30–31 December 1921, 1 January

1922; D'Abernon to Curzon, 3 January: PRO, FO 371, file 7447, fos. 7, 15–19, 24, 28f.

211. D'Abernon to Foreign Office, 5, 8 and 9 February 1922: ibid., fos. 56, 58, 60.

212. Kilmarnock to Curzon, 27 March 1920: ibid., file 3782, fo. 256.

213. Kilmarnock to Curzon, 8 April 1920: ibid., file 3783, fo. 335f.

214. Kilmarnock to Curzon, 23 April 1920: ibid., file 3801, fo. 327f.

215. Reports by Major Piggott and Captain Barrett, 8 May 1920: ibid., file 3785, fos. 199f., 210A.

216. Kilmarnock to Curzon, 20 May 1920: ibid., file 3785, fo. 490.

217. Kilmarnock to Curzon, 11 June 1920: ibid., file 3786, fo. 548.

218. Intelligence Report, Rotterdam, 14 July 1920: ibid., file 4832, fos. 69, 73.

219. Minute by G. Saunders, 2 September, on expulsions from the KAPD report of 18 August 1920: ibid., file 4834, fos. 150, 152.

220. Seeds to Curzon, 17 October 1920: ibid., file 4810, fo. 182.

221. The same to same, 18 October 1920: ibid., file 4845, fo. 182.

222. Monthly Review of Revolutionary Movements, no. 27, January 1921: PRO, Cab. 24, vol. 120, fo. 109.

223. D'Abernon to Curzon, 7 February 1921: FO 371, file 5937, fo. 76f.

224. Kilmarnock to Curzon, 26 February 1921: ibid., file 5937, fo. 140f.

225. D'Abernon to Curzon, 27 March, 1921: ibid., file 5938, fo. 178.

226. Captain G. Lawson to British Commissioner at Cologne, 6 April 1921: PRO, FO 894, file 8, fo. 365f., file 10, fo. 168 (decision to rescind the order).

227. British Army of the Rhine, reports of 20 April and 30 June 1921: FO 371, file 5958, fos. 196, 290.

228. Monthly Review of Revolutionary Movements, no. 34, August 1921: PRO, Cab. 24, vol. 128, fo. 119.

229. D'Abernon to Curzon, 30 September 1921: PRO, FO 371, file 5976, fo. 44.

230. Report by E.C. Campbell, 3 October 1921: ibid., file 6000, fo. 192.

231. D'Abernon to Curzon, 21 November 1922: ibid., file 7519, fo. 131.

232. Weissmann, State Commissioner for Public Order, to Addison, 29 December 1922: ibid., file 8700, fo. 80f.

233. Minute by G. Saunders, 17 June 1919: ibid., file 3777, fo. 151.

234. Captain H.L. Farquhar to Foreign Office, 17 October, and minute by Saunders, 23 October 1919: ibid., file 3794, fos. 133f., 140ff.

235. Robertson to Curzon, Coblenz, 24 January 1921: ibid., file 6007, fo. 2f.

236. Kilmarnock to Curzon, 19 May and 8 September 1922: ibid., file 7521, fos. 35, 230.

237. The same to same, 27 February 1922: ibid., file 7542, fo. 20f.

238. Robertson to Curzon, 25 May, 7 and 15 July 1921: DBFP, 1st series, xvi, no. 785, p. 884; PRO, FO 371, file 5883, fo. 71f., file 5973, fo. 9.

239. Robertson to Curzon, 18 July and 1 August 1921: ibid., file 5858, fos. 20, 43.

240. R.S. Ryan to Kilmarnock, 11 August 1922: ibid., FO 894, file 12, fo. 705f.

CHAPTER III

1. Acton to Curzon, 26 July 1919: PRO, FO 371, file 3790, fo. 310f. For Foerster see Heinrich Lutz, 'Friedrich Wilhelm Foerster', in Peter Glotz (ed.), *Vorbilder für Deutsche – Korrektur einer Heldengalerie*, Munich, 1974, pp. 47–62.
2. Report by Captain J.J.W. Herbertson, 26 November 1919: FO 371, file 3778, fo. 418f.
3. Minutes by J.W. Headlam Morley, 25 and 27 October 1919, 27 January and 19 February 1920, George Saunders of 24 October 1919 and 19 February 1920, L.O. of 18 February Crowe of 20 February and Curzon of 23 February, 1920: ibif., file 3793, fos. 380ff., 426, 505, 545–49.
4. Minutes by S.P. Waterlow, 14 July, and Curzon, 16 July 1920: ibid., file 4725, fos. 10f., 15f.
5. Kilmarnock to Curzon, 20 May 1920: DBFP, 1st series, ix, no. 475, p. 488f.
6. R.T. Smallbones to Curzon, 4 April and 1 July 1920: ibid., nos. 326, 553, pp. 354, 587.
7. Report by General Malcolm, circulated by Churchill, 28 May 1920: PRO, Cab. 24, vol. 106, fo. 200.
8. D'Abernon, *Ambassador of Peace*, i, p. 94.
9. Intelligence Summary by Lieut.-Colonel A.L. Longhurst, 30 September, and report of 15 November 1920: PRO, FO 371, file 4794, fo. 45f., file 4849, fo. 95.
10. Kilmarnock to Foreign Office, 23 December 1920: ibid., file 4852, fo. 50f.
11. Seeds to Foreign Office, 4 January 1921: ibid., file 5853, fo. 138.
12. General Staff Memorandum, 15 January 1921: ibid., Cab. 24, vol. 118, fo. 369.
13. Curzon to Kilmarnock, 3 January 1921: DBFP, 1st series, xvi, no. 561, p. 601f.
14. Cecil Gosling to Curzon, 13 January 1921: PRO, FO 371, file 5941, fo. 170.
15. Smallbones to Curzon, 26 July, and minute by A. Cadogan, 16 November 1920: ibid., file 4748, fo. 167, file 4752, fo. 4. In general see F.L. Carsten, *Fascist Movements in Austria*, London, 1977, pp. 47ff.
16. Military Notes, 5 October 1920: FO 371, file 4784, fo. 208.
17. Smallbones to Curzon, 17 November 1920: ibid., file 4758, fo. 27f.
18. Seeds to Curzon, 12 April 1921: ibid., file 5856, fo. 74.
19. Smallbones to Curzon, 7 July 1920: ibid., file 4798, fo. 133f.
20. Seeds to Curzon, 23 December 1920: ibid., file 4742, fo. 150.
21. Seeds to Curzon, 12 May 1921: ibid., file 5856, fo. 103f.
22. Minute by George Saunders, 1 September 1920: ibid., file 4836, fo. 131.
23. Seeds to Curzon, 6 and 11 January 1921: ibid., file 5968, fos. 157f., 178.
24. Seeds to Curzon, December 1920: ibid., file 4802, fo. 135.

25. Seeds to Curzon, 20 May and 2 June 1921: ibid., file 5856, fo. 146, file 5857, fo. 63f.
26. Seeds to Curzon, 7 June, and Kilmarnock to Foreign Office, 23 June 1921: ibid., file 5857, fo. 46, file 5972, fo. 59. R. then was the Minister for Reconstruction.
27. Report by G.E. Ellington Wright, 19 September 1921: ibid., file 5997, fos. 70ff. In general see Eyck, *History of the Weimar Republic*, pp. 188ff.
28. Smallbones to Curzon, 29 October 1921: FO 371, file 5977, fo. 193.
29. D'Abernon to Foreign Office, 24 November 1921: ibid., file 5978, fo. 184.
30. Seeds to Foreign Office, 22 June 1922: ibid., file 7574, fo. 175.
31. Seeds to Curzon, 9 February 1922: ibid., file 7501, fo. 556f.
32. Seeds to Curzon, 25 May 1922: ibid., file 7501, fo. 20.
33. Seeds to Curzon, 23 March and 6 April 1922: ibid., file 7564, fos. 29f., 35.
34. Seeds to Foreign Office, 21 October 1922: ibid., file 7579, fo. 35f.
35. L.C. Hughes-Hallett to Foreign Office, 22 December 1924; Geoffrey Knox to Miles Lampson, 26 November 1925, with minutes of 10–11 December 1925: ibid., file 9799, fo. 68f., file 10762, fo. 281f.
36. Smallbones to Curzon, 28 September 1920: ibid., file 4798, fo. 159f.
37. Seeds to Curzon, 1 September 1921: ibid., file 5975, fo. 28.
38. Seeds to Curzon, 4 January 1922: ibid., file 7525, fo. 11.
39. Seeds to Curzon, 13 June 1922: ibid., file 7525, fo. 51f.
40. Seeds to Curzon, 2 and 23 November 1922: ibid., file 7525, fos. 86f., 110.
41. Memorandum by Addison, 13 November 1922: ibid., file 7502, fos. 137–41.
42. Notes by Lieutenant F.G.E. Warburton, 2 January 1923: PRO, WO 190, file 2.
43. Seeds, 'Bavaria in 1922', 9 January 1923: FO 371, file 8769, fos. 241ff.
44. Seeds to Curzon, 24, 25, 31 January 1923: ibid., file 8790, fo. 45, file 8753, fos. 181f., 211.
45. Seeds to Curzon, 2 February and 2 April 1923: ibid., file 8753, fo. 215, file 8754, fo. 40.
46. Seeds to Curzon, 20 February 1923: ibid., file 8716, fo. 135f.
47. Addison to Miles Lampson, 29 January 1923: ibid., file 8710, fo. 23.
48. Seeds to Curzon, 23 January 1923: ibid., file 8792, fo. 160f.
49. Seeds to Curzon, 22 February 1923: ibid., file 8794, fo. 66.
50. Seeds to Curzon, 2 May 1923: ibid., file 8754, fo. 71f. For the May Day events in Munich, see F.L. Carsten, *The Rise of Fascism*, London, 1980, pp. 109f.
51. Seeds to Curzon, 15 May 1923: FO 371, file 8754, fo. 95.
52. Addison to Lampson, private, 11 September 1923: ibid., file 8667, fo. 68ff.
53. Addison to Cadogan, 2 October 1923: ibid., file 8817, fo. 103.

Lossow, like the other officers of the 7th Division, was a Bavarian, hence his attitude.

54. Clive to Curzon, 27–28 September, 4, 10, 16 and 26 October 1923: ibid., file 8754, fos. 198, 219, file 8755, fos. 26, 43, 50 and 87.
55. Colonel A.T. McGrath to Lampson, 2 July 1923: ibid., file 8641, fo. 180f.
56. General Bingham to Director of Military Intelligence, 27 September 1923: ibid., file 8781, fo. 53.
57. J.L. Likeman to Bingham, 10 October 1923: ibid., file 8699, fo.180.
58. Joint Committee of the Jewish Board of Deputies and Anglo-Jewish Association to Curzon, 18 January and 7 November 1923; Seeds to Foreign Office, 19 January, and Clive to Curzon, 29 November 1923: ibid., file 8776, fos. 187, 193, 197, 200, 209f.
59. Telephone message of Lord Crewe to Foreign Office and Crowe's minute of 9 November 1923: ibid., file 8818, fos. 5–8.
60. D'Abernon, *Ambassador of Peace*, ii, p. 270; Viscountess D'Abernon, *Red Cross and Berlin Embassy*, p. 117 (both with the wrong date of 10 November 1923). For the events in Munich on 8–9 November, see Carsten, *The Rise of Fascism*, pp. 113ff.
61. Odo Russell to Curzon, 10 November 1923: PRO, FO 371, file 8661, fo. 93.
62. Clive to Curzon, 11 November, and to Lampson, 14 November 1923: DBFP, 1st series, xxi, London, 1978, no. 632, p 887, and p. 889 n. 1.
63. Clive to MacDonald, 22 February 1924: PRO, FO 371, file 9828, fo. 99f.
64. Clive to Curzon, 13, 16, 26 November, 20 December 1923: ibid., file 8756, fos. 56, 119, file 8784, fo. 211, file 8757, fo. 22.
65. Clive to Foreign Office, 25 March 1924: ibid., file 9799, fos. 297, 300.
66. Addison's Report for 1924, 27 April 1925: ibid., file 10726, fo. 93.
67. D'Abernon to MacDonald, 4 March 1924: ibid., file 9802, fo. 183.
68. Clive to Foreign Office, 12 March 1924: ibid., file 9831, fo. 148ff.

CHAPTER IV

1. D'Abernon, *Ambassador of Peace*, i, p. 66 (14 July 1920).
2. Reports by Major R.T.G. Tangye, 29 October, and Captain W.C.H.M. Georgi, 14 September 1920: PRO, FO 371, file 4785, fo. 67f., file 4773, fo. 97.
3. D'Abernon to Curzon, 23 November, and Army Council to Foreign Office, 24 December 1920: ibid., file 4758, fos. 48, 172.
4. George Grahame to Curzon, Brussels, 21 September 1920: ibid., file 4728, fo. 33f.
5. Briand's memorandum, 24 April, and Wigram's minute, 21 April 1921: ibid., file 6025, fos. 187ff., file 6024, fo. 132f.
6. W.I. to Curzon, 22 August 1922: ibid., file 7482, fo. 188.
7. Earl of Ronaldshay, *Life of Lord Curzon*, iii, London, 1928, p. 345; Crewe to Curzon, 4 January 1923: DBFP, 1st series, xxi, no. 4, p. 5.

8. D'Abernon to Curzon, 6 January 1923: ibid., no. 6, p. 7.

9. Foreign Office to Kilmarnock, 11 January 1923: ibid., no. 20, p. 25.

10. Colonel R.S. Ryan to Miles Lampson, 5 January 1923: PRO, FO 371, file 8626, fo. 302.

11. Kilmarnock to Curzon, 23–24 January 1923: ibid., file 8707, fos. 17f., 72. According to Ferdinand Tuohy, *Occupied 1918–1930*, London, 1931, p. 269, K. was 'markedly pro-French'.

12. Memorandum by Colonel Ryan, Foreign Office, 24 January 1923: FO 371, file 8787, fo. 40.

13. Memorandum of the Central Department, 8 February 1923: ibid., file 8710, fo. 124.

14. Julian Piggott to Lampson, 20 January 1923: ibid., file 8706, fo. 3.

15. Report by Colonel James D. McLachlan, 28 February 1923: ibid., file 8721, fos. 168ff. The conference was concerned with technical problems and was 'terminated amid mutual expressions of good will'.

16. Kilmarnock to Curzon, 16 April 1923: ibid., file 8801, fo. 47.

17. Curzon's speech of 20 March 1923: ibid., file 8728, fos. 189–92.

18. D'Abernon to Curzon, 31 March 1923, with extract from *Paris Midi* of 24 March: ibid., file 8792, fos. 135, 147.

19. D'Abernon, *Ambassador of Peace*, ii, p. 238 (20 August 1923).

20. D.G. Williamson, 'Great Britain and the Ruhr Crisis', *British Journal of International Studies*, iii, 1977, p. 81f.; Earl of Ronaldshay, *Life of Curzon*, iii, p. 360; Harold Nicolson, *Curzon: The Last Phase*, London, 1934, p. 364.

21. D'Abernon, *Ambassador of Peace*, ii, p. 233 (16 August 1923).

22. Draft statement without signature, 12 July 1923: PRO, FO 371, file 8643, fos. 56ff.

23. D'Abernon to Curzon, 16 January 1923: ibid., file 8704, fo. 204f.

24. E.W.P. Thurstan to D'Abernon, 12 February and 4 August 1923: British Library, Additional MS. 48927A, fos. 198, 231.

25. D'Abernon, *Ambassador of Peace*, ii, pp. 159, 164 (21 and 29 January 1923).

26. D'Abernon to Curzon, 20 February 1923: PRO, FO 371, file 8716, fo. 29f.

27. D'Abernon to Foreign Office, 18 March 1923: ibid., file 8723, fo. 144.

28. Kilmarnock to Curzon, 30 March 1923: ibid., file 8726, fo. 8.

29. J.B. Browne to E.W.P. Thurstan, 26 March 1923: ibid., file 8725, fo. 211f.

30. Williamson, 'Great Britain and the Ruhr Crisis', p. 73 n. 4; Mary Agnes Hamilton, *Arthur Henderson*, London, 1938, p. 230.

31. J.B. Browne to Thurstan, 21 February, 1923: PRO, FO 371, file 8718, fo. 20.

32. Thurstan to D'Abernon, 1 March 1923: DBFP, 1st series, xxi, no. 124, p. 132.

33. Thurstan to D'Abernon, 5 and 9 March 1923: FO 371, file 8719, fo. 222, file 8722, fo. 3.

34. Minutes of 15 May 1923: ibid., file 8730, fos. 208f., 214.

35. Addison to Lampson, 14 June 1923: ibid., file 8780, fo. 23ff.
36. Addison to Curzon, 10 July 1923: ibid., file 8735, fo. 196f.
37. Memorandum by Commercial Secretary, 1 August 1923: ibid., file 8737, fos. 134–37.
38. C. Ralph Curtis to D'Abernon, 4 August 1923: ibid., file 8741, fo. 52.
39. C.W. Elphick to A. Cadogan, 12 November 1923: ibid., file 8796, fo. 9.
40. Thurstan to D'Abernon, 15 November 1923: ibid., file 8749, fo. 177.
41. Kilmarnock to Curzon, 15 and 26 May 1923: ibid., file 8803, fo. 167f., file 8804, fo. 21f.
42. Kilmarnock to Curzon, 6–7 June 1923: ibid., file 8804, fos. 105, 109f.
43. Kilmarnock to Foreign Office, 7 August 1923: ibid., file 8805, fo. 180f.
44. D'Abernon to Curzon, 4 January 1923: ibid., file 8696, fo. 61f.
45. Sir Somerville Head to Curzon, 21 March 1923: ibid., file 8724, fos. 186–89.
46. D'Abernon to Foreign Office, 6 May 1923: ibid., file 8634, fo. 213f.
47. D'Abernon to Foreign Office, 29 July 1923: ibid., file 8795, fo. 63f.
48. Addison to Lampson, 26 June 1923: PRO, WO 190, file 14, pp. 3ff., 11.
49. Kilmarnock to Lampson, 26 July 1923: FO 371, file 8814, fo. 196.
50. D'Abernon to Curzon, 26 May 1923: ibid., file 8637, fo. 188.
51. D'Abernon to Curzon, 13–14 August, 1923: ibid., file 8699, fo. 109, file 8649, fo. 127.
52. D'Abernon to Foreign Office, 7 September 1923: ibid., file 8740, fo. 166.
53. D'Abernon to Curzon, 13 August 1923: ibid., file 8795, fo. 137.
54. D'Abernon to Foreign Office, 18 September 1923: ibid., file 8656, fo. 3.
55. Addison to Lampson, 18 June 1923: DBFP, 1st series, xxi, no. 271, p. 354.
56. Addison to Lampson, private, 11 September 1923: PRO, FO 371, file 8667, fo. 66.
57. Colonel Ryan to Curzon, 8 September 1923: ibid., file 8741, fo. 10
58. D'Abernon to Foreign Office, 11 and 14 September 1923: ibid., file 8654, fo. 235, file 8655, fo. 181. Stresemann's own exposition of 18 September is in Henry Bernhard (ed.), *Gustav Stresemann Vermächtnis*, Berlin, 1932, i, p. 127.
59. Minute by A. Cadogan, 7 September 1923: FO 371, file 8654, fo. 182.
60. D'Abernon to Foreign Office, 23 September 1923: ibid., file 8741, fo. 214.
61. Clive to Foreign Office, 26 September 1923: ibid., file 8742, fo. 109.
62. D'Abernon to Foreign Office, 29 September 1923: ibid., file 8743, fo. 73f.

63. Addison to Foreign Office, 2 and 5 October 1923: ibid., file 8817, fos. 20, 22, 32f. Hilferding was a leading Marxist theoretician and particularly obnoxious to the People's Party.
64. Addison to Curzon, 4 October 1923: ibid., file 8817, fo. 59f.
65. D'Abernon to Foreign Office, 20 October 1923: ibid., file 8817, fo. 139.
66. For details see Carsten, *The Reichswehr and Politics*, p. 167.
67. General Bingham to War Office, 13 November 1923: PRO, FO 371, file 8786, fo. 194.
68. Sir Somerville Head to Curzon, 24 March 1923: ibid., file 8670, fo. 165f.
69. Reports by M.I.3.b, 28 May 1923 and s.d.: PRO, WO 190, files 9 and 10.
70. Report by Colonel J.H. Morgan, 1 August 1923: PRO, FO 371, file 8780, fo. 125f.
71. Robert Dell to MacDonald, 14 June 1924: ibid., file 9726, fo. 89f.
72. Minute by J.C. Sterndale, 21 June 1923: ibid., file 8664, fo. 173.
73. D'Abernon to Curzon, 8 August 1923: ibid., file 8738, fo. 102f.
74. D'Abernon to Foreign Office, 18 August 1923: ibid., file 8666, fo. 48.
75. D'Abernon to Foreign Office, 13 August 1923: ibid., file 8795, fo. 136f.
76. For details see Eyck, *History of the Weimar Republic*, p. 265f.
77. D'Abernon to Curzon, 11 and 29 October 1923: PRO, FO 371, file 8668, fos. 9, 85.
78. Official French communiqué, 15 November 1923: ibid., file 8749, fo. 185.
79. Official French communiqué, 11 December 1923: ibid., file 8752, fo. 124; D'Abernon, *Ambassador of Peace*, ii, p. 283 (25 December 1923).
80. Kilmarnock to Curzon, 8 January 1924: FO 371, file 9798, fo. 5f.
81. D'Abernon, *Ambassador of Peace*, ii, p. 274. In general cp. Eyck, *History of the Weimar Republic*, pp. 281ff.
82. D'Abernon to Curzon, 1 December 1923, based on private talk with Stresemann: PRO, FO 371, file 8818, fo. 219f.
83. Note of the Food Committee, s.d.: PRO, FO 894, file 16, fo. 419f.; communiqué of 15 August 1923: FO 371, file 8739, fo. 23.
84. Memorandum by Addison, 22 December 1923: FO 371, file 9761, fo. 205f.
85. *The Times*, 10 January 1924: ibid., file 9762, fo. 174.
86. Viscountess D'Abernon, *Red Cross and Berlin Embassy*, p. 112f.
87. Odo Russell to MacDonald, 15 March 1924: PRO, FO 371, file 9762, fo. 328f.
88. French communiqués of 15 August and 9 October 1923: ibid., file 8739, fo. 23, file 8745, fo. 113f.
89. Kilmarnock to Curzon, 5 October 1923: ibid., file 8744, fo. 118.
90. Thurstan to D'Abernon, 29 October 1923: ibid., file 8748, fo. 24.
91. D'Abernon to Foreign Office, 6 November 1923: ibid., file 8817, fo. 189.

92. French communiqué, 9 November 1923: ibid., file 8749, fo. 61.
93. Thurstan to D'Abernon, 15 November 1923: ibid., file 8749, fo. 176.
94. Report by W.J. Larke, s.d.: ibid., file 8750, fo. 55.
95. Thurstan to D'Abernon, 27 November, 1923; Annual Report for 1923, 31 December 1926: ibid., file 8750, fo. 171a, file 12130, fo. 13.
96. R.S. Ryan to President Rhineland High Commission, 26 November 1923: PRO, FO 894, file 17, fo. 224f.
97. French communiqués, 10, 11 and 18 December 1923: FO 371, file 8752, fos. 101, 124; file 8753, fo. 30.
98. Section 1 to Lampson, 4 July 1923: ibid., file 8809, fo. 76f. In general see Werner T. Angress, *Stillborn Revolution*, Princeton, 1963, pp. 320–24. According to him, Soviet agents were active in the Ruhr, but not Radek who was more cautious.
99. D'Abernon to Curzon, 31 July 1923: FO 371, file 8809, fo. 83f.
100. Colonel A.T. McGrath to Lampson, secret, 2 July 1923: ibid., file 8641, fo. 179f.
101. Addison to Lampson, 11 September 1923: ibid., file 8667, fo. 69.
102. Thurstan to D'Abernon, 18 August 1923: ibid., file 8739, fo. 54.
103. D'Abernon to Foreign Office, 14 August 1923: ibid., file 8649, fo. 127.
104. William Peters to Curzon, Moscow, 28 August 1923, quoting *Gudok* of 25 and 27 August: ibid., file 8795, fo. 171.
105. French communiqué, 27 September, and Kilmarnock to Curzon, 5 October 1923: ibid., file 8743, fos. 6, 118.
106. French communiqué, 9 October 1923: ibid., file 8745, fo. 113f.
107. F. Oliver to D'Abernon, Hamburg, 24 and 26 October 1923: ibid., file 8809, fos. 126, 132. For the Hamburg rising, see Angress, *Stillborn Revolution*, pp. 444ff.
108. Viscountess D'Abernon, *Red Cross and Berlin Embassy*, p. 124 (27 November 1923).
109. General Bingham to Director of Military Intelligence, 17 November 1923: PRO, FO 371, file 8783, fo. 64.
110. Minutes of meetings of the I.A.R.H.C., 28 May, 12 and 19 June 1923: PRO, FO 894, file 15, fos, 384, 531, 539.
111. Kilmarnock to President I.A.R.H.C., 3 November 1923: ibid., file 17, fo. 35.
112. Report by Colonel Wallace Wight, 12 February 1924: PRO, WO 106, file 447.
113. Proclamation of the Provisional German Government, 12 November 1918: E.R. Huber, *Dokumente Zur deutschen Verfassungsgeschichte*, iii, Stuttgart, 1966, no. 7, p. 6.
114. Memorandum by W.J. Larke, private and confidential, s.d.: PRO, FO 371, file 8748, fo. 56.
115. Report by Thelwall on position in the Ruhr, 11 October 1923: ibid., file 8746, fos. 43, 46f.
116. French communiqués of 7, 9 and 10 November 1923: ibid., file 8748, fo. 216, file 8749, fos. 61f., 106f.

117. Report by Colonel Wallace Wight, 12 February 1924: PRO, WO 106, file 447, pp. 1–2.
118. Memorandum by Kavanagh, 3 April 1924 PRO, FO 371, file 9764, fo. 214f.
119. R.D. Moarse to D'Abernon, 29 August 1923: ibid., file 8814, fo. 211f.
120. Rhine Army Military Notes, 3 December 1923: ibid., file 8758, fo. 15.
121. idem, 20 March 1923: ibid., file 8757, fo. 97.
122. Sir Somerville Head to Curzon, 24 March 1923: ibid., file 8670, fo. 165f.
123. Addison to Curzon, 1 and 4 October 1923: ibid., file 8816, fo. 229, file 8817, fo. 60.
124. D'Abernon to Foreign Office, 5 November 1923: ibid., file 8817, fo. 174.
125. D'Abernon to Foreign Office, 2 February 1923: ibid., file 8709, fo. 215.
126. Addison to Lampson, 14 June 1923: ibid., file 8780, fo. 25.
127. D'Abernon, Ambassador of Peace, ii, p. 251f. (17 September 1923).
128. D'Abernon to Austen Chamberlain, 8 November 1924: PRO, WO 190, file 45, fo. 3.
129. Theo Russell to Curzon, 29 March, enclosing a copy of Maxse's report of 8 March 1920: FO 371, file 3800, fos. 97ff. One line is missing in the copy.
130. Gosling to Curzon, 15 October 1920: ibid., file 4741, fos. 144–47.
131. Minute by George Saunders, 22 October 1920: ibid., file 4741, fo. 141f.
132. Colonel Ryan to President I.A.R.H.C., 18 March, President I.A.R.H.C. to Chief Representative in the British Zone, 20 March, and J.G. Birch to President I.A.R.H.C., 27 March 1923: PRO, FO 894, file 14, fos. 493f., 618f.
133. Colonel Ryan to President I.A.R.H.C., 29 August and 3 September 1923: ibid., file 16, fos. 443f.
134. The same to Lampson, 5 June 1923: PRO, FO 371, file 8681, fos. 157–60.
135. Memorandum by the same, 22 November 1923: ibid., file 8690, fo. 14f.
136. J.I. Piggott to Kilmarnock, 11 December 1923: ibid., file 8691, fo. 124.
137. Colonel Ryan to Foreign Office, 23 October 1923: ibid., file 8685, fo, 56f,
138. Thurstan to Foreign Office, 26 October 1923: ibid., file 8685, fo. 117f.
139. Piggott to Kilmarnock, 26 October 1923: ibid., file 8686, fo. 223.
140. Declaration of 23 October 1923: PRO, FO 894, file 16, fo. 767.
141. Memorandum of 3 November 1923: FO 371, file 8660, fo. 122f.
142. Curzon at Imperial Conference on 31 October 1923: ibid., file 8687, fo. 33.
143. Curzon to Kilmarnock, 31 October 1923: DBFP, 1st series, xxi, no. 429, p. 613.

144. H. Bernhard (ed.), *Stresemann Vermächtnis*, i, p. 213.
145. Kilmarnock to Foreign Office, 5 November 1923: PRO, FO 371, file 8687, fo. 39f.
146. Thurstan to D'Abernon, 27 October, 8 and 20 November 1923: ibid., file 8686, fo. 100, file 8688, fo. 34, file 8689, fo. 236f.
147. Kilmarnock to Curzon, 17 November 1923: ibid., file 8689, fo. 78f.
148. Kilmarnock to Curzon, 15 December 1923: ibid., file 8691, fos. 116ff.
149. Kilmarnock to Foreign Office, 2 January 1924: ibid., file 9770, fo. 204.
150. Kilmarnock to Curzon, 4 January 1924: ibid., file 9771, fo. 6f.
151. Foreign Office to Lord Crewe, 4 January 1924: ibid., file 9770, fo. 214f.
152. Foreign Office to Eric Phipps, 9 January 1924: ibid., file 9771, fo. 49f., also for the following sentences.
153. Foreign Office to Lord Crewe, 12 January 1924: ibid., file 9771, fo. 101f.
154. Minute of meeting of the I.A.R.H.C., 9 January 1924: PRO, FO 894, file 17, fo. 406.
155. British Consul-General Frankfurt to Foreign Office, 15 January 1924: FO 371, file 9772, fo. 83.
156. Kilmarnock to Foreign Office, 18 January 1924: ibid., file 9772, fo. 145f. Clive's full report, 22 January 1924: ibid., file 9773, fos. 143–48.
157. British Consul-General Munich to Foreign Office, 28 January 1924: ibid., file 9773, fo. 109.
158. Clive to Foreign Office, Munich, 6 February 1924: ibid., file 9774, fo. 67; Kilmarnock to Foreign Office, 13 February: ibid., fos. 197–201; and Clive to Foreign Office, 13 February 1924: ibid., fo. 203; on the organization of the attack see von Salomon, *Die Geächteten*, p. 441f.
159. Kilmarnock to Foreign Office, 19–20 February 1924: PRO, FO 371, file 9775, fos. 65a, 80, 133.
160. Report of the Special Committee for the Palatinate, 18 March 1924: PRO, FO 894, file 18, fo. 309.

CHAPTER V

1. D'Abernon, *Ambassador of Peace*, ii, pp. 233, 280 (16 August and 28 November 1923).
2. D'Abernon to MacDonald, 3 June 1924: PRO, FO 800, file 219, fo. 41.
3. D'Abernon to MacDonald, 28 May 1924: FO 371, file 9802, fo. 4.
4. D'Abernon to MacDonald, 25 May 1924: FO 800, file 219, fo. 38.
5. Addison to Harold Nicolson, 18 October 1924: FO 371, file 9803, fo. 215. The name is misspelled as Nicholson. Italics in the original.
6. D'Abernon to Foreign Office and to MacDonald, 3 May 1925: ibid., file 10731, fo. 16f.; British Library, Additional MS. 48926A, fo. 242.

7. D'Abernon to Foreign Office, 2 March, and minute by Lampson, 4 March 1925: FO 371, file 10728, fos. 2ff.
8. D'Abernon to Lampson, 11 March 1925: ibid., file 10728, fo. 125.
9. Lord Crewe to Foreign Office, Paris, 5 May 1925: ibid., file 10731, fo. 27.
10. Minute by J.C. Sterndale Bennett, 5 June 1925: ibid., file 10732, fo. 20.
11. W.G. Max Muller to Lampson, private, Warsaw, 20 May 1925: ibid., file 10732, fos. 21ff.
12. Foreign Office to D'Abernon, 22 and 24 September and D'Abernon's replies, 22–24 September 1925: ibid., file 10740, fos. 52, 81f., 87, 97.
13. Chamberlain to D'Abernon, 17 October 1925: DBFP, series IA, i, London, 1966, no. 4, p. 20.
14. D'Abernon to Foreign Office, 23, 24, 27 October, 3 and 28 November 1925: PRO, FO 371, file 10744, fos. 8, 10, 99 and 182, file 10747, fos. 26ff. In general cp. Eyck, *A History of the Weimar Republic*, ii, Cambridge, Mass., 1964, pp. 39–42.
15. D'Abernon to Sir William Tyrrell, 1 November, and Foreign Office to D'Abernon and to Crewe, 8 November 1925: FO 371, file 10760, fo. 62f. DBFP, series IA, i, no. 73, p. 112.
16. D'Abernon, *Ambassador of Peace*, iii, pp. 184, 204 (11 August and 18 November 1925).
17. D'Abernon to Foreign Office, 3–4 February 1926: PRO, FO 371, file 11262, fos. 115ff. Conclusions of a Cabinet Meeting, 3 March, and Foreign Office précis of Geneva telegrams, 16 March 1926: ibid., file 11265, fo. 91, file 11266, fo. 139f.
18. E.M.B. Ingram to Chamberlain, 9 September 1926: ibid., file 11270, fos. 77–82.
19. D'Abernon to Foreign Office, 26 September 1926: ibid., file 11330, fo. 152f.
20. R.C. Lindsay to Chamberlain, 30 March, and minute by O.E. Sargant, 2 April 1927: ibid., file 12148, fos. 121, 125.
21. Lindsay to Chamberlain, 29 April 1927: ibid., file 12148, fos. 141, 146.
22. Figures of French and Belgian strength: Colonel R.G. Finlayson to Lampson, 4 April 1924, and of 'colonial' troops: Kilmarnock to Chamberlain, 4 December 1924: ibid., file 9720, fos. 30, 90.
23. Chamberlain to Crewe, 2 June, and minute by M.H. Huxley, 3 June 1926: ibid., file 11298, fos. 41, 44f.; minute by Stresemann, Geneva, 6 March 1927: *Akten zur deutschen auswärtigen Politik*, series B, iv, Göttingen, 1970, no. 220, p. 478f.
24. Minutes by Schubert and Stresemann, 5 and 26 August 1927: ibid., vi, Göttingen, 1974, no. 89, pp. 188–91, no. 141, p. 311; Tuohy, *Occupied 1918–1930*, p. 239.
25. Rumbold to Chamberlain, 28 December 1928: PRO, FO 371, file 12907, fos. 109ff.
26. Chamberlain's notes on conversation with Stresemann on 12 December 1927: DBFP, series IA, iv, 1971, no. 91, p. 181f.

27. Lindsay to Howard Smith, 1 May, and to Chamberlain, 3 May 1928: ibid., v, 1973, no. 14, p. 25, no. 16, p. 28.
28. Arthur Yencken to Henderson, 26 June 1929: PRO, FO 371, file 13618, fo. 39.
29. Rumbold to Lord Cushendun, 8 November 1928: DBFP, series IA, v, no. 210, p. 448f.
30. Chamberlain to D'Abernon, 23 April 1926: British Library, Additional MS. 48926B, fo. 202.
31. Minute by Gesandtschaftsrat Redlhammer, Geneva, 9 December 1926: *Akten zur deutschen auswärtigen Politik*, series B, i 2, Göttingen, 1968, no. 245, p. 572.
32. Chamberlain to Lindsay, 5 February 1927: DBFP, series IA, iii, 1970, no. 6, p. 11f.
33. Kilmarnock to Chamberlain, 12 May, Chamberlain to D'Abernon, 19 May, and D'Abernon to Chamberlain, 22 May 1926: DBFP, series IA, ii, 1968, no. 3, p. 9f., no. 13, p. 25.
34. idem; Chamberlain to D'Abernon, 25 and 31 May; Addison to Chamberlain, 27 May; D'Abernon to Chamberlain, 2 June 1926: ibid., no. 22, p. 34, no. 26, pp. 41–44, no. 32, p. 50, no. 39, p. 59.
35. D'Abernon to MacDonald, 11 February 1924: British Library, Additional MS. 48926A, fo. 9.
36. D'Abernon to MacDonald, 4 March 1924: PRO, FO 371, file 9802, fo. 183f.
37. D'Abernon to MacDonald, 3 May 1924: ibid., file 9802, fo. 277: only that Gessler was not von Gessler as D'Abernon thought.
38. D'Abernon to MacDonald, 1 June 1924: ibid., file 9725, fo. 230.
39. Notes on a conversation with Stresemann, 18 June 1924: ibid., file 9845, fos. 125ff. The name of the officer is not given.
40. Chamberlain to Sir William Tyrrell, 6 December 1926: DBFP, series IA, ii, no. 327, p. 380f.
41. Lindsay to Chamberlain, 14 January 1927: ibid., no. 400, p. 729.
42. Lindsay to Chamberlain, 12 April 1927: ibid., iii, 1970, no. 146, p. 217.
43. For details see Carsten, *The Reichswehr and Politics*, pp. 253–65.
44. Rumbold to Lord Cushendun, 22 November 1928: PRO, FO 371, file 12887, fo. 278f.
45. The same to Henderson, 3 and 10 October 1929: ibid., file 13647, fo. 44f., file 13630, fos. 89ff.
46. Memorandum of 3 October, with minute of 9 October 1929: ibid., file 13608, fos. 159ff.
47. Annual Report for 1929, 12 March 1930: ibid., file 14374, fo. 73, pp. 2–3.
48. Nicolson to Orme Sargent, 22 November 1929: ibid., file 13644, fo. 261f.
49. D'Abernon, *Ambassador of Peace*, iii, 1930, p. 20.
50. V.H.C. Bosanquet to Rumbold, Frankfurt, 9 May 1931: PRO 30/69, file 5 part 3, fo. 17. MacDonald's message is in FO 371, file 15227, fo 68f.
51. *The Times*, 7 March 1933.

CHAPTER VI

1. Addison to Curzon, 22 January, and D'Abernon to MacDonald, 24 January 1924: PRO, FO 371, file 9737, fos. 3, 17. In general cp. John Hiden, *Germany and Europe 1919–1939*, London, 1977, p. 54.
2. D'Abernon to Foreign Office, 6, 29 and 30 April 1924: FO 371, file 9739, fo. 49, file 9783, fo. 154, file 9742, fo. 213.
3. MacDonald on 19 April 1924: ibid., file 9741, fo. 168A.
4. D'Abernon to MacDonald, 25 May , Foreign Office to D'Abernon, 29 May 1924: ibid., file 9746, fos. 91, 99f.
5. D'Abernon to Foreign Office, 4 and 8 July 1924: ibid., file 9749, fos. 161, 172f., file 9750, fo. 24.
6. D'Abernon to Foreign Office, 8 and 11 July 1924: ibid., file 9750, fo. 12, file 9751, fos. 46ff.
7. D'Abernon to Foreign Office, 27 July 1924: ibid., file 9752, fos. 9, 11.
8. D'Abernon to Foreign Office, 3 August 1924: ibid., file 9848, fo. 132.
9. Conclusions of Cabinet Meeting, 30 July 1924: ibid., file 9853, fo. 136.
10. idem, 5 August 1924: ibid., file 9854, fo. 159.
11. Minute by Miles Lampson, 6 August 1924: ibid., file 9855, fo. 26f.
12. Hankey to Lampson, 16 August 1924: ibid., file 9858, fos. 113–16.
13. D'Abernon to Foreign Office, 12, 14 and 18 August 1924: ibid., file 9863, fos. 149, 165, 186.
14. D'Abernon to Foreign Office, 27 August, and Addison to Lampson, 30 August 1924: ibid., file 9864, fo. 162, file 9865, fo. 2, private.
15. A.J.P. Taylor, *English History 1914–1945*, Oxford, 1965, p. 214.
16. Colonel R.S. Ryan to Chamberlain, 13 February 1925: PRO, FO 371, file 10703, fo. 113.
17. Notes by Major-General A.G. Wauchope, 23 June 1925: ibid., file 10710, fos. 11, 15.
18. Crewe to D'Abernon, 27 October, Sir W. Tyrrell to D'Abernon, 26 October 1925: DBFP, series IA, i, nos. 27, 32, pp. 51, 56f.
19. D'Abernon to Foreign Office, 20 November, with minutes of 21 November 1925: PRO, FO 371, file 10704, fo. 198f.
20. D.G. Williamson, 'Cologne and the British 1918–1926', *History Today*, xxvii, 1977, p. 702.
21. Kilmarnock to Chamberlain, 23 March 1926: PRO, FO 371, file 11307, fos. 109–12, with minute by J.M. Troutbeck of 27 March.
22. D'Abernon, *Ambassador of Peace*, iii p. 207f.; Colonel Ryan to Chamberlain, 20 October 1925: DBFP, series IA, i, no. 12, p. 34.
23. J.W. Magowan to Chamberlain, 27 January 1927: ibid., iii, no. 255, pp. 412ff.
24. Minute by O.G. Sargent, 16 July, R.C. Lindsay to Chamberlain, 28 November, and minutes by M.H. Huxley and O.G. Sargent, 23–24 November 1928: PRO, FO 371, file 12883, fo. 204f., file 12884, fos. 137, 139f., 141–52.
25. MacDonald to D'Abernon, 22 March, and D'Abernon's reply, 28

March 1924: PRO, FO 800, file 219, fos. 4, 6f. (MacDonald papers).

26. D'Abernon to MacDonald, 16 June, and to Chamberlain, 8 November 1924: FO 371, file 9803, fo. 76f., file 9804, fo. 308f.

27. Minutes by Crowe and by Chamberlain, 3 February 1925: ibid., file 10724, fo. 110f.

28. D'Abernon to Chamberlain, 15 August, 1925: ibid., file 10722,fo. 76.

29. D'Abernon to Chamberlain, 13 March 1925: ibid., file 10713, fo. 226f.

30. D'Abernon to MacDonald, 3 May, and memorandum by J.C. Sterndale Bennett, 27 April 1925: British Library, Additional MS. 48926A, fo. 242; FO 371, file 10713, fos. 93ff.

31. Chamberlain to D'Abernon, 28 April and 8 May 1926: DBFP, series IA, i, no. 477, p. 686f., no. 510, p. 737.

32. Stresemann's notes, 10 May 1926: Akten zur deutschen auswärtigen Politik, series B, I 1, 1966, no. 215, p. 512.

33. Chamberlain to Sir W. Tyrrell, 12 September 1926: DBFP, series IA, ii, no. 204, p. 361f.

34. Sthamer to Auswärtiges Amt, 19 October 1927: Akten zur deutschen auswärtigen Politik, series B, vii, 1974, no. 37, p. 98f.

35. Counsellor Dieckhoff to the same, 27 October 1928: ibid., x, 1977, no. 85, p. 223f.

36. Chamberlain to Crewe, 30 May 1928: DBFP, series IA, v, 1973, no. 42, p. 77f.

37. J.H. Magowan to Rumbold, 12 October, and Seeds to Lord Cushendun, 22 October 1928: PRO, FO 371, file 12905, fos. 69ff., 114–19.

38. Memorandum by J.V. Perowne, 10 December 1928: ibid., file 12906, fos. 227–31.

39. Vice-Consul Macrae to D'Abernon, 25 April 1924: ibid., file 9842, fo. 29.

40. R.H. Clive to Foreign Office, 15 February and 10 March 1924: ibid., file 9775, fo. 40f., file 9776, fo. 74.

41. C.H. Bentinck to Foreign Office, 5 January 1925: ibid., file 10702, fo. 132f.

42. Kilmarnock to Chamberlain, 8 May and 23 June, and Foreign Office to D'Abernon, 29 May 1925: ibid., file 10757, fos. 12, 81, 93, file 10758, fo. 150.

43. British Department Rhineland High Commission, Annual Report for 1926, p. 35: ibid., file 13640, fo. 212.

44. idem, Annual Report for 1925, p. 13: ibid., file 13640, fo. 199.

45. Kilmarnock to Chamberlain, 1 July 1927: DBFP, series IA, iii, no. 260, p. 423.

46. Rumbold to Howard Smith, 26 September 1929: DBFP, series IA, vii, no. 16, p. 30.

47. Central Department memoranum, 11 April 1924: PRO, FO 371, file 9812, fos. 27ff.

48. G.G. Knox to Lampson, 8 May, and to MacDonald, 13 May 1924: ibid., file 9825, fos. 172ff., 202.

49. Notes by a British officer, apparently of M.I.3.b, 19 May 1924: PRO, WO 190, file 29.
50. War Office to Foreign Office, 12 January 1925: FO 371, file 10707, fo. 146.
51. Vice-Consul Macrae to D'Abernon, 29 March 1924: ibid., file 9837, fos. 25ff. For the *Stahlhelm* see Volker R. Berghahn, *Der Stahlhelm Bund der Frontsoldaten*, Düsseldorf, 1966.
52. D'Abernon to Chamberlain, 8 November, with minutes of 13 November 1924: FO 371, file 9875. fos. 229–38.
53. B.H. Fry to Lindsay, 1 October, and E.M.B.Ingram to Chamberlain, 28 September 1927: ibid., file 12146, fo. 157, file 12139, fo. 105f.
54. Report by M.I.3.b, 10 July 1928: PRO, WO 190, file 52.
55. Rumbold to Sargent, 21 June 1929: FO 371, file 13630, fo. 234f.
56. Rumbold to Foreign Office, 30 November 1928: ibid., file 12914, fos. 128–31, with minute by M.H. Huxley of 3 January 1929.
57. Report by M.I.3.b, 5 January 1929: PRO, WO 190, file 60.
58. Addison to Chamberlain, 26 May 1926: FO 371, file 11326, fo. 4f.
59. Kilmarnock to MacDonald, 18 September 1924: ibid., file 9826, fos. 356ff.
60. D'Abernon to Chamberlain, 26 March 1926: Annual Report for 1925, p. 9: ibid., file 11322, fo. 96.
61. The same to MacDonald, 25 May and 3 June 1924: PRO, FO 800, file 219, fos. 38f., 41.
62. The same to Chamberlain, 26 March 1926: Annual Report for 1925, p. 21: FO 371, file 11322, fo. 96.
63. C.H. Bentinck to Foreign Office, 27 October 1924, and his Annual Report for 1924, 27 February 1925: ibid., file 9799, fo. 25, file 10756, fo. 48, p. 8.
64. Lindsay to Chamberlain, 18 December 1926: DBFP, series IA, ii, no. 365, p. 666f.
65. Rumbold to Cushendun, 24 October 1928: PRO, FO 371, file 12877, fo. 252f.
66. Nicolson to Henderson, 26 November 1929: ibid., file 13631, fo. 186f.
67. Addison to Sargent, 20 January 1927: ibid., file 12131, fos. 146, 155.
68. Clive to Foreign Office, 22 September and L.C. Hughes-Hallett to Foreign Office, 1 December 1924: ibid., file 9799. fos. 373f.. 52.
69. Addison to Nicolson, 1 March, and D'Abernon to Foreign Office, 30 April 1924: ibid., file 9813, fo. 205, file 9742, fo. 213.
70. D'Abernon to Foreign Office, 28 November 1925: ibid., file 10747, fo. 26.
71. Lindsay to Chamberlain, 24 May 1928: ibid., file 12887, fo. 146.
72. Howard Smith to Rumbold, 24 September 1929: ibid., file 13630, fos. 43ff.
73. Nicolson to Henderson, 20 November 1929: DBFP, series IA, vii, no. 87, p. 168f. Soon after Nicolson left the diplomatic service and in 1931 be became the editor of *Action*, the organ of the 'New Party' founded by Sir Oswald Mosley.

74. Rumbold to Henderson, 17 December 1929: ibid., vii, no. 142, pp. 259ff.
75. For National Socialist propaganda, cp. Z.A.B. Zeman, *Nazi Propaganda*, Oxford-London, 1973.
76. Notes by Major-General A.G. Wauchope, secret, 23 June 1925: PRO, FO 371, file 10710, fo. 15f. The civil servant was called Horstmann, not Horsmann.
77. Addison to Lampson, 19 January, D'Abernon to Chamberlain, 12 January 1925: ibid., file 10749, fos. 194f., 179. For the Barmat scandal cp. Eyck, *History of the Weimar Republic*, i, pp. 326ff.
78. D'Abernon to Chamberlain, 26 January 1925: FO 371, file 10712, fo. 162f.
79. Chamberlain to D'Abernon, 28 October and 5 November 1925: ibid, file 10759, fos. 145, 193.
80. D'Abernon to Foreign Office, 20 January 1926: ibid., file 11279, fo. 127.
81. Addison to Chamberlain, 25 May 1926: ibid., file 11280, fos. 80–83.
82. D'Abernon to Chamberlain, 26 November 1925 and 11 August 1926: DBFP, series IA, i, no. 117, p. 173, ii, no. 140, p. 243.
83. D'Abernon *Ambassador of Peace*, iii, p. 147.
84. Lindsay to Chamberlain, 25 January 1928: PRO, FO 371, file 12887, fo. 64.
85. Rumbold to Chamberlain, 13 December, with minutes by Howard Smith and Sargent, 18 December 1928: ibid., file 12906, fos. 199, 201, 206.
86. Rumbold to Chamberlain, 18 January 1929: ibid., file 13592, fo. 264.
87. Rumbold to Chamberlain, 1 May, memorandum by F. Thelwall, 30 April 1929: ibid., file 13594, fos. 112f., 117f. In general see Eyck, *History of the Weimar Republic*, ii, pp. 183–93.
88. Rumbold to Chamberlain, 11 May, and to Henderson, 12 June 1929: ibid., file 13595, fo. 180, file 13617, fo. 208.
89. Arthur Yencken to Henderson, 24–25 June 1929: ibid., file 13598, fos. 26f., 110ff.
90. Nicolson to Henderson, 6 December 1929: ibid., file 13610, fos. 207–10.
91. Rumbold to Sargent, 21 June 1929: ibid., file 13630, fo. 236f.
92. Nicolson to Chamberlain, 20 July 1928: ibid., file 12902, fo. 164f.
93. E.M.B. Ingram for ambassador to Chamberlain, 7 September 1927: ibid., file 12138, fo. 207.
94. Addison to Chamberlain, 5 December 1925, and to Lampson, 21 June 1926: ibid., file 10762, fos. 297–300, file 11321, fo. 109.
95. D'Abernon to Chamberlain, 26 March 1926: ibid., file 11322, fo. 96, p. 9.
96. Report by Lieutenant R.V. Hume, 12 May 1926: DBFP, series IA, i, no. 520, p. 746.
97. Chamberlain to Lindsay, 12 January 1927: ibid., ii, no. 392, pp. 718f.

98. Military Control Commission reports of 16 September and 20 December 1924: PRO, FO 371, file 10707, fo. 145, file 9839, fo. 248.
99. General Staff Intelligence Summary for August 1924: ibid., file 9728, fo. 92. Files 9839 to 9841 contain numerous reports about the training of *Zeitfreiwillige* by the Reichswehr.
100. War Office to Foreign Office, 12 January 1925, and reports by Major J.L. Likeman, 10 January 1924: ibid., file 10707, fo. 145, file 9722, fos. 189f., 193.
101. Caroline E. Playne to Arthur Ponsonby, 19 February 1924: ibid., file 9825, fos. 100–103.
102. Minutes by Lampson, Crowe and MacDonald, 26 March, wire to D'Abernon, 27 March and his reply, 29 March 1924: ibid., file 9825, fos. 115ff., 123, 129.
103. Lindsay to Chamberlain, enclosing opinion of Colonel F.W. Gosset, 28–29 March 1927: DBFP, series IA, iii, no. 287, pp. 490ff.
104. Director of M.I.3.b, 5 February 1929; PRO, WO 190, file 60, p. 4f.
105. Report by Colonel J.H. Marshall-Cornwall, 9 December 1929: FO 371, file 13614, fo. 24. The quotation from Blomberg's autobiography: Carsten, *Reichswehr and Politics*, p. 352.
106. Minute by Ministerialdirektor Köpke, 30 June 1928: *Akten zur deutschen auswärtigen Politik*, series B, ix, 1976, no. 109, p. 254.
107. Nicolson to Howard Smith, 14 August 1928: DBFP, series IA, v, no. 131, pp. 253ff.
108. Sargent to Ralph Wigram, 18 July 1928: ibid., v, no. 96, p. 188.
109. Report by Colonel Andrew Thorne, 13 January 1933: PRO, FO 371, file 16715, fo. 17ff.
110. Minute by Legationsrat Forster, 7 December 1929: *Akten zur deutschen auswärtigen Politik*, series B, xiii, 1979, no. 186, p. 388.
111. Committee of Imperial Defence, 11 February 1930: PRO, WO 190, file 75.
112. War Office to Foreign Office, 4 January 1927: FO 371, file 12115, fo. 79f.
113. Lindsay to Chamberlain, 27 March, and Colonel Gosset to War Office, 9 July 1927: ibid., file 12119, fos. 88ff., file 12122, fo. 2f.; Chamberlain to Stresemann, 18 June 1927: *Akten zur deutschen auswärtigen Politik*, series B, v, no. 245, p. 558.
114. Addison to Lampson, 20 November 1924: FO 371, file 9729, fos. 75ff.
115. Minutes by several Foreign Office officials, 21–23 January 1925: ibid., file 10707, fo. 165.
116. Foreign Office memorandum by A. Balfour, 11 November 1929: DBFP, series IA, vii, no. 65, p. 121.
117. ibid., and Rumbold to Chamberlain, 19 December 1928: ibid., v, no. 298, pp. 588f.
118. D'Abernon to Foreign Office, 9 January, and Addison to Lampson, 24 June 1924: PRO, FO 371, file 9722, fo. 110, file 9726, fo. 130f. Cp. Hans Meier-Welcker, *Seeckt*, Frankfurt, 1967, pp. 442ff., who confirms these reports.
119. Robert Dell to MacDonald, 14 June 1924: FO 371, file 9726, fos. 88, 90f.

120. D'Abernon to MacDonald, 6 June 1924: ibid., file 9803, fo. 53.
121. Lieut.-Colonel A.J. McGrath for Director of Military Intelligence to General Wauchope, 27 January 1925, secret: ibid., file 10706, fo. 11. The *Siegesallee* commemorated the victories of the Franco-Prussian war by endless rows of statues of the rulers of Brandenburg and Prussia from the Middle Ages onwards.
122. D'Abernon to Chamberlain, 8 November, War Office to Foreign Office, 12 November and 1 December 1924: PRO, WO 190, file 45, p. 4; FO 371, file 9728, fos. 206, 218, file 9729, fos. 53ff.
123. *The Times*, 14 January 1924.
124. D'Abernon to Foreign Office, 24 December 1924, and Lieut.-Colonel A.J. McGrath to General Wauchope, 27 January 1925: PRO, FO 371, file 9834, fo. 59f., file 10706, fo 11f.
125. General Staff memoranda of December 1924 and 3 March 1925: ibid., file 10711, fo. 203, file 10708, fo. 265.
126. D'Abernon to Foreign Office, 1 February, and notes by General Wauchope, 23 June 1925: ibid., file 10707, fo. 232f., file 10710, fo. 11.
127. D'Abernon, *Ambassador of Peace*, iii, p. 208 (18 November 1925); Stresemann's notes of 24 November 1926: *Gustav Stresemann Vermächtnis*, iii, p. 66.
128. D'Abernon to Chamberlain, 7 October 1926, and Lindsay to Chamberlain, 13 June 1927: DBFP, series IA, ii, no. 242, p. 425; PRO, FO 371, file 12153, Annual Report for 1926, p. 44.
129. General Wauchope's Notes no. 70, 28 October, no. 72, 3 November 1926: ibid., file 11291, fo. 166f., file 11292, fo. 226.
130. Wauchope's Notes no. 77, 20 December 1926: ibid., file 11296, fo. 79. The Military Control Commission was replaced by a number of Allied military experts.
131. Wauchope's Notes no. 78, 22 December 1926: ibid., file 11296, fo. 247f.
132. Notes by Stresemann and von Schubert, 3 and 9 January and 5 March 1926: *Akten zur deutschen auswärtigen Politik*, series B, I 1, nos. 27, 31, 139, pp. 91, 98, 334f.
133. For Lipetsk see page 260, and Carsten, *Reichswehr and Politics*, pp. 221f., 236f., 278f.
134. Report by Group Captain M.G. Christie, 29 November 1929: PRO, FO 371, file 13655, fos. 132ff.
135. Reports by Colonel J.H. Marshall Cornwall, 4 December 1928 and 9 December 1929: ibid., file 12889, fos. 92, 101, file 13614, fos. 22ff. Blomberg's report on his visit to Soviet Russia of 17 November 1928 is published in *The Slavonic and East European Review*, xli, no. 98, 1962, pp. 218–41.
136. Memorandum by the financial adviser, 9 July 1928, with minute of 31 July: FO 371, file 12877, fos. 211–14.
137. Rumbold to Chamberlain, 30 May 1929: ibid., file 13628, fos. 252ff.
138. Nicolson to Cushendun, 14 and 22 August 1928: ibid., file 12892, fos. 206f., 211ff.

139. Minute by Philip Noel Baker, 26 June 1931: ibid., file 15215, fo. 81f.
140. Memorandum by Finlayson, 9 October 1925: ibid., file 10751, fos. 228ff.
141. Report on Ruhr Steel Trust sent by D'Abernon on 31 March, and D'Abernon to Tyrrell, 23 January 1926: ibid., file 11306, fos. 243–48, file 11248, fos. 67–70.
142. The same to Chamberlain, 29 January 1925: ibid., file 10711, fo. 124f.
143. W.N. Dunn to D'Abernon, 1 February 1924: ibid., file 9782, fo. 158, transmitting a report from Essen, s.d.
144. Report on labour situation, Coblenz, 9 April 1924: ibid., file 9790, fos. 328ff.
145. Report by Colonel Wallace Wright, 12 February 1924: PRO, WO 106, file 447.
146. James H. Causey to Lord Parmoor, 29 March 1924: PRO, FO 371, file 9804, fo. 130.
147. Minute by J. Perowne, 6 November 1924: ibid., file 9783, fo. 18.
148. Minutes of the Rhineland High Commission, 5–8 March 1924: PRO, FO 894, file 18, fo. 144f.
149. Memorandum by C.J. Kavanagh, 2 November, and report by Rumbold, 7 November 1928: PRO, FO 371, file 12911, fos. 74ff., 78.
150. Minute on German-Polish relations by M.H. Huxley, 11 March, and memorandum by the same, 15 June 1927: ibid., file 12136, fo. 77f., file 12138, fo. 159.
151. E.M.B. Ingram to Chamberlain, 15 September 1927: ibid., file 12155, fos. 99–104.

CHAPTER VII

1. Schubert to Auswärtiges Amt, Rome, 27 February 1931: Akten zur deutschen auswärtigen Politik, series B, xvi, no. 237, p. 601.
2. Minute by Count Bernstorff, London, 20 October 1930: ibid., no. 16, p. 35f.
3. The same to Auswärtiges Amt, 25 June 1931: ibid., xvii, 1982, no. 208, p. 493.
4. Minute by Curtius, 24 February 1931: ibid., xvi, no. 230, p. 578f.
5. Minute by Philip Nichols and Orme Sargent, 5 March 1931: PRO, FO 371, file 15220, fos. 243–46. The minute throughout stresses the connection between disarmament and the issue of the Polish Corridor.
6. Minute by Vansittart, 7 March 1931: ibid., file 15220, fo. 246. Italics in the original.
7. Rumbold to Henderson, 26 February 1931: ibid., file 15220, fo. 265.
8. Foreign Office Memorandum of 13 July 1931: ibid., file 15222, fo. 60. Heye is quoted from Schlesische Zeitung, no. 272, 1 June 1931.
9. Minutes by Maurice Hankey and Orme Sargent, 22 September and

4 October 1932: FO 371, file 15930, fo. 365, file 15941, fo. 214.
10. Memorandum by A.W.A. Leeper, 7 December, and minute by Cadogan, 29 December 1932: ibid., file 15935, fos. 315–19.
11. Rumbold to Henderson, 10 December 1930: ibid., file 14354, fo. 184f.
12. Rumbold to Henderson, 6 March 1931: private: PRO, FO 800, file 283, fos. 207–12.
13. Summary of discussion with the German ministers at Chequers, 7 June 1931: PRO 30/69/285.
14. Rumbold to Vansittart, 29 May, and to Henderson, 24 July 1931: PRO 30/69/285, and FO 371, file 15210, fo. 115f.
15. Rumbold to Foreign Office, 9 October 1931: ibid., file 16216, fo. 283.
16. Minutes by Sargent, 17 June, Vansittart, 18 June, and Noel Baker, 8 July 1931: FO 371, file 15209, fos. 133–36.
17. Henderson to B.C. Newton, 2 and 9 July 1931: DBFP, 2nd series, ii, 1947, nos. 113, 172, pp. 119, 161. In general cp. Eyck, *History of the Weimar Republic*, ii, pp. 311–16.
18. Rumbold to Vansittart, 16 July 1931: ibid., ii, no. 210, p. 208.
19. Rumbold to Marquess of Reading, 7 October 1931: ibid., ii, no. 265, pp. 281–84.
20. Minute by Philip Nichols, 2 March 1932: PRO, FO 371, file 15936, fo. 248.
21. R.H. Brand to Sir John Simon, 1 April 1932: ibid., file 15936, fos. 32–35. The writer was a banker sent to Berlin to investigate the financial situation.
22. Memorandum by Sir Frederick Leith-Ross, Berlin, 14 March 1932: ibid., file 15936, fo. 18.
23. Memorandum by F. Thelwall, 25 April 1932: ibid., file 15936, fo. 63.
24. Leith-Ross to Sir Patrick Duff: note on conversation with Major Church, 23 May 1932: PRO 30/69/301.
25. Rumbold to Simon, 9 and 9 June 1932: FO 371, file 15944, fos. 364–70, 376f.
26. B.C. Newton to Simon, 25 November 1931: ibid., file 15216, fo. 99f.
27. Rumbold to Simon, 4 August 1932: ibid., file 15945, fo. 158f.
28. Memorandum by E. Rowe-Dutton, 17 October 1932: ibid., file 15937, fo. 310.
29. Rumbold to Simon, 21 September 1932: DBFP, 2nd series, iv, 1950, no. 26, p. 56.
30. Rumbold to Simon, 19 November 1932: ibid., iv, no. 37, p. 77.
31. Rumbold to Foreign Office, 2 and 7 December 1932: PRO, FO 371, file 15947, fos. 317, 364f.
32. Rumbold to Simon, 21 December, and MacDonald's reply, 24 December 1932: ibid., file 15947, fo. 416f., PRO 30/69/678, fo. 510.
33. Colonel J.H. Marshall-Cornwall to M.I.3.b, 21 July, and to Rumbold, 10 September 1930: FO 371, file 14372, fos. 370, 391.
34. Rumbold to Sargent, 3 November 1930: PRO, FO 800, file 275, fo.

97f. (private papers of Sir Orme Sargent).

35. Report by M.I.3.b, 11 April 1930: PRO, WO 190, file 76. The full text of Groener's *Hirtenbrief* of 22 January 1930 in Otto-Ernst Schüddekopf, *Das Heer und die Republik*, Hanover, 1955, pp. 260ff. It does not contain the passages quoted in the text.
36. Colonel Marshall-Cornwall to Rumbold, 9 October 1930: PRO, FO 371, file 14372, fo. 457.
37. Report by A.F. Yencken, 18 May 1932: ibid., file 15944, fo. 192f. For the story of Groener's fall and Schleicher's role in it, see Carsten, *Reichswehr and Politics*, pp. 346–51.
38. Colonel Andrew Thorne to Rumbold, 19 April 1932, and Colonel Marshall-Cornwall to M.I.3.b, 19 June 1931: PRO, FO 371, file 15943, fo. 115f., file 15224, fos. 232ff.
39. Colonel Marshall-Cornwall to Rumbold, 9 December 1931: DBFP, 2nd series, ii, appendix iv, pp. 523f.
40. Report by Marshall-Cornwall, 8 May, with minute of 21 May 1930: PRO, FO 371, file 14367, fo. 192f.
41. Annual Report for 1930, p. 7: ibid., file 15223, fo. 36.
42. Newton to Henderson, 10 July 1931: DBFP, 2nd series, ii, no. 186, p. 184.
43. Sargent to Rumbold, 18 June, and M.I.3.b report, 25 September 1930: PRO, FO 800, file 275, fo. 93f., WO 190, file 89.
44. Colonel Marshall-Cornwall to Rumbold, 23 January 1932: FO 371, file 15948, fos. 18ff.
45. War Office Memorandum, 2 March 1932: ibid., file 15938, fo. 232.
46. Colonel Marshall-Cornwall to M.I.3.b, 27 May 1931, and Rumbold's Annual Report for 1930, p. 87: ibid., file 15218, fo. 117f., file 15223, fo. 36.
47. Colonel Marshall-Cornwall to Rumbold, 9 December 1931, and Rumbold to Sargent, 3 November 1930, private: ibid., file 15225, fo. 260, FO 800, file 275, fo. 96.
48. Air Ministry to Foreign Office, 5 July 1933: ibid., file 16707, fos. 137, 162f. (extremely detailed). The most detailed German account of Lipetsk by an officer who was trained there: Helm Speidel, 'Reichswehr und Rote Armee', *Vierteljahrshefte für Zeitgeschichte*, i, 1953, pp. 9–45.
49. Minutes by F. Nichols, 16 December 1930 and 25 January 1932: FO 371, file 14359, fo. 335, file 15938, fo. 212f.
50. Reports by Colonel Marshall-Cornwall, s.d. and 9 October 1930: ibid., file 15215, fo. 103, file 14372, fo. 457.
51. Rumbold to Foreign Office, 22 February 1930: ibid., file 14353, fo. 82.
52. Rumbold to Simon, 3 August, and B.C. Newton to Simon, 26 October 1932: DBFP, 2nd series, iv, nos. 8 and 30, pp. 17, 63f.
53. Rumbold to Henderson, 20 June 1930: PRO, FO 371, file 14357, fo. 370.
54. Rumbold to Henderson, 31 January 1930: ibid., file 14371, fo. 227.
55. Rumbold to Henderson, 18 March 1930: ibid., file 14371, fo. 241f.
56. Memorandum by E. Rowe-Dutton, 17 October 1932: ibid., file 15937, fo. 310.

57. Rumbold to Henderson, 5 July 1930: with minutes by Vansittart of 7 and 9 July: ibid., file 14377, fos. 2f., 8f., 12.
58. Rumbold to Henderson, 5 September 1930: ibid., file 14363, fo. 26f.
59. Rumbold to Henderson, 11 December 1930: ibid., file 14364, fo. 245f.
60. Rumbold to Marquess of Reading, 24 September 1931: ibid., file 15215, fo. 262f. Lord Reading was Jewish.
61. Rumbold to Simon, 11 and 18 December 1931: ibid., file 15212, fo. 172, file 15217, fo. 219.
62. 'Germany, Annual Report 1931', p. 73f.: ibid., file 15942, fo. 25.
63. Rumbold to Simon, 3–4 August 1932: DBFP, 2nd series, iv, nos. 8 and 9, pp. 16f., 22f.
64. Memorandum by E. Rowe-Dutton, 17 October 1932: PRO, FO 371, file 15937, fo. 310.
65. Newton to Simon, 27 October 1932: ibid., file 15955, fo. 230f.
66. Rumbold to Simon, 24 November 1932: DBFP, 2nd series, iv, no. 39, p. 85.
67. The same to Vansittart, 29 May, and to Henderson, 24 July 1931: PRO, 30/69/285 and FO 371, file 15210, fo. 115.

CHAPTER VIII

1. Rumbold to Simon, 11 and 18 January 1933: DBFP, 2nd series, iv, nos. 224, 226, cp. 385f., 388; *The Times*, 9 January 1933. For accounts of the Papen-Hitler meeting, see Alan Bullock, *Hitler – A Study in Tyranny*, 1973 edition, pp. 243ff., and Joachim Fest, *Hitler*, Berlin, 1973, p. 496f.
2. Rumbold to Simon, 5 January 1933: PRO, FO 371, file 16716, fo. 12; *The Times*, 16 January 1933.
3. *The Times*, 23 January 1933.
4. Rumbold to Simon, 25 January 1933: FO 371, file 16717, fo. 65f.
5. Rumbold to Simon, 28 January 1933: ibid., file 16717, fos. 69ff., 73.
6. *Manchester Guardian*, 26 January, *The Times*, 28 January 1933.
7. *The Times* and *Manchester Guardian*, both of 30 January 1933.
8. Rumbold to Simon, 1 February 1933: PRO, FO 371, file 16717, fo. 182f.
9. *The Times* and *Manchester Guardian*, both of 31 January 1933.
10. *Daily Mail*, 31 January 1933. For the most recent assessment of the role of the SPD and KPD at the end of the Weimar Republic, see Andreas Dorpalen, 'SPD und KPD in der Endphase der Weimarer Republik', *Vierteljahrshefte für Zeitgeschichte*, xxxi, 1983, pp. 77–107.
11. Rumbold to Simon, 7 and 22 February 1933: DBFP, 2nd series, iv, nos. 238, 243, pp. 409f, 426f.
12. *The Times*, 10 and 15 February, *Manchester Guardian*, 16 February 1933.
13. *The Times*, 16 February 1933.

14. Report by F. Thelwall, 15 February 1933: DBFP, 2nd series, iv, no. 241, p. 421.
15. Rumbold to Simon, 22 February 1933: ibid., iv, no. 243, p. 423f.
16. *Manchester Guardian*, 27 February, *The Times*, 25 February 1933.
17. *News Chronicle*, 28 February, 1 and 2 March 1933.
18. *Manchester Guardian* and *The Times*, both of 1 March 1933.
19. Rumbold to Simon, 1 March 1933: DBFP, 2nd series, iv, no. 246, p. 430f.
20. *The Times*, 4 March, *Manchester Guardian*, 4 and 7 March 1933.
21. Rumbold to Simon, 15 and 21 March 1933: DBFP, 2nd series, iv, nos. 265, 268, pp. 458f., 471f.
22. Rumbold to Simon, 13 April 1933: PRO, FO 371, file 16722, fo. 284.
23. *Manchester Guardian*, 13, 16, 27 and 28 March, *News Chronicle*, 13 and 20 March, *Daily Mail*, 21 March, 1933.
24. Rumbold to Simon, 14 March 1933: PRO, FO 371, file 16719, fo. 179.
25. *News Chronicle*, *Daily Mail* and *The Times*, all of 22 March 1933.
26. *Daily Mail*, 23 March, *News Chronicle*, 21 March 1933.
27. *The Times*, and *Manchester Guardian*, both of 24 March 1933.
28. *News Chronicle*, 7 and 25 March, *The Times*, 9 and 10 March 1933.
29. *The Times*, 11 and 15 March 1933.
30. Rumbold to Simon, 15 March 1933: DBFP, 2nd series, iv, no. 265, pp. 458–62.
31. Rumbold to Simon, 12 April 1933: PRO, FO 371, file 16721, fos. 260–63.
32. Rumbold to Simon, 7 April 1933: ibid., file 16721, fo. 255f.
33. Rumbold to Simon, 7 April 1933: ibid., file 16721, fo. 253f.
34. Memorandum by Vansittart, 15 June 1933: ibid., file 16696, fo. 239.
35. *The Times*, *Manchester Guardian* and *News Chronicle*, all of 10 March 1933.
36. *Daily Mail*, *News Chronicle* and *Manchester Guardian*, all of 30 March, *The Times*, 29 and 31 March 1933.
37. Rumbold to Simon, 13 April 1933: PRO, FO 371, file 16722, fo. 275.
38. Rumbold to Simon, 28 March and 5 April 1933: ibid., file 16720, fos. 426f., 428ff. 70f.
39. Memorandum by Vansittart, 'Some Political Aspects of German Economic Revival', 15 June 1933, 'very secret': ibid., file 16696, fo. 240.

CONCLUSION

1. Addison to MacDonald, 16 October, and to Chamberlain, 25 November 1924: PRO, FO 371, file 9786, fos. 93f., 111, 114f.
2. Foreign Office to Home Office, 14 November, and Home Office reply, 26 November 1919: ibid., file 3795, fos. 418ff.
3. Home Office to Foreign Office, 1 June, with minutes of 3 and 4

June, and Home Office to Foreign Office, 22 June 1920: ibid., file 3796, fos. 422ff., 430.
4. Minutes by R.F. Wigram and Crowe, 12 March, and Foreign Office wire to Kilmarnock, 14 March 1921: ibid., file 6046, fos. 209f. 217.
5. Minute by Sir Eyre Crowe, 4 April 1920: ibid., file 3782, fo. 37.

BIBLIOGRAPHY

A. UNPUBLISHED SOURCES

British Library

D'Abernon Papers, Additional Manuscripts 48925 A–B, 48926 A–B, 48927 A.

Public Record Office

Cabinet Papers, Files 67–140, 158–168;
Foreign Office 371, Files 3776–3803, 4725–4852, 5849–6076, 7447–7583, 8625–8821, 9720–9877, 10702–10762, 11247–11333, 12115–12156, 12875–12917, 13592–13647, 14352–14379, 15209–15228, 15935–15955, 16693–16762;
Foreign Office 800, Files 219, 272–284;
Foreign Office 984, Files 1–18;
War Office 106, File 447;
War Office 144, Files 1–35;
War Office 155, Files 2–5;
War Office 190, Files, 2, 4, 9, 10, 12, 14, 20, 23, 24, 26, 29, 31, 39, 40, 44, 45, 48, 52, 53, 56–60, 65, 66, 75, 76, 78, 81, 89, 93, 94, 110, 127, 146, 147, 163, 166, 174;
MacDonald Papers, PRO 30/69, Files 5, 25, 97, 102, 282, 285, 292, 301, 668, 672, 678, 752.

B. PUBLISHED SOURCES

Akten zur deutschen auswärtigen Politik, Serie B: 1925–1933, vols. I 1, I 2, IV, V, VI, VII, IX, X, XI, XIII, XV, XVI, XVII, Göttingen, 1966–82.

Bernhard, Henry (ed.), Gustav Stresemann Vermächtnis, 3 vols., Berlin, 1932–33.

D'Abernon, An Ambassador of Peace – Pages from the Diary of Viscount D'Abernon, 3 vols., London, 1929–30.

D'Abernon, Red Cross and Berlin Embassy 1915–1926 – Extracts from the Diaries of Viscountess D'Abernon, London, 1946.

Documents on British Foreign Policy 1919–1939 (quoted as DBFP), First Series, vols. VII, IX, X, XVI, XX, XXI, London 1958–78.

Series IA, vols. I, II, III, IV, V, VII, London, 1966–75.

Second Series, vols, II, IV, London, 1947–50.

Hubert, Ernst Rudolf (ed.), Dokumente zur deutschen Verfassungsgeschichte, vol. III, Stuttgart, 1966.

Schüddekopf, Otto-Ernst, Das Heer und die Republik – Quellen zur Politik der Reichswehrführung 1918–1933, Hanover-Frankfurt, 1955.

C. SECONDARY WORKS

Angress, Werner T., Stillborn Revolution – The Communist Bid for Power in Germany 1921–1923, Princeton, 1963.

Berghahn, Volker R., Der Stahlhelm Bund der Frontsoldaten 1918–1935, Düsseldorf, 1966.

Bullock, Alan, Hitler – a Study in Tyranny, revised edition, London, 1973.

Carsten, F.L., The Reichswehr and Politics 1918–1933, Oxford, 1966.

Revolution in Central Europe 1918–1919, London, 1972.

The Rise of Fascism, London, 1980.

Cole, G.D.H., A History of the Labour Party from 1914, London, 1948.

Dockrill, Michael L., and Goold, Douglas J., Peace without Promise – Britain and the Peace Conferences 1919–1923, London, 1981.

Eliasberg, George, Der Ruhrkrieg von 1920, Bonn, 1974.

Erger, Johannes, Der Kapp-Lüttwitz Putsch, Düsseldorf, 1967.

Eyck, Erich, *A History of the Weimar Republic*, 2 vols., Cambridge Mass., 1962–64.

Fest, Joachim C., *Hitler*, Berlin, 1973.

Gilbert, Martin, *Winston Churchill*, vol. IV – 1916–1922, London, 1975.

Gumbel, E.J., *4 Jahre politischer Mord*, Berlin, 1922.

Hamilton, Mary Agnes, *Arthur Henderson – A Biography*, London, 1938.

Heideking, Jürgen, *Aeropag der Diplomaten – Die Pariser Botschafterkonferenz der alliierten Hauptmächte und die Probleme der europäischen Politik*, Husum, 1979.

Hiden, John, *Germany and Europe 1919–1939*, London–New York, 1977.

Kluge, Ulrich, *Soldatenräte und Revolution*, Göttingen, 1975.

Meier-Welcker, Hans, *Seeckt*, Frankfurt, 1967.

Nicolson, Harold, *Curzon – The Last Phase 1919–1925*, London, 1934.

Ronaldshay, The Earl of, *The Life of Lord Curzon being the authorized Biography of George Nathaniel Marquess Curzon of Keddleston*, vol. III, London, 1928.

Rosenberg, Arthur, *Geschichte der deutschen Republik*, Karlsbad, 1935.

Salomon, Ernst von, *Die Geächteten*, Gütersloh, 1930.

Taylor, A.J.P., *English History 1914–1945*, Oxford, 1965.

Tuohy, Ferdinand, *Occupied 1918–1930*, London, 1931.

Williamson, D.G., 'Great Britain and the Ruhr Crisis 1923–1924', *British Journal of International Studies*, III, 1977, pp. 70–91. 'Cologne and the British 1918–1926', *History Today*, November 1977, pp. 695–702.

INDEX

Index

337

Index

Index

341

Index

William II, Emperor, 1, 2, 157;
  birthday of, 15;
  lack of support for, 210;
  support for, 15;
  a war criminal? 25, 56.
Winterfeldt, General Detlof von, 29.
Wirth, Dr Joseph, 52, 54, 72, 74ff., 77f., 92,
  111, 134.
Wolff, Theodor, 155.
Workers' and soldiers' councils, 2f., 5, 8,
  12ff., 298 n. 20;
  in Bavaria, 16f.;

national congress of, 9.
Württemberg, 49, 149, 232;
  army of, 4, 17;
  government of, 49, 282.
Wuppertal, 40.
Young, Owen D., 218.
Young Plan, the, 212f., 218f., 247f., 262;
  referendum against, 219, 262.
Zetkin, Clara, 91f., 173.
Zinoviev, Grigori, 90, 150.
Zörgiebel, Karl, 95f.